FOUNDATIONS OF PROGRAMMING, STATISTICS & MACHINE LEARNING FOR BUSINESS ANALYTICS

Sara Miller McCune founded SAGE Publishing in 1965 to support the dissemination of usable knowledge and educate a global community. SAGE publishes more than 1000 journals and over 800 new books each year, spanning a wide range of subject areas. Our growing selection of library products includes archives, data, case studies and video. SAGE remains majority owned by our founder and after her lifetime will become owned by a charitable trust that secures the company's continued independence.

Los Angeles | London | New Delhi | Singapore | Washington DC | Melbourne

FOUNDATIONS OF
PROGRAMMING, STATISTICS & MACHINE LEARNING FOR BUSINESS ANALYTICS

RAM GOPAL, DAN PHILPS, TILLMAN WEYDE

Los Angeles | London | New Delhi
Singapore | Washington DC | Melbourne

Los Angeles | London | New Delhi
Singapore | Washington DC | Melbourne

SAGE Publications Ltd
1 Oliver's Yard
55 City Road
London EC1Y 1SP

SAGE Publications Inc.
2455 Teller Road
Thousand Oaks, California 91320

SAGE Publications India Pvt Ltd
B 1/I 1 Mohan Cooperative Industrial Area
Mathura Road
New Delhi 110 044

SAGE Publications Asia-Pacific Pte Ltd
3 Church Street
#10-04 Samsung Hub
Singapore 049483

Editor: Ruth Stitt
Editorial assistant: Charlotte Hegley
Production editor: Ian Antcliff
Marketing manager: Lucia Sweet
Cover design: Naomi Robinson
Typeset by: C&M Digitals (P) Ltd, Chennai, India
Printed in the UK

Library of Congress Control Number: 2022947084

British Library Cataloguing in Publication data

A catalogue record for this book is available from the
British Library

ISBN 978-1-5296-2090-0
ISBN 978-1-5296-2091-7 (pbk)

At SAGE, we take sustainability seriously. Most of our products are printed in the UK using responsibly sourced papers
and boards. When we print overseas, we ensure sustainable papers are used as measured by the PREPS grading
system. We undertake an annual audit to monitor our sustainability.

CONTENTS

ABOUT THE AUTHORS

Ram D. Gopal is the Information Systems Society's *Distinguished Fellow* and Alan Turing Institute's *Turing Fellow*, a Professor of Information Systems and Management, and Pro-Dean for Research, Engagement, and Impact at the Warwick Business School. He also serves as the Academic Director of the Gillmore Centre for Financial Technology at the Warwick Business School. He previously served as the Head of the Department of Operations and Information Management in the School of Business, University of Connecticut from 2008–2018. As the Department Head, he initiated a new Master of Science degree program in Business Analytics and Project Management in 2011 and an undergraduate business major in Business Data Analytics in 2014. He has a diverse and a rich portfolio of research that spans big data analytics, health informatics, financial technologies, information security, privacy and valuation, intellectual property rights, online market design, and business impacts of technology. At the Warwick Business School, he teaches courses on 'Digital Transformation' for the Full-time MBA and Executive MBA (London), as well as 'Digital Finance, Blockchain & Cryptocurrencies' for the MSc Management of Information Systems and Digital Innovation, and 'Text Mining' for the MSc Business Analytics degrees.

Dan Philps is a veteran quantitative investment manager and a widely published artificial intelligence (AI) researcher. He is the founding head of Rothko Investment Strategies and has over 20 years of quantitative investment experience, having managed numerous top-performing strategies across both equities and fixed income asset classes. Prior to developing and leading Rothko's AI-driven Emerging and International equities investment businesses, he was a senior portfolio manager in Mondrian Investment Partners' Global Fixed Income and Currencies group. Before 1998, he specialized in the design and development of trading and risk models at several major investment banks. His career history is one of successfully applying AI to solve complex real-world business challenges and includes leading the development of an advanced form of AI called Temporal Continual Learning. He holds a PhD in AI and Computer Science from City, University of London, a BSc (Hons) from King's College London, is a CFA charterholder, a member of the CFA Society of the UK, co-leads AI research strategy at the Gillmore Centre for FinTech at Warwick Business School, and is an Honorary Research Fellow at the University of Warwick.

Tillman Weyde is a Reader in Computer Science at City, University of London. Before joining City in 2005, he worked as a researcher in the Research Department for Music and Media Technology at the University of Osnabrück, Germany. His research focuses on machine learning and artificial intelligence addressing both fundamental and applied questions. The applications focus on language, speech, and music. At City, he leads the Machine Intelligence and Media

Informatics Research Group and regularly leads research projects funded by the AHRC, EPSRC, Innovate UK, ESRC, and the European Commission. He has published over 150 peer-reviewed papers and as well as software. He was awarded several prizes, including the Comenius Medal for exemplary educational software and best paper awards at international conferences. He has co-founded the MSc degree program in Data Science at City and teaches Big Data, Digital Signal Processing, as well as several other technical topics. He is a fellow of the Higher Education Academy. He regularly advises industry and has co-founded startups that address challenges in data science and AI, including health, finance, and business operations.

ACKNOWLEDGEMENTS

There are several people to whom we are thankful and wish to acknowledge their contributions to the book.

- Maya Gopal for creating the initial versions of the R notebooks for the R programming and statistical analysis.
- Alessandro Alviani, Chaeyoon Kim, Stefan Diener, and Lawrence Ramsey from City, University of London, and Jeong Woo Yang from University of Glasgow for programming and proofreading.
- Ruth Stitt, Charlotte Hegley, and Ian Antcliff from Sage Publishers and the external reviewers who helped to improve this book from its early version.
- Tillman Weyde's students for valuable feedback and inspiration over many years of teaching related courses that helped develop this book.
- Ram Gopal's wife Mary-Catherine Gopal and kids Astro Gopal and Maya Gopal for the encouragement, support, and help throughout this journey.
- Ram Gopal's students in Connecticut, whose feedback over the years has been an important source of inspiration for the book.
- Dan Philps' wife Ruth for her support and encouragement.

ONLINE RESOURCES

Foundations of Programming, Statistics and Machine Learning for Business Analytics is supported by a wealth of online resources for both students and lecturers to aid study and support teaching, which are available at **study.sagepub.com/gopal**

FOR LECTURERS

- **Interactive coding notebooks** – Instructor version (will have additional materials to aid your teaching). For instructors, we provide the full executable code and background information that will help with your teaching. This will come as an editable notebook that you can customize according to your students' needs and your teaching style.

- **Exercises solutions** – Code solutions for the exercises which are customizable.

- **Use case notebooks** – Full executable code for the use cases which are customizable.

- **Datasets** – All the datasets used in the book are provided.

FOR STUDENTS

- **Interactive coding notebooks** – Student version (will have the code from the book for practise). We provide the full executable code but without background information. The code is fully functional and can serve as a starting point for experimentation.

- **Datasets** – All datasets used in the book which you will need to complete the exercises at the end of each chapter.

ABOUT THIS BOOK

Starting the journey into analytics and not sure where to begin? Then this is the book for you. It covers all the fundamentals, from statistics to programming to business applications, to equip you with the solid foundational knowledge to work in the field of business analytics. The book provides an introduction (or a refresher) to the principles behind developing robust and powerful business analytics and predictive models, with detailed use cases in how to apply them. We introduce key statistical concepts, programming techniques, and applied machine learning approaches, giving the reader critical skills to robustly design and develop insightful and powerful models in the age of data science and artificial intelligence. This book aims to equip students with a comprehensive and cohesive foundational knowledge of business analytics to make them industry-ready to design, develop, and implement robust and effective analytics and models in a business context.

Over the years, we have developed deep expertise in business analytics, statistics, machine learning, and their application in software systems. We have carried out cutting-edge research on business analytics, machine learning, and artificial intelligence and we have run businesses, founded businesses, and engaged with businesses, where analytics and machine learning have been critical ingredients for decision-making and business operations. We have developed and taught a variety of courses in business analytics, finance, and computer science across many leading universities. Our joint experience forms the foundation for this textbook.

Business analytics has become a key competency in the information age, as global companies seek to digitally transform themselves and leverage their data resources to realize a competitive advantage. Business analytics combine business acumen, computing, and statistics as drivers of decisions. Students often struggle with business analytics as they tend to either lack direct business experience or the appropriate knowledge in one or more of the core domains of business, statistics, and programming. The intensely mathematical treatment of statistics in many textbooks is often an unneeded diversion for business students, for whom developing a solid conceptual understanding of how statistics really drives business analytics is crucial. Additionally, the rapidly expanding take-up of machine learning in business now requires top-flight business students to be conversant with these technologies and how they link back to traditional statistics.

We started with the premise that this book should be accessible to a wide swathe of students and practitioners interested in entering the field of business analytics. As such, the book is designed to be accessible to students with no prior programming experience or knowledge of statistics. The *learning-through-coding* approach that we take provides a thorough grounding and a deep intuition that would be abstract and challenging with a more traditionally theoretical and mathematical treatment of the subject. Using business use cases, we are also able to provide students with the knowledge to develop their own statistical and machine learning approaches, from scratch, for real-world business problems.

Interactive coding notebooks for R and Python are provided for each chapter, building knowledge progressively and providing the learning-through-coding experience. Real-world business applications get progressively more involved and range from profit forecasting, bad credit prediction, and cyber-threat monitoring, through to venture capital-based performance monitoring. Most chapters in the book come with several exercises to help gain competence and confidence in both statistical and machine learning concepts and applied programming skills.

The book is structured as follows. The first four chapters introduce readers to programming fundamentals using popular analytics open-source software (R and Python). Data structures, data management and manipulation, and visualizing data are covered. This is followed by an intuitive development of statistical concepts, without the use of excessive mathematical treatment, in Chapters 5, 6, and 7. This is achieved by developing intuition through programming and visualization. Students then learn how to design and conduct basic statistical tests from first principles in Chapters 8, 9, and 10. Throughout these chapters, students are provided with practical examples from actual business applications of analytics. Chapter 10 is fully dedicated to a practical application of investigating how COVID-19 infections affected nursing homes in the State of California. Chapter 11 introduces estimation, the core building block of many statistical and machine learning models. The concept of the maximum likelihood principle is detailed with numerous examples. This chapter provides the foundation for building advanced models that follow in the subsequent chapters. Chapters 12, 13, 14, and 15 build on this foundation and cover important topics of linear models, general linear models, regression structure and diagnostics, and timeseries analysis. Chapters 16 to 20 delve into machine learning models most frequently used in analytics applications.

Throughout the book, we provide side-by-side code examples in both R and Python. The two languages are differentiated by the background colour so that the reader can immediately focus on the language of interest. While the book is certainly accessible to those who are only interested in one of the languages, we believe gaining competency in both will serve the students well. As readers will notice, some techniques are easier to implement in one language and in some cases, they are only readily available in one language. From a practical perspective, it will prove to be effective to be able to switch from one to the other within an analytics project to leverage the strengths of each, and this book will enable the reader to gain from the advantages offered by both individually.

1

INTRODUCTION TO PROGRAMMING AND STATISTICS

Chapter Contents

In this first chapter, we will cover some fundamentals of computer programming and statistics that will become the foundation on which we will learn and conduct statistical analysis and elements of machine learning. The *learning-through-coding* approach that we take provides a deep intuition that may be difficult for many to grasp through a more theoretical and mathematical treatment of the subject. Along the way, this will also provide us with the practical skills to quickly code and execute statistical analyses and machine learning models for projects we wish to undertake.

Of course, even just covering the broad essentials of computer programming in a single chapter of a book would be an impossible task. This chapter does not attempt that and is mainly aimed at readers who have no computer programming background and those who need a bit of a refresher to get started. In this chapter, we will focus on aspects of programming relevant to the topic of the book: statistics and machine learning. Since much of what we will learn is about data manipulation, and how to extract insights and knowledge from data, we will cover the elements of programming necessary to accomplish these important activities. Along the way, we will gain familiarity and comfort with coding, and with ample support from numerous resources available online, the jump to becoming expert coders in statistics and machine learning will become much easier.

What programming language should one use for statistics and machine learning? The easy answer is that any well-developed programming language will enable us to conduct statistical analysis and implement machine learning methods. Yet, some are better to use since they are either purposefully built for this type of analysis or enable more efficient and easier coding to enable statistical and machine learning tasks. Even among these languages there are many available options, and the choice set is continually growing. For this textbook, we will use R and Python. Both are powerful open-source software with a large, committed user base that continually works to enhance their capabilities. R is a 'statistical computing and programming' software platform that has been enthusiastically embraced by the applied statistics research community, and Python is a more general-purpose programming language with excellent capabilities for machine learning. Of course, nothing prevents us from mixing and matching these languages for projects we may undertake.

The main body of this book will explore and implement concepts using R and Python. The equivalent code in R and Python is illustrated in sequence, R on blue and Python on yellow background.

Box 1.1

Horses for courses

Which programming language?

Deciding which language to learn or to select for a project can be difficult. The table below is provided to help with this, but it is a generalization, and the ratings are subjective and contended. Individual cases have their own requirements that should be considered. For statistics and data analysis, we recommend using R or Python, due to the availability of many excellent libraries. For maximizing execution speed, use low-level C/C++, and for many large systems, Java is required. In terms of popularity, for Windows applications, we find C#, for Linux and Mac applications, C++. Below is a table presenting the different languages and their performance on different systems and applications:

Table 1.1 Programming languages and performance on different applications

Programming language	Stats?	Machine learning	Windows apps	Linux apps	Android apps	macOS iOS apps	Web	Speed of operation	Development speed
Python	✓✓✓	✓✓✓✓	✓✓	✓✓	✓	✓	✓✓✓	✓	✓✓✓
R	✓✓✓✓	✓✓	n/a	n/a	n/a	n/a	n/a	✓	✓✓✓✓
C# (.Net)	✓	✓	✓✓✓✓	✓	✓	✓	✓✓✓	✓✓	✓✓
Java	✓	✓	✓✓	✓✓✓	✓✓✓	✓✓	✓✓✓	✓✓	✓✓✓
C/C++	✓	✓	✓✓	✓✓✓	✓✓✓	✓✓	✓	✓✓✓✓	✓
JavaScript	✓	✓	✓	✓	✓✓✓	✓✓✓	✓✓✓✓	✓✓	✓✓✓
Swift	✓	✓	✓	✓	✓	✓✓✓✓	✓	✓✓✓	✓✓✓

CODE REPOSITORY AND QUICK START FOR R AND PYTHON

We recommend to students and instructors to run all examples yourself. All code and data are in the online resources at:

https://study.sagepub.com/gopal

We describe below how to install R and Python tools on your own computer. Alternatively you can run the Python code in an online service like Google Colab (https://colab.research.google.com/) or Amazon SageMaker Studio Lab (https://studiolab.sagemaker.aws/).

Downloading and Installing R

The first step is to download and install R from the CRAN (Comprehensive R Archive Network) site. The illustrations in the book use a Windows environment but the examples work as well on other operating systems, such as Mac OS X and various Unix/Linux:

https://cran.r-project.org/

It is often preferred to download and use an IDE (Integrated Development Environment) to create code as it makes the process of coding and managing projects significantly easier. While there are several choices (both free and paid) of IDE, we will use the free version of RStudio for our illustrations. This can be downloaded and installed at the following link:

www.rstudio.com/products/rstudio/download/

R Studio

Once both are installed, open R Studio and the following windows should appear:

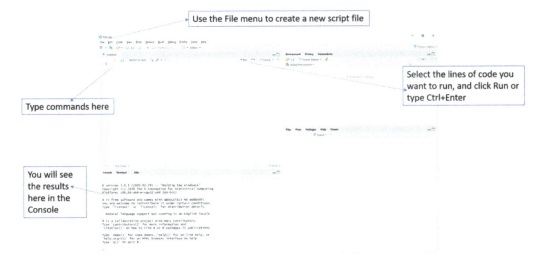

Use the File menu to create a new script file

Select the lines of code you want to run, and click Run or type Ctrl+Enter

Type commands here

You will see the results here in the Console

Figure 1.1   R Studio

Downloading and Installing Python

There are different versions and distributions of Python available. We will use Python 3 in a Jupyter Notebook. An easy way to install that environment is to use Anaconda, which combines Python with several tools, including the Jupyter Notebook, and can be downloaded at the following link: www.anaconda.com/products/individual

For extensive work with Python, we recommend installing Anaconda. If you do use Anaconda on your local computer, you can start the Jupyter Notebook environment (or JupyterLab which is similar with some additional functionality) by running the Anaconda Navigator, as shown below:

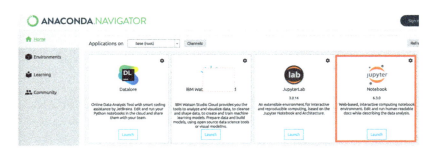

Figure 1.2   Anaconda

Jupyter Notebook

In a Jupyter notebook, we find text cells that contain text in Markdown format, or Python cells that contain code and can be executed directly, with the output displayed underneath the cell:

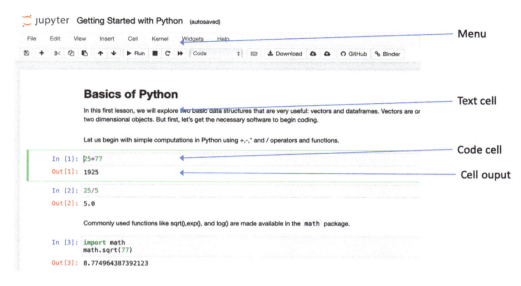

Figure 1.3   Jupiter Notebook

Programming Simple Computations

Create a new script file (see Figure 1.3). At the simplest level, one can use R or Python as a glorified calculator. Let us begin with simple computations in R using multiplication (*) and division (/) operators, and square root (`sqrt()`), exponential (`exp()`), and natural logarithm (`log()`) functions.

In Python, the code looks generally very similar, but we need to import the *math* package for the square root (`sqrt()`), exponential (`exp()`), and natural logarithm (`log()`) functions. In both R and Python, the value of the last line of code is displayed, without the need to call a function like `print()`.

R

```
25*77
## [1] 1925
25/5
## [1] 5
sqrt(77)
## [1] 8.774964
exp(2.5)
## [1] 12.18249
log(55)
## [1] 4.007333
```

Python

```
In [1]: 25*77
Out[1]:   1925
```

```
In [2]:25/5
Out[2]: 5
In [3]: import math
        math.sqrt(77)
Out[3]: 8.774964
In [4]: math.exp(2.5)
Out[4]:    12.18249
In [5]: math.log(55)
Out[5]:    4.007333
```

Notice that the calls to functions are followed by parentheses and typically take one or more arguments to produce an answer.

Since statistics and machine learning are fundamentally about data, let us turn our attention to how we create, manage, and manipulate data. A very useful data structure (or a data object where we store some data) is a vector. A vector is used to store a collection of data items of the same type. The simplest way to think of a data type is as an agreement over how to use data, e.g., as a number. Another common data type is a character, which may be used to store names of individuals. Let us start with vectors of numbers. A ubiquitous function in R is the c() function, which stands for combine or concatenate. This function is used to combine and put together individual items into a vector.

Creating Vectors

To create a vector in R, the appropriate syntax is v = c(...), **where '...' stands for the elements of the vector**. An example is:

```
v = c(1,2,4,63,7,5)
```

The above creates a vector of numbers and stores it in a vector data object that is named **v**.

For most numerical and statistical uses in Python, it is practical to use the *NumPy* package and its **ndarray** class:

```
In [1]: import numpy as np
        v1 = np.array([1,2,3,4])
        v1
Out[1]: array([1, 2, 3, 4])
```

While we can manually create a vector as above, it is often useful to automate the creation of vectors that have a particular structure. Useful functions in this regard are the sequence and repetition functions, illustrated below.

To create a vector of a sequence in R, we use seq(a,b), which creates a sequence from **a** to **b**, including both values. The option by in the sequence function allows to increment by any value.

In Python, we can also create a vector with a regular sequence over a range of numbers, we can use **arange(a,b)**, where the argument **a** is the starting point of the sequence (inclusive), and **b** is the end point (exclusive). We can add a third argument to specify a step size in the sequence.

In the next example, we do not create a variable to contain the second sequence so that the value of the vector is directly displayed on screen. This works for testing, but it means that the value we created will not be available for later use:

R

```
vec1 = seq(1,5)
vec1
## [1] 1 2 3 4 5
seq(2,25,by = 3)
## [1]  2  5  8 11 14 17 20 23
```

Python

```
In [1]: vec1 = np.arange(1,6)
        vec1
Out[1]:    array([1, 2, 3, 4, 5])
In [1]: np.arange(1,25,3)
Out[1]:    array([2, 5, 8, 11, 14, 17, 20, 23])
```

To create a vector in R that repeats a number, character, or a vector of numbers or characters, we use **rep()**. Characters must be in quotations. The second element in parentheses is the number of times we want the first element to be repeated.

To create a vector in Python that repeats a number, character, or a vector of numbers or characters, we use **tile()** and the rest of the code is similar to R. In Python, we can use single or double quotation marks. Since our script is on two lines now, we will need to use the print function to display both outputs:

R

```
rep(1, 5)
## [1] 1 1 1 1 1
rep(c(3,4,5),3)
## [1] 3 4 5 3 4 5 3 4 5
rep("c", 5)
## [1] "c" "c" "c" "c" "c"
```

Python

```
In [1]: np.tile(1,10)
Out[1]: array([1, 1, 1, 1, 1])
In [2]: print(np.tile((3,4,5),3))
        print(np.tile(('c'),5))
[3 4 5 3 4 5 3 4 5]
['c' 'c' 'c' 'c' 'c']
```

In the above Python example, we see two different ways of outputting a value. If we provide just a single expression on the last line of a cell (without an assignment with '='), that value will be output below the cell. The function **print()** can be used on any other line in the code to display the outputs of interest, which otherwise will not appear.

Equally, in R, we can use `print()`, but this is not needed for now, as the expression in each line will be printed automatically.

Vector Computations

Once a vector is created, we can perform computations on its elements. A major feature of R is its ability to conduct vectorized calculations. This makes writing code for statistical purposes significantly easy and efficient. For example, to find the sum of all the elements of a vector, we simply use the command `sum()`:

R

```
sum(vec1)
## [1] 10
```

Python

```
In [1]: np.sum(vec1)
Out[1]: 10
```

The following are other vector-based functions in R that will prove useful for conducting the statistical analysis we will delve into later in the chapter.

In Python, we have the same vectorized functions defined in the *NumPy* package. They have almost the same names as in R (note the different name for the standard deviation):

R

```
min(x) # minimum value of vector x
max(x) # maximum value of vector x
mean(x) # mean value of vector x
median(x) # median value of vector x
quantile(x, p) # pth quantile of vector x
sd(x) # standard deviation of vector x
var(x) # variance of vector x
```

Python

```
np.min(x)  # minimum value of vector x
np.max(x)  # maximum value of vector x
np.mean(x)  # mean value of vector x
np.median(x)  # median value of vector x
np.quantile(x, p)  # pth quantile of vector x
np.std(x)  # standard deviation of vector x
np.var(x)  # variance of vector x
```

Let us create three vectors to store information about *weight*, *height*, and *gender* of some individuals. Since *gender* is not numerical data, we use quotation marks when creating the vector.

Note that initially, the *gender* vector contains elements of type character. This can be seen using the `class()` function:

R

```
weight = c(60,72,57,90,95,72)
height = c(1.75,1.8,1.65,1.9,1.74,1.91)
gender = c("m","f","m","f","f","m")
gender
## [1] "m" "f" "m" "f" "f" "m"
class(gender)
## [1] "character
```

In Python, we can use the `type()` function for the same purpose, but we need to apply it to the elements, as the vector is always of type `numpy.ndarray`, as illustrated in the code snippet below:

Python

```
In [1]:  weight = np.array([60,72,57,90,95,72])
         height = np.array([1.75,1.8,1.65,1.9,1.74,1.91])
         gender = np.array(['f','m','f','m','m','f'],dtype='str')
         print(type(gender))
         print(type(gender[0])
```

```
<class 'numpy.str_'>
<class 'numpy.ndarray'>
```

As working with textual data is becoming increasingly common, it is helpful to understand how text is treated in terms of the data type. A basic data type is *character*, as seen above, or more generally a *string*, which is just a sequence of characters.

Dataframes

A dataframe is a two-dimensional variable with added information, such as names and a row index. They are immensely useful for many common data analysis tasks.

Creating Dataframes

In R, we use the command `data.frame()` to create a dataframe, in this case, it is called **ghw** and uses the three vectors we defined above. `View()` is a key function that allows us to see the dataframe as a table in a separate tab in the R Studio Environment:

R

```
ghw=data.frame(gender,height,weight)
ghw
##    gender height weight
```

```
## 1       m    1.75     60
## 2       f    1.80     72
## 3       m    1.65     57
## 4       f    1.90     90
## 5       f    1.74     95
## 6       m    1.91     72
View(ghw)
```

In Python, we need to import the *Pandas* package to use dataframes. To create a dataframe, we need to provide column names and data in a Python dictionary, as defined in the curly brackets:

Python

```
In [1]: import pandas as pd
        ghw = pd.DataFrame(data = {'gender':gender,'weight':weight,
            'height':height})
         print(ghw)
        df
    gender  weight  height
0      f       60    1.75
1      m       72    1.80
2      f       57    1.65
3      m       90    1.90
4      m       95    1.74
5      f       72    1.91
```

Plotting Variables in R

Let's plot *gender* against *weight*. Using the `plot()` command, we can plot the above vectors as scatterplots or boxplots. Within parentheses, we first define the variable we want on the *x* axis, then the variable we want on the *y* axis. `col` can be used to change the colour of the dots in a scatterplot, and `pch` changes the design of the dots.

```
plot(weight,height,col = "red",pch=9)
```

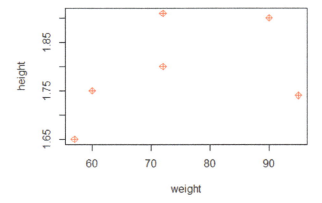

Figure 1.4   Scatterplot of gender versus weight

If we want to plot two variables from the dataframe with the **plot()** function, we must specify both the dataframe and the variable from the dataframe. The appropriate syntax is, in our example, ghw$weight, ghw$height, and ghw$gender:

```
plot(ghw$weight,ghw$height)
```

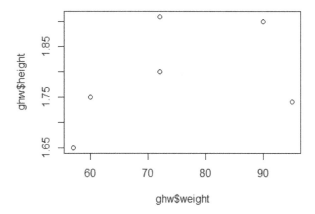

Figure 1.5   Scatterplot of height versus weight

When working with textual data, it is helpful to transform the **character/string** data type into a **factor** data type. Factors organize character/string data into levels, i.e., the unique values of that variable, and this often aids the analysis of the data. For example, let us see what the vector gender looks like if converted to a *factor* data type:

```
factor(gender)
[1] m f m f f m
Levels: f m
```

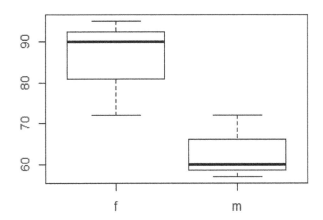

Figure 1.6   Boxplot of weights by gender

Once defined as a *factor* variable, the data are organized into two levels **f** and **m**. This is useful to get insights to what the data are capturing. When using a factor variable, the `plot()` function automatically generates a boxplot that visualizes information about distribution of one column's values grouped by the values for *gender*.

```
plot(factor(gender),weight)
```

Plotting Variables in Python

In Python, we start by importing the popular *Matplotlib* plotting package, specifically its subpackaged *Pyplot*. We can then create a scatterplot by using the function `scatter()`. We can specify the colour and shape of the points in the plot using the `c` and `marker` arguments.

```
In [1]: import matplotlib.pyplot as plt
        plt.scatter(height,weight,c='red',marker='x')
```

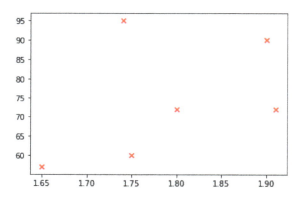

Figure 1.7   Scatterplot of height versus weight with changed data points colour and shape

Matplotlib in the background. Here, we scatter the same data as above (but with the default colour and shape):

```
ghw.plot.scatter('weight','height')
```

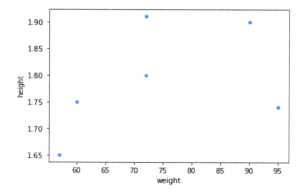

Figure 1.8   Scatterplot of height versus weight with default colours

We can select individual columns by providing their name as a character string (i.e., surrounded by quotes) in square brackets. For example, we can look at the third column named ghw['gender'] and use unique() to see the different values in the data.

```
print(df['gender'].unique())
array(['f', 'm'], dtype=object)
```

A scatterplot is not very interesting for just two different values. In this case, we can create a box plot, like in R, to visualize the distribution of height grouped by gender. The call to 'tight_layout()' in the example below is not strictly necessary, but it makes the layout tidier.

```
sp = df.boxplot(column='height',by='gender')
sp.get_figure().tight_layout()
```

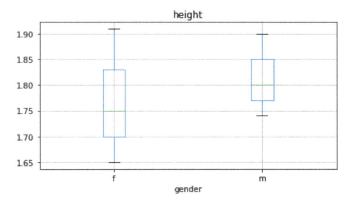

Figure 1.9   Boxplot of heights grouped by gender

Information about Dataframes

When we need a quick summary of the structure or contents of a dataframe, there are a few helpful commands we can use.

In R, **summary()** returns the min, max, mean, median, and 1st and 3rd quartiles of the numerical data, and the length, class, and mode of categorical data. **dim()** returns the number of rows and columns of the dataframe. **str()** provides the first few elements of each variable and **head()** the first few rows of the dataframe:

```
summary(ghw)
##   gender      height            weight
##   f:3     Min.   :1.650     Min.    :57.00
##   m:3     1st Qu.:1.742     1st Qu.:63.00
##           Median :1.775     Median :72.00
##           Mean   :1.792     Mean    :74.33
##           3rd Qu.:1.875     3rd Qu.:85.50
##           Max.   :1.910     Max.    :95.00
```

```
dim(ghw)
## [1] 6 3
str(ghw)
## 'data.frame':    6 obs. of  3 variables:
##  $ gender: Factor w/ 2 levels "f","m": 2 1 2 1 1 2
##  $ height: num  1.75 1.8 1.65 1.9 1.74 1.91
##  $ weight: num  60 72 57 90 95 72
head(ghw)
##   gender height weight
## 1      m   1.75     60
## 2      f   1.80     72
## 3      m   1.65     57
## 4      f   1.90     90
## 5      f   1.74     95
## 6      m   1.91     72
```

To see the full dataframe in another tab, use the `View()` function.

```
View(ghw)
```

In Python, we can obtain similar results using `describe()`, `shape`, `dtypes`, and `head()`.

```
ghw.describe()
```

	weight	height
count	6.000000	6.000000
mean	74.333333	1.791667
std	15.422927	0.100283
min	57.000000	1.650000
25%	63.000000	1.742500
50%	72.000000	1.775000
75%	85.500000	1.875000
max	95.000000	1.910000

```
ghw.shape
(6, 3)
```

```
df.dtypes
gender     object
weight      int64
height    float64
dtype: object
```

```
ghw.head()
```

	gender	weight	height
0	f	60	1.75
1	m	72	1.80
2	f	57	1.65
3	m	90	1.90
4	m	95	1.74

Adding Columns

We can add new columns to a dataframe using data in the already existing columns. Let us calculate the Body Mass Index which is defined as:

$$bmi = \frac{weight}{height^2}$$

```
ghw$bmi = ghw$weight/ghw$height^2
ghw
```

gender	height	weight	bmi
m	1.75	60	19.59184
f	1.80	72	22.22222
m	1.65	57	20.93664
f	1.90	90	24.93075
f	1.74	95	31.37799
m	1.91	72	19.73630

```
ghw['bmi'] = ghw ['weight'] / ghw ['height']**2
ghw
```

	gender	weight	height	bmi
0	f	60	1.75	19.591837
1	m	72	1.80	22.222222
2	f	57	1.65	20.936639
3	m	90	1.90	24.930748
4	m	95	1.74	31.377989
5	f	72	1.91	19.736301

Working with Data

Thus far, we have worked with data that we created ourselves by manually typing in the data values. In reality, this is often not the way we access and work with data. There are two ways in which we can access data from other sources: packages (for example, datasets) and external files (as a general mechanism). Let us first understand what packages are and then how we can access interesting datasets from these packages.

R and Python are open-source languages to which a vibrant community of contributors continually adds new features and functionalities. These enhancements are offered through packages, where some packages offer a collection of functions, e.g., to perform advanced analyses, and some contain datasets available for public use.

Packages in R

The number of packages available is in excess of 18,000 and is constantly growing. You can view the list of all currently available packages at the following link: http://cran.r-project.org/web/packages/available_packages_by_date.html.

The typical process to access a particular package is by installing it and then loading it. For example, there is a package called *moments*. To install and load it, the commands are

```
install.packages("moments")
library(moments)
```

The following command provides a list of all packages loaded in the current project:

```
library()
```

There are three types of packages in R.

Base Packages: These packages are critical for the core functioning of R. They are always loaded and available to use.

Recommended Packages: These are highly recommended packages. Examples include packages named *MASS, boot, Matrix*, and *nnet*. To use a recommended package, we do not need to install it, but we need to load it with the `library(name of the package)` command.

Optional Packages: These are the packages that must be both installed and loaded prior to use.

Let us take a look at the recommended *MASS* package. Since this is a recommended package, it does not need to be installed, but just to be loaded prior to its use:

```
library(MASS)
```

When we want to investigate what a package offers and what data it provides, we can use the following command:

```
library(help=MASS)
```

We can access and work with any of the datasets made available in a package. Let us explore a dataset named *whiteside* that comes with the *MASS* package. To get information about the background and details of the available data, we use the following command:

```
help(whiteside)
```

━━━━━ **Box 1.2** ━━━━━

Whiteside data description

House Insulation: Whiteside's Data

Description

Mr Derek Whiteside of the UK Building Research Station recorded the weekly gas consumption and average external temperature at his own house in south-east England for two heating seasons, one of 26 weeks before, and one of 30 weeks after cavity-wall insulation was installed. The object of the exercise was to assess the effect of the insulation on gas consumption.

Usage

whiteside

Format

The **whiteside** dataframe has 56 rows and 3 columns:

Insul

   A factor, before or after insulation.

Temp

   Purportedly the average outside temperature in degrees Celsius. (These values are far too low for any 56-week period in the 1960s in South-East England. It might be the weekly average of daily minima.)

Gas

   The weekly gas consumption in 1000s of cubic feet.

We can now work with this dataset, for example to compute the average *Temp* in the *whiteside* dataset, we use:

```
mean(whiteside$Temp)
[1] 4.875
```

Packages in Python

Python is a general-purpose programming language, with the main repository *pypi.org* listing over 334,000 packages, and ever growing. We can view the list of all currently available packages at the following address:

https://pypi.org/search/

The typical process to access a particular package is to install it first and then import it. For the installation, we can use Anaconda, which we recommend as the best tool. Many popular packages, including those we use, are included in the full Anaconda installation. We can search for installed packages in the navigator, as shown below:

Figure 1.10 Anaconda Navigator - Environments and packages

Using packages that are not available with Anaconda can be done on the command line using the `pip` command, but that will not be necessary for now. If we want to use a package in our code, we need to import it like we did before with `import numpy`.

Let us now import the popular *Scikit-Learn* package, which comes with some datasets. To know the package name and the available subpackages and functions, we need to look at the package documentation on the internet, e.g., at https://scikit-learn.org/ for scikit-learn. There we can see that the package name to import is *sklearn*, and that we need the subpackage *datasets*, which can be imported as follows:

```
import sklearn.datasets
```

Once we have the package imported, we can use one of its methods (which we can look up here: https://scikit-learn.org/stable/modules/classes.html?highlight=datasets#module-sklearn.datasets) to load the classic *Iris* dataset and get its description:

```
iris = sklearn.datasets.load_iris()
print(iris.DESCR)
.. _iris_dataset:

Iris plants dataset
--------------------

**Data Set Characteristics:**

    :Number of Instances: 150 (50 in each of three classes)
    :Number of Attributes: 4 numeric, predictive attributes and the class
    :Attribute Information:
        - sepal length in cm
        - sepal width in cm
[...]
```

We can now create a *DataFrame* from the data like this:

```
iris_df = pd.DataFrame(iris.data, columns=iris.feature_names)
iris_df
```

	sepal length (cm)	sepal width (cm)	petal length (cm)	petal width (cm)
0	5.1	3.5	1.4	0.2
1	4.9	3.0	1.4	0.2
2	4.7	3.2	1.3	0.2
3	4.6	3.1	1.5	0.2
4	5.0	3.6	1.4	0.2
...	...	...	...	...
145	6.7	3.0	5.2	2.3
146	6.3	2.5	5.0	1.9
147	6.5	3.0	5.2	2.0
148	6.2	3.4	5.4	2.3
149	5.9	3.0	5.1	1.8

Like before, we can now calculate the mean of a variable by using its column name:

```
iris_df['sepal length (cm)'].mean()
5.843333333333334
```

Reading and Writing External Files

R and Python provide tremendous flexibility in the format of the external data they can import and work on. These include text files in CSV (comma-separated values) format, Excel, a variety of database formats, and even data made available on websites. We will prevalently work with CSV files since these are the most common format and other types of files can generally be converted to them before being fed to R or Python. Before we do this, let us first understand how to work with directories where these files are stored.

Files and Directories in R

To get information on the current default directory, use the command:

```
getwd()
"C:/Users/rgopal/Google Drive/Maya R"
```

This is the directory where files will be saved. We can change the default directory with the command:

```
setwd("C:/Users/rgopal")
```

The functions to read and write CSV files are **read.csv()** and **write.csv()**. Let us save the ghw dataframe we created to an external text file with the name 'Sample Data.csv'.

```
write.csv(ghw,file="Sample Data.csv")
```

Similarly, reading external files can be done with the **read.csv()** function. However, RStudio makes reading external files even more trivial thanks to the menu-driven process presented below:

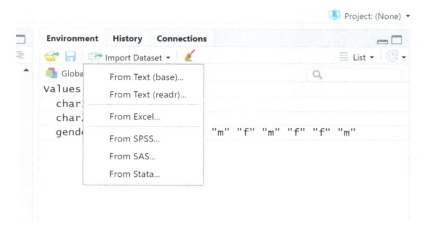

Figure 1.11 RStudio environment

Files and Directories in Python

In Python, there are different ways of interacting with the file system. We will use the 'magic' commands that are available in Jupyter notebooks. They start with the '%' sign and can be used to run a number of commands. To display the current working directory, we use %pwd (for 'print working directory'):

```
%pwd
/Users/tweyde/Documents/projects/Textbook/binder-test/data
```

We can also change the working directory with %cd ('change directory'):

```
%cd ../data
```

If you have cloned our repository from Github, or are using our setup on Binder, the Whiteside data, previously used in R, can also be loaded from a file:

```
whiteside = pd.read_csv('whiteside.csv')
```

We can calculate the mean like before:

```
whiteside['Temp'].mean()
4.87
```

Alternatively, we can load a CSV file directly from the Internet. For example, the Whiteside file is available from the package repository:

```
whiteside = pd.read_csv('https://forge.scilab.org/index.php/p/
    rdataset/source/file/master/csv/MASS/whiteside.csv')
```

Statistics - A First Look

Formally speaking, statistics is a branch of mathematics that transforms data into useful information for decision makers. There are two major areas of statistics – descriptive statistics and inferential statistics. As the name indicates, the objective of descriptive statistics is to describe and understand features of a given set of data. The much broader area of inferential statistics aims to study a sample of data to infer insights on the larger population from which the sample was drawn. Descriptive statistics allow us to detect outliers (i.e., underperforming sales executives), to compare different stock returns in relation to the oil price, use correlations, and more.

The concepts of inferential statistics and population may seem murky to you at this point. Let us focus on descriptive statistics for now and delve deeper into inferential statistics in Chapters 7–10.

Descriptive Statistics

Consider a simple scenario with two individuals, A and B. Suppose the age of A is 21 and that of B is 34. In this trivial scenario, it is easy to note that A is younger than B, and that B is 13 years older than A. Now, instead of two individuals, suppose we have two groups with 10 individuals in each group. Their ages are listed below:

Table 1.2 Age data

Group	Age
1	34, 49, 64, 38, 60, 78, 67, 36, 19, 37
2	77, 75, 78, 41, 51, 20, 61, 73, 76, 38

It becomes a bit more challenging to understand and draw insights within and across the two groups. There are individuals in group 1 who are older than some individuals in group 2, and similarly there are individuals in group 2 who are older than some individuals in group 1. How to make sense of this? This is where descriptive statistics comes in handy.

There are three types of descriptive statistics. These are central tendency, variation, and shape. *Central tendency* captures the extent to which all the data values group around a typical or central value. *Variation* is a measure of the amount of dispersion or spread of the data values. *Shape* measures the pattern of the distribution of values. In this chapter, we will focus on the first two measures and postpone the discussion on shape measures to Chapters 6 and 7 where we delve into distributions.

The most common measures of central tendency are the *mean* and the *median*. Others, not as widely used, yet useful in some instances, include *mode, geometric mean*, and *harmonic mean*. Let us briefly introduce some notation. Let x_i, $i=1,...,n$ represent the values in a dataset of size n. The mean is simply the average of these values. Mathematically, the mean $\bar{x}$ is computed as

$$\bar{x} = \frac{x_1 + x_2 + x_3 + ... + x_n}{n}$$

Strictly speaking, this should be called the *arithmetic mean* as there are other measures of mean as well, as we will see shortly. However, we will continue to call it the mean, which by convention refers to the arithmetic mean. Let us compute the mean for our two groups. The code is:

R

```
g1 = c(34, 49, 64, 38, 60, 78, 67, 36, 19, 37)
g2 = c(77, 75, 78, 41, 51, 20, 61, 73, 76, 38)
mean(g1)
[1] 48.2
mean(g2)
[1] 59
```

Python

```
g1 = (34, 49, 64, 38, 60, 78, 67, 36, 19, 37)
g2 = (77, 75, 78, 41, 51, 20, 61, 73, 76, 38)
print(np.mean(g1))
print(np.mean(g2))
48.2
59.0
```

We can conclude that the average age of individuals in the second group is higher than in the first group. A first glimpse of insights on our data! The mean as a measure of the central tendency, however, is susceptible to extreme values, also termed *outliers*. Let us see an example of this. Consider the following two groups of data:

R

```
g1a = c(34, 49, 64, 38, 60, 78, 67, 36, 19, 37)
g2a = c(34, 49, 64, 38, 60, 400, 67, 36, 19, 37)
```

Python

```
g1a = (34, 49, 64, 38, 60, 78, 67, 36, 19, 37)
g2a = (34, 49, 64, 38, 400, 78, 67, 36, 19, 37)
```

They are both identical except for the sixth value in the second group. The value of 400 is quite far off from the rest of the values in that group. This constitutes an outlier. Let us see how this impacts the mean of the groups:

R

```
mean(g1a)
[1] 48.2
mean(g2a)
[1] 80.4
```

Python

```
np.mean(g1a)
48.2
```

```
np.mean(g2a)
80.4
```

A single outlier value in our data nearly doubles the value of the mean, which highlights the great impact of outliers on it. Extreme outliers can distort the findings, so we often need to pay attention to their presence in the data. Where do they come from? One common source is just errors in the data. In the above example, assuming the values represent ages of individuals, a value of 400 is clearly an error. Perhaps a typo. In other cases, outliers are real and genuine values. In a dataset of salaries, the values for senior management and especially the CEO's will look like an outlier compared to the majority of employees in the same company. It is important to detect and manage outliers before we begin the process of conducting any rigorous statistical analysis or machine learning task. We will return to this later.

A more robust measure to outliers is the median. The median is simply the 'middle value' such that half the data has values less than or equal to the median, and half larger than or equal to it. Let us compute the median of the two groups:

R

```
median(g1a)
[1] 43.5
median (g2a)
[1] 43.5
```

Python

```
np.median(g1a)
43.5
np.median(g2a)
43.5
```

The values are identical. An extreme outlier did not have any impact on the median, proving that outliers do not distort the values of the median.

Let us see how the median was computed. The first step is to sort the data, as shown below:

R

```
sort(g1a)
 [1] 19 34 36 37 38 49 60 64 67 78
```

Python

```
np.sort(g1a)
array([19, 34, 36, 37, 38, 49, 60, 64, 67, 78])
```

Because there are 10 values, the median is between the 5th and 6th values, which are 38 and 49. The median is calculated as the average of these two numbers. We can easily verify that the average is 43.5.

There are other measures of central tendency, such as mode, geometric mean, and harmonic mean. We will not delve into these measures, but put briefly, the mode is defined as the most frequently occurring value. The geometric mean is defined as follows:

$$g(x) = \sqrt[n]{x_1 x_2 x_3 \ldots x_n}$$

Geometric means are useful for values that grow over time, such as house prices, stock prices, populations, and in cases where growth rates need to be multiplied together to get the correct answer. It is a critical concept, particularly in finance, that can be illustrated by house price changes and the related concept of geometric returns. Should you buy a house for \$100k? If the next year prices fell by 50% and the following year rose by 50%, your house would be worth \$100k * (1 − 50%) * (1 + 50%) = \$75k, i.e., the return would be −25%. Differently, an arithmetic mean of the changes would suggest a return of 0% (average of 50% and −50% = 0%), resulting in a wrong estimate. The harmonic mean is defined as:

$$h(x) = \frac{n}{\dfrac{1}{x_1} + \dfrac{1}{x_2} + \dfrac{1}{x_3} \ldots + \dfrac{1}{x_n}}$$

The harmonic mean is useful when the data capture ratios, such as price to earnings (PE) ratios, where very large PE ratios, i.e., a stock has reported a fall to near zero earnings, can distort arithmetic averages. To calculate the average PE of a basket of stocks, it is more meaningful (and more widely accepted) to use the harmonic mean.

The common measure of variation is variance or equivalently the standard deviation. Variance is defined as

$$var(x) = \frac{\left(x_1 - \bar{x}\right)^2 + \left(x_2 - \bar{x}\right)^2 + \left(x_3 - \bar{x}\right)^2 + \ldots + \left(x_n - \bar{x}\right)^2}{n - 1},$$

where $\bar{x}$ is the mean. As the equation above indicates, it measures how spread out the data values are around the mean. The standard deviation σ is also often used and it simply is the square root of the variance. Let us compute the values of the variance for the groups g1 and g2. Note that in Python, we need to add the **ddof=1** parameter to use the sample variance:

Box 1.3

Samples, populations, and estimators

In this chapter, and generally in the book, we use the sample-based definition of the variance and standard deviation, with the denominator $n - 1$. If we had access to all possible values, the whole *population*, we would use just n as the denominator.

The difference is because in statistics and probability, we think of data as a sample from a larger population, e.g., in medicine, we test a few patients to learn for all patients, or think of the data source as a process that can produce infinitely many samples. The true mean of the population or process is often called μ. The sample mean $\bar{x}$ is closer to the sample points than the true mean μ and the smaller denominator compensates for this.

Using the sample-based definition is the default in R, but in Python it is not. In Python, we need to add argument **ddof=1**, to switch to sample-based calculations.

R

```
var(g1)
[1] 340.4
var(g2)
[1] 420
```

Python

```
np.var(g1,ddof=1)
340.4
np.var(g2,ddof=1)
420
```

In addition to a larger mean, group g2 has a higher variance than g1, indicating that the values in the second group are more spread out than in the first group. The code below computes the standard deviation, and we can verify that it is indeed the square root of the variance. Again, we need to provide the *ddof=1* in Python to switch from variance to sample-based standard deviation:

R

```
sd(g1)
[1] 18.44993
sd(g2)
[1] 20.4939
```

Python

```
np.std(g1,ddof=1)
18.44993
np.std(g2,ddof=1)
20.4939
```

Simply comparing two groups of data by variance can be misleading. Consider two stocks A and B with mean prices of $500 and $50, respectively. A fluctuation in the price of $5 for stock A, given its high average price, would be considered minor. However, similar fluctuation of $5 for stock B would be much more significant given its lower average price. A more apples-to-apples comparison of the variance for two different datasets is the coefficient of variation, defined as follows:

$$cv(x) = \frac{\sigma(x)}{\bar{x}}$$

The table below shows that stock C has higher fluctuation despite having lower standard deviation (and thus variance) than stock D:

Table 1.3 Stock returns

Stock	Mean	Standard Deviation	Coefficient of Variation
C	25	3	0.12
D	100	5	0.05

The following code computes the coefficient of variation for groups g1 and g2:

R

```
sd(g1)*100/mean(g1)
[1] 38.27787
sd(g2)*100/mean(g2)
[1] 34.73543
```

Python

```
np.std(g1,ddof=1)/np.mean(g1)
0.38277867736925514
np.std(g2,ddof=1)/np.mean(g2)
0.3473542632528677
```

This again shows that group g1 has a higher coefficient of variance in the data despite having lower variance than group g2.

This brings us to an interesting question. Is variance in a dataset a good thing or a bad thing. Consider an extreme case where all the values are identical as in the simple example below:

R

```
g3 = rep(4,10)
 g3
 [1] 4 4 4 4 4 4 4 4 4 4
 var(g3)
[1] 0
```

Python

```
g3 = np.tile(4,10)
g3
[4 4 4 4 4 4 4 4 4 4]
np.var(g3)
0.0
```

The variance in this case is obviously 0. This is not interesting as these data do not tell us much. When there is variation in the data value, there is a richer story to unfold. We may want to examine why these values vary or how the variation in these values influences other outcomes of interest. In a dataset of salaries, if there is a good amount of variation in pay, then we can analyse factors (perhaps education and age) contributing to this variation or how income impacts outcomes of interest, such as charity giving. Therefore, we want to see variance in the data.

However, we do not want high variance that stems from outliers because these artificially inflate the variance and do not capture the essence of the data, resulting in likely misleading insights.

As mean and variance can vary across datasets, another useful measure is the *z-score*. This, in essence, scales the data values to make them more easily comparable to each other. The z-score is one of the simplest, yet most powerful statistical tools used in business because it helps detect outliers. This measure scales the data as follows:

$$z\_score(x) = \frac{x - \bar{x}}{\sigma}$$

The z-score indicates how many standard deviations a data point is away from the mean. It is a key business analytic that can be used for anything from identifying mis-sized widgets on a factory line to determining historic extremes in valuations of credit spreads. For instance, if we were considering whether borrowing costs are reasonable based on the past, we could use a z-score. Take the current interest rate, x, and look at the history of this number, calculating $\bar{x}$ and σ over this period. A z-score > +3 would indicate an extremely high current interest rate. A z-score of <−3 would indicate an extremely low current interest rate.

The code to compute the above is the following:

R

```
(g1-mean(g1))/sd(g1)
 [1] -0.76965052  0.04336059  0.85637171 -0.55284756  0.63956874  1.61518208
  1.01897393 -0.66124904 -1.58266164 -0.60704830
```

Python

```
(g1-np.mean(g1))/np.std(g1,ddof=1)
array([-0.76965052,  0.04336059,  0.85637171, -0.55284756,  0.63956874,
        1.61518208,  1.01897393, -0.66124904, -1.58266164, -0.6070483 ])
```

Alternately, an easier way to compute z-scores is to use the **scale()** function in R or the **zscore** function from the *scipy* package in Python:

R

```
scale(g1)
          [,1]
 [1,] -0.76965052
 [2,]  0.04336059
 [3,]  0.85637171
 [4,] -0.55284756
 [5,]  0.63956874
 [6,]  1.61518208
 [7,]  1.01897393
 [8,] -0.66124904
 [9,] -1.58266164
[10,] -0.60704830
```

Python

```
from scipy import stats
stats.zscore(g1,ddof=1)
array([-0.76965052,  0.04336059,  0.85637171, -0.55284756,  0.63956874,
        1.61518208,  1.01897393, -0.66124904, -1.58266164, -0.6070483 ])
```

Values close to 0 are near the mean, and the higher or lower the value, the farther away it is from the mean. This means that larger positive or negative values are indicative of outliers. A general rule of thumb is that z-score values approaching +3 or −3 are potential outliers and more extreme values are often branded as extreme outliers. Let's see the z-scores for the group g2a:

R

```
scale(g1a)
          [,1]
 [1,] -0.4094642
 [2,] -0.2770943
 [3,] -0.1447244
 [4,] -0.3741656
 [5,] -0.1800230
 [6,]  2.8203611
 [7,] -0.1182504
 [8,] -0.3918149
 [9,] -0.5418341
[10,] -0.3829902
```

Python

```
stats.zscore(g1s,ddof=1)
array([-0.40946419, -0.2770943 , -0.14472441, -0.37416555, -0.18002305,
        2.82036111, -0.11825043, -0.39181487, -0.54183408, -0.38299021])
```

The sixth observation has a z-score of 2.82 suggesting a possible outlier. Z-scores are a simple, easy tool to detect possible outliers in our data.

An extension of the median is the measure quartile, and it illustrates how the data values are distributed, as shown in the figure below:

Figure 1.12 Quartiles

The second quartile, Q2, is the same as the median. Half the values in the data are below Q2 and half above. The first quartile Q1 is the value where a quarter or 25% of the data are below this value. Similarly, the third quartile Q3 is the value where three quarters or 75% of the data are below this value. Computing the quartiles is rather simple in R. In Python, it is straightforward too, using the **mquantiles** function from the *SciPy* package. The **alphap, betap** parameters adjust the interpolation behaviour so to create the same results as in quantiles R. We can easily drop them to obtain the Python standard behaviour. These subtle differences are not important for now:

R

```
quantile(g1)
    0%   25%   50%   75%  100%
19.00 36.25 43.50 63.00 78.00
```

Python

```
from scipy.stats.mstats import mquantiles
        mquantiles(g1,alphap=1,betap=1)
array([36.25, 43.5 , 63.  ])
```

Let us summarize what the above results tell us. The minimum value is 19 and the maximum value is 78. Here, 25% of the data values are below 36.25 and 75% are below 63. Notice that half the values are between Q1 and Q3. This is the middle half of our data. The difference between Q3 and Q1 is called the *interquartile range,* which indicates the spread of the middle half of the data. We can get a visual of the quartiles with the `boxplot()` function:

R

```
boxplot(g1)
```

Python

```
import matplotlib.pyplot as plt
plt.boxplot(g1)
```

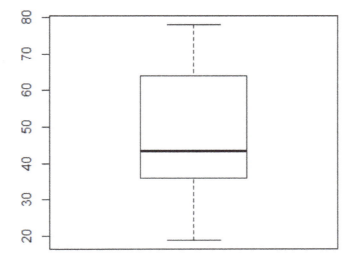

Figure 1.13   Boxplot showing the quartiles

Box plots are a great way to eye ball our data, spot outliers, and visualize whether the distribution is skewed towards higher values, i.e., stock prices, or skewed to lower values, i.e., profits on individual loan decisions.

Correlation

Correlation is a powerful business analytic that allows us to compare data series for similarities (or dissimilarities), i.e., sales patterns over time between different product lines, or to define strong or weak relationships between margin performance of different companies. Covariance, highly related to correlation, forms the basis of diversifying stock market portfolios by combining stocks with different price tendencies, in an attempt to balance them. For instance, one of the most popular hedge fund strategies, statistical arbitrage, attempts to combine stocks with similar price movements, such as PepsiCo and Coca-Cola, and take advantage of divergences and convergences in price.

Consider the `ghw` dataframe we created and let's visually inspect how weight and height may be related:

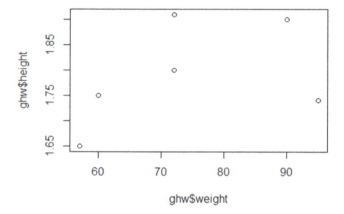

Figure 1.14   Height versus weight for the `ghw` dataframe

Roughly speaking, it appears that as weight values increase (i.e., we move from left to right on the x axis), the height values also tend to increase. Covariance and correlation are mathematical measures of linear association between two numeric variables. Covariance between two variables X and Y (in our case, **height** and **weight**) is defined as follows (in the sample-based version):

$$cov(X,Y) = \frac{1}{n-1}\sum_{i=1}^{n}(x_i - \bar{x})(y_i - \bar{y})$$

When the covariance is positive, higher values in one variable generally correspond to higher values in the second variable. Note the expression in the summation function, $(x_i - \bar{x})(y_i - \bar{y})$. This term is positive when both x and y values are either below the mean or both above the mean $\bar{x}$ or $\bar{y}$, respectively. Thus, when the covariance is positive, both values tend to be below or above their mean. The correlation coefficient ρ (the Greek letter 'rho') scales the covariance values to lie between −1 and +1 and is defined as follows:

$$\rho(X,Y) = \frac{cov(X,Y)}{\sigma(X)\,\sigma(Y)}$$

The figure below provides a visual illustration of correlation:

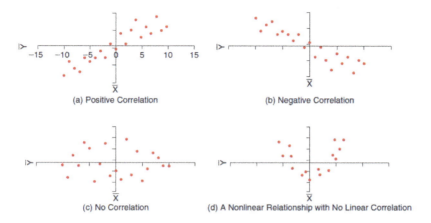

(a) Positive Correlation

(b) Negative Correlation

(c) No Correlation

(d) A Nonlinear Relationship with No Linear Correlation

Figure 1.15 Illustration of correlation

Let us code the computation of covariance and correlation between height and weight. In Python, we get the complete covariance matrix, i.e., the covariance of the individual vectors with themselves too:

R

```
cov(ghw$height,ghw$weight)
[1] 0.6773333
cor(ghw$height,ghw$weight)
[1] 0.437934
```

Python

```
stats.cov(df['height'],df['weight'])
[[1.00566667e-02 6.77333333e-01]
 [6.77333333e-01 2.37866667e+02]]
stats.pearsonr(df['height'],df['weight'])
(0.4379339635990291, 0.38509389043540027)
```

A value of 0.437 for the correlation between height and gender indicates that they are positively associated with each other. This descriptive statistic provides a first glimpse on how different variables in the dataset may be related to each other. In Python, we also get the p-value, that is, the probability of this being the result of random variation in the data, which we will explain in more detail in Chapter 8.

Use Case: Descriptive Statistics and Correlations to Determine US Supermarket Sales Strategy

Descriptive statistics and correlations help us understand more about business problems, and can improve our decision making. For instance, a supermarket chain needs to maximize sales at the lowest marketing cost, determining whether in-store promotion or out-of-store advertising is most effective in driving profits by product line. Should they invest more in Promotions or Advertising?

We have data in a CSV file listing product lines (rows), profit reported on each over the sales period, what was spent on promoting each, and what was spent on advertising. First, we can load the CSV file into a **Pandas** dataframe, and examine some of the data. In what follows, the output is shown for the Python code. We get a very similar output when the R code is run.

R

```
df_supermarket = read.csv("50_SupermarketBranches.csv")
head(df_supermarket)
```

Python

```
import pandas as pd
df_supermarket = pd.read_csv("50_SupermarketBranches.csv")
df_supermarket.head()
```

	Advertisement Spend	Promotion Spend	Administration Spend	State	Profit
0	165349.20	136897.80	471784.10	New York	192261.83
1	162597.70	151377.59	443898.53	California	191792.06
2	153441.51	101145.55	407934.54	Florida	191050.39
3	144372.41	118671.85	383199.62	New York	182901.99
4	142107.34	91391.77	366168.42	Florida	166187.94

We can examine the simple statistics of our data to understand more:

R

```
summary(df_supermarket)
```

Python

```
df_supermarket.describe()
```

	Advertisement Spend	Promotion Spend	Administration Spend	Profit
count	50.000000	50.000000	50.000000	50.000000
mean	73721.615600	121344.639600	211025.097800	112012.639200

std	45902.256482	28017.802755	122290.310726	40306.180338
min	0.000000	51283.140000	0.000000	14681.400000
25%	39936.370000	103730.875000	129300.132500	90138.902500
50%	73051.080000	122699.795000	212716.240000	10978.902500
75%	101602.800000	144842.180000	299469.085000	139765.977500
max	165349.200000	182645.560000	471784.100000	192261.830000

There are several interesting points to note about our marketing approach that we can see from the descriptive statistics immediately. The range of spend on Advertising ($0 to $165,349) is wider than on Promotion ($51,283 to $182,645) across product lines, as in some cases nothing is spent on Advertising. All lines are promoted, but not all are advertised. Mean Promotion Spend ($121,344) is considerably more than mean Advertising Spend ($73,721).

Now we can examine the correlations between Advertising Spend and Profits and Promotion Spend and Profits. We can use charts to examine the correlations. If there is no relationship, we will see a cloud of dots with no form:

R

```
plot(df_supermarket$Promotion.Spend,df_supermarket$Profit,
    main = 'Relationship between Promotion Spend and profit
            (each point is a product line)',
    xlab = 'Promotion Spend',
    ylab = 'Profit')
```

Python

```
plt.scatter(df_supermarket['Promotion Spend'],df_supermarket['Profit'])
plt.title('Relationship between Promotion Spend and profit (each point is a
product line)');
plt.xlabel('Promotion Spend')
plt.ylabel('Profit')
plt.show()
```

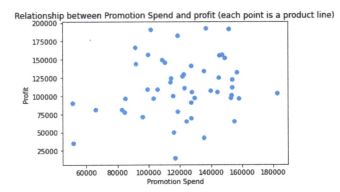

Figure 1.16　Relationship between Promotion Spend and Profit

There is no apparent relationship between Promotion Spend and Profits. In this case, it appears that every extra dollar we spend on promoting a product line does not contribute to the profits from that line. We now examine Advertisement Spend:

R

```
plot(df_supermarket$Advertisement.Spend,df_supermarket$Profit,
     main = 'Relationship between Advertisement Spend and profit
             (each point is a product line)',
     xlab = 'Advertisement Spend',
     ylab = 'Profit')
```

Python

```
plt.scatter(df_supermarket['Advertisement Spend'],df_supermarket['Profit'])
plt.title('Relationship between Advertisement Spend and profit (each point is
    a product line)');
plt.xlabel('Advertisement Spend')
plt.ylabel('Profit')
plt.show()
```

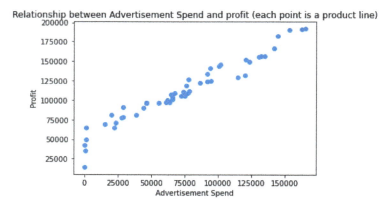

Figure 1.17 Relationship between Advertisement Spend and Profit (each point is a product line)

Advertisement Spend is quite different and shows a strong relationship between profits and out-of-store advertising spending. The dots follow an upwards sloping line, described as a linear relationship with a positive slope. This means that with every product line where more has been spent on advertising, more profit has resulted. Where less has been spent on advertising, less profit has resulted. The amount of US$s in profit we gain from and extra US$1 spent on advertising is described by the slope of the line. We can now calculate the correlation coefficients, and sort them in order of the highest correlation:

R

```
cor(df_supermarket$Profit,df_supermarket[-c(4,5)])
```

Python

```
corr.sort_values(['Profit'], ascending=False)[['Profit']]
```

	Profit
Profit	1.000000
Advertisement Spend	0.972900
Administration Spend	0.747766
Promotion Spend	0.200717

The correlation coefficients show what we already know that Advertisement Spend has a high correlation (0.97), while Promotion Spend has a low correlation (0.20). While correlation is not necessarily causational, from this analysis we can clearly see that Advertising has the stronger relationship with profits. It would make sense to review possible increases in Advertisement Spend by product line as a priority, and to review reductions in Promotion Spend too.

Caution: Independence? Spurious Correlation?

A note of caution is needed. This simple analysis assumes no relationship between Advertising and Promotion, we are also associating correlation with causation. Both assumptions need to be treated with care, and we need to do more work to make sure these assumptions are valid. For instance, some product promotion may be necessary to allow advertising to be effective. If we cut promotional spending to zero for all products, this could have very poor results. Equally, the relationship between Advertising and Profits could be spurious. It may be that management have taken all product lines profitability and assigned Advertisement Spend based on the past profits. Statistics will get us a long way to understanding a problem, but there is no substitute for grey matter.

Summary

We covered quite a bit of ground in the first chapter. This introduction to R and Python programming covered working with important data structures. In addition to manually creating the data, we discussed how to bring in external data files and start the analysis to gain insights. The section on descriptive statistics covered measures of central tendency and variation which are useful to analyse and compare data.

Now that we have developed a good intuition on these concepts, we are ready to study them in more detail in the following chapters. We recommend first doing the programming exercises below to become fluent with the programming, statistics, and applications. The key take-aways are:

Programming

- R and Python as programming environments for statistics and machine learning.
- Most common data objects – vectors/arrays and dataframes.
- Numeric and factor/categorical data types.
- Simple computations and plotting.
- Working with data files from external sources.
- Using packages to enhance functionality of code.

(Continued)

Statistics

- Introduction to descriptive statistics to describe and understand features of a dataset.
- Measures of central tendency – mean, median, mode, geometric mean, and harmonic mean.
- Measures of variation – variance, standard deviation, coefficient of variation, and quantiles.
- Z-score as a simple measure to detect outliers in the data.
- Useful measures to compare similarities between two numeric variables – covariance, correlation, and R^2.

Practical Applications

- Work with data files in R and Python environments.
- Useful insights through the application of descriptive statistics.
- Detect patterns and outliers in data to begin to gain deeper insights on the phenomenon that generated the data.

Exercises

To complete the activity below, you will need to visit the companion website to the book and download the relevant dataset: https://study.sagepub.com/gopal

Now that we have covered various approaches to work with data, we are ready to import some data and run simple analysis and plots to explore it.

1 Create a vector called x and place values 10 to 1000. Create a y vector that takes the square root of the log of numbers in x. Plot x and y.
2 In the R *datasets* package, there is a dataset called `airquality`. In Python, load the airquality.csv data file from the GitHub repository.

The information is as follows:

The `airquality` dataframe has 153 rows and 6 columns. It contains daily air quality measurements in New York, between May and September 1973. The dataset contains information of the factors affecting the air quality on a daily basis, over the same period. It also contains parameters such as *Ozone, Solar.R, Wind, Temp, Month,* and *Day*.

Compute the following.

i Mean, median, and 75th percentile values of `Temp`.
ii Create a subset dataframe called **s1** which has data for all days in June.
iii Draw a plot from **s1** of *Temp* and *Solar.R*.
iv What is the median value of *Solar.R* in the **s1** dataframe?

3 In R, load the *MASS* package. There is a dataset called `Cars93`. In Python, load the 93cars.csv data file.

The information is as follows:

The `Cars93` dataframe has 93 rows and 26 columns. It contains data for 93 cars on sale in the USA in 1993. Cars were selected at random from among 1993 passenger car models that were listed in both the Consumer Reports issue and the PACE Buying Guide. It includes the price, mpg, horsepower, capacity, etc. of the cars.

Compute the following.

i   Mean, median, and 25th percentile values of *MPG* on a highway.

ii   Create a subset dataframe called **p1** which has data for all Non-4WD cars that weigh over 3500 pounds.

iii   Draw a plot from *p1* of price and horsepower.

iv   What is the median luggage room in the **p1** dataframe?

4   In R, install the package `plm`, load the library, and load the data using the command `data(Males)`. In Python, load Males.csv from the repository.

Compute the following:

i   Create a frequency table between industry and residence. Where do people in manufacturing mostly live and in what proportion? What proportion of people in the south are in transportation? What is the most popular industry for people living in rural areas?

ii   Compute the average wage based on industry and marriage status. Which industry has the highest wage on average among married people?

Some Useful Resources

R

- The R reference card is very useful if you want to look up the basic syntax. You are strongly recommended to download and keep it handy as you work to get comfortable with coding in R. https://cran.r-project.org/doc/contrib/Short-refcard.pdf
- There are several other cheatsheets for specific packages and functionalities. You can find a list of them at https://rstudio.com/resources/cheatsheets/
- Quick-R
- The R Journal: https://journal.r-project.org/
- Books: https://rstudio.com/resources/books/

Python

- General information and links www.python.org
- Python reference cards

  http://sixthresearcher.com/wp-content/uploads/2016/12/Python3_reference_cheat_sheet.pdf
  https://perso.limsi.fr/pointal/_media/python:cours:mementopython3-v1.0.5a-english.pdf
- Documentation of the Python language: https://docs.python.org/3/
- NumPy reference: https://numpy.org/doc/stable/reference/
- SciPy reference: https://docs.scipy.org/doc/numpy-1.17.0/reference/
- Pandas reference: https://pandas.pydata.org/docs/reference/index.html

2

SUMMARIZING AND VISUALIZING DATA

Chapter Contents

In the first chapter, we covered the basics of programming and learnt how to work with data and compute descriptive statistics to draw initial insights from the data. To draw further insights, in this chapter, we will turn to the most powerful sense we humans possess, vision. The sense of sight provides 80% of the information we receive about the world surrounding us. We will focus on two important tools – summarization and visualization – which can explain trends, patterns, and exceptions by leveraging our visual skills. In fact, the goal of these tools is to use visual representations to explore, make sense of, and communicate with data. It is often said that statistics is about proving what we expect, whereas visualization is about making sense of and discovering what we did not expect. We will explore the data visualization packages *ggplot* and *plotly*, along with the grammar of graphics principles that aid in the design of effective visualizations to drive insights and understanding.

Dataframes are the most common data structure we use in R and Python to work with data. Before we start the process of summarizing and visualizing data in dataframes, it is useful to first understand how to 'slice and dice' the data so that we can focus our attention on parts of the dataframe that are of current interest. We will begin with indexing and subsetting to select and exclude variables and observations from dataframes.

INDEXING AND SUBSETTING

Indexing and subsetting are ways of viewing specific parts of a dataframe. For example, we use them if we want to see the first four rows of the dataframe **df**, or the first, third, and sixth columns. The syntax is as follows:

R

```
df[rows,columns]
df[,1]


# all rows, 1st column
```

Python

```
df.iloc[rows,columns]
df.iloc[:,0]


# all rows, 1st column
```

There are some differences in the syntax and operation of working with dataframes between R and Python.

1   Data in a Python dataframe can be addressed in many ways, the default is by the row and column names. For numeric addressing, we need to use the `iloc` syntax as shown above. In R, you can mix name-based and numeric addressing.

2   If we want all the rows or all the columns, in R, leave that argument blank, in Python, write a colon (':').

3 Indexing in R starts from 1, like in mathematics, while in Python, we use offsets starting from 0, as in most programming languages.[1]

4 Ranges in R include both arguments, i.e., 1:3 is 1,2,3. In Python, 1:3 means 1,2, i.e., the second argument is exclusive.

Below are some examples using the **ghw** dataframe that we created in the first chapter:

R

```
weight = c(60,72,57,90,95,72)
height = c(1.75,1.8,1.65,1.9,1.74,1.91)
gender = c("m","f","m","f","f","m")

ghw=data.frame(gender,height,weight)

ghw[1,1]
## [1] m
## Levels: f m

ghw[,1:3]

##   gender height weight
## 1      m   1.75     60
## 2      f   1.80     72
## 3      m   1.65     57
## 4      f   1.90     90
## 5      f   1.74     95
## 6      m   1.91     72

ghw[2:5,]

##   gender height weight
## 2      f   1.80     72
## 3      m   1.65     57
## 4      f   1.90     90
## 5      f   1.74     95

ghw[,1]

## [1] m f m f f m
## Levels: f m
```

---

[1]The use of offsets means that the first element of a vector **v** is accessed as **v[0]** in a Python array, or as **v.iloc[0,0]** in a Python dataframe (using the *Pandas* package). The use of offsets stems from addressing Random Access Memory, where the memory address of the first array element in v is the memory address of **v** and the address **v+1** already points to the second element of **v**. This method is used in most programming languages, including C, C++, Java, and JavaScript.

```
ghw[c(1,3,6),2:3]
```

```
##   height weight
## 1   1.75     60
## 3   1.65     57
## 6   1.91     72
```

Python

```python
weight = np.array([60,72,57,90,95,72])
height = np.array([1.75,1.8,1.65,1.9,1.74,1.91])
gender = np.array(["m","f","m","f","f","m"])
ghw = pd.DataFrame({"gender":gender,"height":height,"weight":weight})
```

```python
ghw.iloc[0,0]
'm'
```

```python
ghw.iloc[:,1:3]
```

```
     height    weight
0     1.75        60
1     1.80        72
2     1.65        57
3     1.90        90
4     1.74        95
5     1.91        72
```

```python
ghw.iloc[1:5,:]
```

```
     gender    height    weight
1       f       1.80       72
2       m       1.65       57
3       f       1.90       90
4       f       1.74       95
```

```python
ghw.iloc[:,0]
```

```
0    m
1    f
2    m
3    f
4    f
5    m
Name: gender, dtype: object
```

```python
ghw.iloc[[0,2,5],1:3]
```

	height	Weight
0	1.75	60
2	1.65	57
5	1.91	72

It is sometimes useful to store the subset in a new variable. In the code below, the variable x is created as a dataframe with the first three rows of the **ghw** dataframe:

R

```
x = ghw[1:3,]
dim(x)
```

```
## [1] 3 3
```

Python

```
x = ghw.iloc[0:3,:]
x.shape
```

```
(3, 3)
```

SPECIFYING CONDITIONS

A key element of indexing and subsetting is using conditions to select specific rows. We use the comparison symbol == to specify which elements we desire. Other symbols include:

Table 2.1 Symbols for conditions

R	Meaning	Python (bitwise)
&	and	and (&)
|	or	Or (|)
<, >,>=,<=	less than, greater than, greater than or equal to, less than or equal to	<,>,>=,<=
!	not	not (~)
is.na(x)	x is NA	pd.isna(x)

In R, the last line in the above table, NA means 'Not Available' and depicts missing values. Missing values are very common in many datasets. This function allows us to detect and manage missing values. Another symbol used in R is NAN, which stands for 'Not a Number'. This arises, as shown below, when you have an impossible operation, such as dividing 0 by 0.

```
> 0/0
[1] NaN
```

In Python, *Pandas* uses the NaN ('Not a Number') value to indicate missing values. These values occur if a value was not set or if a computation yielded this result, like above. However, there are several subtle differences in the handling of NaN between R, standard Python, and *Pandas*, e.g., the expression above in pure Python yields an error message:

```
0/0
...
ZeroDivisionError: division by zero
```

If that computation is done inside a `Pandas` dataframe, however, it yields -inf, inf, or NaN, depending on the dividend (the number being divided), and will be treated as a missing value in subsequent operations:

```
df = pd.DataFrame({'a': [0,-1], 'b': [2,3]})
print(df)
df /= 0
print(df)
   a  b
0  0  2
1 -1  3
      a    b
0   NaN  inf
1  -inf  inf
```

Let us show some examples on the student dataframe (you can download the file from the online source provided):

R

```
student = read.csv("student.csv")
```

Python

```
student = pd.read_csv("../data/student.csv")
```

For factor variables, remember to use quotations to specify the elements:

R

```
x1 = student[student$daysabs==0,]
head(x1)
     id gender math prog daysabs
16 1016      0   89    2       0
18 1018      1   35    2       0
22 1022      0   61    2       0
24 1024      0   63    2       0
28 1028      1   21    2       0
31 1031      0    1    2       0
```

```
x2 = student[student$daysabs==0 & student$math>60,]
head(x2)
     id gender math prog daysabs
16 1016      0   89    2       0
22 1022      0   61    2       0
24 1024      0   63    2       0
35 1035      0   68    2       0
71 1071      0   72    2       0
85 1085      0   75    2       0
```

Python

```
x1 = student[student['daysabs']==0]
x1.head()
     id  gender  math  prog  daysabs
15  1016       0    89     2        0
17  1018       1    35     2        0
21  1022       0    61     2        0
23  1024       0    63     2        0
27  1028       1    21     2        0
```

```
x2 = student[(student['daysabs']==0) & (student['math']>60)]
x2.head()
     id  gender  math  prog  daysabs
15  1016       0    89     2        0
21  1022       0    61     2        0
23  1024       0    63     2        0
34  1035       0    68     2        0
70  1071       0    72     2        0
```

It is also useful to use formulae to create conditions. We can do this in R by saving a condition as a variable as shown below:

```
f1 = student$gender==0 & student$prog==3 & student$math>60
```

The variable *f1* is stored as a logical data type as shown below:

```
class(f1)
[1] "logical"
```

In Python, this works similarly to R and creates a Pandas Series object that contains values of type Boolean (i.e., logical):

```
f1 = (student['gender']==0) & (student['prog']==3) &
(student['math']>60)
f1
```

```
0        False
1        False
2        False
         ...
311      False
312      False
313      False
Length: 314, dtype: bool
```

Now we can use the formula to subset the dataframe:

R

```
x3 = student[f1,]
head(x3)
     id gender math prog daysabs
89  1089      0   84    3      4
165 2007      0   71    3      0
167 2009      0   71    3      0
169 2011      0   77    3      2
173 2015      0   65    3      1
175 2017      0   77    3      0
```

Python

```
x3 = student[f1]
x3.head()
       id  gender  math  prog  daysabs
88   1089       0    84     3        4
164  2007       0    71     3        0
166  2009       0    71     3        0
168  2011       0    77     3        2
172  2015       0    65     3        1
```

Use of formulae can make our code more comprehensible and a bit easier to manage, especially when we need to use complicated sets of conditions.

In terms of writing succinct and easy-to-read code, here is another trick we can use in R. As we mentioned before, we refer to variables by prefixing them with the name of the dataframe, for example, **student$gender.** This can get tedious if the amount of code we need to write is extensive. We can skip prefixing variables with their associated dataframe by first attaching the dataframe. The above example could be rewritten more simply as follows:

```
attach(student)
f1 = gender==0 & prog==3 & math>60
```

We must exercise some caution here as this may create name conflicts across different dataframes and with reserved words. A good practice is to attach the dataframe, when convenient, and then detach it with the *detach()* function to avoid further conflicts.

In Python, there is no functionality like *attach* and it is not recommended to use variable names without context information as above (even though we could write our own attach function). The reason is the different philosophy of R as a specialist tool, where convenience in typically small projects is important, while Python is used more widely and sometimes as part of very large systems, where it can be difficult to keep track of names.

SUMMARIZING DATA

Summaries are a quick and simple way to see our data in an organized fashion. In R, we will be using the `whiteside` dataframe in the *MASS* package, and the `Arthritis` dataframe in the *vcd* package, which need to be installed. As mentioned in Chapter 1, we can install packages manually in R Studio (see the bottom right-hand pane in the R Studio window) or through the command `install.packages("name of the package")`. Once installed, we load the package and start using it with the command `library("name of the package")`. Remember that, while packages require to be installed only once, we must load them in our script every time we want to use them.

In Python, we will use the same data, but we will load them from files. As mentioned before, there is a vast number of packages available in Python for additional functionality (typically not including data). How we install Python packages on our system depends on what Python distribution we are using. If we use Anaconda (recommended), we can conveniently install the most common packages with a Graphical User Interface (GUI) using the Anaconda Navigator (under 'Environments') or with the *conda* command line tool.[2]

FACTOR VARIABLES

The command we use to create summary tables of factor variables is *table()*. In Python, we don't have factor variables as a programming element, but we can use other functionality to achieve the same effect, in particular the `value_counts()` method, often combined with `unstack()` to change the stacked index created by `value_counts()` into a lattice. Let us start off by creating a few tables from the `Arthritis` dataframe:

R

```
table(Arthritis$Sex)
```

```
##
## Female    Male
##     59      25
```

---

[2]See here for more information: https://docs.conda.io/projects/conda/en/latest/user-guide/concepts/installing-with-conda.html

Python

```
arthritis['Sex'].value_counts()
```

```
Female    59
Male      25
Name: Sex, dtype: int64
```

We can see that there are 59 females and 25 males.

Next, let us create a two-way table with *Treatment* and *Improved* variables:

R

```
x = table(Arthritis$Treatment,
    Arthritis$Improved)
x
##
##          None Some Marked
##   Placebo  29    7      7
##   Treated  13    7     21
```

Python

```
arthritis[['Treatment','Improved']].
  value_counts().unstack()
```

```
Improved    Marked  None  Some
Treatment
Placebo          7    29     7
Treated         21    13     7
```

Let us say that instead of a count, we want proportions in our table. For this, we use the command `prop.table()`:

R

```
prop.table(x)

##
##               None       Some     Marked
##   Placebo 0.34523810 0.08333333 0.08333333
##   Treated 0.15476190 0.08333333 0.25000000

prop.table(x, margin = 1)

##
##              None      Some     Marked
##   Placebo 0.6744186 0.1627907 0.1627907
##   Treated 0.3170732 0.1707317 0.5121951

prop.table(x, margin = 2)
```

```
##
##              None      Some     Marked
##   Placebo 0.6904762 0.5000000 0.2500000
##   Treated 0.3095238 0.5000000 0.7500000
```

Python

```
arthritis[['Treatment','Improved']].
  value_counts(normalize=True).unstack()


Improved       Marked      None       Some
Treatment
Placebo       0.083333   0.345238   0.083333
Treated       0.250000   0.154762   0.083333


arthritis.groupby('Improved')['Treatment'].
  value_counts(normalize=True).unstack()


Treatment       Placebo      Treated
Improved
Marked         0.250000     0.750000
None           0.690476     0.309524
Some           0.500000     0.500000


arthritis.groupby('Treatment')['Improved'].
  value_counts(normalize=True).unstack()


Improved       Marked      None       Some
Treatment
Placebo       0.162791   0.674419   0.162791
Treated       0.512195   0.317073   0.170732
```

Note that no **margin** gives percentages of the total population, a **margin** of 1 gives percentages across the rows, and a **margin** of 2 gives percentages across the columns.

If we want to create a table with 3 factor variables, we use the command **ftable()**. Let us give an example:

R

```
y = table(Arthritis$Sex,Arthritis$Treatment,Arthritis$Improved)
ftable(y)
##                 None Some Marked
##
## Female Placebo   19    7     6
##        Treated    6    5    16
## Male   Placebo   10    0     1
##        Treated    7    2     5
```

Python

```
df3 = arthritis[['Sex','Treatment','Improved']].
        value_counts().unstack()[['None','Some','Marked']]
df3
```

Improved		None	Some	Marked
Sex	Treatment			
Female	Placebo	19.0	7.0	6.0
	Treated	6.0	5.0	16.0
Male	Placebo	10.0	NaN	1.0
	Treated	7.0	2.0	5.0

NUMERIC VARIABLES IN R

To create a table with a factor variable and a numeric variable, we use the following syntax:

```
aggregate(numeric variable, list(factor variable), simple statistic
command).
```

Let us give an example using the `whiteside` dataframe:

```
z = aggregate(whiteside$Temp,list(whiteside$Insul),mean)
head(z)
```

```
##    Group.1        x
## 1   Before 5.350000
## 2    After 4.463333
```

Thus far, we have covered Base R commands to work with dataframes. Later, we will discuss a popular package called *dplyr* that provides much more functionality and efficiency for data management.

NUMERIC VARIABLES IN PYTHON

In Python, the factors variables can be used by applying the *groupby()* and *aggregate()* methods. We combine these by what is called method chaining. The idea is that methods applied to a dataframe object using the '.' return a new object on which we can apply another method. In this example, we first apply *groupby* to determine *Insul* as a factor, then we select *Temp* as the column of interest (using square brackets) and then aggregate with the mean function from the *NumPy* package:

```
whiteside.groupby(['Insul'])['Temp'].aggregate(np.mean)
     mean
```

```
Insul
After   4.463333
Before  5.350000
Name: Temp, dtype: float64
```

GRAPHING WITH *ggplot2*

We will now explore graphing with the *ggplot2* package, one of the most powerful and popular packages in R. To access this package, we will install and load a package called *tidyverse* which includes *ggplot2* along with other useful packages for data manipulation. We will explore some of these other packages later.

First, we will install the *tidyverse* package with the command

```
install.packages("tidyverse",dependencies = TRUE).
```

The option **dependencies = TRUE** will ensure all the packages necessary to run *tidyverse* are properly installed. After installation, we load the package. We will also load the *MASS* package, as we will use a dataset from there:

```
library(tidyverse)
library(MASS)
```

Let us take a look at the dataframe **whiteside,** which we used before:

R

```
head(whiteside)
##     Insul Temp Gas
## 1 Before -0.8 7.2
## 2 Before -0.7 6.9
## 3 Before  0.4 6.4
## 4 Before  2.5 6.0
## 5 Before  2.9 5.8
## 6 Before  3.2 5.8
```

Python

```
whiteside.head()

    Insul  Temp  Gas
0  Before  -0.8  7.2
1  Before  -0.7  6.9
2  Before   0.4  6.4
3  Before   2.5  6.0
4  Before   2.9  5.8
```

We will now explore graphing with this dataframe.

The *ggplot2* package allows you to create data visualizations. The process involves starting with a basic canvas, and then layering in new aspects of the graphics using +. To create the basic canvas, we use the `ggplot()` command. Inside the parentheses, we define the dataframe and variables we want on the *x* and *y* axes. `aes()` is used to create the axes. Note that for a single variable, we can choose either the *x* or *y* axis and ignore the other. The other key command is `geom`, which stands for geometric object. This is used mainly to create different types of graphs. We will start creating one-dimensional graphs and then move on to two or more dimensions.

ONE VARIABLE PLOTS

One Factor Variable

First, let us just create a basic canvas with the *whiteside* dataset, where we want to plot `Insul`:

R

```
ggplot(whiteside,aes(x = Insul))
```

Python

```
plt.style.use('ggplot')
plt.plot()
```

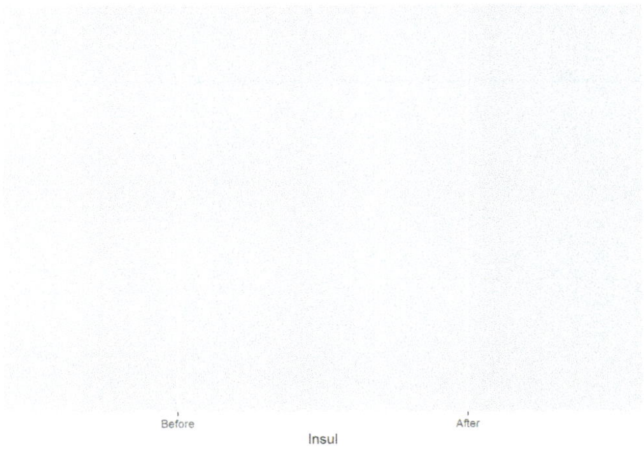

Figure 2.1 Basic canvas

Since this is factor data, we will plot a simple bar graph:

R

```
ggplot(whiteside,aes(x = Insul)) + geom_bar()
```

Python

```
plt.bar(g['Insul'], g['count'])
```

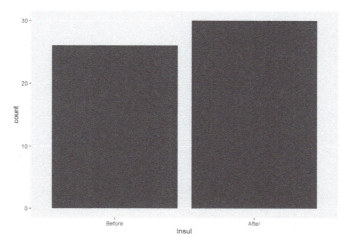

Figure 2.2 Simple bar graph

This is the concept of layering; we added a bar graph on top of the basic canvas. Now we can make a few additional adjustments. *col* makes the outline of the graph the colour of your choice, and *fill* fills the space with the colour of your choice.

R

```
ggplot(whiteside,aes(x = Insul)) + geom_bar(col = "blue", fill = "orange")
```

Python

```
plt.bar(g['Insul'], g['count'], edgecolor='blue', color='orange')
```

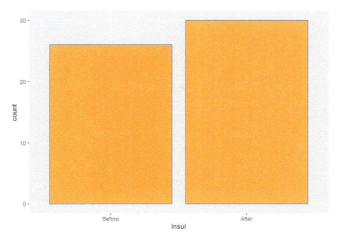

Figure 2.3 Colour added to bar graph

A few more adjustments. Let us change the background theme using *theme*:

R

```
ggplot(whiteside,aes(x = Insul)) + geom_bar(col = "blue", fill = "orange") + theme_light()
```

Python

```
plt.style.use('default')
plt.grid(alpha=.2)
plt.bar(g['Insul'], g['count'], edgecolor='blue', color='orange')
```

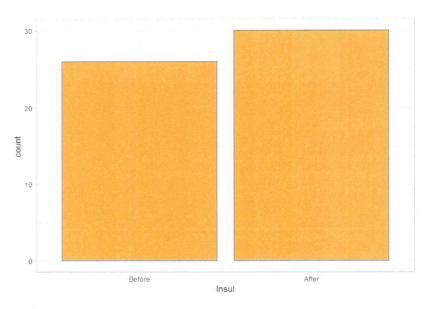

Figure 2.4 Changing background colour

Now, let us flip the axes:

```
ggplot(whiteside,aes(x = Insul)) + geom_bar(col = "blue", fill = "orange")
        + theme_light() + coord_flip()
plt.grid(alpha=.2)
plt.barh(g['Insul'], g['count'], edgecolor='blue', color='orange')
plt.ylabel('Insul')
plt.xlabel('count')
```

We can also flip the graph by assigning the Insul data to the y axis in the `aes()` command:

```
ggplot(whiteside,aes(y = Insul)) + geom_bar(col = "blue", fill = "orange")
        + theme_light()
```

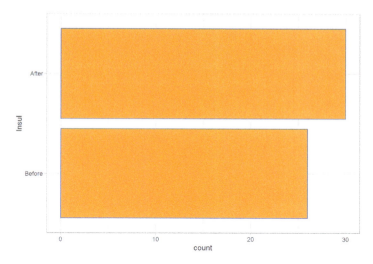

Figure 2.5 Flipping axes

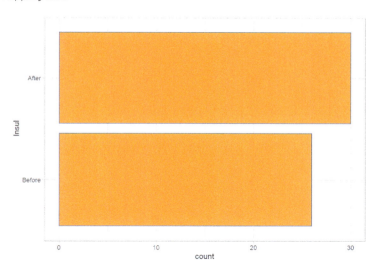

Figure 2.6 Alternate way to flip the axes

Another useful graph for factor data is a dot plot. In the code below, we also add titles and labels using *labs()*:

```
ggplot(whiteside,aes(x = Insul)) + geom_dotplot(col = "blue",
    fill = "orange") + theme_light() + labs(title = "Insulation",
    subtitle = "Observations With and Without Insulation", y = "Percent")
## 'stat_bindot()' using 'bins = 30'. Pick better value with 'binwidth'.

g['percent'] = g['count'].div(g['count'].sum())

fig = plt.figure()
```

```
fig.suptitle('Insulation')
ax = plt.subplot(111)
ax.grid(alpha=.2)
ax.set_title('Observations With and Without Insulation')
ax.scatter(g['Insul'], g['percent'], edgecolor='blue', color='orange')
ax.set_ylim([-.05, 1.05])
ax.set_ylabel('Percent')
ax.set_xlabel('count')
plt.show()
```

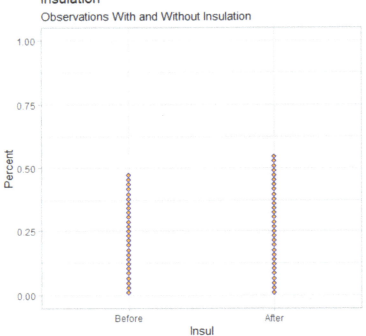

Figure 2.7 Dot plot with titles and labels

ONE NUMERIC VARIABLE

We will now turn our attention to graphing with a single numerical variable. The most basic graph for a numerical variable is a histogram:

R

```
ggplot(whiteside,aes(x = Temp)) + geom_histogram()
```

Python

```
plt.style.use('ggplot')
plt.hist(whiteside['Temp'], bins=30)
plt.ylabel('count')
plt.xlabel('Temp')
plt.show()
```

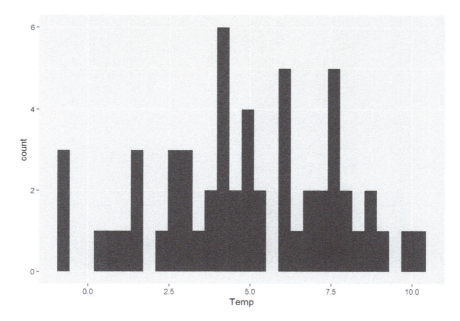

Figure 2.8 Histogram of temperatures from the *whiteside* dataset

By default, the data on the **Temp** variable is grouped into 30 bins and the count of *Temp* values in each bin is plotted on the *y* axis. This can be altered as shown below:

R

```
ggplot(whiteside,aes(x = Temp)) + geom_histogram(bins = 10, col = "purple",
      fill = "yellow") + theme_light()
```

Python

```
plt.style.use('default')
plt.grid(alpha=.2)
plt.hist(whiteside['Temp'], bins=10, edgecolor='purple', color='yellow')
plt.ylabel('count')
plt.xlabel('Temp')
plt.show()
```

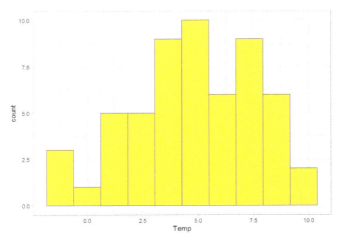

Figure 2.9   Changing the binning in a histogram

As an alternative, instead of binning the data into equal sized bins, we can also specify the length of each bin using the *breaks* option:

R

```
ggplot(whiteside,aes(x = Temp)) + geom_histogram(breaks = c(-2,-1,0,2,5,10),
      col = "purple", fill = "yellow") + theme_light()
```

Python

```
plt.grid(alpha=.2)
plt.hist(whiteside['Temp'], bins=[-2,-1,0,2,5,10], edgecolor='purple', color='yellow')
plt.ylabel('count')
plt.xlabel('Temp')
plt.show()
```

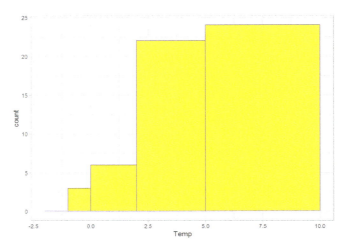

Figure 2.10   Histogram with different sized bins

If we want to create many break points, we can use the *seq()* function as shown below:

R

```
ggplot(whiteside,aes(x = Temp)) + geom_histogram(breaks = seq(-2,10,by = 1),
    col = "purple", fill = "yellow") + theme_light()
```

Python

```
plt.grid(alpha=.2)
plt.hist(whiteside['Temp'], bins=range(-2, 10, 1), edgecolor='purple', color='yellow')
plt.ylabel('count')
plt.xlabel('Temp')
plt.show()
```

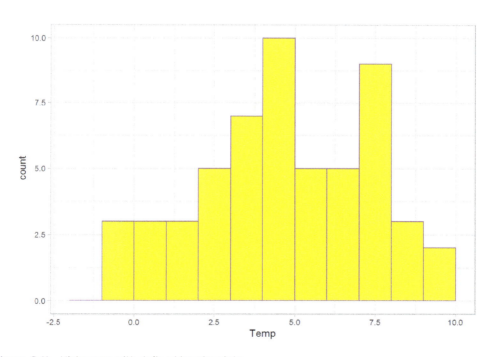

Figure 2.11 Histogram with defined break points

You may have noticed that the shape of the histogram can be quite different as we change the binning settings. Thus, histograms can be misleading and do not always give a completely accurate depiction of the data. Imagine if we increased the number of bins, drew a point in the middle of each bin, and connected them with a line; this is how we create a density graph of our data. Density graphs are more useful than histograms because they provide a more accurate picture of how the data are distributed. In fact, histograms can be a little confusing because their shape looks different depending on how the bins are defined. We can notice this from the previous histograms of the *Temp* variable.

Now, let us create a density graph:

R

```
ggplot(whiteside,aes(x = Temp)) + geom_density(col = "pink", fill = "yellow") +
        theme_light()
```

Python

```
sns.set_style("whitegrid")
ax = sns.displot(whiteside['Temp'], kind = 'kde', color = 'yellow', fill='y')
ax.set(xlim=(-1, 11))
plt.xlabel('Temp')
plt.show()
```

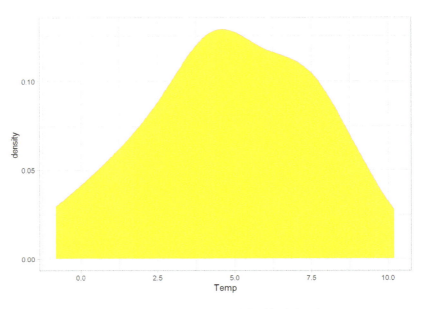

Figure 2.12   Density graph of temperatures from the *whiteside* dataset

What if we want to create a vertical line at the mean, maximum, and minimum values of the temperature? First, we need to compute the mean, max, and min, and then we can draw vertical lines at these values. We can change the colour and size of the lines as follows:

R

```
meantemp = mean(whiteside$Temp)
mintemp = min(whiteside$Temp)
maxtemp = max(whiteside$Temp)

ggplot(whiteside,aes(x = Temp)) + geom_density(col = "pink", fill = "yellow") +
        geom_vline(xintercept = maxtemp, col = "blue", size = 2) +
        geom_vline(xintercept = mintemp, col = "pink", size = 2) +
        geom_vline(xintercept = meantemp, col = "purple", size = 2) + theme_light()
```

Python
```
maxtemp = whiteside['Temp'].max()
mintemp = whiteside['Temp'].min()
meantemp = whiteside['Temp'].mean()

ax = sns.displot(whiteside['Temp'], kind = 'kde', color = 'yellow', fill='y')
plt.axvline(maxtemp, color='blue')
plt.axvline(mintemp, color='pink')
plt.axvline(meantemp, color='purple')
ax.set(xlim=(-1, 11))
plt.xlabel('Temp')
plt.show()
```

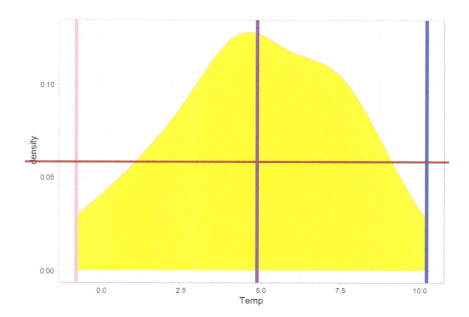

Figure 2.13 Inserting useful indicators into a density graph

With a single numeric variable, we can also create a boxplot. The code is straightforward:

R
```
ggplot(whiteside,aes(x = Temp)) + geom_boxplot(col = "violet", fill = "lightblue",
    size = 1) + theme_light()
```

Python
```
ax = sns.boxplot(x = whiteside['Temp'], linewidth = 1, boxprops = dict (facecolor = 'lightblue',
    edgecolor = 'violet'), medianprops = dict(linewidth = 3, color = 'violet',
    whiskerprops = dict(color = 'violet'), capprops = dict(color = 'violet'))
```

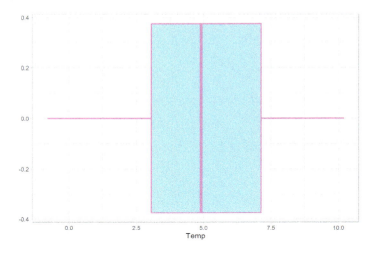

Figure 2.14 Boxplot with a single numerical variable

TWO+ VARIABLE PLOTS

Numeric + Factor Variable

Suppose we want to extend the above boxplot by also considering the insulation. In other words, we want two boxplots, one before insulation and one after insulation:

R

```
ggplot(whiteside,aes(x = Temp, col = Insul)) + geom_boxplot(fill = "lightblue",
        size = 1) + theme_light()
```

Python

```
ax = sns.boxplot(x='Temp', y='Insul', data=whiteside)
```

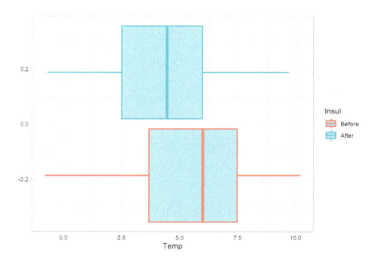

Figure 2.15 Comparing boxplots

The above code creates a legend for the factor variable *Insul*. Another way to create a boxplot for before and after insulation is to write *y = Insul* in the `aes()` command.

```
ggplot(whiteside,aes(x = Temp, y = Insul)) + geom_boxplot
        (col = "violet", fill = "lightblue", size = 1) + theme_light()

ax = sns.boxplot(x='Temp', y='Insul', data=whiteside)
box_before = ax.patches[0]
box_after  = ax.patches[1]
box_before.set_edgecolor('red')
box_after.set_edgecolor('blue')
plt.show()
```

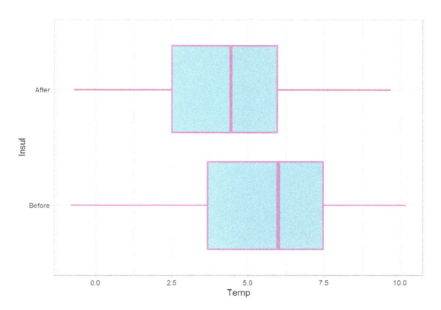

Figure 2.16 Alternate way to compare boxplots

Instead of creating a legend, this method labels before and after *Insul* on the *y* axis. We can use the same logic for a density plot as well:

R

```
ggplot(whiteside, aes(x = Temp, col = Insul)) + geom_density(fill = "yellow")
        + theme_light()
```

Python

```
fig = sns.kdeplot(whiteside.loc[whiteside['Insul'] == 'Before']['Temp'],
      color="pink", shade=True, alpha=1)
fig = sns.kdeplot(whiteside.loc[whiteside['Insul'] == 'After']['Temp'],
      color="lightblue", shade=True, alpha=1)
plt.show()
```

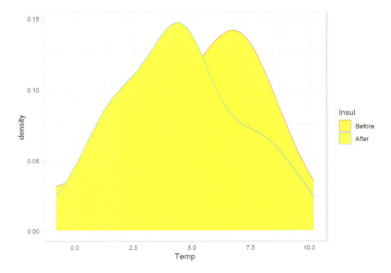

Figure 2.17   Comparing density plots

Below are a few changes that make both graphs clearer:

R

```
ggplot(whiteside, aes(x = Temp)) + geom_density(aes(fill = Insul), alpha = .4) +
    theme_light()
```

Python

```
fig = sns.kdeplot(whiteside.loc[whiteside['Insul'] == 'Before']['Temp'],
    color="pink", shade=True, alpha=.4)
fig = sns.kdeplot(whiteside.loc[whiteside['Insul'] == 'After']['Temp'],
    color="lightblue", shade=True, alpha=.4)
plt.show()
```

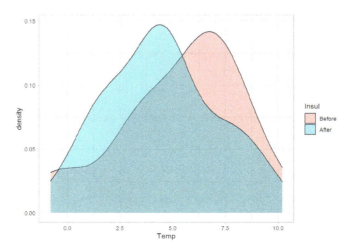

Figure 2.18   A clearer comparison

This works a little better, due to setting **alpha=.4**, which improves the transparency of the graph.

TWO+ NUMERIC VARIABLES

Now, let us plot temperature against gas consumption:

R

```
ggplot(whiteside, aes(x = Temp, y = Gas)) + theme_light() + geom_point(pch = 7,
      col = "purple") + geom_smooth()
```

Python

```
sns.lmplot(x='Temp', y='Gas', data=whiteside, order=3)
plt.show()
```

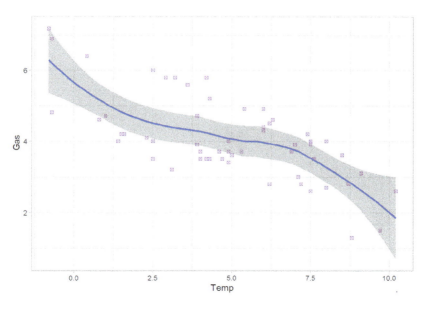

Figure 2.19   Temperature versus gas consumption

The command **geom_point** gives us a scatterplot of the data. As before, we can change the design of the points using *pch* and the colour using **col**. **geom_smooth** gives us the best-fit curve between *x* and *y*. The grey region is the 95% confidence interval, a concept that we will discuss later in the book. We can make a few adjustments as below:

R

```
ggplot(whiteside, aes(x = Temp, y = Gas)) + theme_light() + geom_point(pch = 13,
      col = "purple") + geom_smooth(method = lm, se = FALSE)
```

Python

```
x = whiteside['Temp']
y = whiteside['Gas']
a, b = np.polyfit(x, y, 1)
plt.plot(x, a*x+b)
plt.scatter(x, y, linewidths=.7, color='purple', marker='x')
plt.ylabel('Gas')
plt.xlabel('Temp')
plt.show()
```

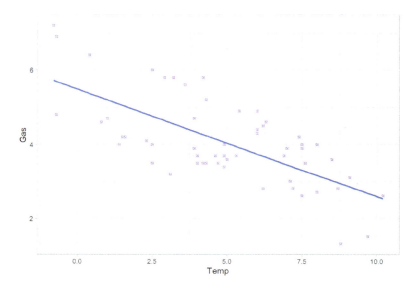

Figure 2.20 Adjusted temperature versus gas consumption

method = lm returns a linear model of the relationship between *x* and *y*. **se = FALSE** removes the confidence interval around the smoothing function.

We can also add a third dimension if it is a factor variable. In this example, suppose we want to plot the relationship between temperature and gas consumption both before and after insulation. A simple way to do this is to use the colour option to add the third dimension:

R

```
ggplot(whiteside, aes(x = Temp, y = Gas, col = Insul)) + theme_light() + geom_point()
    + geom_smooth(method = lm, se = FALSE)
```

Python

```
sns.lmplot(x='Temp', y='Gas', hue='Insul', data=whiteside,
        palette=['pink','lightblue'], ci=None)
plt.show()
```

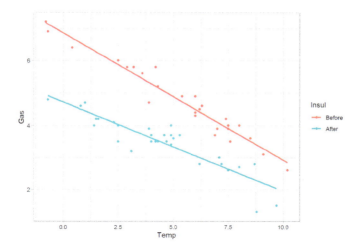

Figure 2.21 Comparing scatter plots

The graph now clearly illustrates how the gas consumption is lower after insulation and the gap between the two narrows as the temperature increases. We can use the **size** option to add another dimension:

R

```
ggplot(whiteside, aes(x = Temp, y = Gas, size = Insul)) + theme_light()
        + geom_point(col = "magenta")
```

Python

```
sns.scatterplot(x = 'Temp', y='Gas', hue='Insul', data = whiteside,
                palette = ['magenta','magenta'], size='Insul', sizes=(100,30))
plt.show()
```

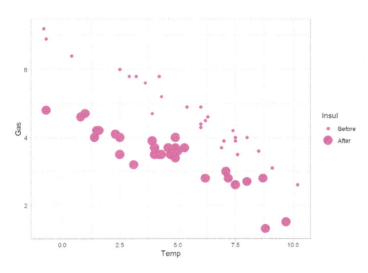

Figure 2.22 Alternate representation for a comparison

We can also use facets for the third dimension using the **facet_grid** command. Facets are a way to create multiple subplots. We use the ~ in the facet function to control how the subplots are displayed. '.' is the replacement for other elements of the plot. We will plot in a few different ways to show the results:

```
ggplot(whiteside, aes(x = Temp, y = Gas)) + geom_point() + facet_
grid(Insul~.)
```

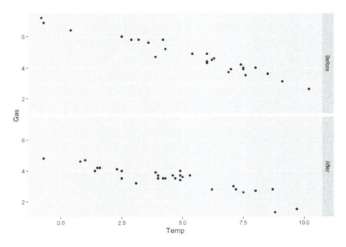

Figure 2.23 Multiple subplots using facets

R

```
ggplot(whiteside, aes(x = Temp, y = Gas)) + geom_point() + facet_grid(.~Insul)
```

Python

```
sns.catplot(x='Temp', y='Gas', col='Insul', data=whiteside, kind='swarm',
            palette=['black','black'], dodge=True)
```

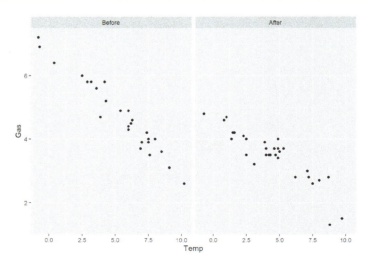

Figure 2.24 Facets for side-by-side comparison

Notice that the variable to the left of the tilde (~) makes up the rows and the variable to the right makes up the columns of the subplots.

TWO+ FACTOR VARIABLES

For graphing two factor variables, we will use the `mpg` dataframe, as the `whiteside` dataframe does not contain two factor variables.

R
```
head(mpg)
```

Python
```
mpg.head()
```

```
## # A tibble: 6 x 11
##    manufacturer model displ  year   cyl trans drv     cty   hwy fl    class
##    <chr>        <chr> <dbl> <int> <int> <chr> <chr> <int> <int> <chr> <chr>
## 1 audi         a4      1.8  1999     4 auto(~ f       18    29 p     comp~
## 2 audi         a4      1.8  1999     4 manua~ f       21    29 p     comp~
## 3 audi         a4      2    2008     4 manua~ f       20    31 p     comp~
## 4 audi         a4      2    2008     4 auto(~ f       21    30 p     comp~
## 5 audi         a4      2.8  1999     6 auto(~ f       16    26 p     comp~
## 6 audi         a4      2.8  1999     6 manua~ f       18    26 p     comp~
```

Let us first plot the class variable:

R
```
ggplot(mpg, aes(x = class)) + geom_bar()
```

Python
```
g = mpg.groupby(['class'])['drv'].count().reset_index()
g.rename(columns={'drv':'count'}, inplace=True)
plt.style.use('ggplot')
plt.bar(g['class'], g['count'])
```

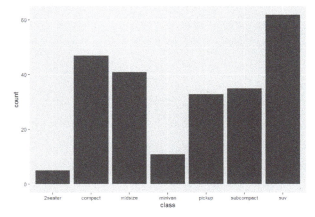

Figure 2.25 Histogram showing class variables

Now, suppose we want to add **drv** to this plot:

R

```r
ggplot(mpg, aes(x = class)) + geom_bar(aes(fill = drv))
```

Python

```python
sns.histplot(mpg.sort_values(by=['class','drv']), x='class', hue='drv',
            multiple='stack', palette=['blue', 'red', 'green'])
```

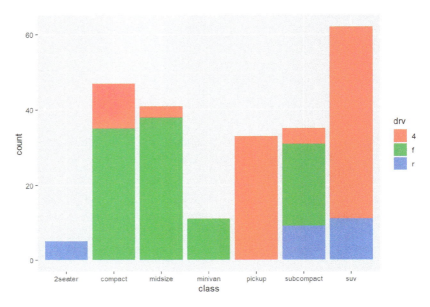

Figure 2.26 Adding additional information

This is a useful visualization as it provides several insights on the data: (a) all two-seaters are rear-wheel drives; (b) the majority of compact and midsize cars are front-wheel drive; and (c) pickups all are 4-wheel drive. We can use the **fill** option to add the second dimension. Here is the result:

R

```r
ggplot(mpg, aes(x = class)) + geom_bar(aes(fill = drv), position = "dodge")
```

Python

```python
sns.histplot(mpg.sort_values (by=['class','drv']), x='class', hue='drv', multiple='dodge',
            palette=['blue', 'red', 'green'])
```

We can also **facet** this.

In R:

```r
ggplot(mpg, aes(x = class)) + geom_bar(aes(fill = drv)) +
    facet_grid(year~.)
```

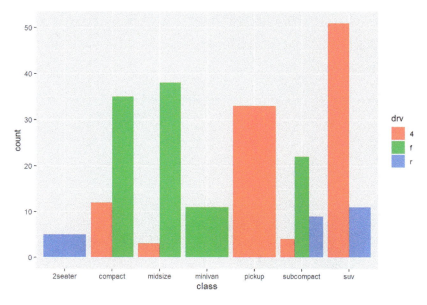

Figure 2.27 Side-by-side representation of all the variables

In Python:

```
g = sns.FacetGrid(mpg, row = "year")
g.map_dataframe(sns.histplot, x = "class",hue = 'drv')
```

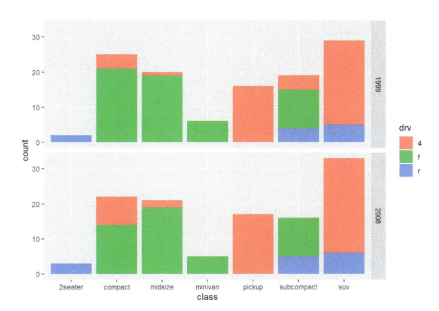

Figure 2.28 Adding an extra dimension to the comparison using `facet`

Note how the above graph incorporates three dimensions from the dataframe.

INTERACTIVE PLOTS

In R, we can add some interactivity with the *plotly* package.

```
library(plotly)
g1 = ggplot(mpg, aes(x = class)) + geom_bar(aes(fill = drv)) + facet_
    grid(year~.)
ggplotly(g1)
```

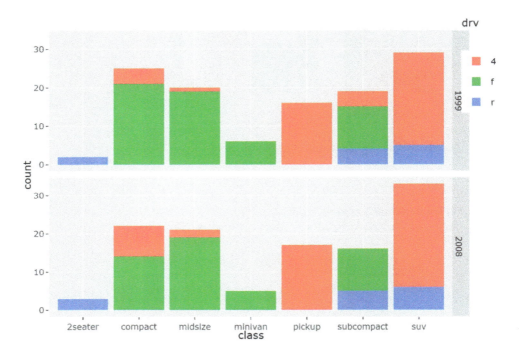

Figure 2.29   Interactive plot of the *mpg* dataset

Here is another example:

```
g2 = ggplot(whiteside, aes(x = Temp, y = Gas, col = Insul)) + theme_
    light() + geom_point() + geom_smooth(method = lm, se = FALSE)
ggplotly(g2)
```

That's it! It's quite simple to use.

In Python, we can achieve interactivity even more simply by starting the code in a cell with plotting using the following two lines:

```
%matplotlib notebook
plt.ion()
```

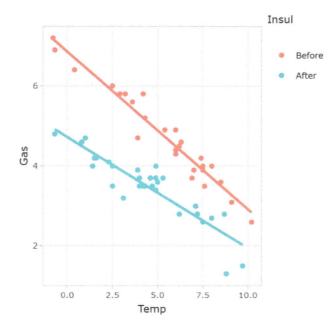

Figure 2.30   Interactive plot of the *whiteside* dataset

```
g = mpg.groupby(['class'])['drv'].count().reset_index()
g.rename(columns={'drv':'count'}, inplace=True)
sns.histplot(mpg.sort_values(by=['class','drv']), x='class', hue='drv',
          multiple='stack')
```

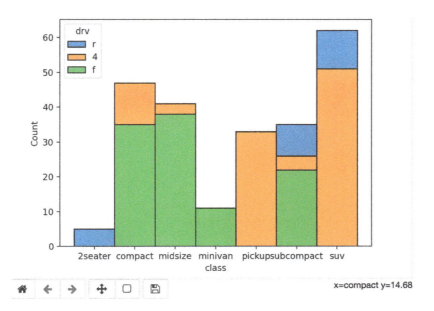

Figure 2.31   Interactivity with Python

USE CASE: VISUALIZING INDUSTRY VALUATIONS

Python and R visualization libraries allow for many ways to infer more from the data. Sometimes, simply sorting and colouring items can help. For instance, if we were an entrepreneur or angel/venture cap investor, visualization can be used to quickly grasp on which industries we should focus, and which we should probably avoid. Earnings before interest tax, depreciation, and amortization (EBITDA) is a commonly used analytic to proxy the cash generated by a business. It is widely used in corporate financial analysis, from credit analysis through to public and private equities analysis. We will use a business analytic called 'EBITDA multiple', which is widely used in venture capital (VC) to value businesses:

EBITDA multiple = EV / EBITDA

where Enterprise Value (EV) is the total value of a company's equity plus debt capital (including minority interests). Different industries will be valued by investors at different EBITDA multiples based on their perceived risk and return potential, or how 'hot' an industry is considered by investors. Two companies in different industries, identical in all other respects, may be valued quite differently given these perceptions. (Investors can make excess returns if these perceptions are incorrect.)

Use of dataseries sorting and colours

We can visualize the EBITDA multiples in which the market is currently pricing, across industries by sorting sectors by EBITDA multiples, and plotting on a column chart:

R

```
df = valuation_multiples
df$EBITDA_margin = df$'EBITDA ($ millions)'/df$'Revenues ($ millions)'
df$Net_Margin = df$'Net Income ( $ millions)'/df$'Revenues ($ millions)'
df$Debt_EV = df$'Total Debt (including leases) ($ millions)'/df$'Enteprise Value ($ millions)'
df$EBITDA_EV = df$'EBITDA ($ millions)'/df$'Enteprise Value ($ millions)'
df$EBITDA_multiple = df$'EBITDA ($ millions)'/df$'Enteprise Value ($ millions)'
ggplot(df,aes(x ='Industry  Name', y = EBITDA_multiple)) + geom_col(size = 1) +
        theme(axis.text.x = element_text(angle = 90))
```

Python

```
#Column chart with sorted EBITDA multiples

plt.figure(figsize = (18,10))

#Chart data, note that the dataframe is sorted by 'EBITDA Multiple' before charting!
ax = sns.barplot(x = 'Industry Name', y = 'EBITDA Multiple', data = df_EBITDA_mul,
dodge = False, order = df_EBITDA_mul.sort_values('EBITDA Multiple')['Industry Name'])

#Labels rotated and with a tight layout so as we can read them....
ax.set_xticklabels(ax.get_xticklabels(), rotation=40, ha = "right")
plt.tight_layout()
```

```
#Label and title the chart...
plt.ylabel('EBITDA Multiple', fontsize=16)
plt.xticks(fontsize=12)
plt.title('Distribution of EBITDA Multiples')

plt.show()
```

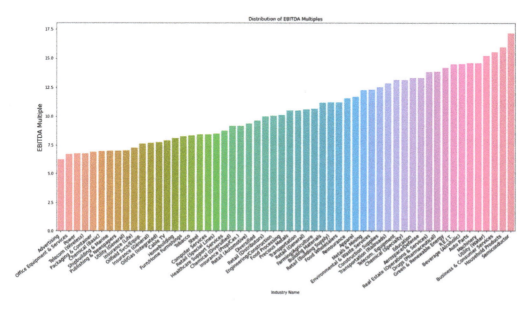

Figure 2.32   Sorted industrial sectors by EBITDA multiples

Examining the column chart above, we can see that semiconductor companies have the highest valuation for every $1 of EBITDA generated, while advertising has the lowest valuation. The former has high barriers to entry, growing demand (at the present), and stable margins. Advertising is quite the opposite and is therefore a riskier proposition.

Boxplots to examine distributions of analytics

Boxplots allow us to visualize the distribution of analytics such as 'EBITDA multiples', as you can see in the boxplot below:

R

```
ggplot(df,aes(x = EBITDA_multiple)) + geom_boxplot(col = "violet",
      fill = "lightblue", size = 1) + theme_light()
```

Python

```
plt.figure(figsize=(17,4))
plt.boxplot(df_EBITDA_mul['EBITDA Multiple'], vert=False)
plt.title('Distribution of EBITDA Multiples')
plt.show()
```

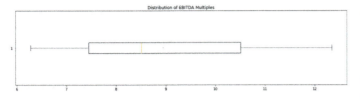

Figure 2.33   Distribution of EBITDA multiples

The box represents the interquartile range of industry EBITDA multiples, where the middle 50% of industries are found. The vertical orange bar is the Industry with the median EBITDA multiple, and the extreme 'T' to the left, the minimum (Advertising), and the 'T' to the right, the maximum (Semiconductor) EBITDA multiple **Industries**.

Scatter plots to explore drivers of valuation

As VC investors, we want to understand what is driving different industry valuations and whether these drivers seem sensible. We can either resolve this question heuristically, i.e., through trial and error and gut instinct, or through a process of data exploration. We previously saw the power of scatter plots; we can expand this idea using bubble plots:

R

```
ggplot(df,aes(x =EBITDA_multiple, y = 'EBITDA ($ millions)'),size='Market Cap
     ($ millions)') +   geom_point(col="magenta")
```

Python

```
plt.figure(figsize = (18,10))
plt.title('EBITDA_margin vs EBITDA Multiple')
sns.scatterplot(data = df, x = "EBITDA Multiple", y = "EBITDA_margin",
          size = "Market Cap ($ millions)", legend = False, sizes = (20, 2000))
plt.show()
```

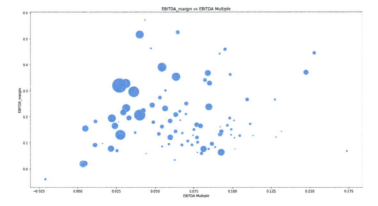

Figure 2.34   EBITDA margin versus EBITDA multiple

The bubble plot above shows all **Industries** plotted by EBITDA multiple and EBITDA margin. In other words, we are examining whether there is a relationship between how profitable an industry is and its valuation. We would expect a correlation, although many other factors should be considered, such as risk and growth potential. We can add a third dimension to our analysis: 'bubbles'. Each point on the scatter plot is sized, in this case, by the median size of the companies (market capitalization) in each industry. This allows us to identify obvious relationships between these three data items.

We can also quickly analyse a pairwise relationship by plotting a line of best fit:

R

```
ggplot(df,aes(x = EBITDA_multiple, y = 'EBITDA ($ millions)')) + geom_point(col = "magenta")
        + geom_smooth()
```

Python

```
plt.figure(figsize = (18,10))
sns.regplot(data = df_key_dis, x = "EBITDA Multiple", y = "EBITDA_margin", robust = True)
plt.show()
```

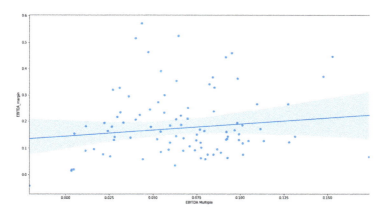

Figure 2.35   Line of best fit for EBITDA margin versus EBITDA multiple

Clustering

We can use our features to group similar instances together. This is called clustering. In this case, we want to see which industries are similar with respect to certain vital statistics: EBITDA margin, EBITDA to EV, and net margin. Hierarchical clustering is a way of doing this without making assumptions about how these data items might be distributed. We only want to know the distance between the vital statistics of different industries and present them in a digestible way. Dendrograms are one approach to understand the similarities between different industries, using more than two features:

R

```
clusters = hclust(dist(df[, c(1,3,6,9,13)]),method = "ward.D")
plot(clusters,labels = df$'Industry  Name')
```

Python

```
import scipy.cluster.hierarchy as shc df_lbs = [x for x in df[df.columns[0]]]
plt.figure(figsize = (16, 10), dpi= 80)
plt.title("Business Performance Clusters", fontsize = 22)
dend = shc.dendrogram(shc.linkage(df[['EBITDA_margin', 'EBITDA_EV', 'Net_Margin']],
                      method = 'ward'), labels=df_lbs, color_threshold = 100)
plt.xticks(fontsize = 12)
plt.show()
```

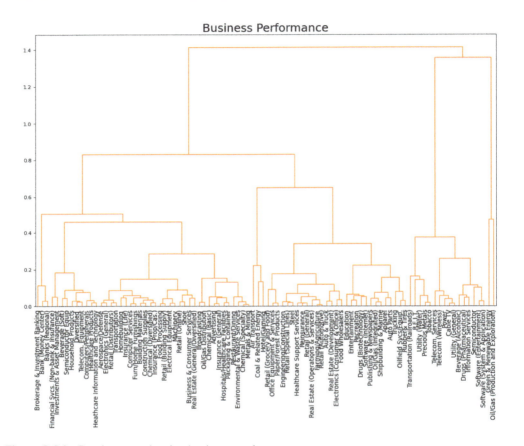

Figure 2.36 Dendrogram showing business performance

We can see three main clusters of industries and two outliers (right) in Oil/Gas Exploration and Green and Renewable Energy. This indicates that these two **Industries** are quite different with respect to the data items we have used to generate these clusters. Focusing on the three main clusters, if the data items we are using on which to cluster are important drivers of valuation, we might expect each cluster to have similar valuations. If there are exceptions, for instance, an industry with a very low EBITDA multiple in a cluster of generally higher EBITDA multiple industries, this may represent an anomaly and a business opportunity to invest in companies in this undervalued industry.

Summary

We have touched upon some of the basics able to be achieved with *ggplot2* and *plotly*. There is much more we can do with these packages. Research these further and do check out some of the links at the end of the chapter. One important thing to remember is that the plots we create should be visually appealing, concise, and most importantly informative. For example, the various visualizations we built on the **whiteside** dataframe helped us uncover the following useful information.

1   There are more observations after insulation compared to before.
2   The median temperature after insulation is higher than before.
3   The gas consumption lowers after insulation, but the difference narrows as the temperature increases.

Good visualizations provide you with good insights.

Exercises

To complete the activity below, you will need to visit the companion website to the book and download the relevant dataset: https://study.sagepub.com/gopal

Read the file gapminder.csv.

1   Calculate the average life expectancy for each year.
2   Plot year versus life expectancy and draw a horizontal line at the average life expectancy value. Colour the points based on the continent.
3   Calculate the total population for each continent for each year. Create an appropriate plot to visualize the data.
4   Plot GDP per capita for each year for African countries. Add appropriate labels to indicate the country name.

Read the file UsedCars2017.csv. The file contains the following information:

Price: Selling price when the vehicle was sold at a dealership (in dollars).

Age: Year 2016 minus the model's year (i.e., a 2012 model would be four years old).

Mileage: Approximate number of miles (in thousands) on the vehicle's odometer at the time of the sale.

MPG: Average fuel economy of the vehicle measured in miles per gallon.

KBB Price: Kelly Blue Book valuation of the vehicle.

CR Reliability Score: Consumer Reports' car reliability score determined as the percentage of survey respondents who reported problems with vehicles of the same model as the sold vehicle.

5   Create a plot of Age and Mileage. What conclusions can you draw from the plot?
6   Explore the data by creating various plots and document any insights from visualization.

Useful Links

https://dereksonderegger.github.io/570L/9-graphing-using-ggplot2.html

https://r4ds.had.co.nz/data-visualisation.html

https://uc-r.github.io/ggplot_intro

www.r-graph-gallery.com/

3

MANAGING AND PREPARING DATA

Chapter Contents

In the previous chapter, we discussed how to summarize and visualize data. While these are important parts of most statistical and business analytics tasks, there are several additional processes associated with data. In many practical settings for instance, it is required to manage and rework the data to make them suitable for subsequent analysis. Both R and Python offer packages that make the task of data manipulation easier and more efficient. These are typically found on the 'grammar of data manipulation'. In essence, they provide a common and consistent set of verbs that help address the most common data manipulation challenges.

These packages derive their inspiration from SQL (Structured Query Language) which is the standardized programming language used to manage relational databases and perform operations on the data residing in these databases. The packages in R and Python simplify the construction and improve the readability of these operations. We will discuss the popular *dplyr* package in R and *Pandas* package in Python.

MANAGING DATA

Managing Data R: dplyr

dplyr is a popular package that, similarly to *ggplot*, provides common verbs useful for data manipulation and management. If we already installed *tidyverse*, we do not need to install *dplyr* because it is included in this package. Once installed, we load the package as follows:

```
library(dplyr)
library(tidyverse)
```

Some of the common verbs equivalent to SQL used in *dplyr* are:

```
Selecting columns: select()
Filter rows: filter()
Re-order or arrange rows: arrange()
Create new columns: mutate()
Summarize values: summarise()
Allows for operating on groups: group_by()
```

To understand the power of *dplyr*, we will work with a fairly complex dataset. There is a dataset called *hflights* in a package also called *hflights*. Let us load and take a look at this dataset:

```
library(hflights)
```

Let us view the dataset:

```
glimpse(hflights)
## Rows: 227,496
## Columns: 21
## $ Year          <int> 2011, 2011, 2011, 2011, 2011, 2011, 2011, 20...
## $ Month         <int> 1, 1, 1, 1, 1, 1, 1, 1, 1, 1, 1, 1, 1, 1, 1,...
## $ DayofMonth    <int> 1, 2, 3, 4, 5, 6, 7, 8, 9, 10, 11, 12, 13, 1...
## $ DayOfWeek     <int> 6, 7, 1, 2, 3, 4, 5, 6, 7, 1, 2, 3, 4, 5, 6,...
```

```
## $ DepTime        <int> 1400, 1401, 1352, 1403, 1405, 1359, 1359, 13...
## $ ArrTime        <int> 1500, 1501, 1502, 1513, 1507, 1503, 1509, 14...
...
```

This dataset includes 227,496 rows and 21 columns. We will use a special function called `kable`, in the *tidyverse* package, to generate a new table:

```
knitr::kable(hflights[1:5,1:8])
```

	Year	Month	Day of Month	Day Of Week	DepTime	ArrTime	UniqueCarrier	FlightNum
5424	2011	1	1	6	1400	1500	AA	428
5425	2011	1	2	7	1401	1501	AA	428
5426	2011	1	3	1	1352	1502	AA	428
5427	2011	1	4	2	1403	1513	AA	428
5428	2011	1	5	3	1405	1507	AA	428

Let us start exploring each of the important 'verbs' in *dplyr*.

Managing Data in Python: *Pandas*

Pandas provides the DataFrame object, which gives access to a powerful table-like data structure, with SQL style functions for data manipulation and management. Once installed, we load the package as follows (where *Pandas* tends to be declared as **pd** but you can call it anything you like):

```
import Pandas as pd
```

Some of the common functions in *pandas* are:

```
df = pd.DataFrame() # declare a Pandas DataFrame
```

Selecting a column:`df['Person']`; or select rows 1–10: `df.loc[1:10, ['Person']]`
Selecting columns: `df[['Person', 'City', 'Earnings']]`
Filter rows: `df[(df['Person'] == 'Ahmed'] ...`where 'Person' equals 'Ahmed'
Create new columns: `df['Debt'] = [1000, 2200, 110000, 670000]`
Operating on groups: `df.groupby(['Person', 'Earnings'])`

SELECTING COLUMNS

Select in R

`select` is used to select columns in a dataframe and the syntax is:

```
select(data, columns)
```

df['...'] in Python

Pandas dataframe allows you to select column(s) by name or by column number. If we have declared and loaded our dataframe, `df`, we can state the column we want to return, `df['Person']`, or return many columns using a list like this: `df[['Person', 'City', 'Earnings']]`, where a list is a data structure containing a list of items, shown in squared brackets: `[item1, item2, ...]`.

We can also return a certain row in a named column using the `.loc` function, `df.loc[1, 'Person']`, or ranges of rows using ':' (denoting 'to'): `df.loc[2:10, 'Person']`.

We can also call a column by number using the `.iloc` function: `df.iloc[:,2]` (column 2 here), or a given cell in the dataframe using the `.iloc` function specifying row number then column number: `df.iloc[3, 2]` (row 3 or column 2 here).

Here is how we can use it on our dataset:

R

```
d1 = select(hflights, ArrTime, DepTime)
knitr::kable(d1[1:5,])
```

	ArrTime	DepTime
5424	1500	1400
5425	1501	1401
5426	1502	1352
5427	1513	1403
5428	1507	1405

Python

```
d1 = hflights.loc[:, ['ArrTime', 'DepTime']]
d1.head()
```

	ArrTime	DepTime
5424	1500.0	1400.0
5425	1501.0	1401.0
5426	1502.0	1352.0
5427	1513.0	1403.0
5428	1507.0	1405.0

We can also search based on column names.

HELPER FUNCTIONS

R Helper Functions

Dplyr comes with a set of helper functions that can help us select groups of variables inside a `select()` call:

```
starts_with("X") - every name that starts with 'X',
ends_with("X") - every name that ends with 'X',
contains("X") - every name that contains 'X',
matches("X") - every name that matches 'X', where 'X' can be a regular expression,
num_range("x", 1:5) - the variables named x01, x02, x03, x04, and x05,
one_of(x) - every name that appears in x, which should be a character vector.
```

Note that when we define the columns directly inside **select()**, we do not use quotes, but if we use the helper functions, we do need to use quotes.

Python Helper Functions

Pandas also comes with a set of helper functions. Python is *object-oriented*, so when we are accessing a text function, for instance, we need to use the **.str** member to access string member functions such as **get()**. To filter the dataframe **df**'s 'Person' column where the first character is 'X': **df[df['Person'].str[0] =='X'])**, where **.str** treats each entry in the 'Person' column as a string, and **.str[0]** references the first character of each entry in the column (note that the first character of the string is referenced as '0' rather than '1'):

```
df[df['Person'].str[0] =='X'] - every name that starts with 'X'
df[df['Person'].str[-1] =='X'] - every name that ends with 'X'
df[df['Person'].isin(['X'])] - every name that contains 'X'
```

For example, let us say we want to see all the columns which contain the word 'time' in the name:

R

```
d2 = select(hflights, contains("time"))
knitr::kable(d2[1:5,])
```

Python

```
d2 = hflights.filter(regex = 'Time')
d2.head()
```

	DepTime	ArrTime	ActualElapsedTime	AirTime
5424	1400	1500	60	40
5425	1401	1501	60	45
5426	1352	1502	70	48
5427	1403	1513	70	39
5428	1405	1507	62	44

All the above columns contain 'time'. Keep in mind that it is not case-sensitive.

Now suppose we want to select columns that contain either 'time' or 'delay':

R

```
d3 = select(hflights, contains("time"), contains("delay"))
knitr::kable(d3[1:5,])
```

Python

```
d3 = hflights.filter(regex = 'Time|Delay')
d3.head()
```

	DepTime	ArrTime	ActualElapsed Time	Air Time	Arr Delay	Dep Delay
5424	1400	1500	60	40	-10	0
5425	1401	1501	60	45	-9	1
5426	1352	1502	70	48	-8	-8
5427	1403	1513	70	39	3	3
5428	1405	1507	62	44	-3	5

Some of the resulting columns are numeric while others are not. The following can be useful to extract columns that are of a particular data type. Let us select all the numeric columns:

R

```
d4 = select_if(hflights, is.numeric)
knitr::kable(d4[1:5,],row.names = F)
```

Python

```
d4 = hflights.select_dtypes(include=np.number)
d4.head()
```

Vice versa, we can extract all the character columns:

R

```
d5 = select_if(hflights, is.character)
knitr::kable(d5[1:5,], row.names = F)
```

Python

```
d5 = hflights.select_dtypes(include = 'object')
d5.head()
```

UniqueCarrier	TailNum	Origin	Dest	CancellationCode
AA	N576AA	IAH	DFW	
AA	N557AA	IAH	DFW	
AA	N541AA	IAH	DFW	
AA	N403AA	IAH	DFW	
AA	N492AA	IAH	DFW	

FILTERING DATA

R filter

The `filter()` function is used to select rows. For example, let us subset the rows with a distance greater than 1000 miles:

Python `df[(... > ...)]`

Pandas allows us to show all rows in a dataframe where row entries of a given column are greater than a certain value, `df[(df['Earnings'] > 10)]`:

R

```
d6 = filter(hflights, Distance>1000)
dim(d6)

## [1] 65389    21
```

Python

```
d6 = hflights.loc[hflights['Distance'] > 1000, :]
d6.shape

(65389, 21)
```

Suppose we want to get all the flights that got cancelled because of weather or security. These are labelled with the characters 'B' and 'D' in the **CancellationCode** column:

R

```
d7 = filter(hflights, CancellationCode == "D" | CancellationCode == "B")
dim(d7)
## [1] 1653    21
```

Python

```
d7 = hflights.loc[(hflights['CancellationCode'] == 'D') | (hflights['Cancellation
Code'] == 'B'), :]
d7.shape

(1653, 21)
```

Another way to write this is:

R

```
d8 = filter(hflights, CancellationCode %in% c("B","D"))
dim(d8)
## [1] 1653    21
```

Python

```python
d8 = hflights.loc[hflights['CancellationCode'].isin(['B', 'D']), :]
d8.shape
```

```
(1653, 21)
```

%in% identifies the elements belonging to the vector `CancellationCode`. Note that we always use `c()`, even when we are only looking for rows containing one element.

Let us provide two more examples.

1   Select all the flights where the total delay, which is `ArrDelay + DepDelay`, is more than one hour. Note that the current time is expressed in minutes.
2   Select all flights where `AirTime` is less than the total delay (what we just calculated):

R

```r
hflights$TotalDelay = hflights$ArrDelay + hflights$DepDelay
d9 = filter(hflights, TotalDelay>60)
dim(d9)
## [1] 22367     22
knitr::kable(d9[1:5,], row.names = F)
```

Python

```python
hflights['TotalDelay'] = hflights['ArrDelay'] + hflights['DepDelay']
d9 = hflights.loc[hflights['TotalDelay'] > 60, :]
d9.shape
d9.head()
```

R

```r
d10 = filter(hflights, AirTime<TotalDelay)
knitr::kable(d10[1:5,],row.names = F)
```

Python

```python
d10 = hflights.loc[hflights['AirTime'] < hflights['TotalDelay'], :]
d10.head()
```

Another way to do this is as follows:

R

```r
d9 = filter(hflights, (ArrDelay + DepDelay)>60)
d10 = filter(hflights, AirTime<(ArrDelay + DepDelay))
```

Python

```python
d9 = hflights.loc[(hflights['ArrDelay'] + hflights['DepDelay']) > 60, :]
d10 = hflights.loc[hflights['AirTime'] < (hflights['ArrDelay'] +
    hflights['DepDelay']), :]
```

Now, suppose we want to create a dataset including only the columns `FlightNum`, `DayOfWeek`, `ArrTime`, `ArrDelay`, and `DepDelay`, for all the flights where `AirTime` is less than the total delay (`ArrDelay` + `DepDelay`):

R

```
d11 = filter(hflights, AirTime<(ArrDelay + DepDelay))
d12 = select(d11, FlightNum, DayOfWeek, AirTime, ArrDelay, DepDelay)
knitr::kable(d12[1:5,])
```

Python

```
d11 = hflights.loc[hflights['AirTime'] < (hflights['ArrDelay'] + hflights
    ['DepDelay']), :]
d12 = d11.loc[:, ['FlightNum', 'DayOfWeek', 'AirTime', 'ArrDelay', 'DepDelay']]
d12.head()
```

FlightNum	DayOfWeek	AirTime	ArrDelay	DepDelay
428	7	41	44	43
428	1	45	43	43
428	2	42	29	29
428	1	48	84	90
428	4	42	72	67

Note that when we have more than one condition, we can simply add them separated by a comma.

SIMPLIFYING CODE

R: Piping

Sometimes doing a series of operations on a variable can become complicated, especially when many parentheses are involved. For example, the following can be difficult to understand; note the number of parentheses involved in creating the function:

R

```
x = c(25,2,72,456,8,34,6,7,2,3,4)
round(exp(sqrt(log(x))), 1)
## [1]  6.0  2.3  7.9 11.9  4.2  6.5  3.8  4.0  2.3  2.9  3.2
```

Python

```
x = np.array([25, 2, 72, 456, 8, 34, 6, 7, 2, 3, 4])
np.round(np.exp(np.sqrt(np.log(x))), 1)

array([ 6. ,  2.3,  7.9, 11.9,  4.2,  6.5,  3.8,  4. ,  2.3,  2.9,  3.2])
```

Piping is an important operator that can make writing such expressions much simpler. The operator for piping is `%>%` and it comes with the *dplyr* package. The above example can be written using piping as follows:

```
x %>% log() %>%
  sqrt() %>%
  exp() %>%
  round(1)
## [1]  6.0  2.3  7.9 11.9  4.2  6.5  3.8  4.0  2.3  2.9  3.2
```

The mathematical reasoning behind piping has to do with composite functions. When solving `f(g(x))`, the input `x` is run through the function `g`, and then `g(x)` is run through `f`. This would be written like so:

```
x   %>%    g()   %>%      f()
```

To explain this further, `function(argument)` is rewritten as `argument %>% function()`. Now, let us rewrite the example in the previous section using piping:

```
d12 = hflights %>%
  filter(ArrTime<(ArrDelay + DepDelay)) %>%
  select(FlightNum, DayOfWeek, ArrTime, ArrDelay, DepDelay)
knitr::kable(d12[1:5,])
```

FlightNum	DayOfWeek	ArrTime	ArrDelay	DepDelay
310	1	2	33	49
467	1	53	58	42
209	7	19	20	37
310	7	5	36	25
467	7	10	15	26

Whenever possible, try to use the pipe operator to write your code. Check out the 'further reading' at the end of this chapter for a more in-depth piping tutorial.

RENAMING COLUMNS

R: Rename Function

The rename function can be used to rename the columns of a dataframe. The syntax is:

```
rename(dataframe, new name = old name)
```

Let us say we want to change the columns DepTime to DepartureTime and ArrTime to ArrivalTime. We will use the piping method in R in the snippet below.

Python: Rename Function

As in R, the dataframe has a **rename()** function.

R
```
d13 = hflights %>%
   rename(DepartureTime = DepTime, ArrivalTime = ArrTime)
knitr::kable(d13[1:5,],row.names = F)
```

Python
```
d13 = hflights.rename(columns = {'DepartureTime': 'DepTime', 'ArrivalTime':
    'ArrTime'})
d13.head()
```

A clean way to do this is presented below:

```
d14 = rename(hflights, DepartureTime = DepTime, ArrivalTime = ArrTime)
knitr::kable(d14[1:5,],row.names = F)
```

COPYING COLUMNS

R: Mutate Function

This option is used to create new columns based on existing columns. The basic syntax is:

```
mutate(dataframe, new column name = expression).
```

Suppose we want to create the following columns using piping:

```
ActualGroundTime = ActualElapsedTime - AirTime
TaxiTime = TaxiIn + TaxiOut
AvgSpeed = 60 (Distance / AirTime)
```

Python: df['col_copy'] = df['col']

Pandas allows you to specify a new column, copy another column into it, or assign other values as you prefer. It is not even necessary to do an explicit insert:

R
```
d15 = hflights %>%
   mutate(ActualGroundTime = ActualElapsedTime - AirTime, TaxiTime = TaxiIn +
         TaxiOut, AvgSpeed = 60 * (Distance/AirTime))
knitr::kable(d15[1:5,])
```

Python

```python
d15 = hflights.copy()
d15['ActualGroundTime'] = d15['ActualElapsedTime'] - d15['AirTime']
d15['TaxiTime'] = d15['TaxiIn'] + d15['TaxiOut']
d15['AvgSpeed'] = 60 * (d15['Distance'] / d15['AirTime'])
d15.head()
```

Again, we can do this with the following code:

```
d16 = mutate(hflights, ActualGroundTime = ActualElapsedTime - AirTime,
TaxiTime = TaxiIn + TaxiOut, AvgSpeed = 60 * (Distance/AirTime))
```

COLUMN SORTS

R: Arrange Function

This function is used to reorder the rows of a dataframe in ascending or descending order. The basic syntax is:

```
arrange(dataframe, columns to arrange by).
```

Pandas: sort_values Function

The dataframe **sort_values()** function executes a column sort.

Let us sort the dataframe **hflights** by **AirTime**:

R

```r
d17 = hflights %>%
  arrange(AirTime)
knitr::kable(d17[1:5,],row.names = F)
```

Python

```python
d17 = hflights.sort_values(by = 'AirTime')
d17.head()
```

We can sort multiple columns by descending order using **desc()**. Note that ascending order is the default setting:

```
d18 = hflights %>%
  arrange(AirTime, UniqueCarrier, desc(Month))
knitr::kable(d18[1:5,])
```

GROUP BY

R: Summarize Function

This function is used to summarize data and it usually goes together with the **group_by()** function. The syntax is:

```
s1 = summarize(g1, variable name = some aggregating function)
g1 = group_by(dataframe, factor variables you want to group by)
```

Let us get the average air time for each unique carrier:

R
```
g1 = group_by(hflights, UniqueCarrier)
s1 = summarize(g1, AvgTime = mean(AirTime, na.rm = T))
knitr::kable(s1)
```

Python: groupby()

The *Pandas* syntax to group a column is as follows:

Python
```
s1 = hflights.groupby('UniqueCarrier').agg({'AirTime': 'mean'})
s1
```

UniqueCarrier	AvgTime
AA	69.65261
AS	254.18407
B6	183.98514
CO	145.45787
DL	97.80124
EV	103.65677
F9	125.34135
FL	92.70630
MQ	93.83948
OO	113.41068
UA	157.40630
US	133.85633
WN	86.73134
XE	83.22215
YV	121.93590

Remember to add `na.rm = T` if the data contains missing values.

We can pipe this to improve readability:

```
s2 = hflights %>%
  group_by(UniqueCarrier) %>%
  summarize(AvgTime = mean(AirTime, na.rm = T))
knitr::kable(s2)
```

We can use a number of statistics other than the mean. The basic aggregating functions that R provides are:

```
min(x) - minimum value of vector x
max(x) - maximum value of vector x
mean(x) - mean value of vector x
median(x) - median value of vector x
quantile(x, p) - pth quantile of vector x
sd(x) - standard deviation of vector x
var(x) - variance of vector x
IQR(x) - Inter Quartile Range (IQR) of vector x
diff(range(x)) - total range of vector x
```

In addition, *dplyr* provides a number of other aggregate functions which include:

```
first(x) - The first element of vector x
last(x) - The last element of vector x
nth(x, n) - The nth element of vector x
n() - The number of rows in the dataframe or group of observations
summarise() - Describes the dataframe
n_distinct(x) - The number of unique values in vector x
```

Additionally, we can get multiple statistics from multiple groups. Here is an example:

R

```
s3 = hflights %>%
  group_by(UniqueCarrier, Origin) %>%
  summarize(AvgTime = mean(AirTime, na.rm = T), NumFlights = n(),
            LongestFlightTime = max(AirTime, na.rm = T))
knitr::kable(s3)
```

Python

```
s3 = hflights.groupby(['UniqueCarrier', 'Origin']).agg({'AirTime': ['mean',
    'count', 'max']})
s3.columns = ['AvgTime', 'NumFlights', 'LongestFlightTime']
s3.reset_index(inplace = True)
s3
```

UniqueCarrier	Origin	AvgTime	NumFlights	LongestFlightTime
AA	IAH	69.65261	3244	161
AS	IAH	254.18407	365	315
B6	HOU	183.98514	695	258
CO	IAH	145.45787	70032	549
DL	HOU	92.38978	388	135
DL	IAH	98.70843	2253	188
EV	HOU	92.87955	472	117
EV	IAH	106.47769	1732	173
F9	HOU	125.34135	838	190
FL	HOU	92.70630	2139	186
MQ	HOU	47.55437	2424	88
MQ	IAH	144.11209	2224	220
OO	IAH	113.41068	16061	225
UA	IAH	157.40630	2072	276
US	IAH	133.85633	4082	212
WN	HOU	86.73134	45343	288
XE	IAH	83.22215	73053	204
YV	IAH	121.93590	79	150

Once a summary is 'created, we can easily plot it using *ggplot2* in R:

R

```
library(ggplot2)
ggplot(s3, aes(x = AvgTime, y = LongestFlightTime, col = Origin)) + geom_point()
        + theme_light() + geom_smooth(method = lm, se = F)
```

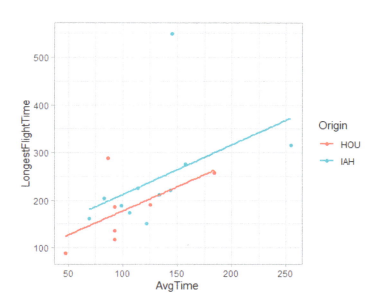

In Python, we can use the package Seaborn, to create this plot:

Python

```
import seaborn as sns

sns.lmplot(x='AvgTime', y='LongestFlightTime', hue='Origin', data=s3, ci=None)
plt.show()
```

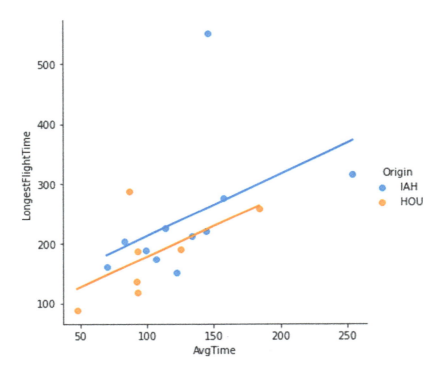

Now, we can pipe the entire code:

```
hflights %>%
  group_by(UniqueCarrier, Origin) %>%
  summarize(AvgTime = mean(AirTime, na.rm = T), NumFlights = n(),
            LongestFlightTime = max(AirTime, na.rm = T)) %>%
  ggplot(aes(x=AvgTime, y = LongestFlightTime, col = Origin)) + geom_
        point()+ theme_light() + geom_smooth(method = lm, se = F)
## 'geom_smooth()' using formula 'y ~ x'
```

We can use the following syntax to generate a summary for the entire dataframe:

```
summarize(dataframe, variable name = some aggregating function)
```

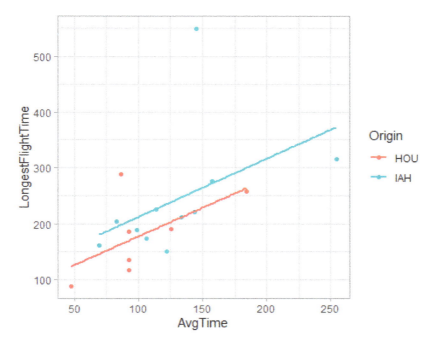

Figure 3.1   Longest flight time versus average air time

RECODING FACTOR VARIABLES

In the long format, the data in the `TotalRainfall` column are too long. Let us suppose we want to recode these values as follows:

TotalRainfall	TotalRainfall_New
Annual total rainfall (mm)	Annual
Winter total rainfall (mm)	Winter
Summer total rainfall (mm)	Summer
Monsoon total rainfall (mm)	Monsoon
Post monsoon total rainfall (mm)	PostMonsoon

The strategy is as follows:

Create a recode table with the existing values and new values of the factor variable. Join the dataframe with the `RecodeTable`:

R

```
TotalRainfall = c("Annual total rainfall (mm)", "Winter total rainfall (mm)",
          "Summer total rainfall (mm)","Monsoon total rainfall (mm)",
```

```
                  "Post monsoon total rainfall (mm)")

TotalRainfall_new = c("Annual","Winter","Summer","Monsoon","PostMonsoon")

RecodeTable = data.frame(TotalRainfall,TotalRainfall_new)

knitr::kable(RecodeTable)
```

Python

```python
RecodeTable = pd.DataFrame({'TotalRainfall': ['Annual total rainfall (mm)',
            'Winter total rainfall (mm)', 'Summer total rainfall (mm)',
            'Monsoon total rainfall (mm)' 'Post monsoon total rainfall (mm)'],
            'TotalRainfall_new': ['Annual', 'Winter', 'Summer', 'Monsoon',
            'PostMonsoon']})

NewRainfall = Rainfall_long.merge(RecodeTable, on='TotalRainfall', how='left')
NewRainfall = NewRainfall.drop('TotalRainfall', axis=1)
NewRainfall.head(10)
```

TotalRainfall	TotalRainfall_new
Annual total rainfall (mm)	Annual
Winter total rainfall (mm)	Winter
Summer total rainfall (mm)	Summer
Monsoon total rainfall (mm)	Monsoon
Post monsoon total rainfall (mm)	PostMonsoon

Now, we need to join `Rainfall_long` and `RecodeTable`:

R

```r
NewRainfall = left_join(Rainfall_long, RecodeTable, by = "TotalRainfall")
## Warning: Column `TotalRainfall` joining character vector and factor,
## coercing into character vector
NewRainfall = NewRainfall %>%
  select(-TotalRainfall)

knitr::kable(NewRainfall[1:10,])
```

Python

```python
RecodeDict = {'Annual total rainfall (mm)': 'Annual',
            'Winter total rainfall (mm)': 'Winter',
            'Summer total rainfall (mm)': 'Summer',
            'Monsoon total rainfall (mm)': 'Monsoon',
            'Post monsoon total rainfall (mm)': 'PostMonsoon'}

NewRainfall['TotalRainfall_new'] = Rainfall_long['TotalRainfall'].map(RecodeDict)
NewRainfall.head(10)
```

State No.	Station Name	Class	Index	Year	Amount(mm)	TotalRainfall_new
1	BOATH	REV	90014	1952	714.9	Annual
1	BOATH	REV	90014	1953	1305.7	Annual
1	BOATH	REV	90014	1954	808.9	Annual
1	BOATH	REV	90014	1955	1245.2	Annual
1	BOATH	REV	90014	1956	1000.8	Annual
1	BOATH	REV	90014	1957	1074.7	Annual
1	BOATH	REV	90014	1958	1049.0	Annual
1	BOATH	REV	90014	1959	1189.8	Annual
1	BOATH	REV	90014	1960	690.9	Annual
1	BOATH	REV	90014	1961	1003.7	Annual

USE CASE: FILTER, SORT, BIN SALES DATA IN PANDAS

After installing *Pandas*, in Python, we can start examining, filtering, and sorting our data. We also show how to bin data to examine sales, in the *Sales* dataset, made at different hours of the day – so we will bin the sales by hour.

First, we install *Pandas*, and then load our CSV. We import the *Numpy* package as **np**, and the *Seaborn* packages as **sns**. Select rows in the **Pandas** dataframe where the 'Gender' column equals 'Female':

R

```
head(df[df$Gender == 'Female',])
```

Python

```
df[df['Gender'] == 'Female']
```

Sort this filtered dataframe by 'Quantity' of sales, with a descending sort (i.e., highest values are first):

R

```
df_female = df[df$Gender == 'Female',]
df_female = df_female[order(df_female$Quantity,decreasing = T),]
```

Python

```
df_females = df[df['Gender'] == 'Female']
df_females = df_females.sort_values(by="Quantity", ascending=False)
```

We now want to examine whether the hour of the day has a bearing on sales volumes, for instance, if most sales happen in the final hour of business of the day, and if so, if we should keep stores open for one hour more to encourage more sales. To do this, we can 'bin' the rows in our dataframe into equally sized bins. This can be done by first converting the 'Time' column to just a time, and removing the date. We then use the *Pandas* '**bin**' function to separate rows into 10 equally sized bins:

Table 3.1 Filtering data

	Invoice ID	Branch	City	Customer type	Gender	Product line	Unit price	Quantity	Tax 5%	Total	Date	Time	Payment	cogs	Gross margin percentage	Gross income	Rating
1	750-67-8428	A	Yangon	Member	Female	Health and beauty	74.69	7	26.1415	548.9715	1/5/2019	1899-12-31 13:08:00	Ewallet	522.83	4.761905	26.1415	9.1
2	226-31-3081	C	Naypyitaw	Normal	Female	Electronic accessories	15.28	5	3.82	80.22	3/8/2019	1899-12-31 10:29:00	Cash	76.4	4.761905	3.82	9.6
3	355-53-5943	A	Yangon	Member	Female	Electronic accessories	68.84	6	20.652	433.692	2/25/2019	1899-12-31 14:36:00	Ewallet	413.04	4.761905	20.652	5.8
4	315-22-5665	C	Naypyitaw	Normal	Female	Home and lifestyle	73.56	10	36.78	772.38	2/24/2019	1899-12-31 11:38:00	Ewallet	735.6	4.761905	36.78	8
5	665-32-9167	A	Yangon	Member	Female	Health and beauty	36.26	2	3.626	76.146	1/10/2019	1899-12-31 17:15:00	Credit card	72.52	4.761905	3.626	7.2
6	692-92-5582	B	Mandalay	Member	Female	Food and beverages	54.84	3	8.226	172.746	2/20/2019	1899-12-31 13:27:00	Credit card	164.52	4.761905	8.226	5.9

R

```
df_female$hour = format(as.POSIXct(df_female$Time, format="%Y-%m-%d %H:%M"),
              format="%H")
df_female$hour = as.numeric(df_female$hour)
breaks = c(0,2,4,6,8,10,12,14,16,18,20,22)
tags = c("[0-2)","[2-4)", "[4-6)", "[6-8)", "[8-10)", "[10-12)","[12-14)",
        "[14-16)","[16-18)", "[18-20)","[20-22)")

df_female$time_bin = cut(df_female$hour, breaks=breaks, include.lowest=TRUE,
                  right=FALSE, labels=tags)
```

Python

```
# define a bin every 2 hours
bins = np.arange(0, 25, 2)
# extract the hours from the time
df_females['Hours'] = df_females.Time.apply(lambda x: x.strftime('%H')). astype(int)
# create the labels to plot the data
labels = ['0-2', '2-4', '4-6', '6-8', '8-10', '10-12', '12-14', '14-16', '16-18',
        '18-20', '20-22', '22-00']
#Bin
df_females['Time_bins'] = pd.cut(df_females['Hours'], bins, labels = labels)
```

We can now plot the relationship between Total sales in each time bin:

R

```
ggplot(df_female,aes(x =time_bin, y = Quantity)) + geom_col(size = 1)
```

Python

```
sns.jointplot(x='Time_bins', y= 'Quantity', data=df_females[df_females
['Customer type'] == 'Member'])
plt.title('Sales by hour - opening time binned in two-hour intervals',
x = -2.5, y=1.25)
plt.show()
```

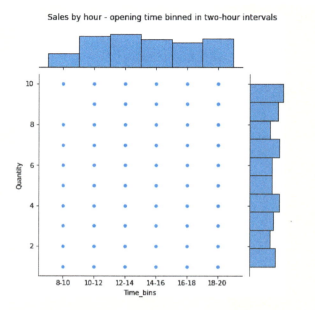

Sales by hour - opening time binned in two-hour intervals

Summary

In this chapter, we introduced R's *dplyr* and Python's *Pandas* packages to store, alter, and manipulate data to get it in the right form for generating insights and for facilitating further analysis. We have seen how to select columns in R dataframes and *Pandas* dataframes, filter rows, sort, create new columns, group by certain column values, and more. Getting fluent in the syntax and operations behind these simple functions will make life easier and your data analysis faster.

Exercises

To complete the activity below, you will need to visit the companion website to the book and download the relevant dataset: https://study.sagepub.com/gopal

Read the file gapminder.csv.

1   How many countries start with the letter A?
2   List all the countries and years when the life expectancy exceeded 70 years.
3   Create a variable termed **totalGDP** which is the product of average GDP per capita (**gdpPercap**) and population (**pop**). Compute the sum of the **totalGDP** for each year and plot it. What does the plot reveal?

4   For each continent, compute the average life expectancy, average GDP per capita, and the average population over the years. Create an appropriate plot to visualize the data.

5   Calculate the total population for each continent for each year. Create an appropriate plot to visualize the data.

6   Reshape the data so that the years are listed in columns.

Further Reading

www.listendata.com/2016/08/dplyr-tutorial.html#select-Function

https://dereksonderegger.github.io/570L/7-data-manipulation.html

https://genomicsclass.github.io/book/pages/dplyr_tutorial.html

www.datacamp.com/community/tutorials/pipe-r-tutorial

4

PROGRAMMING FUNDAMENTALS

Chapter Contents

In addition to providing numerous statistical and analytics capabilities, Python and, to an extent, R are full-blown programming languages. Both allow us to perform complex and repetitive tasks and bring them into operation at any time. In this chapter, we will explore the key programming constructs: functions, conditional statements, and loops for repetition. Their use aids in the development of more complicated statistical and analytics activities.

Functions

Thus far, we have used many functions available in Python, R, and their various packages. Examples of these functions include `mean()`, `std()`, and others. In addition to using these in-built functions, we can create our own functions as well. Why would we want to create our own functions?

We create functions because we often find ourselves using the same sequence of steps multiple times, either in the same project or perhaps in other projects. Instead of repeating a chunk of code several times, it is more efficient to package it all into a function that we can call, with a line of code, whenever required. This also helps cut down on errors as we only need to write the necessary code and package it into a function once.

Let us start with an example. There is no function available in base R to compute the geometric mean. The geometric mean of positive numbers $a_1, a_2, ... a_n$ is defined as:

$$(a_1 \times a_2 \times a_3 ... a_n)^{1/n}$$

Let us create a function ourselves. Before doing this, we write the code to compute the geometric mean of a set of numbers:

R

```
v = c(1,33,4,29,9,90)
gmean = (prod(v))^(1/length(v))
gmean
```

```
## [1] 12.07562
```

Python

```
v = [1,33,4,29,9,90]
gmean = (np.prod(v))**(1/len(v))
gmean
```

```
12.075621482045438
```

The above code computes the geometric mean. What we would like to do now is to package this code into a function so that it can be reused in this script or others we may write.

Programming in Python and R is organized around functions. Think of a mathematical function such as $\log(x)$. This mathematical function takes some inputs (in this case, x) which are called *arguments*, performs a set of calculations on the inputs, and *returns* an output. The same basic idea is used for creating functions in Python and R.

In R, this is the anatomy of a function:

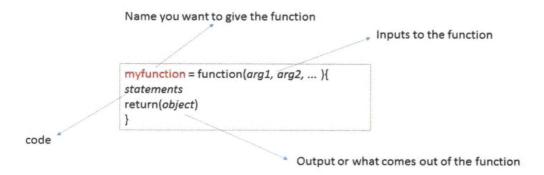

Figure 4.1 Anatomy of a function in R

In Python, the syntax is a bit different, but the main elements are the same:

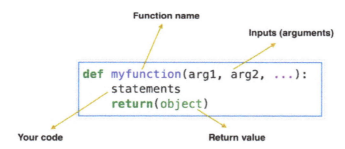

Figure 4.2 Anatomy of a function in Python

The main difference in how to write functions is that in Python, we do not need the curly brackets to structure our code, but we have to use the indentation to mark up where a line of code belongs. In the Python example above, all lines that are indented would be seen as belonging to **myfunction** until a non-indented line. In R, we can be more relaxed with the indentation, but the curly brackets are needed.

The following creates a function, that we name **geomean**, which calculates the geometric mean of a set of numbers in the input vector **v**:

R

```
geomean = function(v){
gmean = (prod(v))^(1/length(v))
return(gmean)
}
```

Python

```
def geomean(v):
    gmean = (np.prod(v))**(1/len(v))
    return(gmean)
```

That is how we create a function! Once the function is created, we can use any numerical vector as an input and the function will return its geometric mean. Here is an example of how we call the function:

R

```r
x = c(1,3,54,9,29,234,6,2,8,2456,2,8)
geomean(x)
```

```
## [1] 13.5207
```

Python

```python
x = [1,3,54,9,29,234,6,2,8,2456,2,8]
geomean(x)
```

```
13.520702172120803
```

As an additional example, let us compute the harmonic mean, defined as:

$$\frac{n}{\dfrac{1}{a_1}+\dfrac{1}{a_2}+\ldots+\dfrac{1}{a_n}}$$

The following code will return the harmonic mean:

R

```r
d = c(2,4,63,6,3)
g = 1/d
hmean = length(d)/(sum(g))
hmean
```

```
## [1] 3.949843
```

Python

```python
d = np.array([2,4,63,6,3])
g = 1/d
hmean = len(d)/(np.sum(g))
hmean
```

```
3.949843260188088
```

Now, let us create a function for the harmonic mean:

R

```r
harmean = function(v){
  a = 1/v
  hmean = length(v)/(sum(a))
  return(hmean)
}
```

Python

```
def harmean(v):
  a = 1/v
  hmean = len(v)/(np.sum(a))
  return(hmean)
```

The following code tests both functions to ensure they work properly:

R

```
v = c(2,23,3456,1,4,6)
geomean(v)
```

```
## [1] 12.5004
```

```
harmean(v)
```

```
## [1] 3.060546
```

Python

```
v = np.array([2,23,3456,1,4,6])
geomean(v)
```

```
12.500396862365385
```

```
harmean(v)
```

```
3.0605463611219847
```

Let us see another example. Suppose we have a vector $v = [4,6,23,6,375,9]$ and we want to find how many elements of the vector are above a cutoff number, say 6. The following code can be used to achieve this. Note that the function `length()` in R returns the number of elements of a vector, just as the function `len()` does in Python:

R

```
v = c(4,6,23,6,375,9)
cutoff = 6
vsub = v[v>cutoff]
vsub
```

```
## [1]  23 375   9
```

```
length(vsub)
```

```
## [1] 3
```

Python

```
v = np.array([4,6,23,6,375,9])
cutoff = 6
```

```
vsub = v[v>cutoff]
vsub
```

```
array([ 23, 375,    9])
```

```
len(vsub)
```

```
3
```

Next, let us package this code into a function. Note that this function should have two inputs: the vector and the cutoff value:

R

```
vecsize = function(v,cutoff = 1){
  vsub = v[v>cutoff]
  return(length(vsub))}
```

Python

```
def vecsize(v, cutoff = 1):
  vsub = v[v>cutoff]
  return(len(vsub))
```

Let us see how this function works:

R

```
v = c(.2,5,2,.6,3,57,34,5)
vecsize(v,10)
## [1] 2
```

```
vecsize(v)
## [1] 6
```

Python

```
v = np.array([.2,5,2,.6,3,57,34,5])
vecsize(v,10)
2
```

```
vecsize(v)
6
```

In the above function, we have set a default cutoff value of 1 by using `cutoff = 1`. If we had not specified a cutoff value when calling the function, this would have defaulted to 1.

Let us see another example. Suppose we have a vector v = [2,2,6,3,546,2346,22,34,7,21,4] and we want to find all the elements between 5 and 100. The following code could be used to achieve this:

R

```r
vec1 = c(2,2,6,3,546,2346,22,34,7,21,4)
cutoff1 = 5
cutoff2 = 100
vsub = vec1[vec1>cutoff1 & vec1<cutoff2]
vsub
```

```
## [1]  6 22 34  7 21
```

Python

```python
vec1 = np.array([2,2,6,3,546,2346,22,34,7,21,4])
cutoff1 = 5
cutoff2 = 100
vsub = vec1[(vec1>cutoff1) & (vec1<cutoff2)]
vsub
```

```
array([ 6, 22, 34,  7, 21])
```

As with the previous example, after testing and ensuring that the code works fine, we can turn this into a function and test it:

R

```r
intermediate = function(vec1, cutoff1,
                        cutoff2){
  vsub = vec1[vec1>cutoff1 &
                vec1<cutoff2]
  return(vsub)
}
vec1 =
    c(2,2,6,3,546,2346,22,34,7,21,4)
intermediate(vec1,5,100)
```

```
## [1]  6 22 34  7 21
```

Python

```python
def intermediate (vec1, cutoff1,
                    cutoff2):
  vsub = vec1[(vec1>cutoff1) & (vec1<cutoff2)]
  return(vsub)

vec1 = np.array([2,2,6,3,546,2346,22,34,7,21,4])
intermediate(vec1,5,100)
```

```
array([ 6, 22, 34,  7, 21])
```

CONDITIONALS

Conditional Statements

Conditional statements are very useful and are an important element in any programming language. In R, there are three varieties of syntax for conditional statements (the brackets are important):

```
1   if (condition) {trueStatement}
2   ifelse (condition,trueStatement,falseStatement)
3   if (condition){trueStatement} else {falseStatement}
```

In Python, the structure is similar, but the syntax is different (the angular brackets are not part of the code):

```
1   if <condition>:
        <trueStatements>
2   if <condition>:
        <trueStatements>
    else:
        <falseStatements>
```

Again, in Python, the indentation is important, but we can dispense with the brackets instead.

The meaning of these statements is in both R and Python that the **condition** is evaluated and if it is found to be true, the **trueStatements** will be executed. In the variants having an else branch, the **falseStatements** will be executed if the **condition** is not true.

For instance, we can check if the sum of a vector is what we expect:

R

```
v = c(1,2,3,4)
if (sum(v) == 10)
{print("Yes, the sum is 10.")}

## [1] "Yes, the sum is 10."
```

Python

```
v = np.array([1,2,3,4])
if sum(v) == 10:
    print("Yes, the sum is 10.")

"Yes, the sum is 10."
```

We can also check the case of the condition being false:

R

```
v1 = c(1,2,3,3)
if (sum(v) == 10){
```

```
    print("Yes, the sum is 10.")
} else {
    print("No, the sum is not 10.")
}
```

```
##  [1] "No, the sum is not 10."
```

Python

```python
v1 = np.array([1,2,3,3])
if sum(v) == 10:
    print("Yes, the sum is 10.")
else:
    print("No, the sum is not 10.")
```

```
"No, the sum is not 10."
```

Conditional Expressions

Conditional expressions include the same logic as conditional statements, but they express a return value that depends on the condition, rather than executing statements.

In R, we can apply this concept directly to vectors. Suppose we have a vector of numbers, and we want to create another vector containing 0s and 1s. If the element in the first vector is 5 or above, we want to put a 1 for the corresponding element in the second vector. Otherwise, we want to put a 0:

R

```r
v1 = c(2,36,83,2,5,7,2,9,3,12)
v2 = ifelse(v1> = 5,1,0)
print(v2)
```

```
##  [1] 0 1 1 0 1 1 0 1 0 1
```

Python

```python
v1 = np.array([2,36,83,2,5,7,2,9,3,12])
v2 = np.where(v1> = 5,1,0)
print(v2)
```

```
[0 1 1 0 1 1 0 1 0 1]
```

Let us show another example with the **whiteside** dataframe:

R

```r
library(MASS)
head(whiteside)
```

```
##     Insul  Temp Gas
## 1 Before -0.8  7.2
```

```
## 2 Before -0.7 6.9
## 3 Before  0.4 6.4
## 4 Before  2.5 6.0
## 5 Before  2.9 5.8
## 6 Before  3.2 5.8
```

Python

```python
whiteside = pd.read_csv('../data/whiteside.csv')
whiteside.head()
```

```
     Insul    Temp    Gas
0    Before   -0.8    7.2
1    Before   -0.7    6.9
2    Before    0.4    6.4
3    Before    2.5    6.0
4    Before    2.9    5.8
```

Suppose we want to create a column in which temperatures below 5 are labelled 'cold' and temperatures above 5 are labelled 'hot':

R

```r
whiteside$hotcold = ifelse(whiteside$Temp<5,"cold","hot")
head(whiteside)
```

```
##     Insul  Temp  Gas hotcold
## 1 Before  -0.8  7.2    cold
## 2 Before  -0.7  6.9    cold
## 3 Before   0.4  6.4    cold
## 4 Before   2.5  6.0    cold
## 5 Before   2.9  5.8    cold
## 6 Before   3.2  5.8    cold
```

Python

```python
whiteside['hotcold'] = np.where(whiteside['Temp']<5, "cold", "hot")
whiteside.head()
```

```
     Insul    Temp    Gas    hotcold
0    Before   -0.8    7.2    cold
1    Before   -0.7    6.9    cold
2    Before    0.4    6.4    cold
3    Before    2.5    6.0    cold
4    Before    2.9    5.8    cold
```

Next, let us create a summary table of average gas consumption for when it is hot and cold, and with and without insulation:

R

```
x = aggregate(whiteside$Gas,list(whiteside$Insul, whiteside$hotcold),mean)
x
```

```
##    Group.1 Group.2       x
## 1  Before    cold 5.94000
## 2   After    cold 3.88500
## 3  Before     hot 4.00625
## 4   After     hot 2.68000
```

Python

```
x = whiteside.groupby(['Insul','hotcold'])['Gas'].mean().reset_index()
x
```

```
     Insul    hotcold      Gas
0    After       cold  3.88500
1    After        hot  2.68000
2   Before       cold  5.94000
3   Before        hot  4.00625
```

As expected, gas consumption is high when it is cold and there is no insulation. Notice that the column names are not very informative. The column names of a dataframe can be changed using the `colnames()` function in R and `.rename()` in Python:

R

```
colnames(x)
x
```

```
## [1] "Group.1" "Group.2" "x"
```

```
colnames(x) = c("Insulation","Weather", "Average_Gas_Consumption")
x
```

```
##    Insulation Weather  Average_Gas_Consumption
## 1      Before    cold                  5.94000
## 2       After    cold                  3.88500
## 3      Before     hot                  4.00625
## 4       After     hot                  2.68000
```

Python

```
x.columns
```

```
Index(['Insul', 'hotcold', 'Gas'], dtype='object')
```

```
x.columns=["Insulation", "Weather", "Average_Gas_Consumption"]
x
```

```
        Insulation    Weather    Average_Gas_Consumption
0           After       cold                     3.88500
1           After        hot                     2.68000
2          Before       cold                     5.94000
3          Before        hot                     4.00625
```

LOOPING

For Loops

Looping, or iterations, is another key element of programming.

The syntax in R is as follows:

```
for (variable in sequence) {statements}
```

It is common to use **i** as the variable in the sequence. The command **print** in R allows to write things out from inside the loop.

The syntax in Python requires no brackets, but the use of the colon ':' and indentation as follows:

```
for variable in sequence:
        statements
```

Let us see an example. Say that we want to print the numbers 1–10 using a loop:

R
```
for (i in 1:10)
{
  print(i)
}

## [1] 1
## [1] 2
## [1] 3
## [1] 4
## [1] 5
## [1] 6
## [1] 7
## [1] 8
## [1] 9
## [1] 10
```

Python
```
for i in range (1, 11):
    print (i)
```

```
1
2
3
4
5
6
7
8
9
10
```

Next, let us print the product of a term and the two terms before it. The code would be as follows:

R

```r
for (i in 1:10)
{
   print(i*(i-1)*(i-2))
}

## [1] 0
## [1] 0
## [1] 6
## [1] 24
## [1] 60
## [1] 120
## [1] 210
## [1] 336
## [1] 504
## [1] 720
```

Python

```python
for i in range (1,11):
    print (i*(i-1)*(i-2))

0
0
6
24
60
120
210
336
504
720
```

As an additional example, let us create a vector that expresses the running sums of the elements in vector $v1 = [1,2,4,2,4,6,7,8,9,12,4,1,5,2]$. The code can be written as follows:

R

```
v1 = c(1,4,5,2,4,6,7,8,9,12,4,1,5,2)
v2 = v1
for (i in 2:length(v1))
{
  v2[i] = v2[i-1]+v1[i]
}
```

```
## [1]  1  5 10 12 16 22 29 37 46 58 62 63 68 70
```

Python

```
v1 = np.array([1,4,5,2,4,6,7,8,9,12,4,1,5,2])
v2 = v1
for i in range (1,len(v1)):
    v2[i] = v2[i-1]+v1[i]
v1
```

```
array([ 1,  5, 10, 12, 16, 22, 29, 37, 46, 58, 62, 63, 68, 70])
```

In the next example, we create a vector containing all the prime numbers between two integers of choice. To do this, we will need to install the package *schoolmath* in R and the package *sympy* in Python:

R

```
library(schoolmath)
ans = c()
a = 20
b = 30
for (i in a:b)
{
  if(is.prim(i) == TRUE){ans = c(ans,i)}
}
ans
```

```
## [1] 23 29
```

Python

```
import sympy
ans = np.array([])
a = 20
b = 30
for i in range (a,b+1):
    if sympy.isprime(i):
        ans = np.append(ans,i)
ans
```

```
array([23., 29.])
```

AVOIDING LOOPS WITH VECTORIZATION

Even though we wrote the above code using loops, we do not necessarily have to use loops in R. This is because R does vectorized calculations. Vectorized operations make the code easier to write and, being computationally efficient, much faster to run. For example, when we did the sum of a vector, to add up all the numbers, we used **sum()**. In other programming languages which do not support vectorized calculations, we would have to write a loop to calculate the sum of the numbers in a vector. In general, it is always preferable to replace loops with vectorized calculations whenever possible.

Now, we will rewrite the above code above without using a loop:

R

```
x = seq(20:30)
y = is.prim(x)
y
```

```
## [1]  TRUE  TRUE  TRUE FALSE  TRUE FALSE  TRUE FALSE FALSE FALSE  TRUE
```

```
x[y]
```

```
## [1]  1  2  3  5  7 11
```

Python

```
x = np.arange(20,30+1)
y = sympy.isprime(x)
y
```

```
False
```

By comparing the two chunks of code, it is evident how writing the code without using loops is much simpler and more elegant.

Now, suppose we have a vector $[a1,a2,...a_n]$ and you want to calculate the following:

$$\sum_{i=1}^{n-1} a_i a_{i+1}$$

Let us first code this using a loop:

R

```
total = 0
v = c(1,4,2,5,73,4,5)
for (i in 1:(length(v)-1))
{
  total = total + (v[i]*v[i+1])
}
total
```

```
## [1] 699
```

Python

```python
total = 0
v = np.array([1,4,2,5,73,4,5])
for i in range (len(v)-1):
    total = total + (v[i]*v[i+1])
total
```

```
699
```

There is a better way to calculate this total, without using loops and by creating vectors $v1 = [a1,a2...,a_n-1]$ and $v2 = [a2,a3,...,a_n]$. The code is:

R

```r
v1 = v[1:(length(v)-1)]
v2 = v[2:length(v)]
total = sum(v1*v2)
total
```

```
## [1] 699
```

Python

```python
v1 = v[:(len(v)-1)]
v2 = v[1:len(v)]
total = sum(v1*v2)
total
```

```
699
```

In some cases, we will have no option but to create a loop. Here is an example.

Let us say we have a vector $v1 = [1,2,3,4,5]$ and we want a loop that reverses the order of the elements in the vector:

R

```r
v1 = c(72,3,57,2,8,24,7)
v2 = c()
n = length(v1)
for (i in 1:n)
{
  v2[i] = v1[n +1 - i]
}
v2
```

```
## [1]  7 24  8  2 57  3 72
```

Python

```python
v1 = np.array([72,3,57,2,8,24,7])
v2 = np.array([])
```

```
n = len(v1)
for i in range (n):
    v2 = np.append(v2,v1[n-1-i])
v2
```

```
array([ 7., 24.,  8.,  2., 57.,  3., 72.])
```

Python still offers built-in methods (i.e., `reversed()`) to achieve that without writing a loop, but effectively, you would be calling a function that runs a `for` loop behind the scenes!

WHILE LOOPS

Another type of iteration is the `while` loop. The `while` loop is used when we want to repeat a set of commands while a condition remains true.

The syntax in R is:

```
while(cond) expr
```

Suppose we have a starting integer value, let us say 19. Now suppose we want to find ten prime numbers that follow 19. In this case, the `for` loop is not useful and the logic to resolve this problem is as follows.

We will create one index called `i` that starts at 19 and will increment by 1 at each iteration. We will create another index `primi` which starts at 0 and will increment by 1 if a prime number is found. The `while` loop will continue until `primi` reaches 10:

R

```
library(schoolmath)
startnumber = 300
numprimes = 3
i = startnumber + 1
primi = 0
primevec = c()
while (primi<numprimes)
{
  if(is.prim(i) == TRUE){
    primi = primi + 1
    primevec = c(primevec,i)
    }
  i = i +1
}
print(primevec)
```

```
## [1] 307 311 313
```

Python

```
startnumber = 300
numprimes = 3
```

```python
i = startnumber + 1
primi = 0
primevec = np.array([])
while primi<numprimes:
    if sympy.isprime(i):
        primi = primi+1
        primevec = np.append(primevec,i)
    i = i+1
print(primevec)
```

```
[307. 311. 313.]
```

As a final step, we will package this into a function so that it can be reused later and test it:

R

```r
nextprimes = function(startnumber, numprimes){
  primi = 0
  i = startnumber + 1
  primevec = c()
  while (primi<numprimes)
  {
    if(is.prim(i) == TRUE){
      primi = primi + 1
      primevec = c(primevec,i)
    }
  i = i +1
  }
  return(print(primevec))
}
nextprimes(3,3)
```

```
## [1]   5   7 11
```

```r
nextprimes(19,10)
```

```
## [1] 23 29 31 37 41 43 47 53 59 61
```

```r
nextprimes(9,3)
```

```
## [1] 11 13 17
```

Python

```python
def nextprimes(startnumber, numprimes):
    primi = 0
    i = startnumber + 1
    primevec = np.array([])
```

```
    while primi<numprimes:
        if sympy.isprime(i):
            primi = primi+1
            primevec = np.append(primevec,i)
        i = i+1
    return(print(primevec))
nextprimes(3,3)
```

```
[ 5.   7. 11.]
```

```
nextprimes(19,10)
```

```
[23. 29. 31. 37. 41. 43. 47. 53. 59. 61.]
```

```
nextprimes(9,3)
```

```
[11. 13. 17.]
```

Summary

In this chapter, we covered core programming elements in Python and R. These will come in handy as we explore and conduct more sophisticated analyses on the data. We will often see these in practice in the upcoming chapters.

Exercises

To complete the activity below, you will need to visit the companion website to the book and download the relevant dataset: https://study.sagepub.com/gopal

1. Create a function that takes two numbers x and y and returns x^3+y^3.
2. Create a function that takes in a numeric vector. The function should do the following: (1) takes all values below the median and calculates the mean of these; (2) takes all values above the median and calculates the mean of these; and (3) returns the difference in the value between the higher and the lower mean. Test it with a few vectors from the datasets.
3. Create a function that takes in a numeric vector. The output should be a vector with running median values. The *ith* element of the output vector should be the median of the values in the input vector from 1 to *i*.
4. Create a function to return TRUE if a given integer is an element of a given vector. For example, a given vector is (1,3,5,7), if the given integer is 7, the function returns TRUE.
5. Create a function that returns the total number of divisors that a certain integer has (other than 1 and itself). List all divisors.
6. Create a function which replaces the missing values in a vector with the median of the input vector and outputs the vector without any missing values.

(Continued)

7   Create a function which calculates the Euclidean distance between two points. The input of this function should be two vectors of form (x_1, y_1) and (x_2, y_2) and the output the calculation of the Euclidean distance. The formula for the Euclidean distance is:

$$\sqrt{\left(x_1 - x_2\right)^2 + \left(y_1 - y_2\right)^2}$$

8   Create a function that takes in a numeric vector and returns the number of outliers. In this case, outliers are defined as values that are 'two standard deviations away from the median'. Test the function with the **Salary** variable in the Baseball.csv file.

5

RANDOM VARIABLES, PROBABILITY, AND DISTRIBUTIONS

Chapter Contents

Statistics is about learning from data. Statistics is important as most phenomena we want to study create data, and the way to understand the phenomena is through analysis of the data that stem from them. An interesting thing about statistics is that we rarely have all the data we need and generally only have access to a sample of the data. Also, we may miss data on relevant variables. Even though we work with a sample that comes from a phenomenon of interest, typically, our goal is to understand and explain the broader phenomenon rather than just the sample we have on hand. A *population* means all data that are relevant for the phenomenon we want to study. This, for example, could be all the people in the world, or all potential customers for a given product. The population can be either finite or infinite. For most practical purposes, we treat populations as infinite. It is often infeasible to get all the data about the entire population and the data we care about in applications will only be produced in the future. For these reasons, we try to infer insights on the population, as best as we can, from the sample of data at hand. This, as a bottom line, is what statistics is all about. In this chapter, we will explore probability, random variables, and distributions, concepts central to statistics.

RANDOM VARIABLES

Consider the simplest example of tossing a coin. *A priori* (i.e., before tossing the coin), we do not know what the outcome of the coin toss is going to be. It is a *random variable* as the outcome is uncertain. *Probability* is the chance that an outcome of interest will occur for a random variable. Probability is always between 0 and 1, with 0 meaning that the event cannot occur and 1 that it is certain to occur.

Figure 5.1 Coin - One pound

Source: kavalenkava from Shutterstock

Let us represent heads as 1 and tails as 0. There are only two possibilities. Therefore, the sample space, which is all the outcomes that can occur, is (0,1). This is also called the support or domain of a distribution. Assuming it is a fair coin, the probability of each is 0.5. This can be represented as follows:

Table 5.1 Coin toss

Outcome	Probability
Heads (1)	0.5
Tails (0)	0.5

This is called a *distribution*. A distribution identifies all possible outcomes and an associated probability for each outcome to occur. The total probability always adds up to 1, as one of the outcomes must occur. In other words, the outcomes are mutually exclusive and collectively exhaustive.

Let us consider another example of rolling a die:

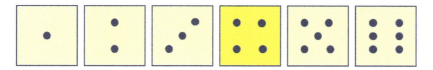

Figure 5.2   Sides of a die

How do we describe this distribution? We need to describe all possible outcomes and a probability for each outcome:

Table 5.2   Die outcome probabilities

Outcome	Probability
1	$\frac{1}{6}$
2	$\frac{1}{6}$
3	$\frac{1}{6}$
4	$\frac{1}{6}$
5	$\frac{1}{6}$
6	$\frac{1}{6}$

In statistics, we often describe and depict a population in terms of a distribution. In that sense, the population is an abstract concept, and a distribution is a mathematical description of this abstract concept. This is what we saw in the two examples above.

A sample simply draws from the distribution. For example, tossing a coin five times is five draws from the distribution we described. Let us see how we create samples from distributions in R and Python:

In R, the basic syntax is:

```
sample(x = , replace = , prob = , size = )
```

In the above syntax, **x** = the domain of the distribution, **prob** = the ordered probabilities of each of the outcomes in the domain, **size** = the number of samples to draw, and **replace** = indicates sampling with or without replacement.

In Python, we can draw a sample from a discrete distribution using *numpy*:

```
numpy.random.choice(domain, size=, replace=, p=)
```

The arguments of the function have the same meaning as above.

Let us simulate tossing a coin ten times. We will first define the domain and the probabilities:

R

```
coindomain = c(0,1)
coinprob = c(.5,.5)
```

```
sample(x = coindomain, size = 10, replace = T,prob = coinprob)

## [1] 0 1 1 1 1 0 0 1 1 1
```

Python

```python
import numpy as np
coindomain = [0,1]
coinprob = [.5,.5]
np.random.choice(coindomain, size = 10, replace = True, p = coinprob)

array([1, 0, 1, 0, 0, 0, 0, 0, 0, 0])
```

We can notice that, due to the randomness of this operation, the outcomes are different each time we run the code. Now, let us simulate rolling a die 15 times.

Note that, different to the corresponding **seq** function in R, the second argument of the **range** function in Python is exclusive, i.e., the value is not included in the output:

R

```
diedomain = seq(1,6)
dieprob = rep(1/6,6)
sample(x = diedomain, size = 15, replace = T, prob = dieprob)

## [1] 2 5 2 1 1 3 2 5 6 5 2 6 6 6 5
```

Python

```python
diedomain = range(1,7)
dieprob = np.repeat(1/6,6)
np.random.choice(diedomain, size = 15, replace = True, p = dieprob)

array([6, 4, 4, 5, 3, 1, 5, 3, 1, 4, 1, 4, 2, 51, 1, 6, 6, 6, 4, 6, 21, 5, 5])
```

SAMPLE SIZE

Let us study the effect of the sample size. We toss the coin five times and from the sample we observe, we compute the probability of heads and tails:

R

```
res1 = sample(x = coindomain, size = 5, replace = T,prob = coinprob)
prop.table(table(res1))

## res1
##   0   1
## 0.2 0.8
```

Python

```
res1 = np.random.choice(coindomain, size = 5, replace = True, p = coinprob)
pd.DataFrame(data=res1).value_counts(normalize=True)
```

```
0    0.6
1    0.4
dtype: float64
```

Now let us toss it 1000 times and compute the probability from the sample:

R

```
res1 = sample(x = coindomain, size = 1000, replace = T,prob = coinprob)
prop.table(table(res1))
```

```
##  res1
##      0     1
## 0.482  0.518
```

Python

```
res1 = np.random.choice(coindomain, size = 1000, replace = True, p = coinprob)
pd.DataFrame(data = res1).value_counts(normalize = True)
```

```
1    0.506
0    0.494
dtype: float64
```

Let us repeat it one more time with a sample of 100,000:

R

```
res1 = sample(x = coindomain, size = 100000, replace = T,prob = coinprob)
prop.table(table(res1))
```

```
## res1
##       0       1
## 0.49741 0.50259
```

Python

```
res1 = np.random.choice(coindomain, size = 100000, replace = True, p = coinprob)
pd.DataFrame(data = res1).value_counts(normalize = True)
```

```
1    0.50005
0    0.49995
dtype: float64
```

We can observe that as the sample size gets larger, the probabilities computed from the sample begin to converge to the true probability of the distribution (which, in this case, is 0.5 and 0.5

for outcomes 0 and 1). This comes from the *law of large numbers*. The distribution computed from the sample is called the *empirical distribution*. The law of large numbers states that the empirical distribution converges to the true population distribution as the sample size tends towards infinity.

The observed difference in the probabilities between the empirical and true distribution is called the *sampling error*. Let us demonstrate this type of error with the die example, using sizes of 5, 100, and 100,000:

R

```
res2 = sample(x = diedomain, size = 5,
  replace = T, prob = dieprob)
prop.table(table(res2))

## res2
##   2   3   4   6
## 0.2 0.2 0.2 0.4

res2 = sample(x = diedomain, size = 100,
  replace = T, prob = dieprob)
prop.table(table(res2))

## res2
##     1     2     3     4     5     6
## 0.165 0.145 0.166 0.182 0.171 0.171

res2 = sample(x = diedomain, size = 1000000, replace = T, prob = dieprob)
prop.table(table(res2))

## res2
##       1       2       3       4       5       6
## 0.16642 0.16629 0.16697 0.16663 0.16664 0.16705
```

Python

```
res2 = np.random.choice(diedomain, size = 5, replace = True, p = dieprob)
pd.DataFrame(data = res2).value_counts(normalize = True).sort_
          index(ascending = True)

2    0.4
3    0.4
6    0.2
dtype: float64

res2 = np.random.choice(diedomain, size = 100, replace = True, p = dieprob)
pd.DataFrame(data = res2).value_counts(normalize = True).sort_
          index(ascending = True)
```

```
1    0.177
2    0.171
3    0.175
4    0.147
5    0.152
6    0.178
dtype: float64
```

```
res2 = np.random.choice(diedomain, size = 100000, replace = True, p = dieprob)
pd.DataFrame(data = res2).value_counts(normalize = True).sort_
            index(ascending = True)
```

```
1    0.16589
2    0.16662
3    0.16685
4    0.16752
5    0.16727
6    0.16585
dtype: float64
```

EMPIRICAL DISTRIBUTION FUNCTIONS

Empirical distribution functions come in handy, especially in environments like R and Python, when the outcome you are interested in studying is rather complicated. It can become complicated because describing the actual distribution function mathematically may be cumbersome or, in some cases, nearly impossible.

To provide an example, let us suppose we are interested in the following outcome:

We toss a coin 50 times, and the outcome in which we are interested is the number of heads we get.

The domain for this distribution is between 0 and 50, but mathematically describing the probabilities for each outcome is a tedious process. This is called a *binomial distribution* and we will show its mathematical formulation later. For now, let us assume we do not want to deal with describing this distribution mathematically. Instead, we want to work with this distribution empirically.

The strategy we will follow to get the empirical distribution is the following:

1 Write the code to simulate one outcome.
2 Put this in a function.
3 Replicate running the function many times to get the empirical distribution.

Let us first create the code to simulate one outcome and wrap this into a function:

R

```
coindomain = c(0,1)
coinprob = c(.5,.5)
```

```
f1 = function(){
  y = sample(x = coindomain, size = 50, replace = T,prob = coinprob)
sum(y)
}


f1()


## [1] 26
```

Python

```
coindomain = [0,1]
coinprob = [.5,.5]


def f1(coindomain, coinprob):
    y = np.random.choice(coindomain, size = 50, replace = True, p = coinprob)
    return sum(y)


f1(coindomain, coinprob)


20
```

The next step is to execute the function repeatedly to generate the empirical distribution function:

R

```
s1 = replicate(n = 10000, f1())
edf1 = prop.table(table(s1))


edf1
```

```
##      11      12      13      14      15      16      17      18      19      20
## 0.0002 0.0001 0.0002 0.0010 0.0028 0.0047 0.0094 0.0155 0.0257 0.0396
##      21      22      23      24      25      26      27      28      29      30
## 0.0602 0.0774 0.0964 0.1103 0.1081 0.1148 0.0927 0.0747 0.0664 0.0407
##      31      32      33      34      35      36      37      39
## 0.0270 0.0170 0.0077 0.0042 0.0021 0.0008 0.0002 0.0001
```

Python

```
s1 = [f1(coindomain, coinprob) for _ in range(10000)]
edf1 = pd.DataFrame(data = s1).value_counts(normalize = True).sort_
        index(ascending = True)
edf1
```

```
11    0.0001
12    0.0001
13    0.0005
```

```
14      0.0009
15      0.0015
16      0.0050
17      0.0093
18      0.0160
19      0.0252
20      0.0430
21      0.0590
22      0.0813
23      0.1005
24      0.1105
25      0.1090
26      0.1034
27      0.0931
28      0.0790
29      0.0577
30      0.0451
31      0.0257
32      0.0177
33      0.0085
34      0.0050
35      0.0013
36      0.0008
37      0.0006
38      0.0002
dtype: float64
```

The output generated is the empirical distribution function as it describes all possible outcomes and associated probabilities.

Note that, in the above R code, we used the **replicate()** function as opposed to the **rep()** function we described earlier. The difference is that the **rep()** function runs the function once and replicates the outcome n times, whereas **replicate()** replicates running the function *n* times. This is an important distinction and a good exercise is to evaluate this difference by replacing the above **replicate()** function with the **rep()** function.

Let us plot the empirical distribution function:

R

```
plot(edf1,type = "h")
```

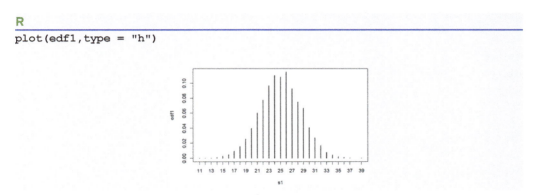

Python

```python
ax = edf1.plot(kind = 'bar')
ax.set_xlabel('s1')
ax.set_ylabel('edf1')
ax.get_figure().tight_layout()
```

Once we have the empirical distribution function, we can compute any probability we wish from this empirical distribution. Let us compute the following probabilities:

1   the number of heads will be less than or equal to 20;
2   the number of heads will be 15 or greater.

The approach we can follow to compute these probabilities is simple. Since the output vector, which represents the empirical distribution, has 10,000 data points, we simply need to count how many of these satisfy the condition to get our probability:

R

```r
length(s1[s1< = 20]) / (length(s1))
```

```
## [1] 0.0992
```

```r
length(s1[s1> = 15]) / (length(s1))
```

```
## [1] 0.9985
```

Python

```python
len([i for i in s1 if i <= 20]) / len(s1)
```

```
0.1016
```

```python
len([i for i in s1 if i >= 15]) / len(s1)
```

```
0.9984
```

The results indicate that the probability of obtaining 20 or fewer heads is 0.1, while the probability of 15 or more heads is nearly 1.

Now let us try something slightly more complicated. We will roll a die multiple times and keep adding the numbers we get from each roll. The outcome of interest is the number of times we need to roll the die until we get a sum of 35.

The domain in this case is [6,35]. Six because the minimum number of rolls needed to obtain a sum of 35 is 6, and the maximum is 35, as we are guaranteed to get to this sum in 35 rolls (in the very unlikely event that every roll results in an outcome of 1).

What coding logic do we use to simulate this distribution? As stated before, the first step is to write the code to simulate one outcome. We will roll the die 35 times to create a vector of 35 outcomes. Then we add the numbers cumulatively from the beginning of the vector until the sum reaches or exceeds 35.

Two useful functions in R to accomplish the above are:

`cumsum(x)` – creates a vector whose ith element is the sum from `x[1]` to `x[i]`

`which(x>c)` – returns the index of all the elements of vector x which are greater than the number c.

The code to simulate one outcome is the following:

R

```
diedomain = seq(1,6)
dieprob = rep(1/6,6)

v1 = sample(x = diedomain, size = 35, replace = T, prob = dieprob)
c1 = cumsum(v1)
which(c1 > 35)[1]

## [1] 12
```

Python

```
diedomain = range(1,7)
dieprob = np.repeat(1/6,6)

v1 = np.random.choice(diedomain, size = 35, replace = True, p = dieprob)
c1 = np.cumsum(v1)
[i for i, x in enumerate(c1) if x > 35][0]
```

8

The final step is to package this into a function and run it repeatedly to create the empirical distribution function:

R

```
f2 = function(){
  v1 = sample(x = diedomain, size = 35, replace = T, prob = dieprob)
  c1 = cumsum(v1)
which(c1 > 35)[1]
}

s2 = replicate(n = 10000, f2())
edf2 = prop.table(table(s2))
plot(edf2, type = "h")
```

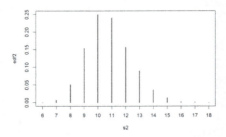

Python

```
def f2(diedomain, dieprob):
    v1 = np.random.choice(diedomain, size = 35, replace = True, p = dieprob)
    c1 = np.cumsum(v1)
    return ([i for i, x in enumerate(c1) if x > 35][0])

s2 = [f2(diedomain, dieprob) for _ in range(10000)]
edf2 = pd.DataFrame(data = s2).value_counts(normalize = True).sort_
    index(ascending = True)
ax = edf2.plot(kind = 'bar')
ax.set_xlabel('s3')
ax.set_ylabel('edf3')
ax.get_figure().tight_layout()
```

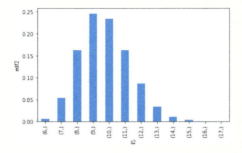

From the above plot, we see that highly likely numbers of rolls of die are 10 and 11. What is the probability that we will hit 35 in 8 rolls or less?

R

```
length(s2[s2< = 8])/(length(s2))
```

```
## [1] 0.0579
```

Python

```
len([i for i in s2 if i < = 8]) / len(s2)
```

```
0.2227
```

A PRACTICAL LOOK

Suppose a drug manufacturer guarantees that a particular drug has a 60% probability of work-ing. If the drug was administered to 300 patients, we would want to compute the probability that no more than 160 patients improved after taking the drug. This situation is like the previ-ous coin toss example. However, this time, the number of tosses and the probability of success are different. To accommodate this type of instance, we will create a more general function that allows us to specify the number of trials and the success probability as inputs to the func-tion. These are the *parameters* of the distribution. The following code creates this empirical distribution function:

R

```
drugdomain = c(0,1)
f3 = function(sz, successprob){
  drugprob = c(1-successprob, successprob)
  v2 = sample(x = drugdomain, size = sz, replace = T, prob = drugprob)
  s3 = sum(v2)
  return(s3)
}

s4 = replicate(n = 100000, f3(300,.6))
edf3 = prop.table(table(s4))
plot(edf3, type = "h")
```

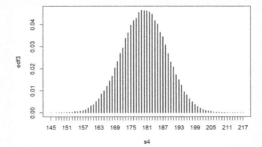

Python

```python
drugdomain = [0,1]

def f3(sz, successprob):
    drugprob = [1-successprob, successprob]
    v2 = np.random.choice(drugdomain, size = sz, replace = True, p = drugprob)
    s3 = sum(v2)
    return (s3)

s4 = [f3(sz=300, successprob = .6) for _ in range(100000)]
edf3 = pd.DataFrame(data = s4).value_counts(normalize = True).sort_
    index(ascending = True)
ax = edf3.plot(kind = 'bar', figsize = (10,5))
ax.set_xlabel('s4')
ax.set_ylabel('edf3')
ax.get_figure().tight_layout()
```

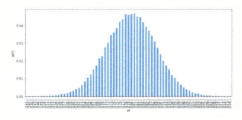

Now we can compute the probability that no more than 160 patients are cured:

R

```r
length(s4[s4 <= 160])/length(s4)
```

```
## [1] 0.01084
```

Python

```python
len([i for i in s4 if i <= 160]) / len(s4)
```

```
0.0116
```

The probability is very small, approximately 1 in a 100.

Now, suppose we know that a medical facility administered the drug to 300 patients and no more than 160 patients improved after taking the drug. What can we say about this situation?

1   The probability of no more than 160 patients getting better is quite small. Even though this is very unlikely, it is not impossible. In fact, it could just be bad luck. For example, we could toss a fair coin ten times and get no heads. The probability is very small, but it is

not zero. If I was at another medical facility, how would I process this information? To rule out the possibility that it was just bad luck, perhaps I would want to see more evidence. This could be satisfied by procuring a larger sample size.

2 If we believe that the sample size is already large enough, then we would not attribute the outcome to just bad luck. Instead, we would begin to question the claims made by the drug manufacturer. Perhaps their claim that the drug is 60% effective could be misleading or even fraudulent. This is the core idea behind hypothesis testing. In this case, the drug manufacturer's claim of 60% success constitutes the null hypothesis. The sample data allow us to either reject the null hypothesis or not reject the null hypothesis. In this case, we would reject the null hypothesis as the probability we computed was very small. We will expand on this concept later.

For now, just note that the null hypothesis describes the population, and the population is described by a distribution. More on this later.

MEAN AND VARIANCE OF A DISTRIBUTION

As we described before, a discrete distribution is defined by a support, which is the set of all possible outcomes, and by the corresponding probability of each outcome. Let $x_1,...,x_N$ denote the possible outcomes. Let $P(x_i)$ denote the probability of outcome x_1. The mean and variance are defined as:

$$\mu = \sum_{i=1}^{N} x_i P(x_i)$$

$$\sigma^2 = \sum_{i=1}^{N} (x_i - \mu)^2 P(x_i)$$

Let us compute the mean and variance of a discrete distribution:

R

```
ddomain = seq(1,4)
dprob = c(.7,.1,.1,.1)
meandistribution = sum(ddomain * dprob)
meandistribution
```

```
## [1] 1.6
```

```
vardistribution = sum((dprob)*(ddomain-meandistribution)^2)
vardistribution
```

```
## [1] 1.04
```

Python

```
ddomain = np.array(range(1,5))
dprob = [.7,.1,.1,.1]
```

```
meandistribution = sum(ddomain * dprob)
meandistribution
```

```
1.6
```

```
vardistribution = sum((dprob)*(ddomain-meandistribution)**2)
vardistribution
```

```
1.04
```

Let us summarize what we know about distributions.

1   A distribution describes all possible outcomes and the corresponding probability for each outcome. Each distribution has its support, which describes the possible outcome values. For tossing a coin, these are 0 and 1. For rolling a die, 1 to 6.
2   A distribution is used to describe a population of interest. In this sense, it is a somewhat abstract concept.

COMMONLY USED DISTRIBUTIONS

There are several distributions that have been developed. These broadly fall into *discrete* and *continuous* distributions. We have looked at several examples of discrete distributions thus far. Below are a few common discrete distributions.

Discrete Distributions

Binomial Distribution

We have already seen a binomial distribution in the examples of tossing a coin 50 times and a drug delivered to 300 patients. A binomial distribution has two parameters: the number of trials n, and the success probability π. Here, x is the random variable that describes the number of successes in n trials. The support for this distribution is $(0,...n)$. The mathematical formulation for a binomial distribution is:

$$P(x) = \frac{n!}{(x!)(n-x)!}(\pi)^x (1-\pi)^{n-x}$$

The mean and variance of a binomial distribution are:

$$mean = n\pi$$

$$variance = n\pi(1-\pi)$$

Negative Binomial Distribution

This is similar to a binomial distribution and it has two parameters: r and π. Here, π is the success probability. The random variable x is the number of failures before the rth success is observed. The support is between 0 and ∞ because the number of failures before the rth success can be 0, as we could start off with r consecutive successes, or it can tend to infinity, since the rth success may never come. The formula is:

$$P(x) = \binom{x-1}{r-1}(\pi)^r (1-\pi)^r$$

$$mean = \frac{r}{\pi}$$

$$variance = \frac{r(1-\pi)}{\pi^2}$$

Poisson Distribution

It is a commonly used distribution for count variables which captures the number of events or occurrences in a given time. It is used to study phenomenon such as the number of claims filed in a year, number of hospital visits in a year, or number of computer crashes in a day. The Poisson distribution has only one parameter λ, which describes the expected number of events. The support is 0 to ∞. The distribution is:

$$P(x) = \frac{e^{-\lambda}\lambda^x}{x!}$$

$$mean = \lambda$$

$$variance = \lambda$$

One interesting thing to note about the Poisson distribution is that the mean and variance are the same. This can be somewhat restrictive compared to the negative binomial distribution, where the variance can be bigger or smaller than the mean. Thus, one can think of a negative binomial distribution as a more flexible and generalized distribution than that of Poisson.

Continuous Distributions

Continuous distributions are used for random variables that can take any value on a continuum. For example, variables like temperature, pressure, age, and salary are often modelled as continuous variables. Since they are continuous, there are an infinite number of possible values that a random variable can take. For this reason, a continuous distribution is depicted through a probability density function $f(x)$. Let the domain of the random variable be denoted as $[a,b]$. A probability density function meets the following criteria:

$$\int_a^b f(x)\,dx = 1$$

The mean and variance are defined as:

$$\mu = \int_a^b xf(x)\,dx$$

$$\sigma^2 = \int_a^b (x - \mu)^2 f(x) \, dx$$

The cumulative density function is defined as:

$$F(\overline{x}) = \int_a^{\overline{x}} f(x) \, dx$$

$F(\overline{x})$ is the probability that x is less than or equal to $\overline{x}$.

Normal Distribution

The normal or Gaussian distribution is perhaps the most common and important distribution in the field of statistics. Many naturally occurring quantities, such as heights and weights, and psychological and educational variables are typically normally distributed, at least approximately. The support for a normal distribution is $[-\infty, \infty]$. The normal distribution is described as follows:

$$f(x) = \frac{1}{\sigma \sqrt{(2\pi)}} e^{-\frac{1}{2}\left(\frac{x-\mu}{\sigma}\right)^2}$$

The mean of the normal distribution is μ and the variance is σ^2.

If x is normally distributed, we write it as:

$$x \sim N(\mu, \sigma)$$

A standard normal variable z is defined as:

$$z = \frac{x - \mu}{\sigma}$$

where:

$$z \sim N(0, 1)$$

Exponential Distribution

This distribution is used to describe the arrival time of randomly reoccurring events. Examples include the time between phone calls to a call centre, between trucks arrivals at an unloading dock, or between transactions at an ATM machine. The support for an exponential distribution is $[0, \infty]$. The probability density function (pdf) of an exponential distribution and its mean and variance are:

$$f(x) = \lambda e^{-\lambda x}, x \geq 0, \lambda > 0$$

$$\mu = \frac{1}{\lambda}$$

$$\sigma = \frac{1}{\lambda}$$

Uniform Distribution

For a uniform distribution in the interval $[a,b]$, the pdf, mean, and variance are:

$$f(x) = \frac{1}{b-a}, a \le x \le b$$

$$\mu = \frac{a+b}{2}$$

$$\sigma^2 = \frac{(b-a)^2}{12}$$

WORKING WITH DISTRIBUTIONS IN R AND PYTHON

Both R and Python provide easy ways to work with various distributions.

Python

Python offers the numerical package *numpy* and the statistical package *scipy.stats*, which together provide all the required utilities to work with numbers and distributions.

To generate random values from a given distribution, we can import the *default_rng* module, from the package *numpy.random,* and call it followed by the name of the distribution of interest, like so:

```
from numpy.random import default_rng as rng
rng().standard_normal(n)
```

A *probability density function* (PDF) defines the probability of a *continuous* random variable to fall in a range of continuous values, often approximated to just a value **x**. In Python, we can compute PDFs using the **.pdf** method on any continuous distribution imported from *scipy.stats*:

```
from scipy.stats import norm
norm.pdf(x, mean, std)
```

A *probability mass function* (PMF) defines the probability that a *discrete* random variable is exactly equal to a value **x**. We can compute PMFs using the **.pmf** method on any discrete distribution imported from *scipy.stats*:

```
from scipy.stats import binom
binom.pmf(x, n, p)
```

A *cumulative distribution function* (CDF) defines the probability of a random variable to take values less than or equal to **x**. To compute this probability, we can use the following syntax:

```
norm.cdf(x, mean, std)
binom.cdf(k, n, x)
```

To compute the *q*th *quantile* of the data along the *x* axis, we can use *numpy.quantile*:

```
import numpy as np
np.quantile(array, quantile)
```

where our array of values can be a randomly generated distribution:

```
np.quantile(rng().standard_normal(n), quantile)
```

How to compute the most relevant distributions we will see in this book:

```
rng().normal(mean = 0, std = 1, size = None)
rng().poisson(lambda = 1, size = None)
rng().binomial(n, p, size = None)
rng().lognormal(mean = 0.0, sigma = 1.0, size = None)
rng().negative_binomial(n, p, size = None)
rng().uniform(low = 0.0, high = 1.0, size = None)
```

R

R provides several distributions with which to work. For each distribution (**dist**), we can get a variety of information, which are based on four possible preceding letters. We precede the distribution name with the letters **r** (for random values from the distribution), **d** (probability or density value), **p** (cumulative probability), or **q** (value of quantile).

How to compute the most relevant distributions we will see in this book:

```
rnorm(n, mean = 0, sd = 1) - Gaussian (normal)
rexp(n, rpois(n, lambda) - Poisson
rbinom(n, size, prob) - Binomial
rlnorm(n, meanlog = 0, sdlog = 1) - Lognormal
rnbinom(n, size, prob) - Negative binomial
runif(n, min = 0, max = 1) - Uniform
```

Recall the drug example with 300 trials and a success rate of 0.6. The probability of having no more than 160 cured patients was 0.0116, based on the empirical distribution. The following code computes the probability directly from the distribution:

R

```
pbinom(160,300,.6)
```

```
## [1] 0.01117726
```

Python

```
from scipy.stats import binom
binom.cdf(160, 300, .6)
```

```
0.011177261497786776
```

which is quite close to the empirically derived probability.

Suppose we want to create 20 random variables from $N(6,3)$:

R

```
rnorm(20,mean = 6, sd = 3)
```

```
##  [1]  1.976763  6.608481  6.277111  5.198196 11.102293  6.572247  5.553133
##  [8]  1.456229  5.903964  5.688421  4.118092  8.246194  8.505609  6.978155
## [15]  5.079688  6.216499  7.427842  9.660354  7.615148 11.065390
```

Python

```
np.random.normal(loc = 6, scale = 3, size = 20)
```

```
array([ 8.50714434,   1.58077139, 10.20295704,   9.59418902,   6.65466507,
3.2954385 ,   3.79275167,  7.12326062,  5.54652208,  7.72761443,  6.95098476,
13.86205514, -1.49168332,  7.12077041,  5.91949799,  2.59593398,  4.91482118,
2.40662953,  9.7909979 ,  5.61188799])
```

As an additional example, let us examine exponential distributions with different parameters and compute the 75th percentile value:

R

```
curve(dexp(x,rate = 1), 0, 10)
curve(dexp(x,rate = 1/2), 0, 10,add = T, col = "blue")
curve(dexp(x,rate = 1/10), 0, 10, add = T, col = "purple")
```

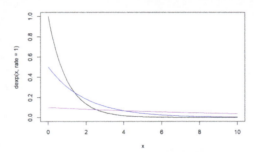

```
qexp(.75, rate = 1/2)
```

```
## [1] 2.772589
```

Python

```python
from scipy.stats import expon
import matplotlib.pyplot as plt

x = np.linspace(0, 10, 1000)
plt.plot(x, expon.pdf(x))
plt.plot(x, expon.pdf(x, scale = 1/.5), color = 'blue')
plt.plot(x, expon.pdf(x, scale = 1/.1), color = 'purple')
plt.xlabel('x')
plt.ylabel('dexp(x), rate = 1')
```

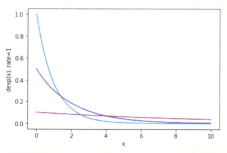

```python
expon.ppf(0.75, scale=1/0.5)
```

```
2.772588722239781
```

Finally, let us plot a normal and an empirical distribution:

R

```r
curve(dnorm(x,mean = 10, sd = 5),-5, 30)
```

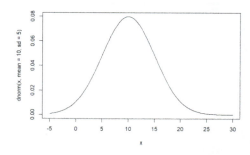

```r
x = rnorm(1000,mean = 10, sd = 5)
plot(density(x))
```

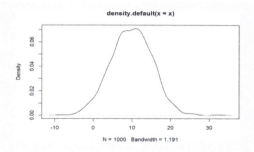

Python

```
from scipy.stats import norm

mu = 10
sigma = 5
x = np.linspace(-5, 30, 1000)
plt.plot(x, norm.pdf(x, mu, sigma))
plt.xlabel('x')
plt.ylabel('stats.norm.pdf(x, mu = 10, sigma = 5)')
plt.show()
```

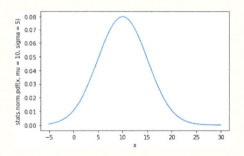

```
x = np.random.normal(loc = 10, scale = 5, size = 1000)
sns.displot(x, kind = 'kde')
plt.xlabel('N = 1000')
plt.ylabel('Density')
plt.title('density.default(x = x)')
plt.show()
```

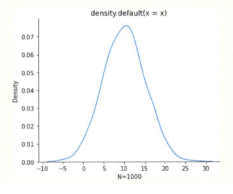

USE CASE: PROBABILITY AND DISTRIBUTIONS IN SALES DATA

As we saw in Chapter 2, data exploration is the first step in learning about the data and building an intuition on its distribution. This process allows us to build a solid knowledge around how useful each data item might be, and how to deal with 'profits?', and 'How do I increase them?'. To answer these questions, we need to collect sales and customer data, to then start understanding the driving forces behind sales and profits. Subsequently, we can propose ways to optimize the sales process such as better target advertising, promotions, areas into which to expand, and those to contract.

In an eCommerce environment, the data we can collect on customers can be potentially huge. For instance, 'click tracking' a customer's journey through our website might help us improve the users experience (UX) and, depending on the products viewed, we might alter advertising, promotions and what we present to customers, together with when to maximize the probability of a purchase during the session.

Supermarket Sales: Examining Distributions

In this use case, we use a small database that reports supermarket sales of various products across three stores. The data include a customer rating (*rating*), as well as other key sales data items. We will study if there are any important patterns that we can exploit.

We can now examine the distribution of key data items such as 'Total', the cash value of a customer transaction. When we examine Total, the frequency of transactions looks similar to the exponential distribution we explored previously in this chapter. To assess this, we can use the Seaborn `distplot()` function, which bins the dataset and counts the frequency of items appearing in each bin. Binning is also known as discretizing, and it is a process of categorizing each row in the dataset as belonging to a range of values of our data item (in this case Total). We can notice that the most frequent transactions have a lower Total value:

R

```
hist(supermarket_sales$Total,main = "Distribution of Total", xlab = "Total")
```

Python

```
import matplotlib.pyplot as plt
import seaborn as sns #charts
plt.figure(dpi=125)
sns.distplot(df['Total'],kde=False)
plt.title('Distribution of Total)
plt.show()
```

We can also examine the distribution of Quantity in our transactions, and see that this is a very different distribution. Again, we use `distplot()` to examine the frequency of transactions. We notice that all the transactions tend to be of random size and evenly distributed with the exception for large quantity sales, which are significantly more frequent. In other words, one in ten transactions were of a significantly higher Quantity. It could be useful to understand what drives this:

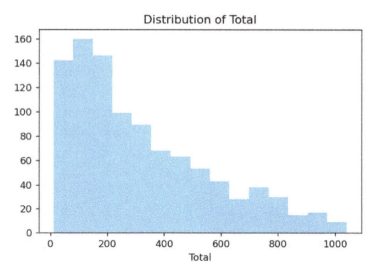

Figure 5.3 Distribution of Total

R

```
hist(supermarket_sales$Quantity,main = "Distribution of Quantity", xlab = "Quantity")
```

Python

```
plt.figure(dpi=125)
sns.distplot(df['Quantity'],kde = False)
plt.title('Quantity')
plt.show()
```

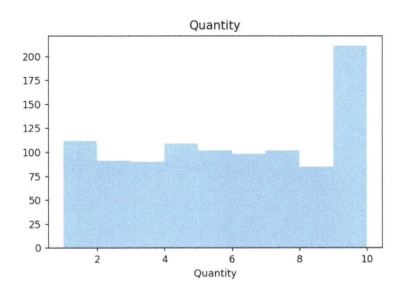

Figure 5.4 Histogram of Quantity

If we look at the distribution of sales using the categorical data item 'City', we can understand how sales are distributed across the three cities where the supermarkets are. In addition, we can show a measure of confidence for each category, as a black line plotted over the horizontal bars, which Seaborn provides to represent the degree of uncertainty around that estimate (i.e., error bars). The larger the black line, the greater the degree of uncertainty:

R

```
ggplot(supermarket_sales,aes(x = City, y = Total)) + geom_col(size = 1)+ oord_flip()
```

Python

```
plt.style.use("default")

plt.figure(figsize = (5,5))
sns.barplot(x = "Total", y = "City", data = df)
plt.title("Total vs City",fontsize = 15)
plt.xlabel("Total")
plt.ylabel("City")
plt.show()
```

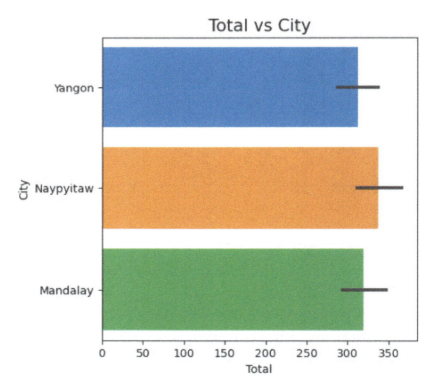

Figure 5.5 Total versus City

We can also drill down into categories within the dataset to examine the distribution of sales. Here we show how sales vary by gender in different product areas, which could be used to optimize our promotions and marketing, for example:

R

```
ggplot(supermarket_sales,aes(x = `Product line`)) + geom_bar(aes
     (fill = Gender),position = "dodge") +  coord_flip()
```

Python

```
plt.figure(dpi = 125)
sns.distplot(df['Rating'],kde = False)
plt.show()
```

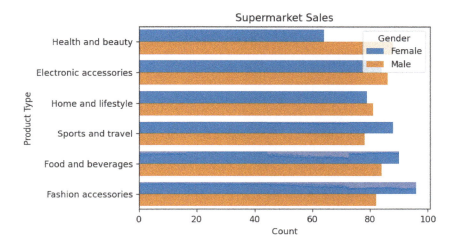

Figure 5.6   Supermarket sales by product type for each gender

---

Summary

In this chapter, we covered the concepts of random variables, probabilities, and distributions, which constitute the foundation on which we develop statistical analysis. We saw how R and Python enable us to empirically create and work with complicated distributions that are often difficult to deal with mathematically. We also saw that, given a distribution, it is fairly simple to create a sample from it and work with it. In practice, however, we will need to do the opposite. We will be given a sample, and then be asked to determine the distribution and more precisely the parameters of the distribution from which the sample was created. This lies at the heart of all statistical analysis, and we will systematically address this problem in the coming chapters.

Exercises

To complete the activity below, you will need to visit the companion website to the book and download the relevant dataset: https://study.sagepub.com/gopal

(Continued)

1   Consider an election with five candidates and 1000 voters. Assuming that the voters cast their vote randomly, what is the probability that there will be a tie for first position?

2   Throw two dice. What is the probability that the difference between them is 1, 2, or 3?

3   Given that a throw of three dice show three different faces, what is the probability that the sum of all the three digits is 11.

4   A club is planning to invest $20,000 to host a golf tournament. They expect to sell tickets worth $30,000. Unfortunately, if it rains on the day of the game, they will not sell any tickets and the club will lose all the money invested. The weather forecast for the day of tournament is a 30% possibility of rain, is this a good investment?

5   A soft-drink company sells its drink in 350-millilitre (ml) bottles. Based on past data, the company knows that the contents of any particular bottle vary according to a normal distribution with mean 348 and variance 9.

   a   What is the probability that a bottle contains less than 345 ml?
   b   What is the probability that less than 10% of the bottles in a case of 100 bottles have a content less than 345 ml?
   c   What is the 99th percentile for the number of millilitres in a single bottle (i.e., the number such that 99% of all bottles have less than this amount)?

6   Accidents occur with a Poisson distribution at an average of four per week. i.e., $\lambda = 4$. Calculate the probability of more than five accidents in any one week.

6

DISTRIBUTIONS

Chapter Contents

In Chapter 5, we explored the concept of distributions. A distribution is a mathematical representation of a population of interest that we use in an attempt to describe and understand a phenomenon or an event of interest. Each distribution captures one event of interest. However, there are occasions where we might be interested in capturing multiple events of interest at once.

MULTIPLE DISTRIBUTIONS

Suppose we are interested in the joint distribution of two events. The first event of interest is tossing a coin and the second event of interest is rolling a die.

To begin with, let us treat them separately and individually. The following creates two empirical distributions, one for the coin and one for the die.

R

```
set.seed(87654321)
coindomain = c(0,1)
coinprob = c(.5,.5)
diesupport = seq(1,6)
dieprob = rep(1/6,6)

coinsmpl = sample(x = coinsupport, size = 10000, replace = T, prob = coinprob)
diesmpl = sample(x = diesupport, size = 10000, replace = T, prob = dieprob)
```

Python

```
import numpy as np
np.random.seed(87654321)
coindomain = [0,1]
coinprob = [.5,.5]

coinsmpl = np.random.choice(coindomain, size = 10000, replace = True, p = coinprob)
```

Now that we have created these distributions, let us look at the empirically computed probabilities:

R

```
prop.table(table(coinsmpl))

## coinsmpl
##      0      1
## 0.5082 0.4918

prop.table(table(diesmpl))

## diesmpl
##      1      2      3      4      5      6
## 0.1623 0.1654 0.1676 0.1650 0.1686 0.1711
```

Python

```
pd.DataFrame(data = coinsmpl).value_counts(normalize = True).sort_
        index(ascending = True)


0 0.5084
1 0.4916
dtype: float64


pd.DataFrame(data = diesmpl).value_counts(normalize = True).sort_
        index(ascending = True)


1 0.1739
5 0.1711
6 0.1685
3 0.1634
4 0.1623
2 0.1608
dtype: float64
```

Suppose we are interested in the following probabilities: the probability of getting a head, and the probability of rolling a 4. Based on the empirical probabilities, we can write:

$$P(coin = heads) = 0.4918$$

$$P(die = 4) = 0.1650$$

Now suppose that the event in which we are interested is the joint probability of getting a head first and subsequently rolling a 4. We can depict this as

$$P(coin = heads \text{ and } die = 4)$$

We can compute this empirically by joining the samples and calculating the empirical distribution:

R

```
prop.table(table(coinsmpl,diesmpl))

##       dieedf
## coinedf    1      2      3      4      5      6
##       0 0.0818 0.0812 0.0860 0.0875 0.0876 0.0841
##       1 0.0805 0.0842 0.0816 0.0775 0.0810 0.0870
```

Python

```
pd.crosstab(coinsmpl, diesmpl, rownames = ['Coins'], colnames = ['Dies'],
    normalize = 'all')
Die       1       2       3       4       5       6
```

```
Coin
0     0.0875     0.0821     0.0848     0.0834     0.0879     0.0827
1     0.0864     0.0787     0.0786     0.0789     0.0832     0.0858
```

From the above distribution (in R), we can see that:

$$P(coin = head \text{ and } die = 4) = 0.0775$$

This is called the *joint probability* of heads and 4. How is this related to the individual probabilities of heads and 4? If the two events A and B were independent, we would have:

$$P(A \text{ and } B) = P(A) \times P(B)$$

In our case, *P(coin = heads)* = 0.4918 and *P(die =4)* = 0.1650. The product of these two numbers (0.4918 × 0.1650) is 0.081147 which, given the magnitude of the data, we can consider close enough to 0.0775 to indicate that these two events are independent. This makes sense because flipping a coin has nothing to do with rolling a die. In other words, the outcome of one should not have any impact on the outcome of the other.

Now, let us consider another example. Read the file called Transactions.csv. The dataset contains transactions of consumers. Here, 0 indicates the item was not purchased, and 1 indicates it was purchased. Suppose we are interested in two items: a toothbrush and perfume. Let us compute the individual and joint probabilities of these two items:

R

```
Transactions = read.csv("Transactions.csv")
prop.table(table(Transactions$Toothbrush))

##
##          0          1
## 0.92784993 0.07215007

prop.table(table(Transactions$Perfume))

##
##          0          1
## 0.90681661 0.09318339

prop.table(table(Transactions$Toothbrush, Transactions$Perfume))

##
##                 0          1
##    0 0.85791141 0.06993852
##    1 0.04890520 0.02324487
```

Python

```
Transactions = pd.read_csv('../data/Transactions.csv')
Transactions['Toothbrush'].value_counts(normalize = True)


0 0.92785
1 0.07215
Name: Toothbrush, dtype: float64


Transactions['Perfume'].value_counts(normalize = True)


0      0.906817
1      0.093183
Name: Perfume, dtype: float64


pd.crosstab(Transactions['Toothbrush'], Transactions['Perfume'],
    normalize = 'all')


Perfume      0            1
Toothbrush
0      0.857911    0.069939
1      0.048905    0.023245
```

We have P(Toothbrush) = 0.07215 and P(Perfume) = 0.09318, and the joint probability P(Toothbrush AND Perfume) = 0.02324. P(Toothbrush) × P(Perfume)= 0.07215 × 0.09318 = 0.006718278, thus we find P(Toothbrush AND Perfume) is significantly bigger than P(Toothbrush) ×P(Perfume). This indicates that the purchases of a toothbrush and perfume are not independent. Let us define a measure called *lift*:

$$Lift = \frac{P(A \text{ and } B)}{P(A) \times P(B)}$$

In our case, the value of lift is 0.02324487/(0.0721 × 0.09318) = 3.459945. The lift value of 3.46 indicates there is a strong association between the purchase of these two items, or more exactly that the probability that a consumer would buy these two together is 3.46 times more than if they were to buy them individually.

This is the basic idea behind a technique called *association rule mining*. This is a very popular machine learning technique to identify which items are strongly associated. Why is this useful?

Once we find items that are strongly associated, we are able to take a number of actions. For example, if a customer bought a toothbrush, a tailored recommendation to buy a perfume as well could be offered to the customer. Other decisions such as inventory levels, pricing, and placement of these items on the shelves could be informed by knowing the relevance of this association.

UNIVARIATE AND MULTIVARIATE DISTRIBUTIONS

Thus far, we have worked with *univariate* distributions. For example, to describe the empirical distribution for the purchase of a toothbrush, our distribution looked like:

Table 6.1 Probability of purchasing a toothbrush

Toothbrush purchase	Probability
0	0.92784993
1	0.07215007

Similarly, the distribution for the purchase of perfume was:

Table 6.2 Probability of purchasing perfume

Perfume purchase	Probability
0	0.90681661
1	0.09318339

However, these figures are incomplete and do not offer the complete picture. What is missing when described as separate distributions is the dependence between the two random variables. When random variables are dependent, we should define them together as a *multivariate* distribution. In this case, the multivariate distribution would look like the following:

Table 6.3 Joint probability for purchasing a toothbrush and perfume

Toothbrush purchase	Perfume purchase	Probability
0	0	0.85791141
0	1	0.06993852
1	0	0.04890520
1	1	0.02324487

All the univariate distributions we have discussed thus far, including normal, Poisson, and exponential, have corresponding multivariate distributions. For example, the pdf for a multivariate normal distribution is the following:

$$f_x\left(x_1,\ldots,x_k\right) = \frac{1}{\sqrt{\left(2\pi\right)^k |\pounds|}} \exp\left(-\frac{1}{2}\left(x-\mu\right)^\mathrm{T} \pounds^{-1}\left(x-\mu\right)\right)$$

The mean and the variance are now described in matrix forms and a bivariate normal distribution is specified as:

$$N\left(\begin{bmatrix} \mu_1 \\ \mu_2 \end{bmatrix}, \begin{bmatrix} \sigma_1^2 & \sigma_{12}^2 \\ \sigma_{12}^2 & \sigma_2^2 \end{bmatrix}\right)$$

where σ_{12}^2 is the covariance between the two variables.

There are a number of packages in R and Python that allow us to work with multivariate distributions. In R, there is a package called *mvtnorm* that we can use to create multivariate normal distributions. This can be installed with `install.packages("mvtnorm")`.

Let us create some random data from the following bivariate normal distribution:

$$N\left(\begin{bmatrix} 4 \\ 10 \end{bmatrix}, \begin{bmatrix} 2 & 1 \\ 1 & 3 \end{bmatrix}\right)$$

Let us create ten random values:

R

```r
library(mvtnorm)
M = c(4,10)
S = matrix(c(2,1,1,3), nrow = 2, ncol = 2)
x = rmvnorm(10,mean = M,sigma = S)
x
```

```
##                [,1]       [,2]
##  [1,]  5.3564159 11.276414
##  [2,]  2.9601619  9.308978
##  [3,]  4.7488148  8.530479
##  [4,]  3.3656003 11.060733
##  [5,]  4.1133432 12.283310
##  [6,]  4.8381692  9.092852
##  [7,]  3.7097776  8.046649
##  [8,]  0.5240409  8.165238
##  [9,]  3.8213304  9.247592
## [10,]  6.5626681 10.172313
```

```r
cor(x[,1],x[,2])
```

```
## [1] 0.3710177
```

Python

```python
M = np.array([4,10])
S = np.array([[2,1],[1,3]])
x = np.random.multivariate_normal(M, S, 10)
x
```

```
array([[ 4.71377233,  9.61154606],
       [ 3.40777927,  9.59450296],
       [ 4.52847425,  8.49964337],
       [ 4.58181931, 10.63656782],
       [ 6.00786783,  9.28934248],
       [ 5.76156183, 10.89942593],
       [ 3.68797012, 11.1444203 ],
       [ 2.29071726,  8.3847295 ],
       [ 2.66167864,  9.00609472],
       [ 5.19767633, 10.39204891]])
```

```
np.corrcoef(x[:,0], x[:,1])[0,1]
```

```
0.418136736581997
```

Now let us plot the bivariate distribution. In R, the *MASS* package has a function called `kde2d()` which allows to create density values that can then be plotted with `persp()`. The two parameters theta and phi are used to specify the viewing angle. The following code creates 1000 random values from the bivariate distribution, and then plots the density function:

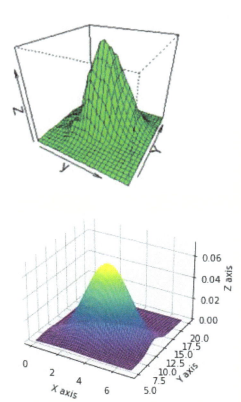

R

```
library(MASS)
x = rmvnorm(1000,mean = M,sigma = S)
y = kde2d(x = x[,1], y = x[,2])
persp(y, col="green",theta = 30, phi = 30)
```

Python

```
#Create grid and multivariate normal
x = np.linspace(0, 7, 500)
y = np.linspace(5, 20,500)
X, Y = np.meshgrid(x,y)
pos = np.empty(X.shape + (2,))
pos[:, :, 0] = X; pos[:, :, 1] = Y
rv = stats.multivariate_normal(M, S)

#Make a 3D plot
fig = plt.figure()
ax = fig.gca(projection = '3d')
ax.plot_surface(X, Y, rv.pdf(pos),cmap =
'viridis',linewidth = 0)
ax.set_xlabel('X axis')
ax.set_ylabel('Y axis')
ax.set_zlabel('Z axis')
plt.show()
```

TRANSFORMATIONS AND CONVOLUTIONS

Let us empirically create a uniform distribution and plot the density function:

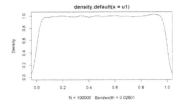

R

```
u1 = runif(10000)
plot(density(u1))
```

Python

```
u1 = np.random.uniform(0,1,10000)
sns.kdeplot(u1)
plt.show()
```

What if we mathematically transformed the random variable, for example, squared the random numbers? Would the resulting distribution still be uniform? Let us take a look:

R

```
u2 = u1^2
plot(density(u2))
```

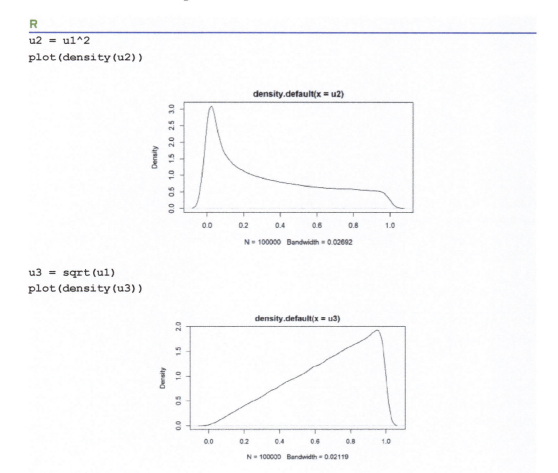

```
u3 = sqrt(u1)
plot(density(u3))
```

Python

```
u2 = u1 ** 2
sns.kdeplot(u2)
plt.show()
```

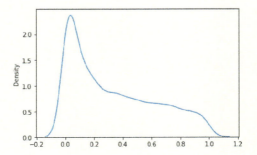

```
u3 = np.sqrt(u1)
sns.kdeplot(u3)
plt.show()
```

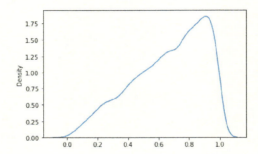

Once we transform a uniform random variable, it is no longer uniform. Squaring will make it right skewed and taking the square root will make it left skewed. This is because when we square numbers between 0 and 1, they trend towards 0; this explains why the first plot is right skewed. In contrast, the second is left skewed because when we take the square root of numbers between 0 and 1, they trend towards 1.

For the next illustration, let us transform a normal distribution through an exponential function:

R

```
n1 = rnorm(10000)
plot(density(n1))
```

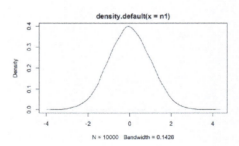

```
n2 = exp(n1)
plot(density(n2))
```

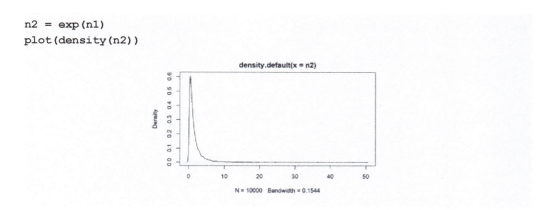

Python

```
n1 = np.random.normal(0,1,10000)
sns.kdeplot(u1)
plt.show()
```

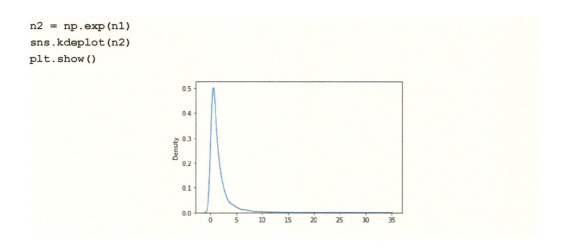

```
n2 = np.exp(n1)
sns.kdeplot(n2)
plt.show()
```

Taking the exponential of a random normal variable changes the domain (to [0,∞]) and induces a right skew. This is called a *lognormal* distribution and it is used to capture variables like income, which can only be positive, and often exhibits a right skew, due to most people having lower incomes as opposite to a few very rich people.

What happens if we keep adding together multiple independent distributions? The following code starts with an empirical uniform distribution, and successively adds a new uniform distribution and plots the resulting distribution with the added distribution. What does it begin to look like?

R

```
newdist = runif(10000)
newdist = (newdist-min(newdist))/max(newdist)
plot(density(newdist),ylim = c(0,2))
for (i in 2:3)
{
  newdist = newdist + runif(10000)
  newdist = (newdist-min(newdist))/max(newdist)
  lines(density(newdist),col = i)
}
```

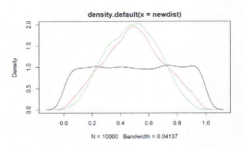

Python

```
newdist = np.random.uniform(0,1,10000)
newdist = (newdist-min(newdist))/max(newdist)
sns.kdeplot(newdist)
for i in range(1,3):
    newdist = newdist + np.random.uniform(0,1,10000)
    newdist = (newdist-min(newdist))/max(newdist)
    sns.kdeplot(newdist, color=sns.color_palette()[i])
plt.show()
```

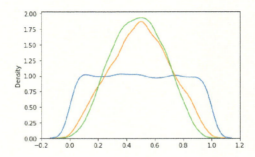

Let us repeat with a larger number of distributions added:

R

```r
newdist = runif(10000)
newdist = (newdist-min(newdist))/max(newdist)
plot(density(newdist),ylim = c(0,2))
for (i in 2:100)
{
  newdist = newdist + runif(10000)
  newdist = (newdist-min(newdist))/max(newdist)
  lines(density(newdist),col = i)
}
```

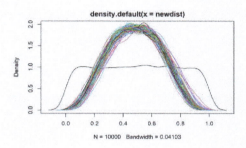

Python

```python
newdist = np.random.uniform(0,1,10000)
newdist = (newdist-min(newdist))/max(newdist)
sns.kdeplot(newdist)
for i in range(1,100):
    newdist = newdist + np.random.uniform(0,1,10000)
    newdist = (newdist-min(newdist))/max(newdist)
    sns.kdeplot(newdist, color=sns.color_palette()[i%10])
plt.show()
```

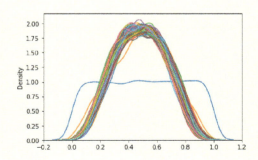

Visually, it appears that the addition of several distributions tends to result in a normal distribution. While the plot above was generated by adding uniform distributions, the end result would have been similar for other distributions as well. This is a very important insight and forms the central point of the famous *central limit theorem*.

The central limit theorem states that when independent random variables are added, their properly normalized sum tends towards a normal distribution, even if the original variables themselves are not normally distributed (from Wikipedia https://en.wikipedia.org/wiki/Central_limit_theorem).

This is an important point to note. Think of variables like SAT (Student Aptitude Test) scores. A student's SAT score is determined by several factors: work ethic, family income, number of siblings, quality of school, peers, family environment, and so on. Each of these factors may have their own distribution, but when we combine them together, the result will be approximately normal, and therefore, it would be appropriate to model SAT scores as being normally distributed. This is also one of the main reasons why the normal distribution is so commonly used. It is quite logical to use it to describe many naturally occurring variables of interest.

SAMPLING DISTRIBUTIONS

The last topic that we will address in this chapter is sampling distributions. Sampling distributions are an important concept when conducting statistical testing.

Let us explore them with the data from the file women.csv. The data are on the height and weight of 15 women. Let us assume that the weight of the women in the dataframe constitutes the *entire population* of interest for us. Let us calculate the population mean and standard deviation:

R

```
mean(women$weight)
sd(women$weight)

[1] 136.7333
[1] 15.49869
```

Python

```
women = pd.read_csv('../data/women.csv')
women['weight'].mean()

136.73333333333332

women['weight'].std()

15.49869426143776
```

In our setting, the population mean is 136.7333 and the population standard deviation is 15.49869. Suppose that from this population, we want to draw a sample of size 5. This is illustrated in the figure below:

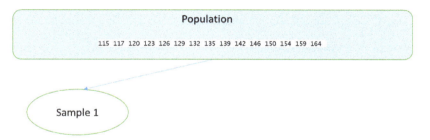

Figure 6.1 Population sample

After drawing a sample of size 5, we want to calculate the mean of the sample. The code is:

R

```
set.seed(87654321)
s = sample(x = women$weight, size = 5, replace = F)
mean(s)

[1] 134.4
```

Python

```
np.random.seed(87654321)
s = np.random.choice(a = women['weight'], size = 5, replace = True)
s.mean()

142.4
```

The sample mean (134.4) is slightly different from the true population mean (136.7333). This difference is called the *sampling error*. While this is not surprising, a question we may ask is how close or far the sample mean should be from the true population mean.

To understand this, let us replicate this process of drawing a sample and computing the sample mean 10,000 times. This is illustrated in the figure below:

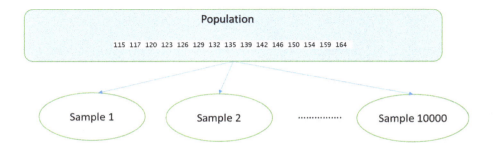

Figure 6.2 Multiple samples drawings

R

```
f1 = function(){
  s = sample(x = women$weight, size = 5, replace = F)
  return(mean(s))
}
samplingdist = replicate(10000, f1())
```

Python

```
def f1():
  s = np.random.choice(a = women['weight'], size = 5, replace = False)
  return s.mean()
samplingdist = np.array([f1() for i in range(10000)])
```

The vector stores the mean of each of the 10,000 samples. How small or large can the sample mean get? What does the average of 10,000 samples look like?

R

```
min(samplingdist)
max(samplingdist)
mean(samplingdist)

[1] 120.2
[1] 154.6
[1] 136.6733
```

Python

```
samplingdist.min()
120.2

samplingdist.max()
154.6

samplingdist.mean()
136.77574
```

While the minimum and maximum values of the sample mean can vary quite a bit from the true mean of the population, the 'mean of the sample means' is in fact very close to the true population mean! This is called the *sampling distribution*. In the current example, we have a sampling distribution when the sample size is 5 and the *statistic* of interest is the mean (of the sample). What does the sampling distribution look like?

R

```
plot(density(samplingdist))
```

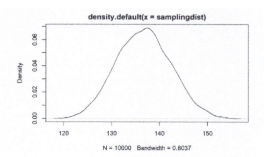

Python

```
sns.kdeplot(samplingdist)
plt.show()
```

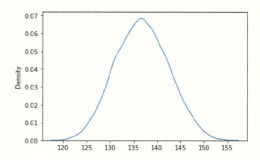

Note how the sampling distribution looks reasonably normal. The characteristics of the sampling distribution are described by the central limit theorem. This theorem, in essence, states that if we take any population distribution and start drawing many samples from it, the distribution of the means from each of the samples will follow a normal distribution. In other words, the sampling distribution of the sample mean becomes almost normal regardless of the shape of the original population from which we created the sampling distribution. Thus, it describes the nature of the sampling distribution. In addition, it states that the standard deviation of the sampling distribution is the standard deviation of the population divided by the square root of the sample size. The sampling distribution of the sample mean becomes almost normal regardless of the shape of the original population from which we created the sampling distribution.

Suppose we changed the statistic of interest from the sample's mean to its median? Let us see what would happen:

R

```
f2 = function(){
  s2 = sample(x = women$weight, size = 5, replace = F)
  return(median(s2))
}
samplingdist2 = replicate(10000, f2())
median(women$weight)
mean(samplingdist2)
```

```
[1] 135
[1] 135.6953
```

```
plot(density(samplingdist2,bw = 3))
```

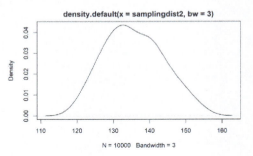

Python

```python
def f2():
    s2 = np.random.choice(a = women['weight'], size = 5, replace = False)
    return s2.mean()
samplingdist2 = np.array([f2() for i in range(10000)])

women['weight'].median()

samplingdist2.mean()

sns.kdeplot(samplingdist2)
plt.show()
```

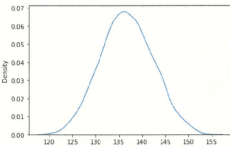

When the statistic of interest is the median, the sampling distribution remains still reasonably normal and the mean of the sampling distribution is close to the true population median. Let us try one more experiment, this time with the 25th percentile value:

R

```r
f3 = function(){
    s2 = sample(x = women$weight, size = 5, replace = F)
    return(quantile(s2,prob = 0.25))
}
```

```
samplingdist3 = replicate(10000, f3())
quantile(women$weight,prob = 0.25)
mean(samplingdist3)
```

```
  25%
124.5
[1] 127.0387
```

```
plot(density(samplingdist3,bw = 3))
```

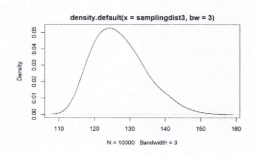

Python

```
def f3():
    s3 = np.random.choice(a = women{'weight'].quantile(0.25), size = 5, replace = False)
    return np.quantile(s3, 0.25)
samplingdist3 = np.array([f3() for I in range(10000)])
```

```
women''weigh''].quantile(0.25)
124.5
```

```
samplingdist3.mean()
```

```
127.1985
```

```
sns.kdeplot(samplingdist3,bw_adjust = 3)
plt.show()
```

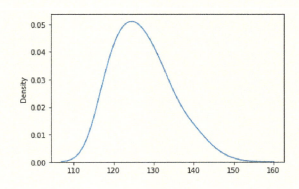

In this case, the resulting distribution exhibits some skew, therefore it cannot be considered normal. This leads us to conclude that the shape of the sampling distribution is only normal when our statistic of interest is the mean, and that there is no guarantee of normality when we use other statistics.

Sampling distributions are the foundation of how we conduct statistical testing. We will explore this in detail in the next chapter. For now, it is important to remember that before creating a sampling distribution, we first need to describe our population. After, we decide the sample size and the statistic in which we are interested. Once we have taken care of these steps, we can easily create the sampling distribution.

Use Case – Data Exploration

Simple plots of the data allow us to understand distributions and relationships. This process is known as data exploration and there are several powerful tools in Python and R to assist. If we are exploring a new dataset to try to understand its distributions, it is a good idea to plot each data item's density function and examine correlations between data items as a starting point. A key tool for data exploration is a bivariate plot such as *pairplot* in Python and *corrgram* in R. These plot each data item in the dataset against each other, showing a simple, visual bivariate analysis plotted on a matrix. In this use case, we will explore and understand the *valuation multiples* dataset, which contains financial analytics for 94 industries, such as Air Transport, Utility (Water), and so on, in the US market. First, we load the dataset from Excel files:

R

```
valuation_multiples = read_excel("valuation multiples.xlsx")
df = valuation_multiples
```

Python

```
loc = "valuation multiples.xlsx"
df = pd.read_excel(loc, engine = 'openpyxl')
```

Now we can calculate some financial analytics that will help us understand the valuation of different industries and create the bivariate plots:

R

```
df$EBITDA_margin = df$'EBITDA ($ millions)'/df$'Revenues ($ millions)'
df$Net_Margin = df$'Net Income ( $ millions)'/df$'Revenues ($ millions)'
df$Debt_EV = df$'Total Debt (including leases) ($ millions)'/df$'Enteprise
            Value ($ millions)'
df$EBITDA_EV = df$'EBITDA ($ millions)'/df$'Enteprise Value ($ millions)'
df$EBITDA_multiple = df$'EBITDA ($ millions)'/df$'Enteprise Value ($ millions)'

library(corrgram)
corrgram(df1,upper.panel = panel.pts,lower.panel= panel.pie,order = T )
```

Python

```
df.insert(df.shape[1],'EBITDA_margin', data['EBITDA ($ millions)']/data['Revenues
    ($ millions)'])
df.insert(df.shape[1],'Net_Margin', data['Net Income ( $ millions)']/data['Revenues
    ($ millions)'])
df.insert(df.shape[1],'Debt_EV', data['Total Debt (including leases) ($ millions)']/
    data['Enteprise Value ($ millions)'])
df.insert(df.shape[1],'EBITDA_EV', data['EBITDA ($ millions)']/data['Enteprise
    Value ($ millions)'])
df.insert(df.shape[1],'EBITDA Multiple', data['EBITDA ($ millions)']/data
    ['Enteprise Value ($ millions)'])

key_dis = ['EBITDA Multiple','EBITDA_margin','Net_Margin','Debt_EV','EBITDA_
EV','Gross Profit ($ millions)']
df_key_dis = df[key_dis]

sns.pairplot(df)
```

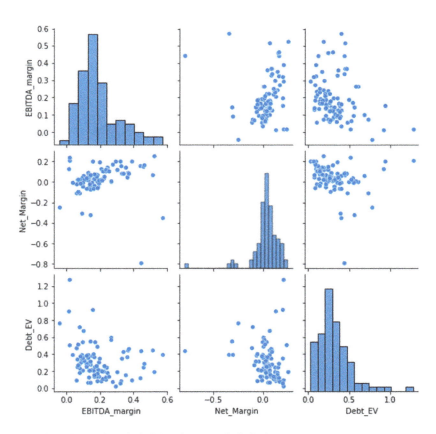

Figure 6.3 Pair plot showing vital stats of corporate industry groups

The diagonal cells in the *pairplot* matrix show the densities of each data item, plotted as a frequency column chart. The non-diagonal cells show a scatter plot of one data item versus another. The frequency distributions allow us to eyeball the data for skews in the distributions, for example. The scatter plots allow us to get an instant impression of whether there is a correlation between two data items, or some other form of relationship.

We can see from the frequency column chart in the lower right-side cell that debt to enterprise value, Debt_EV, which is the ratio of balance-sheet Total Debt (including leases) ($ millions) divided through by Enterprise Value ($ millions), has a positive skew, i.e., there are a number of industries that have a much higher level of debt to enterprise value than the average. We can also see in the middle cell on the right that Debt_EV has a relatively poor relationship with Net_margin, representing industry net profit margins. However, the top middle cell shows there is a more obvious relationship between Net_margin and EBITDA_margin.

We can also examine the pairwise correlations of each of the features by plotting the correlation matrix as a heat map:

R

```
heatmap(cor(df1),Rowv = NA, Colv = NA)
```

Python

```
plt.figure(figsize = (10,7))
plt.title('Correlation matrix: Industry vital stats')

sns.heatmap(corr, xticklabels = corr.columns, yticklabels=corr.columns)

# show plot
plt.show()
```

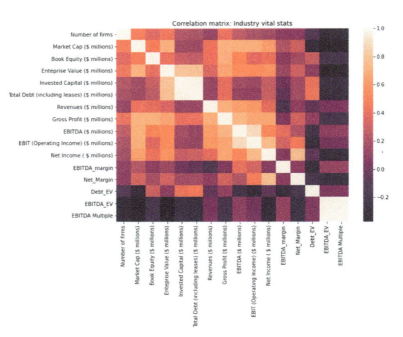

Figure 6.4   Correlation matrix: industry vital statistics

Examining the heat map, we can see how different financial analytics compare across industries. A lighter colour represents a higher correlation between two data items. First, note that the diagonal line, moving top left to bottom right, is correlating a variable against itself, so shows a perfect correlation. We are interested in the off-diagonal areas of the heat map. We can see, for example, that Enterprise Value has a high correlation with Invested Capital (a light colour), and a moderately high correlation with Gross profit, indicating that a more profitable firm results in a higher enterprise value.

This will only look at linear relationships between two features at a time, so there may be more complex nonlinear or multivariate relationships that we will not detect using this. However, it is a good starting point for data exploration.

Summary

In this chapter, we extended our understanding of distributions which typically depict one event of interest to multivariate distributions where we want to depict multiple events of interest together. This becomes important when the events are potentially related to each other and describing them separately through univariate distributions would be incomplete. We then evaluated transformations and convolutions of univariate distributions and discovered that transformations can fundamentally alter the distributional properties. An important discovery in this regard is that adding independent distributions, regardless of what each independent distribution looks like, tends towards a normal distribution. This is an important insight and highlights why normal distribution plays such a prominent role in statistics. Finally, we looked at sampling distributions and their properties. We will explore sampling distributions further in the next chapter and see how this forms the foundation for conducting statistical tests.

Exercises

To complete the activity below, you will need to visit the companion website to the book and download the relevant dataset: https://study.sagepub.com/gopal

Read the Transactions.csv file.

1   Determine if the variables **pens** and **pencils** are independent. Find a pair of variables that are dependent.
2   Create a sample of size 1000 from a bivariate normal distribution where the two variables each have a mean of 15 and the correlation between the two is 0.6. Create a 3D plot to visualize the data.
3   Create a sample of size 1000 from a bivariate normal distribution where the two variables each have a mean of 10 and the correlation between the two is 0.5. Transform the second variable by squaring it and create a 3D plot to visualize the resulting distribution.
4   Simulate 500 samples from standard uniform distributions, with each sample containing 200 data points. Similarly, simulate 500 samples from standard lognormal distributions, with each sample containing 200 data points. Plot the empirical distribution of the sum of all these 1000 samples. Does it appear approximately normal?
5   Consider the population distribution in Table 6.4. Create sampling distributions of size 100 for the following statistics: mean, median, variance, minimum, and maximum. Which sampling distributions exhibit normality?

Table 6.4 Population distribution for task 5

Value	Probability
1	0.5
4	0.1
15	0.1
72	0.3

7

STATISTICAL TESTING - CONCEPTS AND STRATEGY

Chapter Contents

BASIC CONCEPTS

We often conduct a variety of tests on a dataset, but most often, this will only represent a sample of the entire population of interest. In statistics, a population is defined as an entire set of individuals or objects, which may be finite or infinite. Examples of finite populations include the graduate students in the Business programme, the employees of a given company, or the potential consumers in a target market. Infinite populations are not countable – common examples include the outcome of coin tossing and the number of cells in the human body. Collecting data from the entire population is often prohibitively expensive or impossible. For this reason, in most practical settings, we collect and analyse data from a representative subset, or sample, of the population.

Figure 7.1 Population and sample

The concept of population is often a difficult and a murky concept to understand and model. Populations are usually modelled using the concepts of *data generation process* and *distributions*.

Let us try and understand this a bit further. Suppose you toss a coin five times and the following are the outcomes:

HHTHT

The outcome of our experiment represents sample data of all the possible outcomes, and the action of tossing the coin is the data generation process. Since the coin has two sides, H and T, the probability of observing H is p (for a fair coin p = 0.5) and the probability of observing T is (1 – p). This is depicted mathematically in the form of a binomial distribution, expressed as follows:

Outcome	Probability
H	p
T	1 – p

When we think of a population, we often describe it in terms of a distribution that depicts the data generation process from which sample data can be drawn and observed.

Numerical outcomes are often modelled with continuous distributions such as normal, lognormal, or exponential; binary and countable outcomes are modelled with binomial, negative binomial, or Poisson distributions.

The key distinctions between a sample and a population are described in the following table:

Table 7.1 Population and sample characteristics

Characteristic	Population	Sample
Size	Often infinite	Finite
Known?	Often unknown and in fact, unknowable.	Known
Description	As a distribution. For example, $$f_X(x) = e^{-(x-\mu)^2/2\sigma^2}/\sqrt{2\pi\sigma^2}$$	As a data object such as a vector, dataframe, or a table.

Outcome	Probability
H	p
T	$1-p$

Mean	Continuous $$\mu = \int_{-\infty}^{\infty} x f(x)\,dx$$	`mean(whiteside$Temp)`
		
		 `[1]  4.875`

	Discrete $$\mu = E(X) = \sum_{i=1}^{N} x_i P(X = x_i)$$	`whiteside['Temp'].mean()`
		
		 `4.875`

Variance	Continuous $$\sigma^2 = \int_{-\infty}^{\infty} (x-\mu)^2 f(x)\,dx$$	`var(whiteside$Temp)`
		
		 `[1]  7.560091`

	Discrete $$\sigma^2(X) = \sum_{i=1}^{N} [x_i - E(X)]^2 P(X = x_i)$$	`whiteside['Temp'].var()`
		
		 `7.560090`

Quantile	Consider `N(5,7)`, i.e. a normal distribution with a mean of 5 and a standard deviation of 7. The value for 75% quantile is:
	
	 `qnorm(p = 0.75,mean = 5,sd = 7)`
	
	 `[1]  9.721428`
	
	 `stats.norm.ppf(0.75, loc=5, scale=7)`
	 `9.721428251372572`
		To compute the 75% quantile for Temp,
		
		 `quantile(whiteside$Temp, probs = 0.75)`
		
		 `   75%`
		 `7.125`
		 `whiteside['Temp].`
		 `quantile(0.75)`
		
		 `7.125`

STRATEGY FOR STATISTICAL TESTING

The main purpose of statistical testing is to collect a sample of the data to make inferences on the entire population from where the sample was drawn. This is especially useful when all the data are unknown and impossible to retrieve, as often happens in practical settings.

Figure 7.2 Population and sample

How is this done?

Step 1: Choose a statistic of interest (for example, mean or 75th percentile).

Step 2: Create a hypothesis (typically called the null hypothesis) about the population. The stated hypothesis is in essence a conjecture on the population. The hypothesis should describe the population.

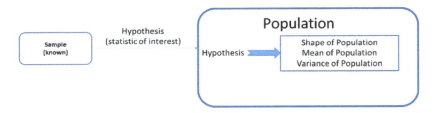

Figure 7.3 Test hypothesis

Step 3: Draw synthetic samples from the population:

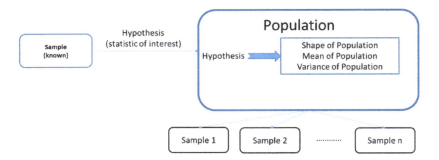

Figure 7.4 Synthetic sampling

Step 4: Compute the test statistic value for each of the synthetic samples drawn. Create a distribution of these values. This is called the *sampling distribution*:

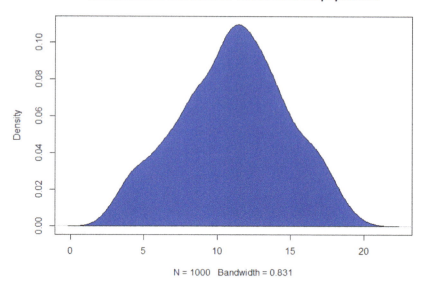

Figure 7.5   Distribution of test statistic values from the population

Step 5: Compute the observed statistic (from the original sample) and locate it on the sampling distribution. A value falling in the tail of the distribution (*rejection region*) would rarely occur by chance, thus the hypothesis can be rejected. Otherwise, there is no evidence to reject the hypothesis:

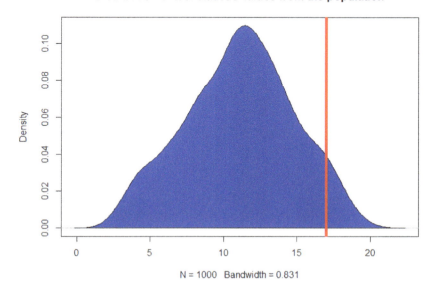

Figure 7.6   Observed statistic on distribution of test statistic values

This, in essence, is how the statistical testing is conducted. One of the key challenges is to create a large number of synthetic samples and generate the sampling distribution. With tools such as R and Python, one can easily create these sampling distributions to conduct any type of statistical test.

PERMUTATION DESIGN FOR STATISTICAL TESTING

Sampling distributions play a central role in conducting statistical testing. Imagine creating sampling distributions before the advent of computing. A sample had to be drawn from a hypothesized population, a test statistic of interest computed for the sample, and this process repeated thousands of times to create the sampling distribution. A near-impossible task without a computer. This prompted statisticians to come up with easier ways to describe and use sampling distributions – and thus we see distributions z, t, F, χ^2, and others that eliminate the need to explicitly create sampling distributions to conduct statistical tests. However, there are some limitations to using these distributions – they work only for certain test statistics, when sample sizes are large enough for certain statistics, and are just approximations of certain tests.

With the availability of ample computing power and statistical software such as R and Python, these limitations no longer exist and creating sampling distributions has become a fairly simple task. The action of creating empirical distributions is termed *permutation* (or *randomization*) *testing*. Instead of comparing the actual value of a test statistic to a standard statistical distribution, a reference sampling distribution is generated from the data and compared to it.

Some key advantages of permutation testing include the following.

1   Fewer assumptions – for example, we do not need large sample sizes.
2   Generality – can be conducted on a wide range of statistics. For example, to test the ratio of means (between males and females), which has no traditional way of testing.
3   Greater accuracy – in many cases, it can be more accurate than classical methods.
4   Promoting understanding – more intuitive and concrete.

The general approach to conduct permutation testing is the following.

1   Choose a statistic of interest (e.g., mean, percentile, correlation, etc.).
2   Generate a null hypothesis that attempts to describe the (hypothesized) population.
3   Draw samples from the population and construct the sampling distribution.
4   Locate the observed statistic on this distribution to draw an inference.

First Example

Suppose that a device manufacturer comes up with a new design and claims that the number of complaints against the device per day will be no more than six. We want to test this claim. Let us follow the process we outlined:

Step 1: State the hypothesis.

H_0: the average number of complaints per day is less than or equal to six.

Step 2: Describe the data generation process and the population.

Since the number of complaints per day is a count variable, we will assume that the data generation process is Poisson. Based on this and the hypothesis, we will describe the population $Pois$ (6).

Step 3: Create a sampling distribution.

Now that the population is defined, we can create the sampling distribution. To create the sampling distribution, we need the *statistic of interest* and the *sample size*. The statistic of interest is the mean. Let us set the sample size as 20 and create the sampling distribution with 10,000 synthetic samples:

R

```
set.seed(87654321)
f1 = function(){
  s1 = rpois(n = 20, lambda = 6)
  return(mean(s1))
}
sampdist = replicate(10000, f1())
plot(density(sampdist))
```

density.default(x = sampdist)

N = 10000 Bandwidth = 0.07878

Python

```
np.random.seed(87654321)
def f1():
  s1 = np.random.poisson(6, 20)
  return np.mean(s1)

sampdist = np.array([f1() for i in range(10000)])
```

Just with a few lines of code, we were able to create the sampling distribution!

Step 4: Get the actual sample and compute the statistic.

Now we need to get a sample of 20 observations and compute the mean of this sample.

Suppose we collected these data and it looked as follows:

Observed number of complaints = (4,3,5,13,7,10,9,9,3,6,4,3,7,10,7,6,7,8,7,7)

Now we can compute the test statistic and plot it on the sampling distribution:

R

```
svalues = c(4,3,5,13,7,10,9,9,3,6,4,3,7,10,7,
            6,7,8,7,7)
tstat = mean(svalues)
plot(density(sampdist))
abline(v = tstat, col = "purple", lwd = 2)



print(tstat)
```

density.default(x = sampdist)

N = 10000 Bandwidth = 0.07878

```
## [1] 6.75
```

Python

```
svalues = np.array([4, 3, 5, 13, 7, 10, 9, 9, 3, 6, 4, 3, 7, 10, 7, 6,
        7, 8, 7, 7])
tstat = np.mean(svalues)

sns.kdeplot(sampdist)
plt.axvline(tstat)
plt.show()

print(tstat)
```

6.75

Now what do we do? It looks like the sample value lies near the right tail, but we are not entirely sure what to make of it. What we need here is a metric that we can use to draw conclusions about the hypothesis. For this, we use the famous, often confusing, and sometimes feared concept of p-values. Let us explore and understand this concept.

P-VALUE

Look at the plot above. All the points to the right of the purple line 'go against' the hypothesis. This is because the area to the right of the purple line represents the samples that we would get where the mean of the sample is even higher than 6.75 complaints per day that we observed with our sample. That area (to the right of the purple line) basically gives us reasons to not support the hypothesis. In other words, points to the left of the vertical line are supportive of the hypothesis compared to our sample, and the points to the right of the line are not supportive of the hypothesis compared to our sample. To the left is the 'green' area, and to the right is the 'red' area. To make this visually clear, let us colour the two parts of the sampling distribution. This will require some coding:

R

```
temp = density(sampdist)
df = data.frame(temp$x, temp$y)
formula1 = df$temp.x<tstat
df1 = df[formula1,]
plot(df, col = "red", type = "h")
points(df1, col = "green", type = "h")
```

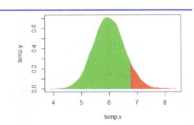

Python

```
points = sns.kdeplot(sampdist).
        get_lines()[0].get_data()
      # get x and y values from plot
x = points[0]
y = points[1]
```

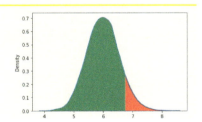

```
plt.fill_between(x,y, where = x >= tstat, color = 'r')
plt.fill_between(x,y, where = x < tstat, color = 'g')
plt.show()
```

Let us figure out the logic of the above code. In the R code, we first coerced the density function into a dataframe with x and y values that describe the x and y coordinates of the density function. Then, we subset the dataframe based on the *tstat* value. The last step is simply to colour the two areas differently.

Now, let us come back to the question of what is a p-value. This simply is the area of the red portion of the sampling distribution. Remember that the red area represents samples that are worse than the sample we have. Let us compute the p-value:

R

```
pvalue = length(sampdist[sampdist>tstat])/(length(sampdist))
print(pvalue)
```

```
## [1] 0.0783
```

Python

```
pvalue = np.sum(sampdist > tstat) / len(sampdist)
print(pvalue)
```

```
0.0821
```

Now we have the p-value! Note that the p-value is always between 0 and 1. What can we conclude from the p-value? A smaller red area results in a lower p-value, meaning the sample we have is increasingly less likely to occur if the hypothesis is indeed true. As the p-value decreases, we are more comfortable in rejecting the null hypothesis.

JUDGEMENT TIME

Our main objective here is to evaluate the hypothesis. If the p-value is very small, then we are very comfortable in rejecting the hypothesis because the evidence (which is the sample) is very inconsistent with the claim (which is the hypothesis). A very common rule of thumb is to reject the null hypothesis if the p-value is less than *0.05*. However, if the p-value is greater than this, we do not reject the hypothesis. In the rest of this book, unless otherwise specified, we will assume that all our tests are conducted at $p \leq 0.05$.

Mind Your Language, Please

Language is important here. With any hypothesis, we have two options: *reject the hypothesis* or *not reject the hypothesis*. Why do we not say *accept the hypothesis* instead of stating *not reject the hypothesis*? Why the double negative? The best way to explain this is to use a legal analogy.

Everyone is presumed to be innocent until proven guilty. Think of this as the null hypothesis. If the evidence against the individual is overwhelming (in our case, the p-value is very small), we term the individual *guilty*. However, if the evidence is not sufficient, we simply say *not guilty*. We do not say the person is *innocent*. Why? It is certainly possible that the person is innocent. It is also possible that the person is truly guilty, but we just do not have enough evidence to prove the guilt. It is safer and more precise to say that the person is *not guilty* instead of claiming innocence about which we are not completely sure.

Coming back to our example, because our p-value is a little above 0.05, we cannot reject the null hypothesis that the mean number of complaints is no more than 6. This does not mean that the actual and correct population mean is indeed 6. It could be 6.5, or 6.2 or some other value for which the hypothesis will not be rejected. All we are saying is: *if our hypothesis is 6 or less, then we do not have evidence to dismiss this hypothesis.*

TALE OF TAILS

In the example we just covered, our null hypothesis was that the mean number of complaints per day was no more than 6. In this case, the 'red' area of the sampling distribution was the 'right tail'. What if we change our null hypothesis to 'mean number of complaints per day is 6 or more'? In this case, we need to rethink the 'red' and 'green' areas of the density plot. As the null hypothesis includes the phrase 'greater than or equal to', the 'red' portion will now be the 'left tail' of the distribution. This is because it represents possible samples that run counter to the stated null hypothesis. Let us colour and compute the p-value for the new null hypothesis:

R

```
temp = density(sampdist)
df = data.frame(temp$x, temp$y)
formula1 = df$temp.x>tstat
df1 = df[formula1,]
plot(df, col = "red", type = "h")
points(df1, col = "green", type = "h")
pvalue = length(sampdist[sampdist<tstat])/
         (length(sampdist))

print(pvalue)

# [1] 0.9079
```

Python

```
points = sns.kdeplot(sampdist).get_lines()[0].
         get_data()
x = points[0]
y = points[1]

plt.fill_between(x,y, where = x < tstat,
    color = 'r')
```

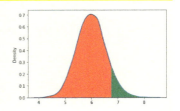

```
plt.fill_between(x,y, where = x >= tstat, color = 'g')
plt.show()
pvalue = np.sum(sampdist < tstat) / len(sampdist)
```

```
print(pvalue)
```

```
0.9049
```

Since the p-value is much larger than 0.05, we are comfortable not rejecting the null hypothesis that the average number of complaints per day is larger than 6. The above two tests are called *one-tailed tests*. This makes sense because we are looking at the tail end of one side of the sampling distribution. If the null hypothesis contains the phrase 'less than or equal to' we employ the right-tail test and if the null hypothesis contains the phrase 'greater than or equal to' we employ the left-tail test to compute the p-value.

What if our null hypothesis was that the average number of complaints per day is equal to 6? How do we compute the p-value? Let us first plot the sampling distribution and the test statistic value:

R

```
plot(density(sampdist))
abline(v = 6, col = "blue")
abline(v = tstat, col = "pink")
```

Python

```
sns.kdeplot(sampdist)
plt.axvline(6, color = 'b')
plt.axvline(tstat, color = 'r')
plt.show()
```

What constitutes our 'red' region in this case? The logic is as follows. The gap between the null hypothesis and the *tstat* is 6.75 – 6 = 0.75. Any sample which deviates from the null hypothesis by more than this amount is worse than our sample statistic. In this example, any sample whose mean deviates from the null hypothesis by more than 0.75, in either direction, provides evidence against the stated hypothesis, and hence should be coloured 'red'. We will employ this logic to colour the sampling distribution and compute the p-value. Also, note that the mean value of the sampling distribution is in fact the hypothesized value, as the sampling distribution is constructed based on the hypothesized value:

R

```
hyp = mean(sampdist)
cutoff1 = hyp - abs(tstat-hyp)
cutoff2 = hyp + abs(tstat-hyp)
temp = density(sampdist)
df = data.frame(temp$x, temp$y)
formula1 = df$temp.x<cutoff1 | df$temp.x>cutoff2
```

```
df1 = df[formula1,]
plot(df, col = "green", type = "h")
points(df1, col = "red", type = "h")
pvalue = length(sampdist[sampdist<cutoff1 | sampdist>cutoff2])/
         (length(sampdist))
print(pvalue)
```

[1] 0.1583

Python

```
hyp = np.mean(sampdist)
cutoff1 = hyp - np.abs(hyp - tstat)
cutoff2 = hyp + np.abs(hyp - tstat)

points = sns.kdeplot(sampdist).get_lines()[0].get_data()
x = points[0]
y = points[1]
```

```
plt.fill_between(x,y, where = (x < cutoff1) | (x > cutoff2), color = 'r')
plt.fill_between(x,y, where = (x >= cutoff1) & (x <= cutoff2), color = 'g')
plt.show()
pvalue = np.sum((sampdist < cutoff1) | (sampdist > cutoff2)) / len(sampdist)

print(pvalue)
```
0.1744

We cannot reject the null hypothesis of this *two-tail test* either. This is an interesting outcome because our hypothesis of less than 6 was not rejected, our hypothesis of greater than 6 was also not rejected, and finally our hypothesis of equal to 6 was also not rejected! You may be scratching your head at this point! How does it make sense to not reject any of the three possibilities? This happened in this example because there is not enough information in the sample we have to draw a more precise conclusion (i.e., reject one of three hypotheses). The solutions then are to either increase the sample size or adjust the hypothesis.

CREATING FUNCTIONS TO COMPUTE P-VALUES

You may have noticed that computing p-values requires only two inputs: sampling distribution and test statistic. The steps in computing the p-value depend only on these inputs. This applies to any statistical test we wish to conduct. As a result, it makes much sense to create functions that can be reused for any test we may want to perform in the future:

R

```
p_rtail = function(sampdist,tstat)
  {
  temp = density(sampdist)
  df = data.frame(temp$x, temp$y)
  formula1 = df$temp.x<tstat
```

```r
  df1 = df[formula1,]
  plot(df, col = "red", type = "h")
  points(df1, col = "green", type = "h")
  pvalue = length(sampdist[sampdist>tstat])/(length(sampdist))
  return(pvalue)
  }


p_ltail = function(sampdist,tstat)
  {
  temp = density(sampdist)
  df = data.frame(temp$x, temp$y)
  formula1 = df$temp.x>tstat
  df1 = df[formula1,]
  plot(df, col = "red", type = "h")
  points(df1, col = "green", type = "h")
  pvalue = length(sampdist[sampdist<tstat])/(length(sampdist))
  return(pvalue)
  }


p_2tail = function(sampdist,tstat)
  {
hyp = mean(sampdist)
cutoff1 = hyp - abs(tstat-hyp)
  cutoff2 = hyp + abs(tstat-hyp)
  temp = density(sampdist)
  df = data.frame(temp$x, temp$y)
  formula1 = df$temp.x<cutoff1 | df$temp.x>cutoff2
  df1 = df[formula1,]
  plot(df, col = "green", type = "h")
  points(df1, col = "red", type = "h")
  pvalue = length(sampdist[sampdist<cutoff1 | sampdist>cutoff2])/
           (length(sampdist))
  return(pvalue)
  }
```

Python

```python
def p_rtail(sampdist,tstat):
    points = sns.kdeplot(sampdist).get_lines()[0].get_data()  # get x and
            y values from plot
   x = points[0]
   y = points[1]

   plt.fill_between(x,y, where = x > tstat, color = 'r')
   plt.fill_between(x,y, where = x <= tstat, color = 'g')
   plt.show()

   pvalue = np.sum(sampdist < tstat) / len(sampdist)
   return pvalue
def p_ltail(sampdist,tstat):
```

```
    points = sns.kdeplot(sampdist).get_lines()[0].get_data()
    x = points[0]
    y = points[1]

    plt.fill_between(x,y, where = x < tstat, color = 'r')
    plt.fill_between(x,y, where = x >= tstat, color = 'g')
    plt.show()

    pvalue = np.sum(sampdist > tstat) / len(sampdist)
    return pvalue
def p_2tail(sampdist,tstat):
    points = sns.kdeplot(sampdist).get_lines()[0].get_data()
    x = points[0]
    y = points[1]

    plt.fill_between(x,y, where = (x < cutoff1) | (x > cutoff2), color = 'r')
    plt.fill_between(x,y, where = (x >= cutoff1) & (x <= cutoff2), color = 'g')
    plt.show()

    pvalue = np.sum((sampdist < cutoff1) | (sampdist > cutoff2)) / len(sampdist)
    return pvalue
```

YOU BE THE JUDGE

As we mentioned before, a common rule of thumb for p-values is to use a cutoff of 0.05. However, this is just a rule-of-thumb and we should not be following it blindly. We have to think about the underlying problem context. What is the implication of rejecting the null hypothesis? Would this cost someone's life? Does it have significant financial or health consequences? If so, we may want to use a much lower cutoff value. For example, if judging someone as guilty can lead to a long-term prison sentence, or even death, then it is perhaps wiser to set a much lower cutoff for the p-value.

CONFIDENCE INTERVALS

Sometimes, we may not have an explicit hypothesis against which to test. What we do have is a sample of data such as the following:

Observed number of complaints = (4,3,5,13,7,10,9,9,3,6,4,3,7,10,7,6,7,8,7,7)

We want to say something intelligent about the population based on the sample data. For this, we create a sampling distribution. To create a sampling distribution, remember that we need to describe a population. In this case, because we do not have a hypothesis, how do we describe the population? We simply assume that the sample of data we have is 'representative' of the population. This would be reasonable if the sample was drawn purely randomly from the population. In this particular example, we will assume that the population mean is the same as the sample mean. Once we decide this, we can create the sampling distribution.

R

```
v1 = c(4,3,5,13,7,10,9,9,3,6,4,3,7,10,7,
       6,7,8,7,7)
set.seed(87654321)
f1 = function(){
  s1 = rpois(n = 20, lambda = mean(v1))
  return(mean(s1))
}
sampdist = replicate(10000, f1())
plot(density(sampdist))
```

Python

```
v1 = np.array([4,3,5,13,7,10,9,9,3,
    6,4,3,7,10,7,6,7,8,7,7])

def f1():
  s1 = np.random.poisson(np.mean(v1), 20)
  return np.mean(s1)

sampdist = np.array([f1() for i in range(10000)])
sns.kdeplot(sampdist)
plt.show()
```

Once we have the sampling distribution, we can compute the confidence intervals. The following code computes the 95% confidence interval:

R

```
q1 = quantile(sampdist, c(.05/2,1-(.05/2)))
plot(density(sampdist))
abline(v = q1, col = "red")
output = paste0("[",q1[1],",",q1[2],"]")
print(output)
```

```
[1] "[5.6,7.9]"
```

Python

```
q1 = np.quantile(sampdist, [.05/2, 1-(.05/2)])
sns.kdeplot(sampdist)
```

```
plt.axvline(q1[0], color = 'r')
plt.axvline(q1[1], color = 'r')
plt.show()1
ouput = "[" + str(q1[0]) + "," + str(q1[1]) + "]"
print(ouput)


"[5.65,7.95]"
```

In this case, the 95% confidence interval is between 5.6 and 7.9. What does this mean? This means that 95% of the time, if we take a sample and calculate its mean, it will be between 5.6 and 7.9. If the samples are 'representative', then we can also say that we are 95% confident that the population mean is between 5.6 and 7.9. The 95% confidence interval is [5.6,7.9]. If anyone hypothesizes that the population mean is outside this range, we can quickly reject it (at a p value of 0.05). In this sense, it is very useful to construct the confidence interval. It should be noted that we can easily construct other confidence intervals at 90%, or 99%, or at some other confidence level. Let us package this into a function to compute and plot the confidence intervals. The inputs to this function are the sampling distribution and the level of confidence. We set 95% as the default level which implies that if this input is not provided, it automatically computes the 95% confidence interval.

R

```
conf_int = function(sampdist,conlevel = 0.95)
{
  left_v = (1 - conlevel)/2
  right_v = 1 - left_v
  q1 = quantile(sampdist,c(left_v,right_v))
  plot(density(sampdist))
  abline(v = q1, col = "red")
  output = paste0("[",q1[1],",",q1[2],"]")
  return(output)
}
```

Python

```
def conf_int(sampdist, conlevel = 0.95):
  left_v = (1-conlevel)/2
  right_v = 1-left_v
  q1 = np.quantile(sampdist, [left_v, right_v])
  sns.kdeplot(sampdist)
  plt.axvline(q1[0], color = 'r')
  plt.axvline(q1[1], color = 'r')
  plt.show()
  output = "[" + str(q1[0]) + "," + str(q1[1]) + "]"
  return output
```

Let us use the function to compute the 99% confidence interval:

R

```
conf_int(sampdist,0.99)
```

```
[1] "[5.3,8.25024999999996]"
```

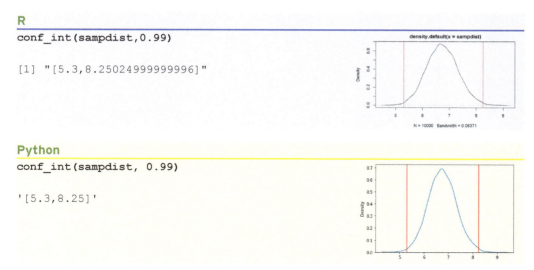

Python

```
conf_int(sampdist, 0.99)
```

```
'[5.3,8.25]'
```

Similarly, we can construct confidence intervals for other statistics of interest. Suppose we want to construct a confidence interval for the population standard deviation:

R

```
set.seed(87654321)
f2 = function(){
  s2 = rpois(n = 20, lambda = mean(v1))
  return(sd(s2))
}
sampdist = replicate(10000, f2())
conf_int(sampdist)
```

```
[1] "[1.75018795983084,3.43517981351968]"
```

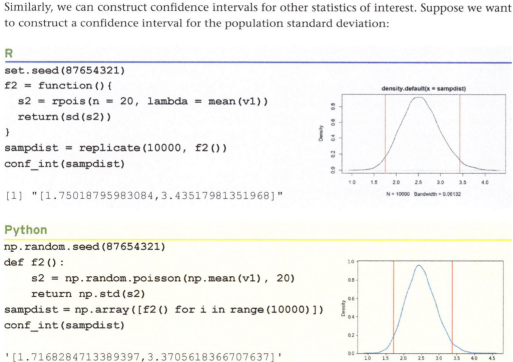

Python

```
np.random.seed(87654321)
def f2():
    s2 = np.random.poisson(np.mean(v1), 20)
    return np.std(s2)
sampdist = np.array([f2() for i in range(10000)])
conf_int(sampdist)
```

```
'[1.7168284713389397,3.3705618366707637]'
```

From this, we can conclude that we are 95% confident that the population standard deviation is between 1.75 and 3.44. As a final example, let us compute the confidence interval for another statistic of interest: 75th percentile.

R

```
set.seed(87654321)
f3 = function(){
```

```
    s3 = rpois(n = 20, lambda = mean(v1))
    return(quantile(s3, probs = .75))
}
sampdist = replicate(10000, f3())
conf_int(sampdist)
```

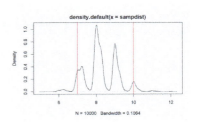

```
[1] "[7,10]"
```

Python

```
np.random.seed(87654321)
def f3():
    s3 = np.random.poisson(np.mean(v1), 20)
    return np.quantile(s3, .75)
sampdist = np.array([f3() for i in range(10000)])
conf_int(sampdist)
```

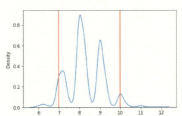

```
'[7.0,10.0]'
```

From this, we can conclude that we are 95% confident that the 75th percentile of the population will lie between 7 and 10.

In this chapter, we covered some core concepts of how statistical testing is conducted. The code we created in this lesson (to create sampling distributions and computing p-values) can be reused in the future when we start to conduct actual statistical tests. In the next chapter, we will use the concepts covered here to conduct a variety of tests from first principles.

Use Case: Outlier Detection in Product Data

Testing whether a sample is likely to have come from a given population is a powerful use of probability, as discussed above. Using the same tools, we can also express whether a certain sample is an outlier in our observations, which is known as outlier detection. Outlier detection is critical for manufacturing processes, detecting components that fall outside of the required tolerances; it can be important in identifying fraudulent transactions in a FinTech environment, along with many other uses in business.

We can use the tools introduced above to identify outliers in a dataset, and once identified, we as business analysts, or managers, will need to determine whether the presence of outliers is acceptable (or indeed, beneficial).

Airbnb Outliers in Boston

Taking the Boston Airbnb Open Data, which has listings, ratings, and so on for different properties advertised and rented through Airbnb, we can examine the different properties on offer for outliers that may or may not benefit Airbnb's offering. Below, you can see the distribution of price for different property types offered in Boston by Airbnb (note that we have to go through some data wrangling steps to clean the data ready for analysis):

R

```
df = read_excel("listings - wrangled.xlsx")
ggplot(df,aes(x = price,y=property_type)) +
  geom_boxplot(col = "violet", fill = "lightblue", size = 1) +
  theme_light()
```

Python

```
plt.figure(figsize=(15,10))
plt.title('AirBnB Boston: Distribution of Apartment Prices')

sns.boxplot(y='price', x='property_type',data=df)
plt.xticks(rotation=90)
plt.ylabel('Price ($)')

plt.show()
```

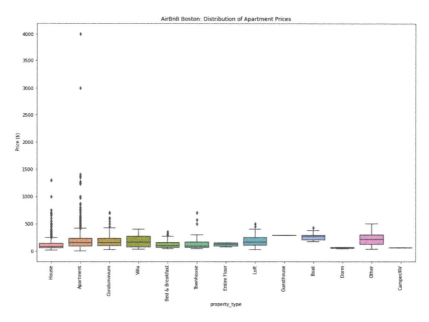

Figure 7.7   Distribution of apartment prices for Airbnb Boston

We can see from the chart that there are outliers in most categories, but particularly the Apartments category, where one apartment is offered for around $4000, whereas the median is $159. There are clearly a few very expensive apartments for rent on Airbnb in Boston. If we drill down into apartment prices, plotting a frequency distribution by binning apartment prices into 50 bins using a column chart, this helps visualize the distribution (note that we remove all outliers over $1000 in this case):

R

```
hist(df$price[df$price<1000],breaks=50,
     main = "AirBnB Boston Distribution of Apartment Prices",
     xlab = "Price")
```

Python

```
plt.figure(figsize=(10,7))
plt.title('AirBnB Boston: Distribution of Apartment Prices')
plt.hist(df_apart['price'], bins=50)
```

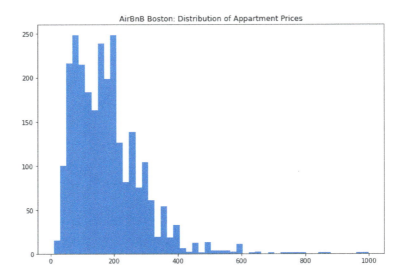

Applying the confidence interval function we have learned above, *conf_int,* we can replot this data distribution with 95% confidence intervals:

R

```
conf_int(df$price[df$price<1000])
```

Python

```
q5pct = conf_int(df_apart['price'])
```

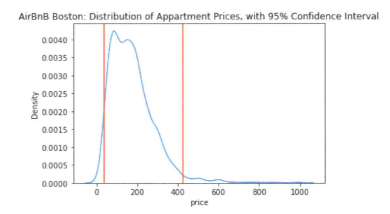

If we prefer to look at the distribution as a boxplot, we can see the extremes more clearly:

R

```
qvalues = quantile(df[df$price<1000,]$price,c(0.05/2,1-0.05/2))
ggplot(df[df$price<1000,],aes(x = price)) + geom_boxplot(col = "violet",
     fill = "lightblue", size = 1) + theme_light() + geom_vline(xintercept =
     qvalues,col = "red")
```

Python

```
plt.figure(figsize = (15,5))
plt.title('AirBnB Boston: Distribution of Apartment Prices')

sns.boxplot(y = 'property_type', x = 'price',data = df_apart)
plt.xticks(rotation = 0)
plt.ylabel('Price ($)')

plt.axvline(q5pct[0], color = 'r')
plt.axvline(q5pct[1], color = 'r')

plt.show()
```

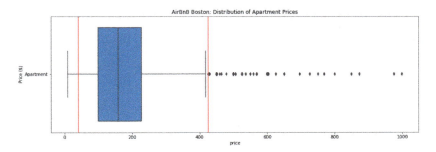

Figure 7.8   Boxplot of distribution of apartment prices for Airbnb Boston

It is certainly the case that the apartments renting for prices above the right-hand confidence interval or below the left-hand confidence interval are significantly different offerings from the majority of the apartments on offer. They are outliers, and perhaps we can consider them different beasts – not from the same population as typical Airbnb rentals. It could be that these apartments rarely rent and represent an overhead for the platform. It could also be that they add prestige (and budget options) to the offering. However, having identified these very different offerings statistically, we are now able to take whatever qualitative business actions are appropriate.

Summary

In this chapter, we covered some core concepts of how statistical testing is conducted. The code we created in this lesson (to create sampling distributions and computing p-values) can be reused in the future when we start to conduct actual statistical tests. In the next chapter, we will use the concepts covered here to conduct a variety of tests from first principles.

Exercises

To complete the activity below, you will need to visit the companion website to the book and download the relevant dataset: https://study.sagepub.com/gopal

Read the Health.csv file.

1   Conduct the following tests on the variable **ofp** (which captures the number of office visits by patients).

   a   Number of office visits is less than or equal to 5.
   b   Number of office visits is more than or equal to 6.
   c   Number of office visits is 5.5.

2   Construct the 95% confidence interval for the average *faminc* (family income). What conclusion can you draw from it?

3   Repeat problem 2, but this time compute the confidence interval for median family income.

4   Compute the 90% confidence interval for median **age** in the data.

8

STATISTICAL TESTS

Chapter Contents

Statistical hypothesis testing is the process of making an assumption about the data and testing whether or not we should reject it. Statistical tests are a rigorous way to gain a deeper understanding of the data and are often carried out in research and business settings. Thanks to these tests, we are, in fact, able to answer questions about the data and inform our decisions that may depend on it. Statistical hypothesis testing is used in demographic studies, drug validation and side-effects discovery, process control and, in general, every time we want to answer a statistical question on a population of interest. Thanks to the rapid technological change, statistical tests that once were challenging and expensive to conduct have now become accessible to most, and are particularly attractive to businesses, often seeking professionals with a good working knowledge of them.

In this chapter, we will conduct several statistical tests based on the principles we discussed in the previous chapter. You will notice that the basic procedure to conduct tests remains the same, regardless of the specific test we perform and, with some practice, conducting these additional tests should become fairly straightforward. We will focus on conducting these tests from the first principles so that we can gain a deeper understanding and we will discuss the standard R and Python functions to carry them out. We will begin with common statistical tests conducted on numerical data. In all the tests, we will assume a significance level of 0.05.

TESTS WITH NUMERICAL DATA

Let us read the file admission.csv which contains three variables: **GMAT**, **GPA**, and **De,** indicating respectively the Graduate Management Aptitude Test, the Grade Point Average scores, and the Admission Decision.

Mean

Suppose we want to create a test where we hypothesize that the population mean of the GMAT score is 510. Let us follow the steps discussed in the previous chapter to test this hypothesis.

Step 1: State the null hypothesis.

The GMAT population mean is 510.

Step 2:

Since the GMAT scores are numerical, we will assume they follow $N(\mu, \sigma)$ where μ is equal to 510, as hypothesized. What about σ? Since we do not have explicit information on σ, we will use the sample standard deviation.

Step 3:

The sampling distribution is created with the following code:

R

```
set.seed(87654321)
sampsize = nrow(admission)
f1 = function(){
  s1 = rnorm(sampsize, mean = 510, sd = sd(admission$GMAT))
  return(mean(s1))
}
sampdist = replicate(10000, f1())
```

Python

```python
np.random.seed(87654321)
sampsize = len(admission)
def f1():
    s1 = np.random.normal(size = sampsize, loc = 510, scale = admission.std()
        ['GMAT'])
    return np.mean(s1)
sampdist = [f1() for _ in range(10000)]
```

Step 4: Get the actual sample and compute the statistic.

Call the function we created in the last chapter to plot and compute the p-value:

R

```r
tstat = mean(admission$GMAT)
p_2tail(sampdist,tstat)
```

[1] 0.0161

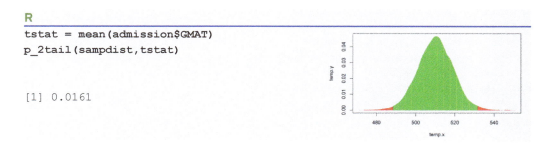

Python

```python
tstat = admission.mean()['GMAT']
p_2tail(sampdist,tstat)
```

0.014

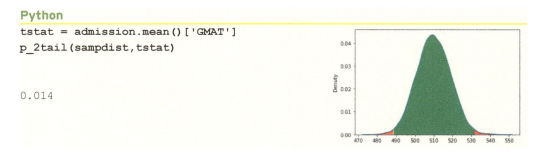

Assuming a significance level α = 0.05, and obtaining a p-value = 0.0161, we can confidently reject the null hypothesis that the mean GMAT population score is 510.

Standard Deviation

We want to test the null hypothesis that the population standard deviation is 78.

Step 1: State the null hypothesis.

The population standard deviation is 78.

Step 2:

Since the GMAT scores are numerical, we will assume they follow $N(\mu,\sigma)$, where μ is equal to 78, as hypothesized. Here, σ will be taken from the sample.

Step 3: Create a sampling distribution.

The sampling distribution is created with the following code:

R

```r
set.seed(87654321)
sampsize = nrow(admission)
f1 = function(){
  s1 = rnorm(sampsize, mean = mean(admission$GMAT), sd = 78)
  return(sd(s1))
}
sampdist = replicate(10000, f1())
```

Python

```python
np.random.seed(87654321)
sampsize = len(admission)
def f1():
    mu = admission.mean()['GMAT']
    s1 = np.random.normal(size = sampsize, loc = mu, scale = 78)
    return np.std(s1)
sampdist = [f1() for _ in range(10000)]
```

Step 4: Get the actual sample and compute the statistic.

Call the function we created in the last chapter to plot and compute the p-value:

R

```r
tstat = sd(admission$GMAT)
p_2tail(sampdist,tstat)
```

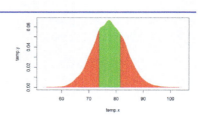

```
[1] 0.5249
```

Python

```python
tstat = admission.std()['GMAT']
p_2tail(sampdist,tstat)
```

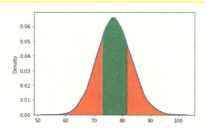

```
0.4737
```

The p-value is far above our confidence threshold (0.05) and hence we cannot confidently reject the null hypothesis that the standard deviation of the GMAT score is 78.

Median

We want to test the null hypothesis that the population median is 500.

Step 1: State the null hypothesis.

The population median is 500.

Step 2:

Since the GMAT scores are numerical, we will assume they follow $N(\mu,\sigma)$. Since a normal distribution is always symmetric about the mean, its median value will be the same as its mean; therefore $\mu = \sigma$.

Step 3:

The sampling distribution is created with the following code:

R

```r
set.seed(87654321)
sampsize = nrow(admission)
f1 = function(){
  s1 = rnorm(sampsize, mean = 500, sd = sd(admission$GMAT))
  return(median(s1))
}
sampdist = replicate(10000, f1())
```

Python

```python
np.random.seed(87654321)
sampsize = len(admission)
def f1():
    s1 = np.random.normal(size = sampsize, loc = 500, scale = admission.
        std()['GMAT'])
    return np.median(s1)
sampdist = [f1() for _ in range(10000)]
```

Step 4: Get the actual sample and compute the statistic. Call the function we created in the last chapter to plot and compute the p-value:

R

```r
tstat = sd(admission$GMAT)
p_2tail(sampdist,tstat)
```

[1] 0.1042

Python

```python
tstat = admission.median()['GMAT']
p_2tail(sampdist,tstat)
```

0.1043

The p-value is slightly above 0.10, and thus we cannot reject the null hypothesis that the median value of the GMAT score in the population is 500.

Percentile

Consider the hypothesis that the 75th percentile value of the GMAT score in the population is 600. We are hypothesizing that 75% of the students in the population will have GMAT scores of 600 or below. Do we reject or not reject this hypothesis based on the data we have?

Step 1: State the null hypothesis.

The 75th percentile value of the GMAT score in the population is 600.

Step 2: Describe the data generation process and the population.

Since the GMAT scores are numeric, we will assume they follow a normal distribution, $N(\mu,\sigma)$. What should the values of μ and σ be to describe the population where the 75th percentile value is 600? Let us first compute the 75th percentile value for a standard normal distribution (remember that a standard normal distribution has a mean of 0 and a standard deviation of 1).

R

```
qnorm(0.75)
```

```
[1] 0.6744898
```

Python

```
norm.ppf(0.75)
```

```
0.6744897501960817
```

From this, we can see that the mean and standard deviation of a normal distribution that results in a 75th percentile value of 600 must satisfy the following condition:

$$\frac{600 - \mu}{\sigma} = 0.6744898$$

Rearranging it, we obtain:

$$\mu + 0.6744898\sigma = 600$$

Now we can select either μ or σ from the sample and compute the other from above. The following computes the appropriate value of μ with the sample standard deviation to ensure that the population 75th percentile value is 600:

R

```
newm = 600-(qnorm(0.75)*sd(admission$GMAT))
print(newm)
```

```
[1] 545.014
```

```
qnorm(p = 0.75,mean = newm,sd = sd(admission$GMAT))
```

```
[1] 600
```

Python

```
newm = 600 - (norm.ppf(0.75) * admission.std()['GMAT'])
print(newm)

545.0140127979766

norm.ppf(q = 0.75, loc = newm, scale = admission.std()['GMAT'])

600.0
```

Step 3: Create a sampling distribution.

The sampling distribution is created with the following code:

R

```
set.seed(87654321)
sampsize = nrow(admission)
f1 = function(){
  s1 = rnorm(sampsize, mean = newm, sd = sd(admission$GMAT))
  return(quantile(s1, probs = .75))
}
sampdist = replicate(10000, f1())
```

Python

```
np.random.seed(87654321)
sampsize = len(admission)
def f1():
    s1 = np.random.normal(size = sampsize, loc = newm, scale = admission.std()
        ['GMAT'])
    return np.quantile(s1, 0.75)
sampdist = [f1() for _ in range(10000)]
```

Step 4: Get the actual sample and compute the statistic. Call the function we created in the last chapter to plot and compute the p-value:

R

```
tstat = quantile(admission$GMAT, probs = .75)
p_2tail(sampdist,tstat)
```

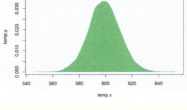

```
[1] 0
```

Python

```
tstat = admission.quantile(.75)['GMAT']
p_2tail(sampdist,tstat)
```

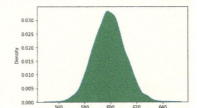

```
0.0
```

The p-value is essentially zero and thus we reject the null hypothesis.

Normality Test

We want to conduct a test to assess whether the population distribution of the GMAT scores is normal. A good pre-processing practice when working with data is to standardize it. Through standardization, we centre the original data around 0, which becomes the new mean, and scale it to a common range (usually between 0 and 1, or –1 and 1). This way, we are able to generate a consistent representation of the data, which enables us to compare it and draw general conclusions from it. Let us first standardize the GMAT scores and visualize the distribution of the sample values:

R

```r
gmat1 = scale(admission$GMAT)
plot(density(gmat1))
```

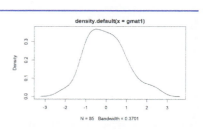

Python

```python
from sklearn.preprocessing import scale

gmat1 = scale(admission['GMAT'])
sns.kdeplot(gmat1)
plt.xlabel('N = 85')
plt.ylabel('Density')
plt.title('density.default(x = gmat1)')
plt.show()
```

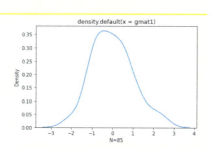

The question we want to answer is whether the `gmat1` follows a normal distribution. Does the above look like a normal distribution? To assess this, let us plot a 'perfect' normal distribution and draw a sample of 50 observations from this normal distribution and plot the distribution of the sample drawn from the normal distribution:

R

```r
set.seed(87654321)
curve(dnorm(x, mean = 0, sd = 1), from = -3,
      to = 3, col = "red")
s1 = rnorm(n = 50, mean = 0, sd = 1)
lines(density(s1), col = "blue")
```

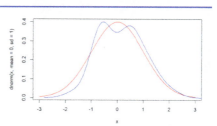

Python

```python
np.random.seed(87654321)
x = np.linspace(-3, 3, 100)

fig, axs = plt.subplots(1, 1)
axs.plot(x, norm.pdf(x, loc = 0, scale = 1),
        color = 'r')
s1 = np.random.normal(size = 50, loc = 0,
        scale = 1)
sns.kdeplot(s1, color = 'b', ax = axs)
```

The plot above indicates that when we take a sample from a normal distribution, it will likely not look perfectly normal, but it should be somewhat close. What we need is a measurement of how similar or dissimilar the two curves are. We will use the following logic to measure similarity.

Let us compute the quantile values of the normal distribution at several different quantile levels. Similarly, we will compute the quantile values from the sample at the same quantile levels:

R

```r
quantiles = seq(.1, .9, by = .1)
qvaluespop = qnorm(p = quantiles, mean = 0, sd = 1)
curve(dnorm(x, mean = 0, sd = 1), from = -3, to = 3, col = "red")
lines(density(s1), col = "blue")
abline(v = qvaluespop, col = "red")
qvaluessamp = quantile(x = s1, probs =
                quantiles)
abline(v = qvaluessamp, col = "blue")
```

Python

```python
quantiles = np.arange(0.1, 1, 0.1) # stop value "1" is excluded
qvaluespop = norm.ppf(quantiles,
    loc = 0, scale = 1)
plt.plot(x, norm.pdf(x, loc = 0,
    scale = 1), color = 'r')
sns.kdeplot(s1, color = 'b')
plt.vlines(x = qvaluespop, ymin=0,
    ymax = np.max(norm.pdf(x = qvaluespop,
    loc = 0, scale = 1)), color ='r',
    linewidth = 0.7)
qvaluessamp = np.quantile(s1, q = quantiles)
plt.vlines(x = qvaluessamp, ymin = 0,
    ymax = np.max (norm.pdf(x = norm.ppf(quantiles, loc = 0, scale = 1),
    loc = 0, scale = 1)), color = 'b', linewidth = 0.7)
```

If the two plots are identical, then the blue and red lines should fully overlap. We will define a measure that is based on the difference between the two sets of quantile values. The metric that we will use is the mean of the absolute differences in quantile values:

R

```
print(round(qvaluespop,3))
```

```
[1] -1.282 -0.842 -0.524 -0.253  0.000
0.253  0.524  0.842  1.282
```

```
print(round(qvaluessamp,3))
```

```
   10%    20%    30%    40%    50%    60%
   70%    80%    90%
-0.819 -0.650 -0.469 -0.254  0.161  0.402
0.595  0.837  1.258
```

```
plot(x = quantiles, y = qvaluespop, type = "l", col = "blue")
points(x = quantiles, y = qvaluessamp, col = "red", pch = 9 )
```

```
normmetric = mean(abs(qvaluespop-qvaluessamp))
print(normmetric)
```

```
[1] 0.1244155
```

Python

```
print(np.round(qvaluespop,3))
```

```
[-1.282  -0.842  -0.524  -0.253   0.  0.253
0.524   0.842   1.282]
```

```
print(np.round(qvaluessamp,3))
```

```
[-1.311  -1.014  -0.622  -0.09  0.136  0.351
0.574 0.912 1.066]
```

```
plt.plot(quantiles, qvaluespop, 'b-')
plt.plot(quantiles, qvaluessamp, 'r.')
plt.show()
```

```
normmetric = np.mean(np.abs(qvaluespop-qvaluessamp))
print(normmetric)
```

```
0.11460909048249418
```

The above example illustrates that a metric value of 0.12 is not unexpected for a sample that is drawn from a normal distribution. This provides us with the basis to construct the statistical test for normality.

Step 1: State the null hypothesis.

Gmat1 follows $N(0,1)$.

Step 2: Describe the data generation process and the population.

The data comes from a standard normal distribution. Create a sample and compute the normmetric.

Step 3: Create a sampling distribution.

The sampling distribution is created with the following code:

R

```
set.seed(87654321)
sampsize = nrow(admission)
f1 = function(){
  k1 = rnorm(sampsize, mean = 0, sd = 1)
  quantiles = seq(.1, .9, by = .1)
  qvaluespop = qnorm(p = quantiles,
    mean = 0, sd = 1)
  qvaluessamp = quantile(x = k1,
    probs = quantiles)
  normmetric = mean(abs(qvaluespop-qvaluessamp))
  return(normmetric)
}
sampdist = replicate(10000, f1())
plot(density(sampdist))
```

density.default(x = sampdist)

N = 10000   Bandwidth = 0.006784

Python

```
np.random.seed(87654321)
sampsize = len(admission)
def f1():
    k1 = np.random.normal(size = sampsize,
            loc=0, scale = 1)
    quantiles = np.arange(0.1, 1, 0.1) #
                stop value "1" is excluded
    qvaluespop = norm.ppf(quantiles,
                loc = 0, scale = 1)
    qvaluessamp = np.quantile(k1, q = quantiles)
    normmetric = np.mean(np.abs(qvaluespop-qvaluessamp))
    return(normmetric)
sampdist = [f1() for _ in range(10000)]
sns.kdeplot(sampdist)
plt.show()
```

Points on the left tail of the sampling distribution are supportive of the null hypothesis whereas points on the right tail support rejecting the null hypothesis. Thus, we employ the right-tail test to assess the hypothesis and compute the p-value.

Step 4: Get the actual sample and compute the statistic. Call the function we created in the last chapter to plot and compute the p-value:

R

```
tstat = mean(abs(qvaluespop-qvaluessamp))
p_rtail(sampdist,tstat)
```

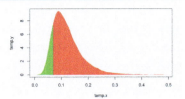

```
[1] 0.8632
```

Python

```
tstat = np.mean(np.abs(qvaluespop-qvaluessamp))
p_rtail(sampdist,tstat)
```

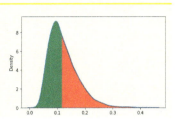

```
0.5259
```

The results of the test indicate that we cannot reject the null hypothesis that the distribution for the GMAT scores is normal.

Inbuilt Functions

As you would expect, R and Python provide functions to do some of the tests we just conducted. The following functions provide tests for the mean and normality of a numeric variable:

R

```
t.test(x = admission$GMAT, mu = 510)

      One Sample t-test

data:  admission$GMAT
t = -2.4375, df = 84, p-value = 0.0169
alternative hypothesis: true mean is not equal to 510
95 percent confidence interval:
 470.8631 506.0310
sample estimates:
mean of x
 488.4471


shapiro.test(x = admission$GMAT)

      Shapiro-Wilk normality test

data:  admission$GMAT
W = 0.98039, p-value = 0.2227
```

Python

```
stats.ttest_1samp(admission['GMAT'], 510)
```

```
Ttest_1sampResult(statistic  =-2.4375, pvalue = 0.0169)
stats.shapiro(admission['GMAT'])
```

```
ShapiroResult(statistic=0.9803898930549622, pvalue=0.2227)
```

The p-value for our test conducted from first principles is quite close to the one from the above function for the mean test. Notice that in the normality test, while the conclusions are the same, the p-values are somewhat different. This is explained by the two tests using a different strategy to test for normality (https://statisticaloddsandends.wordpress.com/2019/08/13/what-is-the-shapiro-wilk-test/). The Shapiro–Wilk test is constructed on the variance of the sample, while the test we designed is based on quantile values. There are other tests for normality as well (www.ncbi.nlm.nih.gov/pmc/articles/PMC3693611/#:~:text=The%20main%20tests%20for%20the,test%20(7)%2C%20and%20the).

An important point needs to be made here: there is no *one and only one way* to conduct any test. The main objective in any test is to describe the population that is consistent with the null hypothesis and design a metric to compute the p-value. For instance, in our test for normality, our chosen metric was based on 10 quantile values but we could have easily used a different or additional one if we had felt the need for it.

Abnormal

In most tests with numeric variables, we tend to assume normality for the population. However, sometimes this assumption may not appropriately describe our data and we may want to consider alternative distributions:

1. When we have count variables, commonly we would use distributions such as Poisson and binomial. In the previous chapter, we have used the Poisson distribution to conduct our test for the number of office visits which is naturally a count variable.
2. Sometimes, if we plot the density of the variable or if we conduct a normality test, as just discussed, the assumption of normality will be evidently unreasonable. When this happens, one option is to try to transform the variable. For example, we may take the log of it to try to make it as normal as possible, and then conduct one of the standard tests. Consider the immer.csv file that contains information on yields for barley from a field trial. The variable **Y1** indicates the yield in the year 1931:

R

```
Immer = read.csv("immer.csv")
plot(density(immer$Y1))
shapiro.test(immer$Y1)
```

```
Shapiro-Wilk normality test
```

```
data:   immer$Y1
W = 0.92973, p-value = 0.04829
```

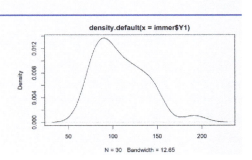

Python
```
Immer = pd.read_csv("../data/immer.csv")
sns.kdeplot(Immer['Y1'])
plt.show()
stats.shapiro(Immer['Y1'])
```

```
ShapiroResult(statistic = 0.9297280311584473,
        pvalue = 0.04829331114888191)
```

Both the plot and the Shapiro–Wilk test indicate that the distribution is not normal. Now let us log transform it and assess normality:

R
```
y = log(immer$Y1)
plot(density(y))
shapiro.test(y)
```

```
Shapiro-Wilk normality test

data:  y
W = 0.96538, p-value = 0.4217
```

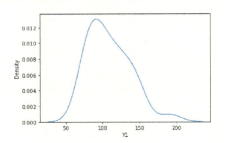

Python
```
y = np.log(Immer['Y1'])
sns.kdeplot(y)
plt.show()
stats.shapiro(y)
```

```
ShapiroResult(statistic=0.9653836488723755,
        pvalue=0.42168083786964417)
```

The p-value is now 0.42, and thus the assumption of normality of the log transformed variable is reasonable. Now we can do the standard tests on this transformed data.

TESTS WITH FACTOR/CATEGORICAL DATA

The factor variable **De** in the admissions dataframe indicates the decisions on student admissions. The three values in the variable are **admit**, **border**, and **notadmit**. Suppose we have a claim that 40% of the applicants are admitted. Let us design a statistical test to verify this claim.

Step 1: State the null hypothesis.

40% of the applicants are admitted.

Step 2: Describe the data generation process and the population.

This is a discrete distribution with two possible outcomes: getting admitted and other. We can describe this as follows:

```
admitdomain = (admit, other)
admitprob = (.4, .6)
```

Step 3: Create a sampling distribution.

The sampling distribution is created with the following code:

R

```r
admitdomain = c("admit", "other")
admitprob = c(.4, .6)
set.seed(87654321)
sampsize = nrow(admission)
f1 = function(){
  k1 = sample(x = admitdomain, size = sampsize, replace = T, prob = admitprob)
  return(prop.table(table(k1))[1])

}
sampdist = replicate(10000, f1())
```

Python

```python
admitdomain = ['admit', 'other']
admitprob = [.4, .6]
np.random.seed(87654321)
sampsize = len(admission)
def f1():
    k1 = np.random.choice(admitdomain, size = sampsize, p = admitprob)
    return(np.mean(k1 == 'admit'))
sampdist = [f1() for _ in range(10000)]
```

Step 4: Get the actual sample and compute the statistic. Call the function we created in the last chapter to plot and compute the p-value:

R

```r
tstat = prop.table(table(admission$De))[1]
p_2tail(sampdist,tstat)
```

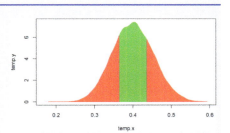

```
[1] 0.4414
```

Python

```
tstat = np.mean(admission['De'] == 'admit')
p_2tail(sampdist,tstat)
```

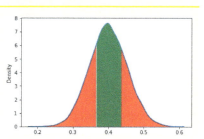

```
0.4379
```

Since the p-value is 0.44, we cannot reject the null hypothesis that 40% of the applicants are admitted.

TESTS WITH TWO NUMERIC VARIABLES

Let us consider the two variables **GMAT** and **GPA**. Recall our discussion in Chapters 5 and 6 about univariate and multivariate distributions. If two variables are independent, we can describe them as separate univariate distributions. However, if they are not independent, we have to describe them together as a multivariate distribution. For numeric variables, if they are independent, their correlation should be 0. Suppose we want to test if **GPA** and **GMAT** are independent.

To simplify, let us first standardize the two variables. There is a function in R called `scale()` that can be used to standardize numeric variables:

```
gmat1 = scale(admission$GMAT)
gpa1 = scale(admission$GPA)
```

It is helpful to first standardize the variables to **gmat1** and **gre1**. The test is conducted as follows:

Step 1: State the null hypothesis.

gmat1 and **gpa1** are independent.

Step 2: Describe the data generation process and the population.

If they are independent, **gmat1** ~ $N(0,1)$ and **gpa1** ~ $N(0,1)$.

Step 3: Create a sampling distribution.

Draw samples from **gpa1** and **gmat1** and compute the correlation. Repeat this process to create the sampling distribution:

R

```
gmat1 = scale(admission$GMAT)
gpa1 = scale(admission$GPA)
set.seed(87654321)
sampsize = nrow(admission)
f1 = function(){
  k1 = rnorm(sampsize, mean = 0, sd = 1)
  k2 = rnorm(sampsize, mean = 0, sd = 1)
  return(cor(x = k1, y = k2))
}
sampdist = replicate(10000, f1())
```

Python

```python
def scale(x):
    return(x - np.mean(x)) / np.std(x)

gmat1 = scale(admission['GMAT'])
gpa1 = scale(admission['GPA'])
np.random.seed(87654321)
sampsize = len(admission)
def f1():
    k1 = np.random.normal(size = sampsize, loc = 0, scale = 1)
    k2 = np.random.normal(size = sampsize, loc = 0, scale = 1)
    return(np.corrcoef(k1, k2)[0,1])
```

Step 4: Get the actual sample and compute the statistic. Call the function we created in the last chapter to plot and compute the p-value:

R

```r
tstat = cor(gmat1, gpa1)[1,1]
p_2tail(sampdist,tstat)
```

```
[1] 0
```

Python

```python
sampdist = [f1() for _ in range(10000)]
tstat = np.corrcoef(gmat1, gpa1)[0,1]
p_2tail(sampdist,tstat)
```

```
0.0
```

The results clearly indicate that we must reject the null hypothesis that **GMAT** and **GRE** are independent. The following are the inbuilt functions in R and Python for the correlation test:

R

```r
cor.test(gmat1, gpa1)
Pearson's product-moment correlation

data:  gmat1 and gpa1
t = 4.728, df = 83, p-value = 9.165e-06
alternative hypothesis: true correlation is not equal to 0
95 percent confidence interval:
 0.2744527 0.6135262
sample estimates:
      cor
0.4606332
```

Python
```
print("p-value: {}, sample estimate: {}".format(pearsonr(gmat1, gpa1)[1],
pearsonr(gmat1, gpa1)[0]))
```

```
p-value 9.16455058014374e-06,
sample estimate 0.4606331976247068
```

Let us complicate things a bit. Suppose our null hypothesis is that the correlation between the two is 0.5. How do we test this hypothesis? Since the null hypothesis states that these two variables are not independent, we have to define the hypothesized population as a bivariate normal distribution. We discussed this in Chapter 6.

Step 1: State the null hypothesis.

The correlation between **gmat1** and **gpa1** in the population is 0.5.

Step 2: Describe the data generation process and the population.

The bivariate normal distribution is defined as:

$$N\left(\begin{bmatrix} 0 \\ 0 \end{bmatrix}, \begin{bmatrix} 1 & 0.5 \\ 0.5 & 1 \end{bmatrix} \right)$$

Note that the covariance is:

$$\rho_{1,2} \times \sigma_1 \sigma_2$$

Step 3: Create a sampling distribution.

Draw samples from the bivariate normal distribution and compute the correlation. Repeat to create the sampling distribution:

R
```
library(mvtnorm)
M = c(0,0)
S = matrix(c(1,.5,.5,1), nrow = 2, ncol = 2)

set.seed(87654321)
sampsize = nrow(admission)
f1 = function(){
  x = rmvnorm(nrow(admission),mean = M,sigma = S)
  return(cor(x[,1],x[,2]))
}
sampdist = replicate(10000, f1())
```

Python
```
M = np.array([0,0])
S = np.array([[1,0.5],[0.5,1]])
np.random.seed(87654321)
sampsize = len(admission)
def f1():
```

```
    x = np.random.multivariate_normal(mean = M, cov = S, size = sampsize)
    return(np.corrcoef(x[:,0], x[:,1])[0,1])
sampdist = [f1() for _ in range(10000)]
```

Step 4: Get the actual sample, compute the statistic and the p-value:

R

```
tstat = cor(gmat1, gpa1)[1,1]
p_2tail(sampdist,tstat)
```

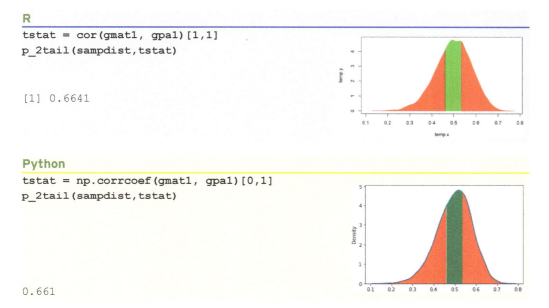

```
[1] 0.6641
```

Python

```
tstat = np.corrcoef(gmat1, gpa1)[0,1]
p_2tail(sampdist,tstat)
```

```
0.661
```

Since the p-value is large, we do not reject the null hypothesis that the correlation between the two variables is 0.5. There is no inbuilt function to do the test for a hypothesized level of correlation, but with some simple code, we are able to quickly design and execute this test.

TESTS WITH TWO FACTOR/CATEGORICAL VARIABLES

Read the file survey.csv. We want to test the hypothesis related to two factor variables **Exer** and **Smoke**. Our null hypothesis is that these two variables are independent. Let us take a look at the empirical distribution of each of them:

R

```
distexer = prop.table(table(survey$Exer))
distsmoke = prop.table(table(survey$Smoke))
distexer
distsmoke
```

```
     Freq      None      Some
0.4852321 0.1012658 0.4135021

     Heavy      Never      Occas      Regul
0.04661017 0.80084746 0.08050847 0.07203390
```

Python

```
distexer = survey.Exer.value_counts() / len(survey)
distsmoke = survey.Smoke.value_counts() / len(survey)
print(distexer)
print(distsmoke)


Freq 0.485232
Some 0.413502
None 0.101266


Never 0.800847
Occas 0.080508
Regul 0.072034
Heavy 0.046610
```

Since the two variables are independent, we can describe them separately. In this case, the joint probability is P (*Smoke* and *Exer*) = P (*Smoke*) × P (*Exer*). Therefore, the probability that someone exercises frequently and is a smoker should be 0.4852321 × 0.04661017. Assuming independence, we can compute the joint probability and the expected number of people in each combination of categories as follows:

R

```
jointdist = distexer %*% t(distsmoke)
round(jointdist,3)


      Heavy Never Occas Regul
 Freq 0.023 0.389 0.039 0.035
 None 0.005 0.081 0.008 0.007
 Some 0.019 0.331 0.033 0.030


n = nrow(survey)
E = n * jointdist
round(E,1)


      Heavy Never Occas Regul
 Freq   5.4  92.1   9.3   8.3
 None   1.1  19.2   1.9   1.7
 Some   4.6  78.5   7.9   7.1
```

Python

```
distexer_colarr = distexer.values.reshape(3,1)
distsmoke_rowarr = distsmoke.values.reshape(1,4)
jointdist = distexer_colarr.dot(distsmoke_rowarr)
jointdist=pd.DataFrame(jointdist, index=distexer.index, columns=distsmoke.
          index).round(3)
jointdist
```

```
      Never Occas Regul Heavy
Freq 0.389 0.039 0.035 0.023
Some 0.331 0.033 0.030 0.019
None 0.081 0.008 0.007 0.005
```

```
n = len(survey)
E = n * jointdist
E.round(1)
```

```
      Never Occas Regul Heavy
Freq  92.2   9.2   8.3   5.5
Some  78.4   7.8   7.1   4.5
None  19.2   1.9   1.7   1.2
```

Now let us generate a sample of data from the two independent distributions:

R

```
o1 = sample(x = c("Freq", "None","Some"), size = n, replace = T, prob = distexer)
o2 = sample(x = c("Heavy", "Never", "Occas","Regul"), size = n, replace = T,
    prob = distsmoke)
O = table(o1,o2)
O
```

```
         o2
o1      Heavy Never Occas Regul
   Freq     3    98     6     8
   None     0    20     2     3
   Some     7    65    10    15
```

Python

```
o1 = np.random.choice(['Freq', 'None','Some'], size = n, replace = True, p = distexer)
o2 = np.random.choice(['Never','Occas','Regul','Heavy'], size=n, replace=True,
    p=distsmoke)
O = pd.crosstab(o1, o2)
O
```

```
      Heavy Never Occas Regul
Freq      3    94     7     7
None      6    70     8    10
Some      0    28     3     1
```

How close are the observed and expected values? A commonly used metric called the *chi-square statistic* is defined as:

$$\sum \frac{(O-E)^2}{E}$$

The more similar the actual data and expected data will result in a lower chi-square value. Identical observed and expected values will yield a chi-square equal to 0. We can easily calculate this:

R

```
sum(((O-E)^2)/E)
```

```
[1] 17.76924
```

Python

```
O = O.reindex(['Never', 'Occas', 'Regul', 'Heavy'], axis = 1)
np.sum((O.values - E.values)**2 / E.values)
```

```
10.59631452129426
```

Thus, a chi-square value of 17.76 in this example is consistent with the assumption of independence of the two factor variables.

With this, we are now ready to conduct the formal test:

Step 1: State the null hypothesis.

Smoke and **Exer** are independent.

Step 2: Describe the data generation process and the population.

Since they are independent, we can describe them separately as:

Table 8.1 Probabilities of exercising and smoking

Exer

Freq	None	Some
0.4852321	0.1012658	0.4135021

Smoke

Heavy	Never	Occas	Regul
0.04661017	0.80084746	0.08050847	0.07203390

Step 3: Create a sampling distribution:

R

```
sampsize = nrow(survey)
f1 = function(){
  o1 = sample(x = c("Freq", "None","Some"), size = sampsize, replace = T,
      prob = distexer)
  o2 = sample(x = c("Heavy", "Never", "Occas","Regul"), size = sampsize,
      replace = T, prob = distsmoke)
  O = table(o1,o2)
  chi = sum(((O-E)^2)/E)
```

```
  return(chi)
}
sampdist = replicate(10000,f1())
```

Python

```
sampsize = len(survey)
def f1():
    o1 = np.random.choice(['Freq', 'None','Some'], size = sampsize,
        replace = True, p = distexer)
     o2 = np.random.choice(['Never', 'Occas','Regul', 'Heavy'], size = sampsize,
        replace = True, p = distsmoke)
    O = pd.crosstab(o1, o2)
    O = O.reindex(['Never', 'Occas', 'Regul', 'Heavy'], axis = 1)
    return(np.sum((O.values - E.values)**2 / E.values))
sampdist = [f1() for _ in range(10000)]
```

Step 4: Get the actual sample, compute the statistic and the p-value. Notice that we use the right-tail test since only points in the tail are not supportive of the null hypothesis:

R

```
O = table(survey$Exer,survey$Smoke)
tstat = sum(((O-E)^2)/E)
p_rtail(sampdist,tstat)
```

```
[1] 0.9124
```

Python

```
tstat = np.sum(((O.values - E.values)**2 /
        E.values))
p_rtail(sampdist,tstat)
```

```
0.5319
```

Thus, we cannot reject the null hypothesis that **Smoke** and **Exer** are independent. The test we just conducted is called the chi-square test. The inbuilt function to conduct the chi-square test is the following:

R

```
chisq.test(x = survey$Exer, y = survey$Smoke)

Pearson's Chi-squared test
data:  survey$Exer and survey$Smoke
X-squared = 5.4885, df = 6, p-value = 0.4828
```

Python

```
chi2, p, df, expected = chi2_contingency(O.values)
print("chi2: {}, p: {}, df: {}".format(chi2, p, df))

chi2: 6.779046167177817, p: 0.3417652182907054, df: 6
```

The p-values are different because the inbuilt function assumes that the sampling distribution is a chi-square distribution. We made no such assumption and created the sampling distribution from the first principles.

One advantage of designing our own testing strategy is that we can customize it. Suppose we are only interested in people who smoke heavily and exercise very frequently. Are these two events independent? If you recall the discussion we had in Chapter 6, we used a concept called *lift* to evaluate independence. Let us use that concept to design a new test.

Step 1: State the null hypothesis.

Heavy smoking and frequent exercising are independent.

Step 2: Describe the data generation process and the population.

Since they are independent, we can describe them separately as:

$P(Exer\ Freq) = 0.4852321$

$P(Smoke\ Heavy) = 0.04661017$

The metric we will use is *lift*, which is the ratio of observed and expected values.

Step 3: Create a sampling distribution:

R

```
set.seed(87654321)
sampsize = nrow(survey)
f1 = function(){
  o1 = sample(x = c("Freq", "None","Some"), size = sampsize, replace = T,
     prob = distexer)
  o2 = sample(x = c("Heavy", "Never", "Occas","Regul"), size = sampsize,
     replace = T, prob = distsmoke)
  O = table(o1,o2)
  lift = O[1,1]/E[1,1]
  return(lift)
}
sampdist = replicate(10000,f1())
```

Python

```
def f1():
  o1 = np.random.choice(['Freq', 'None','Some'], size = sampsize,
     replace = True,      p = distexer)
```

```
o2 = np.random.choice(['Heavy', 'Never', 'Occas','Regul'], size = sampsize,
    replace = True, p = distsmoke)
O = pd.crosstab(o1, o2)
O = O.reindex(['Never', 'Occas', 'Regul', 'Heavy'], axis = 1)
return(O.values[1,1]/E.values[1,1])
sampdist = [f1() for _ in range(10000)]
```

Step 4: Get the actual sample and compute the statistic and the p-value:

R

```
O = table(survey$Exer,survey$Smoke)
tstat = O[1,1]/E[1,1]
tstat
p_rtail(sampdist,tstat)
```

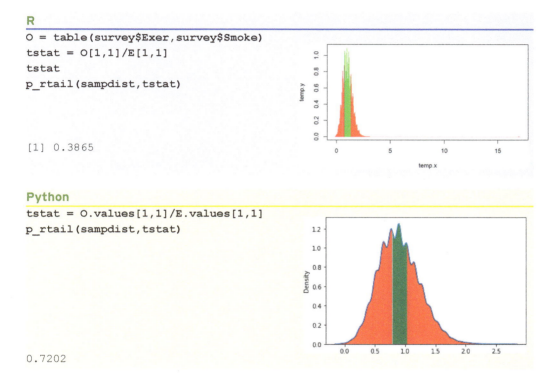

```
[1] 0.3865
```

Python

```
tstat = O.values[1,1]/E.values[1,1]
p_rtail(sampdist,tstat)
```

```
0.7202
```

As the p-value indicates, we cannot reject the hypothesis, and thus someone smoking heavily is unrelated to someone exercising frequently based on the sample data that we have.

Use Case: Statistical Testing to Detect Cyber Attacks

As we have seen, statistical testing separates the exceptions from the usual. We need to consider the right data series to be able to see exceptions, and as we have seen above, we also need to consider the most appropriate distributions to judge is an observation is 'usual'. Cyber-attacks are a rising business risk, and of critical importance to information centric businesses. Statistical testing can be employed to identify anomalies, exceptions from the usual, that can indicate failures, or cyber risks in an industrial or technical setting. The Internet of Things (IoT) poses a large business risk in this context, and hacks have resulted in damaging distributed denial of service attacks (DDOS). The Schneider-Electric dataset shows records of temperature sensor readings, relevant to

IoT devices. Readings outside of the usual indicate a problem. The same principles could apply to monitoring employee activities in the WFH (Work from home) era, or monitoring team members for excellent or weak productivity: we are looking for exceptions.

We will explore two questions: what are the bounds of normal operation of the Schneider sensors (i.e., confidence intervals)? What is the probability that a recent high sensor reading represents failure or cyber-attack (i.e., statistical testing)?

To spot exceptions, outliers, we can plot a frequency distribution of sensor readings taken over several months, using 50 bins and a column chart. By eye, we can see that the distribution is approximately normal, but with several outliers:

R

```
df = read_excel("sensor-fault-detection.xlsx")
hist(df$Value,breaks = 50,
     main = "Schneider-Electric: Distribution of Sensor Readings, Monitoring
             for Faults and Cyber Attacks", xlab="Value")
```

Python

```
plt.figure(figsize=(10,7))
plt.title('Schneider-Electric: Distribution of Sensor Readings, Monitoring
for Faults and Cyber Attacks')
plt.hist(df['Value'], bins = 50)
```

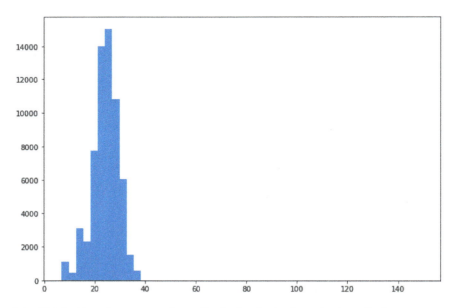

Figure 8.1 Distribution of sensor readings. Monitoring for faults and cyber attacks

To take a clearer look at the outliers we can use a box plot:

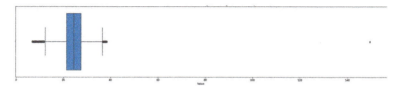

Figure 8.2 Boxplot of distribution of sensor readings

If we remove the extreme outlier to the right, we get a better perspective on the remainder of the distribution, which has multiple outliers to the left and right:

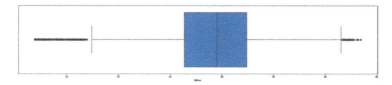

Figure 8.3 Refined boxplot of distribution of sensor readings

First, to determine the limits of normal operation – confidence intervals – we calculate at our desired confidence level, as discussed in Chapter 7. This will allow us to identify outliers as they occur. Alternatively, we may want to investigate an odd sensor reading, for example with a value of 13, to determine if it was an anomaly.

Our null hypothesis: the sensor reading is a typical reading given operation variation; the alternative hypothesis: the sensor reading is not a normal operating reading (an anomaly) and may represent a failure or cyber-attack.

Using our **p_2tail** function, we can test whether the sensor reading of 13 is an anomaly. We use the distribution of our sensor readings to calculate a probability value, p-value, indicating the probability that 13 is a normal operating reading.

R

```
p_2tail(df$Value,13)
```

Python

```
p_2tail(df['Value'],13)
```

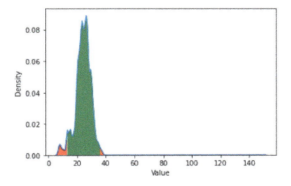

```
Out[57]:  0.0419294575995146
```

In practice, the sensor reading of 13 has a p-value of 0.0419, which tells us that, based on the assumptions of our test, there is only a 4.19% probability the null hypothesis should be not rejected. If we decided to have a 5% significance level, we would reject the null hypothesis, meaning that we would conclude that the sensor reading was not a normal operating reading and may represent a failure or cyber-attack.

Summary

In this chapter, we covered several tests that are frequently used in practice. We designed and executed each test from the first principles. In designing these tests, the key challenges are to describe the population to match the null hypothesis, and then to design the appropriate metric to create the sampling distribution. We also conducted a few tests for which there is no built-in option available. If you understand the core principles of statistical testing, you should be able to design and execute any test that you may need. We will explore one such setting in the next chapter.

Exercises

To complete the activity below, you will need to visit the companion website to the book and download the relevant dataset: https://study.sagepub.com/gopal

Read the file Health.csv.

1   There is a variable called **faminc**, which indicates the income of the family. Conduct a test for the median value of 1.75.
2   There is a variable called **age**. Assuming this follows an exponential distribution, test the hypothesis that the mean value of age is 7.5.
3   There are two variables named **males** and **exclhlth**. The first one refers to gender and the second to the health condition. Both variables have only two values 0 or 1. Conduct (a chi-square) test to see if these two variables are related. Note that the null hypothesis is that there is no relationship between the two.

Read the file UsedCars2017.csv. The file contains the following information:

Price: Selling price when the vehicle was sold at a dealership (in dollars).

Age: Year 2016 minus the model's year (i.e., a 2012 model would be four years old).

Mileage: Approximate number of miles (in thousands) on the vehicle's odometer at the time of the sale.

MPG: Average fuel economy of the vehicle measured in miles per gallon.

KBB Price: Kelly Blue Book valuation of the vehicle.

CR Reliability Score: Consumer Reports' car reliability score determined as the percentage of survey respondents who reported problems with vehicles of the same model as the sold vehicle.

4   Develop a test to evaluate the hypothesis that the population mean **Price** is the same as the population median **Price**. Hint: Assume a normal distribution for the population.

5   Develop a test to evaluate the hypothesis that the population mean **Price** is 1.4 times the population standard deviation of **Price**. Hint: Assume a normal distribution for the population with standard deviation to be the same as the sample and the mean is 1.4 times the sample standard deviation.

6   Develop a test to evaluate the hypothesis that the population correlation between **Age** and **Mileage** is 0.9.

9

NONPARAMETRIC TESTS

Chapter Contents

The tests we have conducted so far are called *parametric tests*. Parametric tests, especially for tests involving numeric data, invoke specific distributions to describe the population and the data generation process. *Nonparametric statistical tests*, however, rely on no or few assumptions about the population distribution from which the sample was drawn. These tests are also suitable to be used when the population sample size is too small or the data are ordinal or nominal. These characteristics make nonparametric tests an important complement to parametric tests and often the best choice in practical settings where the available presents the aforementioned attributes.

The following can be used as a rule of thumb.

When to use Parametric Versus Nonparametric Tests?

Table 9.1 Parametric versus nonparametric tests

	Parametric tests	Nonparametric tests
Assumptions about population?	Many assumptions made	Few assumptions
Distribution?	Specific distribution assumed (e.g., normal, t-distribution, etc.)	Arbitrary distribution
Central tendency?	Mean value	Median value
Prior knowledge of the population needed?	Yes	No

How are nonparametric tests carried out? Remember that we need a sampling distribution to conduct a statistical test. Creating a sampling distribution requires us to specify the population distribution. Therefore, if we cannot specify a population distribution, how can we create the sampling distribution and conduct the test? In certain situations, if we are creative, we can. Let us consider an example.

MEDIAN TEST

In a previous chapter, we conducted a test where the null hypothesis was that the median GMAT score was 500. Let us replicate that code here for a median score of 510.

Step 1: State the null hypothesis.

Population median is 510.

Step 2: Describe the data generation process and the population.

Since the GMAT scores are numerical, we will assume they follow a normal distribution, $N(\mu,\sigma)$. Since a normal distribution is symmetric about its mean, the median value is the same as the mean value. So, $\mu = 510$, and σ will be taken from the sample.

Step 3: Create a sampling distribution.

The sampling distribution is created with the following code:

R

```
set.seed(87654321)
sampsize = nrow(admission)
f1 = function(){
  s1 = rnorm(sampsize, mean = 510, sd = sd(admission$GMAT))
  return(median(s1))
}
sampdist = replicate(10000, f1())
```

Python

```
np.random.seed(87654321)
sampsize = len(admission)
def f1():
    s1 = np.random.normal(size=sampsize, loc = 510, scale = admission.
        std()['GMAT'])
    return np.median(s1)
sampdist = [f1() for _ in range(10000)]
```

Step 4: Get the actual sample and compute the statistic. Call the function we created in the last chapter to plot and compute the p-value:

R

```
tstat = median(admission$GMAT)
p_2tail(sampdist,tstat)
```

[1] 0.0121

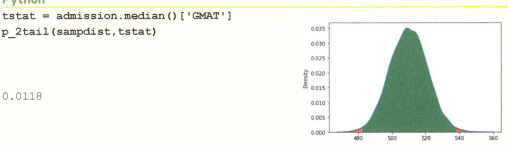

Python

```
tstat = admission.median()['GMAT']
p_2tail(sampdist,tstat)
```

0.0118

The p-value is below 0.05, and thus we reject the null hypothesis that the median value of the GMAT score in the population is 510.

Can we conduct this test without having to assume that the population distribution for GMAT scores is normal?

We know that, regardless of what the population distribution is, by definition, half of the values should lie below the median and half above. This is true for a normal distribution as well as for any other distribution. We will use this basic logic to design our test:

Table 9.2 Parametric versus nonparametric populations

Parametric population description	Nonparametric population description
Normal distribution	Population consists of positives (1) which are above the median and negatives (0) which are below the median with equal probabilities

Now we can conduct the nonparametric test for median.

Step 1: State the null hypothesis.

The population median is 510.

Step 2: Describe the data generation process and the population.

Half the values of the population will be below 510 and the other half above.

Step 3: Create a sampling distribution.

The sampling distribution is created with the following code:

R

```
set.seed(87654321)
sampsize = nrow(admission)
f1 = function(){
  s1 = sample(x = c(0,1), size = sampsize, replace = T, prob = c(.5,.5))
  return(sum(s1)/sampsize)
}
sampdist = replicate(10000, f1())
```

Python

```
np.random.seed(87654321)
sampsize = len(admission)
def f1():
    s1 = np.random.choice([0,1], size=sampsize, replace = True, p = [.5,.5])
    return (sum(s1)/sampsize)
sampdist = [f1() for _ in range(10000)]
```

Step 4: Get the actual sample and compute the statistic. Call the function we created in the last chapter to plot and compute the p-value:

R

```
tstat = length(admission$GMAT
        [admission$GMAT>510])/(sampsize)
p_2tail(sampdist,tstat)
```

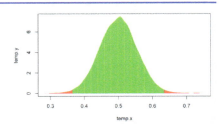

[1] 0.0108

Python

```
tstat = len(admission.loc[admission
        ['GMAT']>510])/sampsize
p_2tail(sampdist, tstat)
```

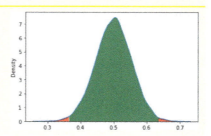

`0.012`

Since the p-value is below 0.05, we reject the null hypothesis. Conducting this test did not require us to specify the population distribution for the GMAT scores!

The main advantage of nonparametric testing is that we make no or few assumptions about the underlying population distribution. The problem is that we may not be able to design a nonparametric version for every test we want to conduct. Another problem with nonparametric testing is that they are less powerful, in the sense that we do not use all the information in the sample. For example, when we coded everything above 510 as 1 and everything below as 0, some useful information was lost.

If we are willing to assume that the population distribution is symmetric, then we can develop a *signed rank test* (called *Wilcoxon signed rank test*) which uses more of the information in the sample. Consider the example below with 10 values for the variable **X** and let us hypothesize that the population median value is 50.

Table 9.3   GMAT scores

X	48	67	56	14	77	41	66	95	52	87
Sign	0	1	1	0	1	0	1	1	1	1
Absolute deviation	2	17	6	36	27	9	16	45	2	37
Rank	1	6	3	8	7	4	5	10	2	9
Positive ranks		6	3		7		5	10	2	9
Negative ranks	1			8		4				

As in the previous example, we code values below the hypothesized median as 0 and the rest as 1. This is noted as a sign (positive/negative or 0/1). In addition to the *sign*, we also do the following.

1   Compute the absolute deviation from the hypothesized median.
2   Rank the observations based on these absolute deviations.
3   Sum of the ranks with positive signs constitutes the test statistic (6+3+7+5+10+2+9).
4   To create a synthetic sample from the population, create the sequence from 1 to 10 (i.e., as large as the sample size). For each value in the sequence, assign a 0 or 1 with equal probability. Add up the numbers with 1 to compute the metric. Repeat this to create the sampling distribution.

With this logic, we can now construct the test.

Step 1: State the null hypothesis.

The population median is 510.

Step 2: Describe the data generation process and the population.

Half the values of the population will be below 510 and the other half above. The population distribution is assumed to be symmetric.

Step 3: Create a sampling distribution.

The sampling distribution is created with the following code:

R

```
set.seed(87654321)
sampsize = nrow(admission)
f1 = function(){
  s1 = sample(x = c(0,1), size = sampsize,
      replace = T, prob = c(.5,.5))
  r1 = seq(1:sampsize)
  x = sum(r1[s1==1])
  return(x)
}
sampdist = replicate(10000, f1())
plot(density(sampdist))
```

density.default(x = sampdist)

N = 10000   Bandwidth = 32.39

Python

```
np.random.seed(87654321)
sampsize = len(admission)
def f1():
    s1 = np.random.choice([0,1], size = sampsize,
        replace = True, p= [.5,.5])
    r1 = np.linspace(1, sampsize, sampsize)
    x = sum(r1[s1==1])
    return x
sampdist = [f1() for _ in range(10000)]
sns.kdeplot(sampdist)
plt.show()
```

Step 4: Get the actual sample and compute the statistic. Call the function we created in the last chapter to plot and compute the p-value:

R

```
sign_gmat = ifelse(admission$GMAT<510,0,1)
dev_gmat = abs(admission$GMAT-510)
df = data.frame(sign_gmat,dev_gmat)
df = df[order(df$dev_gmat),]
```

```
df$rank_gmat = seq(1:sampsize)
tstat = sum(df[df$sign_gmat == 1,]$rank_gmat)
p_2tail(sampdist,tstat)
print(tstat)
```

```
[1] 0.0064
[1] 1223
```

Python

```
sign_gmat = np.where(admission
          ['GMAT']<510, 0, 1)
dev_gmat = np.absolute(admission
          ['GMAT']-510)
df = pd.DataFrame({'sign_gmat':sign_gmat, 'dev_gmat':dev_gmat})
df.sort_values('dev_gmat', inplace = True)
df['rank_gmat'] = np.arange(1, len(df)+1)
tstat = sum(df.loc[df['sign_gmat'] == 1]['rank_gmat'])
p_2tail(sampdist, tstat)
```

```
0.0082
```

```
print(tstat)
1225
```

Since the p-value is smaller than 0.05, we reject the null hypothesis, as before. The test statistic value is 1223. The following demonstrates the inbuilt function to conduct the test. Notice that the test statistic value is very close to the one that we created above:

R

```
wilcox.test(x = admission$GMAT,mu = 510)
```

```
Wilcoxon signed rank test with continuity correction

data:  admission$GMAT
V = 1224.5, p-value = 0.008288
alternative hypothesis: true location is not equal to 510
```

Python

```
from scipy.stats import Wilcoxon
w, p = Wilcoxon(admission['Gmat'])
p
```

```
1.1674527799291764e-15
```

Note that the first test we conducted made no assumptions about the distribution whereas the second test assumed that its symmetry (though we did not specify any particular symmetric distribution).

TWO-SAMPLE TEST

Suppose we have the following data on reading scores of year-4 students (8–9 years old). The treatment group has been subjected to a special reading program. We want to test whether the reading program is effective in improving the reading scores of the students:

Table 9.4 Reading scores

Group	Score
Treatment	24
Treatment	61
Treatment	59
Treatment	46
Treatment	43
Treatment	44
Treatment	52
Treatment	43
Treatment	58
Treatment	67
Treatment	62
Treatment	57
Treatment	71
Treatment	49
Treatment	54
Treatment	43
Treatment	53
Treatment	57
Treatment	49
Treatment	56
Treatment	33
Control	42
Control	33
Control	46
Control	37
Control	43
Control	41

Control	10
Control	42
Control	55
Control	19
Control	17
Control	55
Control	26
Control	54
Control	60
Control	28
Control	62
Control	20
Control	53
Control	48
Control	37
Control	85
Control	42

The null hypothesis is that the treatment is not effective. In other words, there is no difference in the average scores between the two groups. We do not want to assume that the scores follow any particular distribution. How can we conduct this test?

Before we address this, let us take a look at the following code that randomly shuffles entries in a vector. Each time we execute the code, it will generate a new sequence of the vector's elements:

R

```r
v = c(1,2,3,4,5)
sample(v)
```

```
## [1] 4 3 2 5 1
```

Python

```python
v = (1, 2, 3, 4, 5)
np.random.choice(v, size=len(v))
```

```
array([4, 3, 1, 4, 1])
```

The logic that we will use to design the test is the following.

If our null hypothesis is that the treatment has no effect, then it implies that there is no difference between the treatment and the control group. Thus, we can combine all the values into one pool, shuffle them, and randomly reassign them into two groups. The difference between the averages of each group after each shuffle is only due to sampling error, and not because there is any real and substantive difference between them.

Let us read and take a look at the data:

R

```
twosample = read.csv("twosample.csv")
table(twosample$group)


  Control Treatment
       23        21
```

Python

```
twosample = pd.read_csv('../data/twosample.csv')
twosample.groupby('group').count()


            score
group
Control       23
Treatment     21
```

Step 1: State the null hypothesis.

There is no difference in the mean of the treatment and control groups.

Step 2: Describe the data generation process and the population.

Since there is no difference between the two groups, we can pool them all into one large group.

Step 3: Create a sampling distribution.

The sampling distribution is created with the following code:

R

```
set.seed(87654321)
f1 = function(){
  pool = twosample$score
  s1 = sample(pool)
  control1 = s1[1:23]
  treatment1 = s1[24:44]
  return(abs(mean(treatment1)-mean(control1)))
}
sampdist = replicate(10000, f1())
plot(density(sampdist))
```

density.default(x = sampdist)

N = 10000   Bandwidth = 0.3912

Python

```
np.random.seed(87654321)
def f1():
```

```
    pool = twosample['score']
    s1 = np.random.choice(pool, size = len(pool))
    control1 = s1[:23]
    treatment1 = s1[23:]
    return abs(treatment1.mean()-control1.mean())
sampdist = [f1() for _ in range(10000)]
sns.kdeplot(sampdist)
plt.show()
```

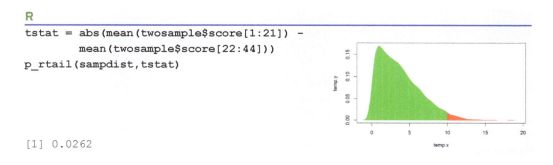

Step 4: Get the actual sample and compute the statistic and the p-value:

R

```
tstat = abs(mean(twosample$score[1:21]) -
        mean(twosample$score[22:44]))
p_rtail(sampdist,tstat)
```

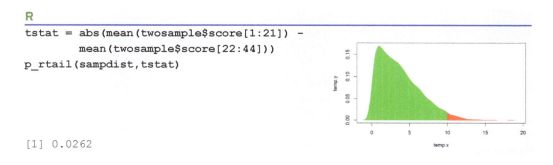

```
[1] 0.0262
```

Python

```
tstat = abs(twosample['score'][:21].mean() -
        twosample['score'][21:].mean())
p_rtail(sampdist, tstat)
```

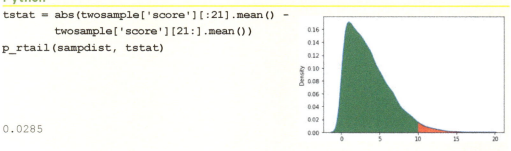

```
0.0285
```

Since the p-value is below 0.05, we reject the null hypothesis that there is no difference between the treatment and control groups. Remember that we made no assumption about the distribution of the student scores. The same basic approach can be used to evaluate if the median or the 75th percentile scores improve with the special reading program.

CORRELATION TEST

Now let us conduct a nonparametric test for the correlation between two numeric variables without assuming any underlying population distribution for either of them.

The basic logic is similar to the two-sample test. Consider the data from the file immer.csv:

Table 9.5 Data from immer.csv

Loc	Var	Y1	Y2
UF	M	81.0	80.7
UF	S	105.4	82.3
UF	V	119.7	80.4
UF	T	109.7	87.2
UF	P	98.3	84.2
W	M	146.6	100.4
W	S	142.0	115.5
W	V	150.7	112.2
W	T	191.5	147.7
W	P	145.7	108.1

Let us suppose that the correlation between **Y1** and **Y2** is positive. What does that mean? When the value of **Y1** is large, then the corresponding value of **Y2** also tends to be large. Similarly, when the value of **Y1** is small, then the corresponding value of **Y2** also tends to be small. The opposite trends happen when the correlation between the two is negative. If there is no correlation between the two variables, then high values in one are not associated with neither high nor low values. In essence, when there is no correlation, we can view it as values in the two being randomly shuffled.

Step 1: State the null hypothesis.

There is no correlation between Y1 and Y2.

Step 2: Describe the data generation process and the population.

Since there is no correlation, we can shuffle the vectors and find their correlation to create a sampling distribution.

Step 3: Create a sampling distribution.

The sampling distribution is created with the following code:

R

```
set.seed(87654321)
f1 = function(){
  s1 = sample(immer$Y1)
  s2 = sample(immer$Y1)
  return(cor(x = s1,y = s2))
}
sampdist = replicate(10000, f1())
plot(density(sampdist))
```

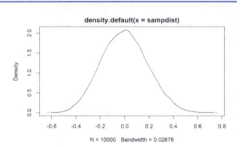

Python

```
from scipy.stats.stats import pearsonr

np.random.seed(87654321)
def f1():
    s1 = pd.DataFrame([immer['Y1'].
        sample(n=len(immer))]).T
    s2 = pd.DataFrame([immer['Y1'].
        sample(n=len(immer))]).T
    return (pearsonr(s1['Y1'], s2['Y1'])[0])
sampdist = [f1() for _ in range(10000)]
sns.kdeplot(sampdist)
plt.show()
```

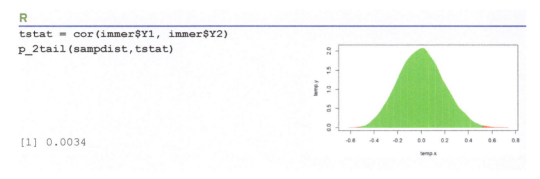

Step 4: Get the actual sample and compute the statistic and the p-value:

R

```
tstat = cor(immer$Y1, immer$Y2)
p_2tail(sampdist,tstat)
```

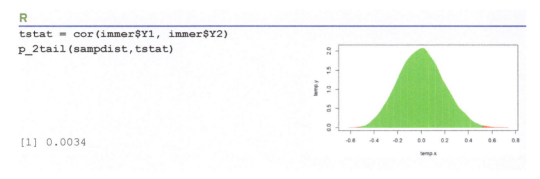

```
[1] 0.0034
```

Python

```
tstat = pearsonr(immer['Y1'], immer['Y2'])[0]
p_2tail(sampdist, tstat)
```

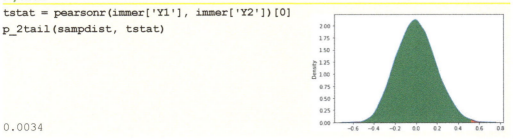

```
0.0034
```

Given the very small p-value, we can reject the null hypothesis of no correlation between the two variables. Additionally, we did not have to make any assumptions about the population distribution of the two variables.

BOOTSTRAPPING

Bootstrapping is a very popular nonparametric technique to define population distributions. Let us first take a look at the Merriam-Webster dictionary definition of the term. Bootstrap is defined as 'to promote or develop by initiative and effort with little or no assistance'. Let us see how this works. Suppose we have the following sample of data:

Observed number of complaints = (4,3,5,13,7,10,9,9,3,6,4,3,7,10,7,6,7,8,7,7)

How do we describe the population that generated this data?

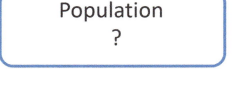

Figure 9.1 Bootstrapping - sample

The bootstrapping approach works as follows:

1   Since the sample came from the population, the sample is clearly part of the population, as shown in the Figure 9.2:

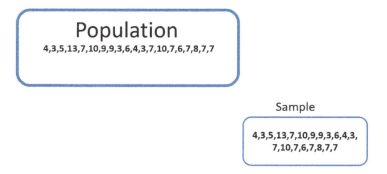

Figure 9.2 Bootstrapping - population

2   Bootstrapping assumes that the data we have are a reasonable representation of the population from which they came and that other data from the population that we did not collect will in fact look like the data we do have. If we do this repeatedly, our population will begin to look like the Figure 9.3:

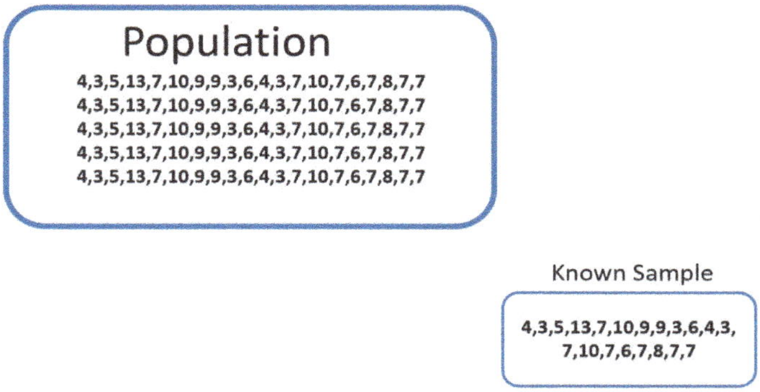

Figure 9.3 Bootstrapping - final population

That's it! This is how we describe the population using the bootstrapping approach.

The notion is that, in the population, we will encounter other instances with the same data values as we observed in the sample. Given this, we can create the sampling distribution by 'taking samples from the one sample we have'. In other words, we sample from the sample with replacement. Once we have the bootstrap sampling distribution, we can use it to create confidence intervals and for hypothesis testing as well.

Let us create the bootstrap sampling distribution and calculate the 95% confidence interval for the variable **Y1** in the immer.csv file:

R

```
bootsampdist = replicate(10000, mean(sample(immer$Y1, replace = T)))

q2 = quantile(bootsampdist, c(.05/2,1-(.05/2)))
plot(density(bootsampdist))
abline(v = q2, col = "red")
paste("95% Confidence interval =
    [", round(q2,2)[1],", ",round(q2,2)[2],"]")
```

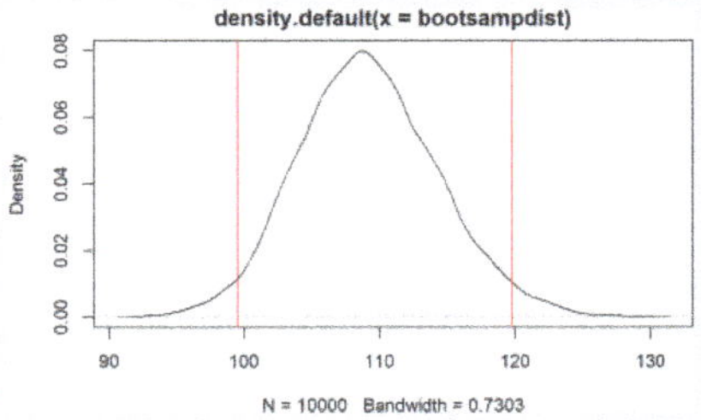

```
[1] "95% Confidence interval = [ 99.5 ,  119.73 ]"
```

Python

```
bootsampdist = [immer['Y1'].sample(n=len(immer), replace=True). mean() for _
                in range(10000)]

q2 = np.quantile(bootsampdist,
      (.05/2, 1-(.05/2)))
sns.kdeplot(bootsampdist)
plt.vlines(x = q2, ymin = 0, ymax = 0.08, color = 'r')
print("95% Confidence interval = [", np.round
      (q2,2)[0], ", ", np.round(q2,2) [1], "]")
```

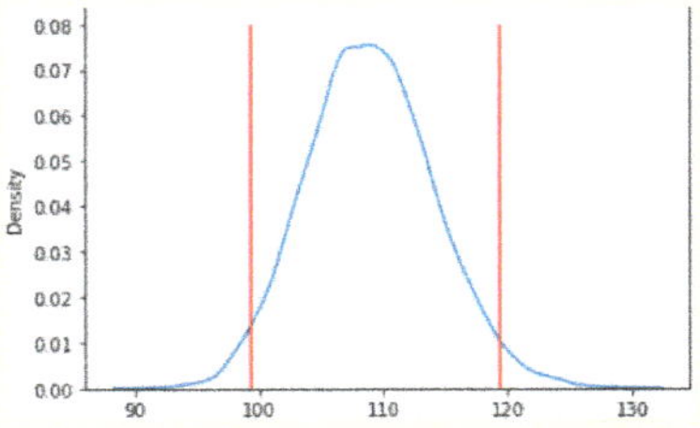

```
95% Confidence interval = [ 99.34 ,  119.4 ]
```

With the confidence interval defined, a null hypothesis which states that the population value is outside of the interval can be rejected.

SYNTHETIC DATA AND GANS

An interesting trend in machine learning is the development of techniques to create *synthetic data*. The idea of synthetic datasets is to develop a process to extract information from an actual dataset and re-express it as artificial or synthetic data. The typical use of this approach is for datasets that contain confidential information which precludes wide sharing of the data for public consumption. Synthetic data derived from the original data retains the characteristics of the original data and at the same time prevents the release of sensitive information. Thus, synthetic data are a powerful tool when the required data are limited or there are concerns to safely share it with the concerned parties. A number of techniques have been developed for the creation of synthetic data and this continues to be an active area of research (see Raghunathan, Trivellore E., 'Synthetic data', *Annual Review of Statistics and Its Application*, 2021, 8: 129–40).

While the primary motivation for synthetic data is to share data while preserving confidential data, it can also be employed as a form of bootstrapping to describe and generate samples from the population. Let us briefly explore this using the *synthpop* package (see www.synthpop.org.uk/ for further information about the package).

R

```
head(admission)
```

1	2.96	596	admit
2	3.14	473	admit
3	3.22	482	admit
4	3.29	527	admit
5	3.69	505	admit
6	3.46	693	admit

```
library(synthpop)
s1 = syn(admission)
head(s1$syn)
```

1	3.47	609	admit
2	2.57	509	notadmit
3	2.90	483	border
4	3.26	467	admit
5	2.51	528	notadmit
6	3.03	596	border

Python

```
admission.head()
```

	GPA	GMAT	De
0	2.96	596	admit
1	3.14	473	admit
2	3.22	482	admit

```
3      3.29      527       admit
4      3.69      505       admit
```

```
from synthpop import Synthpop
spop = Synthpop()
dtypes = {"GPA":'float', "GMAT":'int', 'De':'category'}
spop.fit(admission, dtypes)
s1 = spop.generate(len(admission))
s1.head()
         GPA     GMAT         De
0       2.85      483     border
1       3.60      552      admit
2       2.86      494     border
3       3.69      521      admit
4       3.38      431      admit
```

We can use the above code to create bootstrapped samples to generate confidence intervals and test hypotheses.

Generative adversarial networks (GANs) are an exciting recent innovation in machine learning (see https://developers.google.com/machine-learning/gan). GANs are termed generative models in that they create new synthetic data that resemble the original data. In addition to structured numeric and textual data, GANs have been used to create synthetic images, audio, and videos. GANs have two key components – *Generator*, which aims to generate new instances of the data, and a *Discriminator*, which learns to distinguish true data from that created by the generator. The objective of the generator is to fool the discriminator and the objective of the discriminator is to avoid getting fooled. The end result is a synthetic dataset that 'looks and feels' like the original data.

The basic idea and the principle behind statistical testing are logical and straightforward. With R and Python as tools, we are able to design and execute any statistical test. No more treating statistical testing as a black box, or magic, or a dark art!

Use case: Fast Food Marketing Campaign – Nonparametric Tests

If we are not sure about the distribution of our population, and we do not want to make many assumptions about it, we can use nonparametric tests. This could be sensible in those cases where we just do not know enough about the population, perhaps because our data come from a new process, or we have limited data to judge matters.

One such case is a fast-food chain which launches a new product and has three possible ways of promoting it. Over 500 outlet locations are selected to trial the product promotions, and the trial is conducted over several weeks. However, we cannot wait until the end of the trial to judge the outcome, and the senior management need regular updates on progress. If there is a stand-out 'winner', why wait until the end of the trial to roll it out to other outlets?

We will begin with the null hypothesis that all the Promotions generate equal median sales (**SalesinThousands**).

Which Promotion? A Rough Take from a Small Dataset

We have a problem though due to the store level management taking time to disaggregate the sales numbers for the different promotions. At the end of week 1, only 6 of our stores have reported:

R

```
df = read_excel("WA_Marketing-Campaign.xlsx")
store_locs = c(920, 217, 2, 3, 302, 203)
df_week1 = df[df$week==1 & df$LocationID %in% store_locs,]
df_week1
```

Python

```
# These 5 stores, LocationID, are the first to report in week 1.
store_locs = [920, 217, 2, 3, 302, 203]
df_promos_wk1 = df[(df['week'] == 1) & (df['LocationID'].isin(store_locs))]

df_promos_wk1
```

	MarketSize	LocationID	Age of Store	Promotion	Week	SalesInThousands
MarketID						
1	Medium	2	5	2	1	27.81
1	Medium	3	12	1	1	44.54
3	Large	203	12	3	1	89.70
3	Large	217	5	3	1	91.61
4	Small	302	7	3	1	51.47
10	Large	920	14	2	1	50.20

This is an imbalanced and small sample, with three stores reporting Promotion 3, and only one reporting Promotion 1. We still need to get an idea of Promotion performance. Are **SalesinThousands** of Promotion 3 significantly better or worse than that of Promotion 1? We do not have distribution and other knowledge (yet), but we need to answer the question.

A frequency distribution with so few samples is not that insightful, but it shows the challenge we face to judge the different promotions:

R

```
hist(df_week1$SalesInThousands,breaks=4,
     main="Fast Food Promotion: frequency distribution")
```

Python

```
plt.figure(figsize = (10,7))
plt.title('Fast Food Promotion: frequency distribution')
plt.hist(df_promos_wk1['SalesInThousands'], bins = 5)
```

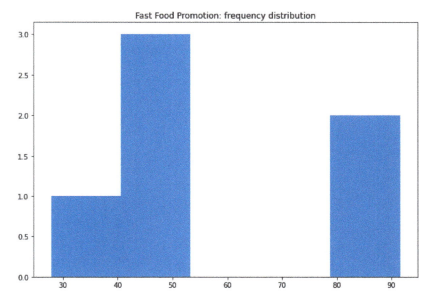

Figure 9.4 Frequency distribution of fast-food promotion

Using bootstrapping, we can construct a distribution and then compare the **SalesInThousands** numbers we have so far, and get a handle on the relative strength of the Promotions.

We create `bootsampdist`, as we did earlier in the chapter, repeatedly sampling from the data we have. We then overlay 95% confidence intervals:

R

```
bootsampdist = replicate(10000, mean(sample(df_week1$SalesInThousands,
            replace = T)))
q2 = quantile(bootsampdist, c(.05/2,1-(.05/2)))
plot(density(bootsampdist))
abline(v = q2, col = "red")
paste("95% Confidence interval = [", round(q2,2)[1],", ",round(q2,2)[2],"]")
```

Python

```
bootsampdist = [df_promos_wk1['SalesInThousands'].sample(n = 10000,
replace = True).mean() for _ in range(10000)]
q2 = np.quantile(bootsampdist, (.05/2, 1-(.05/2)))

plt.figure(figsize = (10,7))
plt.title('Fast Food Promotion: Partial Week 1 SalesInThousands
Distribution From Boot Strapping')
sns.kdeplot(bootsampdist)
plt.vlines(x = q2, ymin = 0, ymax = 1.7, color = 'r')

print("95% Confidence interval = [", np.round(q2,2)[0], ", ",
np.round(q2,2)[1], "]")
```

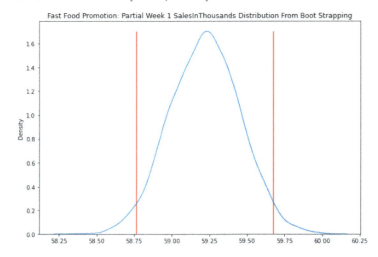

We now compare the median **SalesInThousands** values for each Promotion in turn:

R

```
aggregate(df_week1$SalesInThousands,list(df_week1$Promotion),median)
```

Python

```
# Get median values for each Promotion so far...
df_promos_wk1_grouped = df_promos_wk1.groupby(by="Promotion").median()
df_promos_wk1_grouped
```

Unpromising Promotions? Only 6 Stores Report At the End of Week1

Promotion	AgeofStore	week	SalesInThousands
1	12.0	1.0	44.540
2	9.5	1.0	39.005
3	7.0	1.0	89.700

Promotion 1 **SalesInThousands** < 58.76, the 95% confidence interval, therefore it appears to be a significantly poor performing promotion. Promotion 3 **SalesInThousands** is >59.68, indicating a significantly strong performing promotion. For Promotions 1 and 3, we would reject the null hypothesis. However, it is early days for our trials, so we shall wait for more results and continue testing.

Which Promotion? More Accurate... All Results in for Week 1

We now have received all the week 1 data, significantly more than we did before, with 137 stores reporting. We can run the bootstrapping and testing process again on this larger dataset:

R

```
df1 = df[df$week==1,]
bootsampdist = replicate(10000, mean(sample(df1$SalesInThousands, replace = T)))
q2 = quantile(bootsampdist, c(.05/2,1-(.05/2)))
plot(density(bootsampdist))
abline(v = q2, col = "red")


paste("95% Confidence interval = [", round(q2,2)[1],", ",round(q2,2)[2],"]")
```

Python

```
# All data in for week one
df_promos_all_wk1 = df[(df['week']==1)]
```

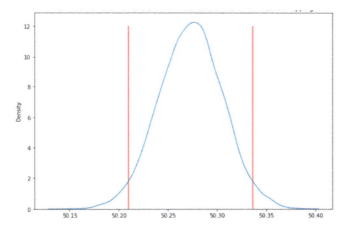

Figure 9.5 Complete week 1 **SalesInThousands** distribution from bootstrapping

And again, we calculate the medians of each promotion and compare them with the 95% confidence intervals from the bootstrapping process:

```
Unpromising Promotions? All Stores Report At the End of Week1
```

Promotion	LocationID	AgeofStore	week	SalesInThousands
1	512	6	1	53.79
2	502	7	1	46.02
3	501	8	1	51.01

Note that the confidence intervals have changed markedly since the initial test we conducted. The lower confidence interval is now 50.21 (it was 58.76 in the first test). This means that Promotion 2 and Promotion 3 could be considered as significantly worse promotions, and we can reject the null hypothesis in both cases. This is quite a different conclusion from the first tests, but as we will see, with a bit more data than we previously had, this is leading us to the right conclusion; Promotion 1 is superior.

All the Data Available: Judging from the Empirical Distribution

At the end of week 4, we have all the data from the trials, but this is still not the full population and we would have to try our Promotions on every fast-food restaurant in the world, and over all time, to obtain this. We repeat the bootstrapping procedure for our much larger dataset:

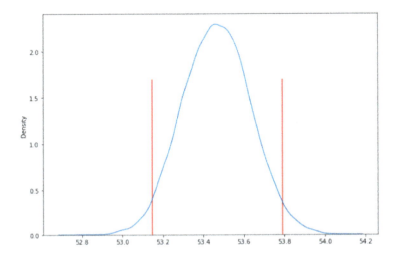

Figure 9.6   Complete week 1 **SalesInThousands** distribution from bootstrapping

Unpromising Promotions? All Stores Report At the End of Week4

Promotion	LocationID	AgeofStore	week	SalesInThousands
1	512.0	6.0	2.5	55.385
2	502.0	7.0	2.5	45.385
3	501.0	8.0	2.5	51.165

The confidence intervals have changed again, but less than between the first two tests, indicating more stability. Promotion 1 median is greater than the upper confidence interval, and Promotions 2 and 3 are below the lower confidence interval. This indicates that we can reject the hypothesis for all Promotions. Our choice is straightforward, Promotion 1 has achieved the best results.

Examining the empirical distributions of the Sales, we can see that Promotion 1 does indeed appear to be the best option. However, we would be well advised to keep monitoring the situation going forward.

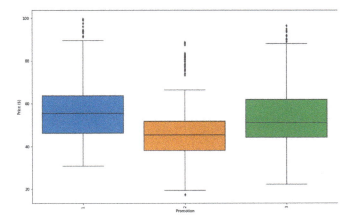

Figure 9.7   Which promotion works best?

═══ Summary ═══

In this chapter, we presented nonparametric tests to conduct hypothesis testing when we do not know the population distribution or our sample data are too small. We demonstrated how to perform a nonparametric test of the population median, which can easily be extended to any test involving population percentiles. We also conducted *two-sample* and *correlation* tests to measure correlation between two variables in the data. Finally, we introduced *bootstrapping,* a *random sampling with replacement* technique that allows us to estimate the properties of a population and construct hypothesis tests when we cannot or do not want to use parametric models.

═══ Exercises ═══

To complete the activity below, you will need to visit the companion website to the book and download the relevant dataset: https://study.sagepub.com/gopal

1   Conduct a nonparametric test for the null hypothesis that the 75th percentile value of *GMAT* score is 600.

2   A customer complains to the owner of an independent fast-food restaurant that the restaurant is discriminating against the elderly. The customer claims that people 60 years old and older are given fewer French fries than people under 60. The owner responds by gathering data, collected without the knowledge of the employees so as not to affect their behaviour. Here are the data on the weight of French fries (grams) for the two groups of customers:

Age less than 60: 75 77 80 69 73 76 78 74 75 81 75 80 79 80
Age greater than 60: 68 74 77 71 73 75 80 77 78 72 69 71 75 78

(Continued)

Conduct a nonparametric two-sample test to evaluate the complaint (i.e., whether the average weight is different in the two groups).

Read the file Real_estate.csv.

1   Conduct a parametric and nonparametric test for the population median *price* of 300. Which test is more reliable?

Read the file UK-Bank-Customers.csv.

2   Conduct a nonparametric two-sample test for the hypothesis that the median value of **Balance** is the same for *Blue Collar* and *White Collar* customers.
3   Use bootstrapping to create the 99% confidence interval for the median value of **Balance** for *Female* customers.

Read the file Baseball.csv.

4   Use bootstrapping to create the 95% confidence interval for the interquartile range of the variable **Average**. The interquartile range is the difference between the 75th and 25th percentile values.

Read the file Health.csv.

5   There is a variable called **faminc**, which indicates the income of the family. Conduct a test for the median value of 1.75 using both parametric and nonparametric tests.
6   There are two variables named **males** and **ofp**. The second variable refers to the number of office visits made by the patients. Conduct a nonparametric two-sample test for the hypothesis that the mean of **ofp** is the same for both males and females.

10

REALITY CHECK

Chapter Contents

In this chapter, we will resolve the practical case of investigating how COVID-19 infections affected nursing homes. Our study will be carried out through the practical application of some of the statistical tests studied in the previous chapters and it will demonstrate how we can transition from theory to practice. In fact, often when we conduct research, we encounter several data-related challenges that impact what and how we conduct statistical tests, making things more complex than in the books. A good knowledge of the different statistical tests is essential to choose the best tests suited to our task and answer complex questions like the ones outlined in this chapter. The case study covered in this chapter is inspired by joint research with colleagues Niam Yaraghi (University of Miami) and Xu Han (Fordham University), both experts in healthcare and statistics and IT research.

COVID-19 IN NURSING HOMES

Nursing homes have been the hot beds of COVID-19 infections, with nearly half of all cases occurring in nursing homes in many countries around the globe. The state of California, which has over 1200 nursing home facilities, has been reporting COVID-19 infections among patients and healthcare staff. The data on infections are available at www.cdph.ca.gov/Programs/CID/DCDC/Pages/COVID-19/SNFsCOVID_19.aspx.

For our analysis, we downloaded the data on infections recorded in early 2022. Below is a snapshot of the data used for our analysis:

In the dataset, *RESIDENTS* refers to patients in the nursing homes and *HCW* to health care workers and other staff working in the nursing homes. *AVAILABLE BEDS* is indicative of the size or capacity of a nursing home. We are interested in the *CUMULATIVE* number of infections and deaths among patients and staff. The following code creates a dataframe with variables of interest for the analysis:

R

```
size = CA.COVID$AVAILABLE.BEDS
patients_I = CA.COVID$CUMULATIVE.POSITIVE.RESIDENTS
patients_D = CA.COVID$COVID.RELATED.RESIDENT.DEATHS
staff_I = CA.COVID$CUMULATIVE.POSITIVE.HCW
staff_D = CA.COVID$COVID.RELATED.HCW.DEATHS
df = data.frame(size,patients_I,staff_I,patients_D,staff_D)
head(df)
```

size <int>	patients_I <chr>	staff_I <chr>	patients_D <chr>	staff_D <chr>
1	7	86	76	0	0
2	54	88	55	<11	0
3	1	<11	<11	0	0
4	3	<11	13	0	0
5	2	0	<11	0	0
6	10	<11	<11	0	0

Table 10.1 Covid-19 infections in nursing homes in California.

County	FACILITY.NAME	COUNTY	FACILITY.ID	AVAILABLE. BEDS	AVAILABLE. BEDS. CAPABLE. OF.ISOLATION	NEW. CONFIRMED. POSITIVE. RESIDENTS	CURRENT. ACTIVE. CASES. RESIDENTS	CUMULATIVE. POSITIVE. RESIDENTS	COVID. RELATED. RESIDENT. DEATHS	NEW. CONFIRMED. POSITIVE. HCW	CURRENT. ACTIVE. HCW	CUMULATIVE. POSITIVE. HCW	COVID. RELATED. HCW. DEATHS
Alameda	ALAMEDA COUNTY MEDICAL CENTER D/P SNF	ALAMEDA	1.4E+08	7	4	0	0	86	0	0	<11	76	0
Alameda	ALAMEDA HEALTHCARE & WELLNESS CENTER	ALAMEDA	20000043	54	8	0	0	88	<11	0	0	55	0
Alameda	ALAMEDA HOSPITAL - SOUTHSHORE CONVALESCENT	ALAMEDA	6.3E+08	1	1	0	0	<11	0	0	0	<11	0
Alameda	ALAMEDA HOSPITAL D/P SNF	ALAMEDA	1.4E+08	3	1	0	0	<11	0	0	0	13	0
Alameda	ALL SAINT'S MAUBERT	ALAMEDA	6.3E+08	2	0	0	0	0	0	0	0	<11	0
Alameda	ALL SAINTS SUBACUTE & TRANSITIONAL CARE	ALAMEDA	20000070	10	0	0	0	<11	0	0	0	<11	0
Alameda	ASHBY CARE CENTER	ALAMEDA	20000010	7	6	0	0	<11	0	0	0	<11	0
Alameda	AVONDALE VILLA POST-ACUTE	ALAMEDA	1.4E+08	6	6	0	0	22	<11	0	0	21	0
Alameda	BANCROFT HEALTHCARE CENTER	ALAMEDA	20000015	7	1	0	0	<11	0	0	0	<11	0

Python

```
size = CA_COVID['AVAILABLE BEDS']
patients_I = CA_COVID['CUMULATIVE POSITIVE RESIDENTS ']
patients_D = CA_COVID['COVID-RELATED RESIDENT DEATHS']
staff_I = CA_COVID['CUMULATIVE POSITIVE HCW ']
staff_D = CA_COVID['COVID-RELATED HCW DEATHS ']
df = pd.DataFrame(data = {'size':size, 'patients_I':patients_I,
    'staff_I':staff_I, 'patients_D':patients_D, 'staff_D':staff_D})
df.head()
```

size	patients_I	staff_I	patients_D	staff_D	
0	7	86	76	0	0
1	54	88	55	<11	0
2	1	<11	<11	0	0
3	3	<11	13	0	0
4	2	0	<11	0	0

1   A couple of things to notice about the data. For privacy reasons, if the number of infected individuals was between 1 and 10, it was reported as **<11**. This is called *censored data*. In particular, these data are left-censored as we do not have precise values for below 11.

2   Number of infections is count data, and thus assuming normality, may or may not be reasonable.

Staff Infections and Deaths

For our initial analysis, we wish to understand how infections translate to deaths among the nursing home staff. Let us take a look at the number of deaths among the staff:

R

```
table(df$staff_D)
```

```
<11    0
 166 1057
```

Python

```
df['staff_D'].value_counts()
```

```
0      1057
<11     166
Name: staff_D, dtype: int64
```

Most nursing homes fortunately did not experience any deaths of their staff and when they did, it always was 10 or less deaths.

How many nursing homes had more than 0 infections among their staff?

R

```
nrow(df[!staff_I=="0",])
```

```
[1] 1201
```

Python

```
len(df[df['staff_I'] != "0"])
```

```
1201
```

Given the nature of the data at hand, we can hypothesize that 15% of nursing homes that had staff infections experienced death among their staff. This is a proportions test (similar to one used in Chapter 8 to hypothesize that 40% of applicants gain admission).

R

```
prop.test(166,1201,p=0.15)
```

```
1-sample proportions test with continuity correction

data:  166 out of 1201, null probability 0.15
X-squared = 1.2168, df = 1, p-value = 0.27
alternative hypothesis: true p is not equal to 0.15
95 percent confidence interval:
 0.1194592 0.1593331
sample estimates:
        p
0.1382182
```

Python

```
import scipy.stats
scipy.stats.chisquare([166, 1201-166], [0.15*1201, 0.85*1201])
```

```
Power_divergenceResult(statistic = 1.3075541623810225,
pvalue = 0.25283796546318715)
```

Given the high p-value, we cannot reject the null hypothesis.

To better understand the relationship between infections and deaths, we can also factorize the data. We will proceed in the following way:

1   Create a new dataframe including only the nursing homes that had staff infections.
2   Create a new variable **staff_D_1** coded as *none* if there are no staff deaths and as *some* otherwise.
3   Create a new variable **staff_I_1** coded as *small* if the value is <11 and as *large* otherwise.
4   Conduct a chi-square test with null hypothesis that the level of infections (small or large) is unrelated to the level of deaths (none or some).

R

```
df1 = df[!staff_I == "0",]
staff_D_1 = ifelse(df1$staff_D == 0, "none", "some" )
staff_I_1 = ifelse(df1$staff_I == "<11", "some", "large" )
chisq.test(staff_I_1,staff_D_1)
```

```
Pearson's Chi-squared test with Yates' continuity correction

data:  staff_I_1 and staff_D_1
X-squared = 4.1481, df = 1, p-value = 0.04168
```

Python

```
df1 = df[staff_I != "0"]
staff_D_1 = np.where(df1['staff_D'] == "0", "none", "some")
staff_I_1 = np.where(df1['staff_I'] == "<11", "small", "large")
# chi square contingency table
no_d_large_inf = ((staff_D_1 == 'none') & (staff_I_1 == 'large')).sum()
no_d_small_inf = ((staff_D_1 == 'none') & (staff_I_1 == 'small')).sum()
some_d_small_inf = ((staff_D_1 == 'some') & (staff_I_1 == 'small')).sum()
some_d_large_inf = ((staff_D_1 == 'some') & (staff_I_1 == 'large')).sum()
test_arr =np.array( [[no_d_large_inf, no_d_small_inf], [some_d_large_inf,
some_d_small_inf]])
scipy.stats.chi2_contingency(test_arr)
```

```
(4.148092869278095,
 0.041681444354659966,
 1,
 array([[1007.42298085, 27.57701915],
        [ 161.57701915, 4.42298085]]))
```

Given the obtained values, we reject the null hypothesis that the number of staff infections and number of deaths are unrelated, indicating that nursing homes with large levels of staff infections are likely to experience staff deaths.

In the above approach, there is a clear loss of information in the staff infections data. Observe how values of 14 and 205 are both categorized as 'large'. To avoid this loss, we can try an alternative way to deal with the censored data. Since the data that are coded as <11 should be in the range 1–10, we may assume it is reasonable to replace it with 5. This way, we can keep the data as numeric without losing the significant variation present in the data. The logic is the following:

1   Recode <11 as 5 for data on staff infections.
2   Conduct a nonparametric two-sample test with null hypothesis that the average number of infections for nursing homes with no deaths is the same as that for the nursing homes that experienced death among their staff.

R

```
staff_I_2 = ifelse(df1$staff_I == "<11",5,df1$staff_I)
staff_I_2 = as.numeric(staff_I_2)
table(staff_D_1)


staff_D_1
 none small
 1035   166
```

```
set.seed(87654321)
f1 = function(){
  s1 = sample(staff_I_2)
  control1 = s1[1:1035]
  treatment1 = s1[1036:length(s1)]
  return(mean(treatment1)-mean(control1))
}
sampdist = replicate(10000, f1())
t1= mean(staff_I_2[staff_D_1 == "none"])
t2 = mean(staff_I_2[staff_D_1 == "small"])
tstat = t2-t1
p_2tail(sampdist,tstat)


[1] 0
```

Python

```
staff_I_2 = np.where(df1['staff_I'] == "<11", 5, df1['staff_I'])
staff_I_2 = staff_I_2.astype(int)
pd.DataFrame(staff_D_1).value_counts()


none    1035
some     166
dtype: int64


np.random.seed(87654321)
def f1():
    s1 = np.random.choice(staff_I_2, size = len(staff_I_2))
    control1 = s1[:1035]
    treatment = s1[1035:]
    return(np.mean(treatment)-np.mean(control1))
sampdist = [f1() for _ in range(10000)]
```

```
t1 = np.mean(staff_I_2[staff_D_1 == "none"])
t2 = np.mean(staff_I_2[staff_D_1 == "some"])
tstat = t2 - t1
p_2tail(sampdist, tstat)
```

0.0

Our test yields a p-value equal to 0, thus we can reject the null hypothesis that there is no difference between the number of infections and deaths of nursing home staff.

One issue with the above approach is that some data were attributed based on a guess around the mean. It becomes hard to quantify the impact of replacing censored data with a value of 5 and, ultimately, this leaves us to wonder whether to trust the results of our test. Since the median is a more robust statistic than the mean (as we discussed in Chapter 1), it is worth conducting the same test but with the median values instead:

R

```
set.seed(87654321)
f1 = function(){
  s1 = sample(staff_I_2)
  control1 = s1[1:1035]
  treatment1 = s1[1036:length(s1)]
  return((median(treatment1)-median(control1)))
}
sampdist = replicate(10000, f1())

t1 = median(staff_I_2[staff_D_1 == "none"])
t2 = median(staff_I_2[staff_D_1 == "small"])
tstat = (t2-t1)
p_2tail(sampdist,tstat)
```

[1] 0

Python

```
np.random.seed(87654321)
def f1():
    s1 = np.random.choice(staff_I_2, size = len(staff_I_2))
    control1 = s1[:1035]
    treatment = s1[1035:]
    return(np.median(treatment)-np.median(control1))
sampdist = [f1() for _ in range(10000)]
t1 = np.median(staff_I_2[staff_D_1 == "none"])
t2 = np.median(staff_I_2[staff_D_1 == "some"])
```

```
tstat = t2 - t1
p_2tail(sampdist, tstat)
```

```
0.0
```

The results are again consistent with our earlier findings and thus boost our confidence that nursing homes with more infections are likely to experience staff deaths from the pandemic.

Patient and Staff Infections

Let us attempt to understand the relationship between the number of staff infected and the number of patients infected. Since both sets of data have some left-censored values, we will replace these with 5 as before.

R

```
staff_I_3 = ifelse(df$staff_I == "<11",5,df$staff_I)
staff_I_3 = as.numeric(staff_I_3)
patient_I_3 = ifelse(df$patients_I == "<11",5,df$patients_I)
patient_I_3 = as.numeric(patient_I_3)
```

Python

```
staff_I_3 = np.where(df['staff_I'] == "<11", 5, df['staff_I'])
staff_I_3 = staff_I_3.astype(int)
patient_I_3 = np.where(df['patients_I'] == "<11", 5, df['patients_I'])
patient_I_3 = patient_I_3.astype(int)
```

Are the number of infections reasonably normal?

R

```
shapiro.test(staff_I_3)
shapiro.test(patient_I_3)

Shapiro-Wilk normality test

data:  staff_I_3
W = 0.88486, p-value < 2.2e-16


Shapiro-Wilk normality test

data:  patient_I_3
W = 0.92823, p-value < 2.2e-16
```

Python

```python
from scipy.stats import shapiro
shapiro(staff_I_3)

ShapiroResult(statistic = 0.884861171245575, pvalue = 3.3410557211274747e-29)

shapiro(patient_I_3)

ShapiroResult(statistic = 0.9282321929931641, pvalue = 9.703639944465253e-24)
```

Neither appears to be normal, and hence we should use a nonparametric test. In addition, given the lack of data, it is more appropriate to use the median as a metric for estimation.

A reasonable null hypothesis is that the median value of the cumulative infections in a nursing home is the same for both the staff and the patients. The following code performs the nonparametric median test:

R

```r
set.seed(87654321)
n = length(patient_I_3)
f1 = function(){
  pool = c(staff_I_3,patient_I_3)
  s1 = sample(pool)
  control1 = s1[1:n]
  treatment1 = s1[(n+1):(2*n)]
  return(median(treatment1)-median(control1))
}
sampdist = replicate(10000, f1())

tstat = median(patient_I_3)-median(staff_I_3)
p_2tail(sampdist,tstat)
```

```
[1] 0.1559
```

Python

```python
np.random.seed(87654321)
n = len(patient_I_3)
def f1():
    pool = np.r_[staff_I_3, patient_I_3]
    s1 = np.random.choice(pool, size=2*n)
    control1 = s1[:n]
    treatment = s1[n:2*n]
    return(np.median(treatment)-
        np.median(control1))
sampdist = [f1() for _ in range(10000)]
tstat = np.median(patient_I_3) - np.median(staff_I_3)
p_2tail(sampdist, tstat)
```

```
0.1589
```

The results indicate that we cannot reject the null hypothesis that the median cumulative number of infections among staff and patients are equal.

To assess the robustness of our findings, let us repeat the above test with the mean, although we already know this metric is more negatively affected by the censored data than the median:

R

```
set.seed(87654321)
n = length(patient_I_3)
f1 = function(){
  pool = c(staff_I_3,patient_I_3)
  s1 = sample(pool)
  control1 = s1[1:n]
  treatment1 = s1[(n+1):(2*n)]
  return(mean(treatment1)-mean(control1))
}
sampdist = replicate(10000, f1())


tstat = mean(patient_I_3)-mean(staff_I_3)
p_2tail(sampdist,tstat)
```

```
[1] 0.1984
```

Python

```
np.random.seed(87654321)
n = len(patient_I_3)
def f1():
    pool = np.r_[staff_I_3, patient_I_3]
    s1 = np.random.choice(pool, size=2*n)
    control1 = s1[:n]
    treatment = s1[n:2*n]
    return(np.mean(treatment)-np.mean(control1))
sampdist = [f1() for _ in range(10000)]
tstat = np.mean(patient_I_3) - np.mean(staff_I_3)
p_2tail(sampdist, tstat)
```

```
0.1984
```

Once again, the results are consistent. As a final check, instead of replacing <11 with 5, we replace it with 1 to evaluate whether the results continue to hold and, as indicated below, they do:

R

```
staff_I_3 = ifelse(df$staff_I=="<11",1,df$staff_I)
staff_I_3 = as.numeric(staff_I_3)
patient_I_3 = ifelse(df$patients_I=="<11",1,df$patients_I)
```

```
patient_I_3 = as.numeric(patient_I_3)

set.seed(87654321)
n = length(patient_I_3)
f1 = function(){
  pool = c(staff_I_3,patient_I_3)
  s1 = sample(pool)
  control1 = s1[1:n]
  treatment1 = s1[(n+1):(2*n)]
  return(mean(treatment1)-mean(control1))
}
sampdist = replicate(10000, f1())

tstat = mean(patient_I_3)-mean(staff_I_3)
p_2tail(sampdist,tstat)
```

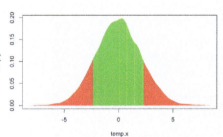

[1] 0.2544

Python

```
staff_I_3 = np.where(df['staff_I'] == "<11", 1, df['staff_I'])
staff_I_3 = staff_I_3.astype(int)
patient_I_3 = np.where(df['patients_I'] == "<11", 1, df['patients_I'])
patient_I_3 = patient_I_3.astype(int)

np.random.seed(87654321)
n = len(patient_I_3)
def f1():
    pool = np.r_[staff_I_3, patient_I_3]
    s1 = np.random.choice(pool, size=2*n)
    control1 = s1[:n]
    treatment = s1[n:2*n]
    return(np.mean(treatment)-np.mean(control1))
sampdist = [f1() for _ in range(10000)]
tstat = np.mean(patient_I_3) - np.mean(staff_I_3)
p_2tail(sampdist, tstat)
```

0.2538

Summary

The variety of tests that we conducted led us to interesting and deeper insights on the impact of COVID-19 in Californian nursing homes. In this case study, because of the data challenges, we had to come up with a variety of different ways to conduct the tests. Facing the problem from different perspectives made our findings more robust and reliable. The lesson from this chapter is that when we understand the basic principles of statistical testing, we can conduct reliable and robust tests despite the challenges we encounter in our research. Challenges are often found in real settings, but now we know how to tackle them!

Exercises

To complete the activity below, you will need to visit the companion website to the book and download the relevant dataset: https://study.sagepub.com/gopal

1   Explore the impact of the size of the nursing home on infections and deaths.
2   Are the deaths among patients and staff related?
3   Explore the relationship of total available beds with those equipped for isolation.
4   Suppose you are interested in conducting analysis at the county level. Note that each county has several nursing homes. Is there a relationship between *AVAILABLE BEDS CAPABLE OF ISOLATION* and staff infections at the county level?
5   At the county level, are the deaths among patients and staff related? Is this consistent with the findings from Exercise 2?

11

FUNDAMENTALS OF ESTIMATION

Chapter Contents

Suppose we have a sample of data as follows:

```
x = (4,3,5,13,7,10,9,9,3,6,4,3,7,10,7,6,7,8,7,7)
```

We believe that this sample comes from a population with the data generation process that can be described by a Poisson distribution. This is depicted in the figure below.

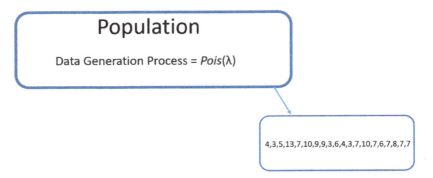

Figure 11.1   Sample from a Poisson distribution

When we conducted *statistical testing*, we started with a hypothesis about the population parameter λ and we developed tests to either reject or not reject the hypothesis. However, in *statistical estimation*, we want to ask the question: what is the estimate of λ that best explains the data that we observe? In other words, with statistical testing, we ask **IS IT?** In statistical estimation, we ask **WHAT IS IT?** The most popular approach for estimation is called *maximum likelihood estimation*.

LIKELIHOOD PRINCIPLE

Our objective is to find the value of λ that best explains the data we have. Let us start this quest with an initial value of 6 for λ. Notice that the first observation in our sample has a value of 4. If λ is 6, what is the probability of finding a value of 4? Similarly, the second observation has a value of 3. What is the probability of observing this? We can answer these questions with the following code:

R
```
x = c(4,3,5,13,7,10,9,9,3,6,4,3,7,10,7,6,7,8,7,7)
lam = 6
dpois(x = 4, lambda = lam)

[1] 0.1338526
dpois(x = 3, lambda = lam)

[1] 0.08923508
```

Python

```
x = np.array([4,3,5,13,7,10,9,9,3,6,4,3,7,10,7,6,7,8,7,7])
lam = 6
scipy.stats.poisson.pmf(k = 4, mu = lam)
0.13385261753998332
```

If λ is 6, the probability of observing a value of 4 is 0.1338526 and the probability of observing 3 is 0.08923508. What about the probability of observing both 4 and 3? Assuming the two observations are independent, this is 0.1338526 × 0.08923508.

Let us compute the probabilities of each of the values in the sample:

R

```
lam = 6
p = dpois(x = x, lambda = lam)
print(round(p,3))
```

```
[1]  0.134 0.089 0.161 0.005 0.138 0.041 0.069 0.069 0.089 0.161 0.134
[12] 0.089 0.138 0.041 0.138 0.161 0.138 0.103 0.138 0.138
```

Python

```
lam = 6
p = scipy.stats.poisson.pmf(k = x, mu = lam)
print(np.round(p,3))
```

```
[0.134 0.089 0.161 0.005 0.138 0.041 0.069 0.069 0.089 0.161 0.134 0.089
0.138 0.041 0.138 0.161 0.138 0.103 0.138 0.138]
```

Having computed the probabilities of individual observations, let us now compute the probability of observing the entire sample of data.

Let us introduce some notation first. Let $x_1,...,x_n$ denote the sample observations and $P(x_1|\lambda),...,$ $P(x_n|\lambda)$ denote the corresponding probabilities for a given λ. If the observations are *independent*, then the probability of observing the entire sample is:

$$\prod_{i=1}^{n} P(x_i | \lambda)$$

This is termed the *likelihood function*:

$$L = \prod_{i=1}^{n} P(x_i | \lambda)$$

The likelihood function as defined above is based on the 'iid' assumption, which stands for independent and identically distributed observations. This is an important assumption to keep in mind. It essentially states that each observation is drawn independently from the underlying population and has no relationship with the next or any other observation drawn to constitute the sample.

Let us calculate the likelihood value for our sample with $\lambda = 6$:

R

```
lam = 6
p = dpois(x = x, lambda = lam)
L = prod(p)
L
```

```
[1] 1.559274e-21
```

Python

```
lam = 6
p = scipy.stats.poisson.pmf(k = x, mu = lam)
L = np.prod(p)
print(L)
1.559273542483997e-21
```

We notice that the likelihood value is very small. Such low values are difficult to work with from a computational standpoint and may even result in errors when they become too small. For this reason, it is more convenient to use the log of likelihood:

$$LL = log\left(\prod_{i=1}^{n}P\left(x_i \mid \lambda\right)\right)$$

$$LL = log\left(P\left(x_i \mid \lambda\right),...P\left(x_n \mid \lambda\right)\right)$$

$$LL = \sum_{i=1}^{n}log\left(P\left(x_i \mid \lambda\right)\right)$$

Let us compute the loglikelihood for our sample:

R

```
lam = 6
p = dpois(x = x, lambda = lam)
LL = sum(log(p))
LL
```

```
[1] -47.91007
```

Python

```
lam = 6
p = scipy.stats.poisson.pmf(k = x, mu = lam)
LL = np.sum(np.log((p)))
print(LL)
-47.91006691797001
```

Note how the loglikelihood yields significantly fewer extreme values, thus becomes much easier to work with. Let us package this into a function:

R

```
LLpois = function(lam){
  p = dpois(x = x, lambda = lam)
  LL = sum(log(p))
  return(LL)
}
LLpois(5)
```

```
[1] -52.52348
```

Python

```
def LLpois(lam):
  p = scipy.stats.poisson.pmf(k = x, mu = lam)
  LL = np.sum(np.log((p)))
  return LL
LLpois(5)
-52.5234770851539
```

The *maximum likelihood principle* states that the best estimate of λ is one that maximizes the likelihood of the observed sample. This is because L is, in essence, the joint probability of observing the entire sample of data. The loglikelihood value for $\lambda = 6$ is -47.91007 and for $\lambda = 5$ it is -52.52348. Since -47.91007 is larger than -52.52348, we can state that a value of 6 is more likely to be the value of λ than 5. The best estimate of λ is the one that maximizes L. Note that maximizing L is equivalent to maximizing the loglikelihood LL.

How do we find the best value of λ? By optimizing the loglikelihood function. The problem now is to find the value of λ that maximizes LL.

OPTIMIZING MATHEMATICALLY

Can we solve this optimization problem analytically? Let us write out the probability for a Poisson distribution:

$$P(x \mid \lambda) = \frac{e^{-\lambda} \lambda_i^x}{x_i!}$$

$$LL = \sum_{i=1}^{n} \log \left(P(x_i \mid \lambda) \right)$$

$$LL = \sum_{i=1}^{n} \log \left(\frac{e^{-\lambda} \lambda_i^x}{x_i!} \right)$$

simplifying, we get:

$$LL = -n\lambda + \log(\lambda)\left(\sum_{i=1}^{n} x_i\right) - \sum_{i=1}^{n} \log(x_i!)$$

Taking the first derivative yields:

$$\frac{dLL}{d\lambda} = -n + \frac{\sum_{i=1}^{n} x_i}{\lambda}$$

which gives the solution:

$$\lambda^* = \frac{\sum_{i=1}^{n} x_i}{n}$$

The second derivative is:

$$\frac{d^2 LL}{d\lambda^2} = -\frac{\sum_{i=1}^{n} x_i}{\lambda^2}$$

Mathematically, we just demonstrated that the maximum likelihood estimate of λ is simply the sample average:

R

```
mean(x)
```

```
[1] 6.75
```

Python

```
np.mean(x)
```
```
6.75
```

Thus, the maximum likelihood estimate of λ, for our sample, is 6.75.

In more complicated settings, we may not be able to solve the optimization problem analytically. In such cases, we use numerical computational methods to get the maximum likelihood estimates. We will explore these shortly.

In terms of terminology, the first-order condition above is called the *gradient* and the second-order condition is called the *Hessian*. When we have multiple parameters to estimate, the gradient is a vector and the Hessian is a matrix.

YET ANOTHER DISTRIBUTION!

Based on our sample of data, the maximum likelihood estimate for λ is 6.75.

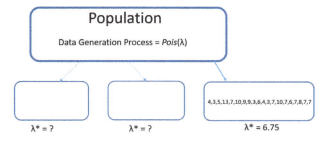

Figure 11.2   Maximum likelihood estimate

What if we take another sample from the same population? A different sample drawn from the population could potentially yield a different estimate for λ. Let us create other samples using the bootstrapping approach and compute the estimate for each:

R

```
set.seed(987654321)
paramdist = replicate(10000, mean(sample(x = x, replace = T)))
plot(density(paramdist))
```

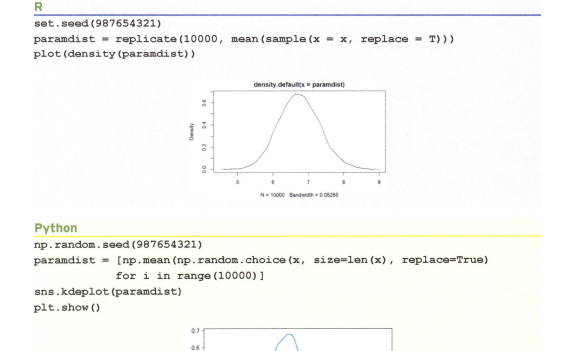

Python

```
np.random.seed(987654321)
paramdist = [np.mean(np.random.choice(x, size=len(x), replace=True)
            for i in range(10000)]
sns.kdeplot(paramdist)
plt.show()
```

What we have is called a *parameter distribution*. Let us compute the 95% confidence interval and the standard deviation for this distribution:

R

```
sd(paramdist)
q2 = quantile(paramdist, c(.05/2,1-(.05/2)))
plot(density(paramdist))
abline(v = q2, col = "red")
paste("95% Confidence Interval = ", "[",q2[1], q2[2],"]")
```

```
[1] 0.5794236
```

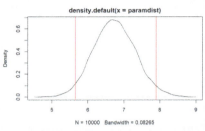

```
[1] "95% Confidence Interval =   [ 5.65 7.9 ]"
```

Python

```
q1 = np.percentile(paramdist, 0.05/2 * 100)
q2 = np.percentile(paramdist, (1-(0.05/2)) * 100)
sns.kdeplot(paramdist)
plt.axvline(q1, color='r', linestyle='-')
plt.axvline(q2, color='r', linestyle='-')
plt.show()
print("95% Confidence Interval = [{:.2f}, {:.2f}]".format(q1,q2))
```

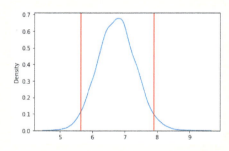

```
95% Confidence Interval = [5.65, 7.90]
```

When we take a different sample, we will obviously get a different estimate. Based on the parameter distribution, we can say the following:

1   The maximum likelihood estimate based on the observed sample is 6.75. This is also called the *point estimate*.
2   We are 95% confident that the population value of λ is between 5.65 and 7.9.

3   The standard deviation for the parameter distribution is 0.579. This is also called the *standard error* of the parameter estimate.

Also, notice that the parameter distribution looks reasonably normal.

OPTIMIZING COMPUTATIONALLY

There are a number of packages in R and Python that provide functions to obtain maximum likelihood estimates through computational methods. Available packages in R include *maxLik*, *likelihood*, *mle*, and *bbmle*. Available packages in Python include *statsmodels*.

R

We will explore the *bbmle* package in R. The main function in the *bbmle* package that does the optimization is `mle2()`. The process is as follows:

1   Create a function that computes the loglikelihood value for a given set of parameters. The parameters are the inputs to the function. The output of the function should be the negative of the loglikelihood as most optimization routines attempt to minimize a function.

2   Use the `mle2()` function to attempt to find the maximum likelihood parameter values. The basic syntax is

```
mle2(minuslogl=function to minimize, start=list("starting values of the
parameters"))
```

Python

The *statsmodels* package has a good implementation of the maximum likelihood expectation (MLE). We will use *scipy* for some helper functions. It is an object-oriented approach so the way we apply it is different to R, in which it requires us to use classes.

```
from statsmodels.base.model import GenericLikelihoodModel
import statsmodels.api as sm
from scipy import stats
```

1   We will copy the class `GenericLikelihoodModel` (which contains all the functions we need). We now declare the class function `loglike` (with base class `GenericLikelihoodModel`). Behind the scenes, after we instantiate our class and call its `fit()` function, fit will now call our function `loglike`.

We declare a new class that has `GenericLikelihoodModel` as its base class, and therefore inherits all members of the class. We now need to override the member function `loglike`, which is called by `GenericLikelihoodModel` during the fitting process when we call `fit()`:

```
class MyProbit (GenericLikelihoodModel):
    def loglike(self, params):
        exog = self.exog
        endog = self.endog
        q = 2 * endog - 1
        return stats.norm.logcdf(q*np.dot(exog, params)).sum()
```

2   Now fit the model. When we call **fit()**, *it* will call our **loglike** function:

```
sm_probit_manual = MyOLS(data_endog, data_ exog).fit()
print(sm_probit_manual.summary())
```

Let us estimate the parameter for the sample we analysed before:

R

```
library(bbmle)
LLpois = function(lam){
  p = dpois(x = x, lambda = lam)
  LL = sum(log(p))
  return(-1*LL)
}


res1 = mle2(minuslogl = LLpois, start = list(lam = 10))
summary(res1)



Maximum likelihood estimation

Call:
mle2(minuslogl = LLpois, start = list(lam = 10))

Coefficients:
    Estimate Std. Error z value      Pr(z)
lam   6.75003    0.58095   11.619 < 2.2e-16 ***
---
Signif. codes:  0 '***' 0.001 '**' 0.01 '*' 0.05 '.' 0.1 ' ' 1

-2 log L: 94.01871
```

Python

```
def LLpois(lam):
  p = scipy.stats.poisson.pmf(k = x, mu = lam)
  LL = np.sum(np.log((p)))
  return(-1*LL)
res1 = scipy.optimize.minimize(LLpois, x0 = 10, method = 'Nelder-Mead')
print(res1)

final_simplex: (array([[6.75 ], [6.75006104]]), array([47.0093571 ,
```

```
47.00935711]))
fun: 47.009357104358216
message: 'Optimization terminated successfully.'
nfev: 36
nit: 18 status: 0
success: True
x: array([6.75])
```

Note that the results are the same as before, when we mathematically optimized the likelihood. Another point worth observing is the reported p-value (2.2e-16 ***). What hypothesis is this testing? Essentially, this is the p-value corresponding to the null hypothesis that the estimated population parameter value is 0. In this example, since the p-value is very small, we can reject the null hypothesis that λ is 0. This reported p-value is computed from the parameter distribution that we covered earlier.

We will explore maximum likelihood estimation computationally with a few more examples.

NUMERIC OUTCOME

Read the admission.csv file. Let us assume that the data generation process for the variable **GMAT** is normal. This is depicted in the figure below. We want to obtain the maximum likelihood estimates of the population mean and standard deviation:

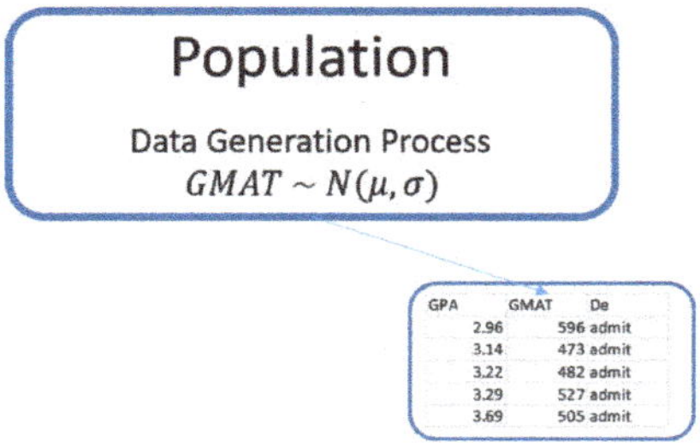

Figure 11.3 Data generation process for the variable **GMAT**

R

```
LLnorm = function(mean1, standdev){
  p = dnorm(x = admission$GMAT, mean = mean1, sd = standdev)
  LL = sum(log(p))
  return(-1*LL)
}


res1 = mle2(minuslogl = LLnorm, start = list(mean1 = 500, standdev = 100))
summary(res1)
```

```
Maximum likelihood estimation
```

```
Call:
mle2(minuslogl = LLnorm, start = list(mean1 = 500, standdev = 100))

Coefficients:
          Estimate Std. Error z value     Pr(z)
mean1     488.4456     8.7902  55.567 < 2.2e-16 ***
standdev   81.0414     6.2156  13.038 < 2.2e-16 ***
---
Signif. codes:  0 '***' 0.001 '**' 0.01 '*' 0.05 '.' 0.1 ' ' 1

-2 log L: 988.3627
```

Python

```
def LLnorm(mean1, standdev):
  p = scipy.stats.norm.pdf(x = admissions.GMAT, loc = mean1, scale = stand-
  dev)
  LL = np.sum(np.log(p))
  return(-1*LL)
res1 = scipy.optimize.minimize(LLnorm, x0 = 500, args = (100,), method = 'Nelder-
Mead')
print(res1)

final_simplex: (array([[488.44709396], [488.4469986 ]]), array([497.46199172,
497.46199172]))
fun: 497.4619917196255 message: 'Optimization terminated successfully.'
nfev: 38
nit: 19
status: 0
success: True
x: array([488.44709396])
```

BINARY OUTCOME

We want to estimate the probability of *admit* based on the sample of data, as shown in the figure below:

Figure 11.4   Data generation process for the variable **admit**

R

```
LLbinary = function(pi){
  p = ifelse(admission$De == "admit", pi, 1 - pi)
  LL = sum(log(p))
  return(-1*LL)
}

res1 = mle2(minuslogl = LLbinary, start = list(pi= .5))
summary(res1)

Maximum likelihood estimation

Call:
mle2(minuslogl = LLbinary, start = list(pi = 0.5))

Coefficients:
   Estimate Std. Error z value    Pr(z)
pi 0.364706   0.052209  6.9854 2.84e-12 ***
---
Signif. codes:  0 '***' 0.001 '**' 0.01 '*' 0.05 '.' 0.1 ' ' 1

-2 log L: 111.5332
```

Python

```
def LLbinary(pi):
  p = np.where(admissions.De == "admit", pi, 1 - pi)
  LL = np.sum(np.log(p))
  return(-1*LL)
constraint = ({'type': 'eq', 'fun': lambda x: x[0]+(1-x[0])})
res1 = scipy.optimize.minimize(LLbinary, x0 = .5, constraints = constraint,
method = 'Nelder-Mead')
print(res1)

final_simplex:  (array([[0.36474609], [0.36464844]]), array([55.76661524,
55.76661555]))
fun: 55.76661524475624 message: 'Optimization terminated successfully.'
nfev: 26
nit: 13
status: 0
success: True
x: array([0.36474609])
```

A FEW CAUTIONARY NOTES

When using computational methods to find the maximum likelihood values, we should be aware of two potential issues.

1   Starting values.

The function *mle2()* in R requires specifying starting values for the parameters to be optimized (not so of *statsmodels* in Python). For complicated likelihood functions, it is important to specify good starting values so that the search for optimal values can converge. As we will see in the next chapter, using starting values from a *baseline model* is a reasonable approach to take. We will explain the concept of a baseline model in the next chapter.

2   Errors.

In an attempt to get the optimal values of the parameters, optimization algorithms can potentially search in the entire domain of values from $-\infty$ to ∞. Sometimes this can be a problem and lead to an error. Below is an example:

R

```
dpois(3,lambda = -10)
```

```
Warning in dpois(3, lambda = -10) : NaNs produced
[1] NaN
```

Python

```
scipy.stats.poisson.pmf(k = 3, mu = -10)
```

```
nan
```

Obviously, the mean of a Poisson distribution cannot be negative. However, the optimization algorithms may try negative values in their search to find the optimal value of λ. This may throw an error and cause the script to fail. When this happens, the best practice is to place bounds on the parameter values.

It also turns out that the *bbmle* package supports several different methods for optimization (see https://en.wikipedia.org/wiki/Limited-memory_BFGS if you are interested in the details on the approach used for optimization). The optimization method **L-BFGS-B** allows box constraints, that is, each variable can be given a lower and/or upper bound. We do so using the **lower** and **upper** commands in the function as shown in the example below:

R

```
res = mle2(minuslogl = LLmeansd,
start = list(M=10,sigma = 1),
lower = c(M = -Inf,sigma = 0),
method = "L-BFGS-B")
```

Python

```
class MyProbit(GenericLikelihoodModel):
    def loglike(self, params):
        exog = self.exog
```

```
        endog = self.endog
        q = 2 * endog - 1
        return stats.norm.logcdf(q*np.dot(exog, params)).sum()

sm_probit_manual = MyProbit(endog, exog, method = 'lbfgs').fit()
print(sm_probit_manual.summary())
```

Summary

In this chapter, we discussed the maximum likelihood principle for estimation. We worked through a few simple examples where we primarily estimated parameters of the distribution from which the sample was generated. We also learnt that we can use numerical optimization techniques to simplify the process of estimating the likelihood functions. In the next chapter, we will explore a variety of more interesting and practical models for estimation.

Exercises

To complete the activity below, you will need to visit the companion website to the book and download the relevant dataset: https://study.sagepub.com/gopal

Read the file diabetes.csv.

1 Assuming that the variable **Pregnancies** follows a Poisson distribution, obtain the maximum likelihood estimate of the mean of the distribution.
2 What is the 95% confidence interval for the parameter?
3 Assuming that the variable **BMI** follows a normal distribution, obtain the maximum likelihood estimate of the mean and the standard deviation.
4 Compute the 95% confidence intervals for the two parameters.
5 Using the maximum likelihood approach estimate the population parameter for the binary variable **Outcome**.
6 Compute the 95% confidence interval and the standard of the parameter estimate.

12

ESTIMATION OF LINEAR MODELS

Chapter Contents

In this chapter, we will explore linear regression models, one of the most widely used modelling techniques in statistics and business analytics. We will work with the file MASchools.csv (Stock, J.H. and M.W. Watson, *Introduction to Econometrics*, 2nd ed. Boston: Addison Wesley, 2007) which contains data on test performance, school characteristics, and student demographic backgrounds for school districts in Massachusetts in 1998. Our main variable of interest is **score4**, which is the average score of fourth grade students in that school. Along with this, we will work with a few other variables from this dataframe.

A brief explanation of the variables is provided below:

Table 12.1 MASchools.csv dataset

Variable	Description
score4	4th grade score (Math + English + Science)
exptot	Expenditures per pupil, total
scratio	Students per computer
special	Special education students (per cent)
stratio	Student-teacher ratio
salary	Average teacher salary

Let us extract these variables into a new dataframe:

R

```
df = MASchools[,c(13,7,8,9,11,15)]
df[1:7,]
```

```
1    714    4646    16.6    14.6    19.0    34.3600
2    731    4930     5.7    17.4    22.6    38.0630
3    704    4281     7.5    12.1    19.3    32.4910
4    704    4826     8.6    21.1    17.9    33.1060
5    701    4824     6.1    16.8    17.5    34.4365
6    714    6454     7.7    17.2    15.7         NA
7    725    5537     5.4    11.3    17.1    41.6150
7 rows
```

Python

```
df = MASchools.iloc[:, [12, 6,7,8,10,15]].copy()
df.head(7).round(2)
```

```
0    714    4646    16.6    14.6    19.0    34.36
1    731    4930     5.7    17.4    22.6    38.06
2    704    4281     7.5    12.1    19.3    32.49
3    704    4826     8.6    21.1    17.9    33.11
4    701    4824     6.1    16.8    17.5    34.11
5    714    6454     7.7    17.2    15.7      NaN
6    725    5537     5.4    11.3    17.1    41.62
```

Dealing with Missing Data

There are missing values in the dataframe which are marked as *NA*. Let us first detect which variables and what percentage of the values in these variables are missing:

R

```
round((colMeans(is.na(df)))*100,3)
```

```
score4   exptot scratio special stratio   salary
 0.000    0.000   4.091   0.000   0.000   11.364
```

```
table(complete.cases(df))
```

```
FALSE   TRUE
   34    186
```

Python

```
df.isna().mean()*100
```

```
score4   0.000000
exptot   0.000000
scratio  4.090909
special  0.000000
stratio  0.000000
salary  11.363636
```

```
num_na = df.isna().any(axis=1).sum()
# no if incomplete rows
num_complete = len(df) - num_na
print("True: ",num_na, "False: ", num_complete)
```

```
True: 34 False: 186
```

The results indicate that the variable **scratio** has approximately 4% of values missing and **salary** has approximately 11% missing values. A total of 34 observations have missing data. The problem of missing data is quite common in many settings and could potentially have a significant effect on the conclusions that can be drawn from the data. Missing values need to be dealt with before we embark on extensive analysis of the data. How to effectively deal with missing data depends critically on how much data are missing and whether the data are 'missing at random'. Missing data occur at random if the data that are missing are not related to a specific value which is supposed to be obtained. This can arise in cases where someone forgets to fill in appropriate values or where a random failure leads to missing data. 'Missing not at random' can arise, for example, when a certain demographic is hesitant to provide financial information. These cases need to be determined and dealt with in different ways.

There are two broad approaches to handling missing data – *removing data* and *imputation*. If we reasonably believe that the missing data are at random and the loss of sample size is not very significant, then the simple approach is to remove all observations that have missing values.

In our example, it would mean dropping 34 observations from further analysis. Imputation, however, attempts to reasonably guess what the values of the missing data are and replace missing values with imputed values. There are several techniques for imputation. A simple approach is to replace missing values with the average of the non-missing variable values. In the case of salary, it would be the following:

R

```
salarymean = mean(df$salary,na.rm = T)
salarymean = mean(df$salary,na.rm = T)
salaryimputed = ifelse(is.na(df$salary),salarymean,df$salary)
salarymean
mean(salaryimputed)
sd(df$salary,na.rm = T)
sd(salaryimputed)
```

```
[1]  35.9927
[1]  35.9927
[1]   3.190556
[1]   3.002929
```

Python

```
salarymean = df['salary'].mean()
salaryimputed = df['salary'].fillna(salarymean)
print(salarymean)
print(salaryimputed.mean())
print(df['salary'].std())
print(salaryimputed.std())
```

```
5.992697446774216
35.99269744677423
3.1905555712426232
3.0029293928495764
```

With this approach to imputation, the mean remains unaltered after imputation while the variance (standard deviation) is reduced as there will be more values clustered at the mean. More sophisticated imputation techniques attempt to build a model to predict missing values based on other available variables in the data.

In our example, let us choose to drop all observations that contain missing values:

R

```
df1 = df[complete.cases(df),]
table(complete.cases(df1))
```

```
TRUE
 186
```

Python

```python
df1 = df.dropna().copy()
len(df1)
```

186

Now the data are ready for analysis!

Baseline Model

Our outcome of interest is the variable **score4**, which is numeric, and its data generation process is shown in the figure below:

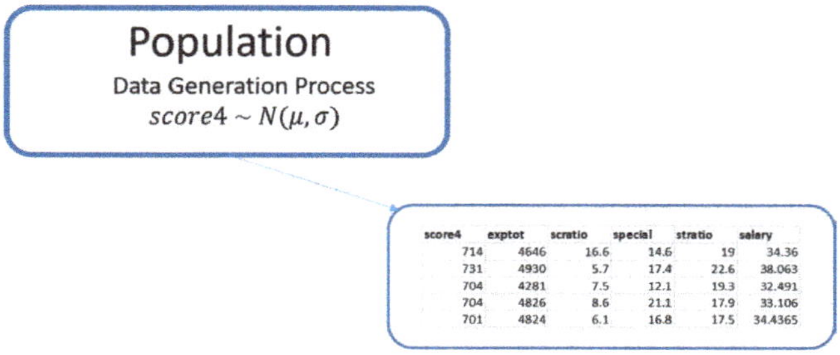

Figure 12.1 Data generation process for **score4**

We will estimate the population parameters of **score4**:

R

```r
library(bbmle)
LLnorm = function(mean1, standdev){
  p = dnorm(x = df1$score4, mean = mean1, sd = standdev)
  LL = sum(log(p))
  return(-1*LL)
}

res1 = mle2(minuslogl = LLnorm, start = list(mean1 = 700, standdev = 50))
summary(res1)
Maximum likelihood estimation

Call:
mle2(minuslogl = LLnorm, start = list(mean1 = 700, standdev = 50))

Coefficients:
         Estimate Std. Error z value                  Pr(z)
mean1    709.03763    1.12886 628.099 < 0.00000000000000022 ***
```

```
standdev  15.39563    0.79823  19.287 < 0.00000000000000022 ***
---
Signif. codes:  0 '***' 0.001 '**' 0.01 '*' 0.05 '.' 0.1 ' ' 1

-2 log L: 1544.924
```

In Python, this can be programmed either using numeric optimization directly (e.g., *scipy.optimize.minimize*) or by using an object-oriented framework. The object requires somewhat more code, but produces a richer evaluation. Therefore, we used this method here. In the online notebook, you can also find a code version that uses the optimizer directly.

Python

```python
from statsmodels.base.model import GenericLikelihoodModel
from scipy import stats

class myMLEbase(GenericLikelihoodModel):
    def loglike(self, params):
        return stats.norm.logpdf(self.endog,loc=params[0],scale=params[1]).sum()

exog = pd.DataFrame(np.ones([len(df1),2]),columns=['mean','std'],
        index= df1.index)
endog = df1[['score4']] # target

mybase = myMLEbase(endog,exog) # setup
print((mybase.fit(start_params=[700, 50],maxiter=2000)).summary())

Optimization terminated successfully.
        Current function value: 4.153022
        Iterations: 64
        Function evaluations: 126
                        myMLEbase Results
==============================================================================
Dep. Variable:                 score4   Log-Likelihood:            -772.46
Model:                       myMLEbase   AIC:                         1547.
Method:            Maximum Likelihood   BIC:                         1550.
Date:                Sun, 21 Aug 2022
Time:                        15:01:31
No. Observations:                 186
Df Residuals:                     185
Df Model:                           0
==============================================================================
                 coef    std err          z      P>|z|      [0.025      0.975]
------------------------------------------------------------------------------
mean         709.0376      1.129    628.098      0.000     706.825     711.250
std           15.3957      0.798     19.287      0.000      13.831      16.960
==============================================================================
```

Let us unpack the results and understand this a little more. Our estimation results show that:

score4 ~ N(709,15.4)

we can write this as:

score4 = 709 + N(0,15.4)

score4 = 709 + ε, ε ~ N(0,15.4)

We interpret the above as that our estimation or prediction for **score4** is 709 for any school district. Of course, there is a possibility for errors in prediction, and this error is normally distributed with a standard deviation of 15.4. Why is there an error in our prediction? This is because there are several variables about which we do not have information, which impact the score of fourth graders. These are our *omitted variables*. For example, these variables could be family income, extracurricular activities available in the district, parental involvement, quality of teachers, and so on. These represent *what we do not know*. The higher the standard deviation of the error term, the more we do not know. From this perspective, it is good to develop models that lower the variance or standard deviation in the error term.

Let us plot the errors:

R

```
x = seq(1,nrow(df1))
plot(x = x, y = df1$score4)
abline(h = 709, col = "blue")
segments(x,709,x,df1$score4,col = "red")
```

Python

```
plt.stem(df1['score4']-709)
# diff to baseline
ticks = np.arange(-49,40,20)
# ticks from 660-baseline
plt.yticks(ticks=ticks, labels=ticks+709) # show full values
plt.show()
```

Let us compute the sum of squared errors for all the observations. This is called *SST (sum of squares total)*. We will come back to this later:

R

```
SST = sum((df1$score4 - 709)^2)
SST
```

```
[1] 44087
```

Python

```
SST = np.sum((df1['score4'] - 709)**2)
SST
```

```
44087
```

LINEAR REGRESSION MODEL

In the baseline model, our estimation or prediction of **score4** for every school district is the same at 709. Now suppose we believe that we can explain why some school districts have higher scores and others have lower scores. The new, better data generation process we propose is the following:

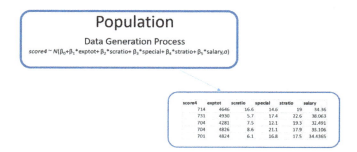

Figure 12.2 Optimized data generation process for *score4*

The model is based on the belief that variables **exptot**, **scratio**, **special**, **stratio**, and **salary** are related to the outcome of interest, **score4**. What we want to estimate are the parameters β_1, β_2, β_3, β_4, β_5, and σ. Let us write the code to estimate this data generation process. First, we will create the function to compute the loglikelihood.

R

```
LLnorm = function(b0,b1,b2,b3,b4,b5, standdev){
  mean1 = b0 + b1*df1$exptot + b2*df1$scratio + b3*df1$special + b4*df1$stratio
        + b5*df1$salary
  p = dnorm(x = df1$score4, mean = mean1, sd = standdev)
  LL = sum(log(p))
  return(-1*LL)
}
```

Python

```python
from numpy import ma
def LLnorm(params):
  b0, b1, b2, b3, b4, b5, standdev = params
  mean1 = b0 + b1*df1['exptot'] + b2*df1['scratio'] + b3*df1['special'] +
          b4*df1['stratio'] + b5*df1['salary']
  p = scipy.stats.norm(mean1, standdev).pdf(df1['score4'])
  LL = np.sum(np.log(p))
  return(-1*LL)
```

Before we optimize to find the parameter values, we need to set some starting values for all the parameters. A reasonable set of starting values can be obtained from the baseline model we developed previously.

With this, we write the R code similar to before.

In Python, we use this time numeric optimization directly, to keep the code more compact. In the online notebook, you can find versions using two *statsmodels* frameworks:

R

```r
res2 = mle2(minuslogl = LLnorm, start = list(b0 = 709, b1 = 0, b2 = 0,
        b3 = 0,b4 = 0,b5 = 0,standdev = 15.4))
summary(res2)


Maximum likelihood estimation

Call:
mle2(minuslogl = LLnorm, start = list(b0 = 709, b1 = 0, b2 = 0,
    b3 = 0, b4 = 0, b5 = 0, standdev = 15.4))

Coefficients:
          Estimate   Std. Error    z value              Pr(z)
b0       714.7610960  0.0041688 171455.3616 < 0.00000000000000022 ***
b1        -0.0050297  0.0014255    -3.5284            0.0004181 ***
b2        -0.1083852  0.3516757    -0.3082            0.7579329
b3        -0.7167440  0.2541550    -2.8201            0.0048008 **
b4        -2.6472217  0.3969816    -6.6684   0.000000000025865 ***
b5         2.2096528  0.3155365     7.0028    0.000000000002508 ***
standdev  13.1042240  0.6794141    19.2875 < 0.00000000000000022 ***
---
Signif. codes:  0 '***' 0.001 '**' 0.01 '*' 0.05 '.' 0.1 ' ' 1


-2 log L: 1484.98
```

Python

```python
res2 = scipy.optimize.minimize(LLnorm, x0 = [709, 0, 0, 0, 0, 0, 15.4],
method = 'Nelder-Mead', options={'maxiter':2000}) # many iterations needed
print(res2)
```

```
fun: 742.4899093887489
    message: 'Optimization terminated successfully.'
       nfev: 2034
        nit: 1343
     status: 0
    success: True
          x: array([ 7.14703557e+02, -5.02906439e-03, -1.07875748e-01,
-7.16282665e-01,
       -2.64688018e+00,  2.21067219e+00,  1.31043293e+01])
```

Understanding Regression Results

Regression Equation

Our regression result is the following.

$$score4 = 714.8 - 0.005 \times exptot - 0.108 \times scratio - 0.717 \times special - 2.65 \times stratio + 2.21 \times salary$$

Let us write out the estimation or prediction for each observation, both from our baseline model and from the regression model. We will also write out the error from the regression equation. The first thing to note is that the estimated parameters are stored in the ***res2*** or ***res2.x*** object, in R or Python, respectively, which contains the results of the optimization and we can obtain the values as follows:

R
```
coef(res2)
```

```
          b0             b1             b2             b3             b4
714.761095996  -0.005029656  -0.108385172  -0.716743984  -2.647221680
          b5        standdev
  2.209652848   13.104224004
```

Python
```
res2.x
```

```
array([ 7.14703557e+02, -5.02906439e-03, -1.07875748e-01,-7.16282665e-01,
-2.64688018e+00, 2.21067219e+00, 1.31043293e+01])
```

To compute the predictions from the regression model and the errors between the actual and predicted values of **score4**, we use matrix multiplication (in R, the command is %*% and in Python, it is **.dot**).

R
```
df1$baseline = 709
df1$regression = as.matrix(df1[,2:6]) %*% coef(res2)[2:6] + coef(res2)[1]
```

```
df1$regerror = df1$score4 - df1$regression
round(df1[1:5,c(1,7,8,9)],3)
```

```
score4
<dbl>
baseline
<dbl>
regression
<dbl>
regerror
<dbl>
1      714      709      704.756      9.244
2      731      709      701.155     29.845
3      704      709      704.446     -0.446
4      704      709      700.200      3.800
5      701      709      707.562     -6.562
```

Python

```
df1['baseline'] = 709
df1['regression'] = df1[['exptot','scratio','special','stratio','salary']].
dot(res2.x[1:6]) + res2.x[0]
df1['regerror'] = df1['score4'] - df1['regression']
print(df1.head().round(3).iloc[:, [0,6,7,8]])
```

```
     score4   baseline   regression   regerror
0      714       709       704.758      9.242
1      731       709       701.157     29.843
2      704       709       704.440     -0.440
3      704       709       700.199      3.801
4      701       709       707.559     -6.559
```

Let us plot the errors from the regression equation:

R

```
x = seq(1,nrow(df1))
plot(x = x, y = df1$regerror, col = "purple", pch = 19)
abline(h=0)
segments(x,df1$regerror,x,0,col = "red")
```

Python

```
x = np.arange(1, len(df1)+1)
plt.stem(x, df1[,regerror'])
plt.axhline(0, color='red')
plt.show()
```

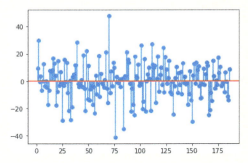

Model Fit

If the regression model is better than the baseline model, then we expect the errors to be smaller. Similar to before, let us compute the sum of the squared errors. This is called *SSE (sum of squares errors)*:

R

```
SSE = sum((df1$regression - df1$score4)^2)
SSE
```

```
[1] 31940.57
```

Python

```
SSE = np.sum((df1['regression'] - df1['score4'])**2)
round(SSE,2)
```

```
31940.56
```

Clearly, the overall error is lower than in the baseline model, which was 44,087. Thus, the regression model is giving us a better approach to estimate **score4**. There is a measure called the *coefficient of determination*, R^2, which is defined as

$$R^2 = 1 - \frac{SSE}{SST}$$

The value for us is

R

```
Rsquare = 1 - (SSE/SST)
round(Rsquare,3)
```

```
[1] 0.276
```

Python

```
Rsquare = 1 - (SSE/SST)
print(Rsquare)
```

```
0.276
```

R^2 is a measure of the overall goodness of fit. When R^2 is 0, we know that *SSE = SST*, which means the regression model is the same as the unintelligent baseline model. When *SSE* = 0, which indicates that there are no errors in the regression, then we get an R^2 of 1.

Another way to understand R^2 is by looking at the standard deviation (or equivalently, variance) of the error terms in the baseline and regression models.

$$R^2 = 1 - \frac{\text{variance of error term in the regression model}}{\text{variance of error term in the baseline model}}$$

Let us check this with the code:

R

```
varbaseline = 15.39563^2
varregression = 13.1042240^2
round(1 - (varregression/varbaseline),3)
```

```
[1] 0.276
```

Python

```
varbaseline = 15.39563**2
varregression = 13.1042240**2
print(1 - (varregression/varbaseline))
```

```
0.276
```

R^2 is an indication of what proportion of the variation observed in the outcome is being explained by the model. Our regression model is able to explain 27.6% of the variation in **score4**. The purpose of building a good regression model is to lower the standard deviation of the error term from the baseline model as much as possible.

Marginal Effects

Assuming all the assumptions of the regression model hold, the coefficients for each of the independent variables (these are the variables on the right-hand side of the regression equation) are called the *marginal effects*. For example, a unit increase in **salary** is expected to increase **score4** by 2.209652848 (this is the coefficient value for $b5$). We have to be careful with this statement. We will have more to say about this in the discussion that follows.

Statistical Significance

Let us take a look at the regression result for the variable **scratio**. The estimated value is −0.108385172 and the standard error is 0.3516757. As we discussed in the previous lesson, the point estimate based on the data is −0.108385172. The value of the coefficient in the population follows a normal distribution with a standard deviation of 0.3516757. Let us plot this parameter distribution and compute the 95% confidence interval:

R

```
m1 = -0.1083852
se1 = 0.3516757
curve(dnorm(x,mean = m1, sd = se1),
    from = -1, to = 1)
abline(v = m1)
qvalues = qnorm(p = c((.05/2),
1-(.05/2)))
qvalues
```

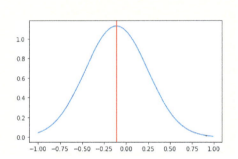

```
[1] -1.959964  1.959964
```

Python

```
m1 = -0.1083852
se1 = 0.3516757
x = np.arange(-1, 1, 0.01)
p = scipy.stats.norm(m1, se1).pdf(x)
plt.plot(x, p)
plt.axvline(m1, color='red')
plt.show()
stats.norm.ppf([.05/2,1-.05/2])
```

```
array([-1.95996398,  1.95996398])
```

Since the 95% confidence interval [−1.959964,1.959964] contains 0, we cannot statistically rule out the possibility that the true population coefficient value is 0. This means that there is a possibility that *scratio* has no effect on the outcome. Thus, we term this as *not statistically significant*. Since we cannot say with 95% confidence that the true value of the coefficient is not 0, we cannot rule out that *scratio* has no effect on the outcome **score4**.

We can also compute a p-value here, similar to what we did earlier with statistical testing:

R

```
gap = abs(m1 - 0)
curve(dnorm(x,mean = m1, sd = se1), from = -1, to = 1)
abline(v = m1)
abline(v = m1 - gap, col = "blue")
abline(v = m1 + gap, col = "blue")
```

```
a = pnorm(q = m1 + gap, mean = m1, sd = se1)
b = pnorm(q = m1 - gap, mean = m1, sd = se1)
pval1 = 1 - (a - b)
pval1
```

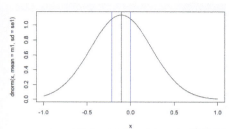

```
[1] 0.7579329
```

Python

```python
gap = abs(m1 - 0)
x = np.arange(-1, 1, 0.01)
p = scipy.stats.norm(m1, se1).pdf(x)
plt.plot(x, p, color='purple', linestyle='-')
plt.axvline(m1, color='black')
plt.axvline(m1 - gap, color='blue')
plt.axvline(m1 + gap, color='blue')
plt.show()
a = scipy.stats.norm(m1, se1).cdf(m1 + gap)
b = scipy.stats.norm(m1, se1).cdf(m1 - gap)
pval1 = 1 - (a - b)
round((pval1),6)
```

```
0.757933
```

The p-value we just computed is identical to what the **mle2()** function generated. When the p-value is small (typically less than 0.05), we say that the variable has a statistically significant impact on the outcome, and otherwise, not.

Based on the results we obtained, we can conclude that all the variables except **scratio** have an effect on **score4**. Furthermore, all statistically significant variables except **salary** have a negative effect on **score4**. Interestingly, the regression results suggest that higher expenditure per pupil is associated with lower grade-four scores.

Assumptions of the Regression Model

As you can imagine, regression models are very widely used. Many important decisions and policies are implemented based on regression studies. These actions and policies entail expending significant time, energy, and resources based on the results of the regression analysis. Given the importance of this, before implementing or taking critical actions, it is important that you understand that the model you built satisfies all the key assumptions on which the model is built. Violations of these assumptions may provide misleading insights and put you down the wrong path in terms of actions taken. Let us look at some of the important assumptions.

Normality

A key assumption made is that error terms are normally distributed. Is this true in our case? We can check this easily:

R

```
plot(density(df1$regerror))
shapiro.test(x = df1$regerror)


Shapiro-Wilk normality test

data:  df1$regerror
W = 0.98869, p-value = 0.1456
```

Python

```
sns.kdeplot(df1['regerror'], color = 'purple')
plt.show()
shapiro = scipy.stats.shapiro(df1['regerror'])
print(shapiro)

ShapiroResult(statistic = 0.9886723160743713,
              pvalue=0.14497749507427216)
```

We can notice an interesting outcome. The plot and the Shapiro–Wilk normality test confirm that the errors are reasonably normally distributed.

If we find significant deviations from normality, a good approach to take is to re-examine the regression structure. This, for example, could be to transform the independent or dependent variables. We will discuss this in detail in Chapter 14.

Homoscedasticity

The regression model assumes a constant standard deviation. This assumption means that the variance or standard deviation of the error term is not correlated to the dependent or outcome variable. In other words, we should not see the magnitude of errors varying with the values of the outcome. Let us take a look at this through a plot of predicted outcomes and the errors:

R

```
plot(df1$regression, df1$regerror)
abline(h = 0)
segments(df1$regression, 0, df1$regression, df1$regerror, col = "red")
```

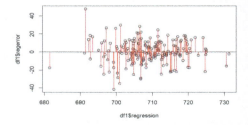

Python

```
plt.stem(df1['regression'], df1['regerror'])
plt.axhline(0, color='red')
plt.xlabel('Regression')
plt.ylabel('Regression Error')
plt.show()
```

Visually, there does not appear to be a violation of this assumption in our model. There are formal tests that we can conduct to check for *heteroscedasticity* and we will explore this in Chapter 14.

Multicollinearity

Suppose we are interested in the effect of salary on **score4**. To place our focus on the effect of salary, let us express the regression equation as follows:

$$\text{score4} = \beta_0 + \beta_1 \text{salary} + \beta_{2x2} + \beta_{3x3} + \beta_{4x4} + \epsilon$$

Take the first derivative with respect to salary:

$$\frac{d(\text{score4})}{d(\text{salary})} = \beta_1 + \beta_2 \frac{dx_2}{d(\text{salary})} + \beta_3 \frac{dx_3}{d(\text{salary})} + \beta_4 \frac{dx_4}{d(\text{salary})} + \frac{d\epsilon}{d(\text{salary})}$$

For now, let us assume that $\frac{d\epsilon}{d(\text{salary})} = 0$. The problem of *multicollinearity* exists when the independent variable **salary** is correlated to the other independent variables x_2, x_3, and x_4. The marginal effect of salary on the outcome is β_1 only valid if the **salary** is uncorrelated to other independent variables. There are formal tests available to check for multicollinearity. The approaches to deal with multicollinearity, when it exists, include dropping, combining, and transforming variables. Be cautious of multicollinearity before interpreting β_1 as the marginal effect of salary on **score4**. We will revisit this issue in Chapter 14.

Endogeneity

A much bigger problem is with the assumption $\frac{d\epsilon}{d(\text{salary})} = 0$. What does this really mean? As we discussed before, the error term encompasses all the omitted variables that impact our outcome. Some possible omitted variables are illustrated in the figure below:

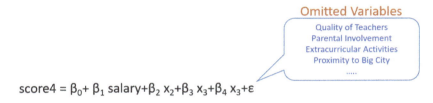

$$\text{score4} = \beta_0 + \beta_1 \text{ salary} + \beta_2\, x_2 + \beta_3\, x_3 + \beta_4\, x_3 + \varepsilon$$

Figure 12.3   Omitted variables and endogeneity

The assumption $\frac{d\varepsilon}{d(\text{salary})} = 0$ implies that none of the omitted variables are correlated with salary. If this assumption is violated, then our coefficient β_1 cannot be correctly interpreted as the marginal effect of **salary** on **score4**. This estimate then becomes unreliable and biased. This is termed *endogeneity* (see https://en.wikipedia.org/wiki/Endogeneity_(econometrics) for more details and www.youtube.com/watch?v=dLuTjoYmfXs for an introduction).

In our example, it is possible that one of the omitted variables, let us say 'quality of teachers', is related to **salary**. It is possible that high-quality teachers command a higher salary and high-quality teachers are the main reason for high values of **score4**. If this is the case, the effect of salary we observe from the regression result is spurious and misleading. One can argue that salary has no *causal effect* on **score4**. It is just that high-quality teachers have high salaries and high-quality teachers are the main cause of high student scores. In other words, there is cor-relation between **salary** and **score4** but there is no direct causation. This is an example of the famous phrase in statistics: *correlation does not imply causation*. If this argument is true, then one should not invest in paying higher salaries to current teachers with the hope that this will lead to higher student scores. This is illustrated in the figure below:

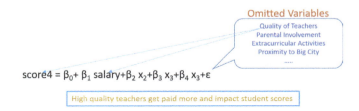

Figure 12.4   Omitted variables and endogeneity - 1/3

There are, of course, other possible causal links as shown in the figures below:

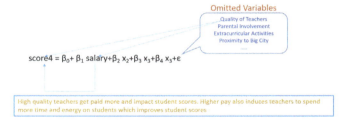

Figure 12.5   Omitted variables and endogeneity - 2/3

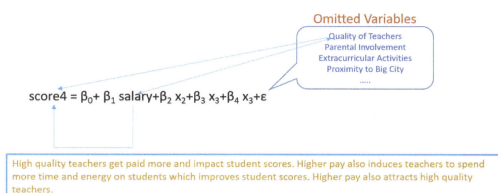

Figure 12.6 Omitted variables and endogeneity - 3/3

Interpreting the coefficient of **salary**, 2.2096528, from the regression result as the marginal causal effect on **score4** means the following: if the **salary** is increased by one unit, then the **score4** will increase by 2.21 units. This is reasonable only if we make the strong assumption that there are no omitted variables that are correlated with **salary**. There are many stories where important policy decisions (such as increasing the salaries of teachers with the expectation that scores will go up) have been made assuming causality which subsequently backfired (see the article at https://allabouthealthychoices.wordpress.com/2016/03/17/associationcorrelation-vs-causation/ for a discussion in the context of healthcare).

One major practical problem is that there is no conclusive way to check for this assumption. We have omitted variables because we do not have information on them. Often, we do not know what and how many omitted variables there are. In this case, how can we really check for the validity of the assumption? After all, we don't know what we don't know!

At the core, this is a *data* problem. This problem arises because of how we collect data and what data we collect. If the data are collected through a *randomized, controlled experiment*, then we can easily rule out problems with omitted variables. In our case, it could work as follows. We randomly identify some school districts as the control group and the rest as the treatment group. We then randomly assign teachers to school districts. Teachers assigned to the treatment group are paid a higher salary than the teachers in the control group. We then observe and collect data over a period of time. If we were to do this, then we will not face the problem of bias induced by the omitted variables. Why? Because of the random assignment of teachers, salary is no longer correlated to any omitted variables. Quite obviously, this is simply not practical in our context. However, this is a standard approach in clinical trials to study the effect of medical treatments and drugs.

When we are restricted to *observational data*, it becomes impossible to prove or guarantee causality (stat.cmu.edu/~larry/=stat401/Causal.pdf). However, we can take steps to alleviate the concerns with causality. For example, with panel data (i.e., data collected on individuals or entities at multiple points in time), we can address some of the concerns that omitted variables might cause. Another approach is through *instrumental variables* which are variables related to **salary** but uncorrelated with the error term. These are hard to find in many situations. Please read one of the author's research papers on the use of instrumental variables to examine the link between music piracy and sales (https://pubsonline.informs.org/doi/abs/10.1287/mnsc.1070.0699). The omitted variable that we had to deal with was 'popularity' which impacts both piracy and sales.

Independence and Identical Distribution

The observations should be independent and identically distributed. This is called the *iid* assumption. We need this assumption because in computing the likelihood, we multiply the probabilities of the observations. We can do so only if the observations are independent. This assumption is true for all maximum likelihood estimations. Examples where this is not true are time series data and network data. In such cases, the approach is to specify the data generation process in a way that the errors will be independent. Consider an example of time series data where one wants to predict sales this year. Since the sales this year can be correlated to sales last year, the observations from this year will be correlated to observations from the past year. If we include last year's sales as one of the independent variables, one can then argue that the errors after incorporating this lag variable would be independent and thus, we can continue to use the maximum likelihood approach for estimation.

REGRESSION FUNCTIONS IN R AND PYTHON

While we developed and estimated a regression model from first principles to derive deep intuition and understanding, R and Python provide functions to conduct regression analysis easily by writing the regression factors:

R

```
res3 = lm(score4~exptot+scratio+special+stratio+salary,data=df1)
summary(res3)

Call:
lm(formula = score4 ~ exptot + scratio + special + stratio +
    salary, data = df1)

Residuals:
    Min      1Q  Median      3Q     Max
-41.324  -7.458  -0.518   8.777  47.569

Coefficients:
             Estimate Std. Error t value            Pr(>|t|)
(Intercept) 714.703519  16.343429  43.730 < 0.0000000000000002 ***
exptot       -0.005029   0.001500  -3.353            0.000974 ***
scratio      -0.107875   0.367331  -0.294            0.769346
special      -0.716282   0.280464  -2.554            0.011480 *
stratio      -2.646880   0.491597  -5.384          0.0000002250 ***
```

```
salary          2.210672    0.373808    5.914          0.0000000165 ***
---
Signif. codes:   0 '***' 0.001 '**' 0.01 '*' 0.05 '.' 0.1 ' ' 1

Residual standard error: 13.32 on 180 degrees of freedom
Multiple R-squared:  0.2755,     Adjusted R-squared:  0.2554
F-statistic: 13.69 on 5 and 180 DF,  p-value: 0.00000000002504
```

Python

```python
from statsmodels.formula.api import ols
res3 = ols("score4 ~ exptot + scratio + special + stratio + salary",
data=df1).fit()
print(res3.summary())
```

```
OLS Regression Results
==============================================================================
Dep. Variable:                 score4   R-squared:                       0.276
Model:                            OLS   Adj. R-squared:                  0.255
Method:                 Least Squares   F-statistic:                     13.69
Date:                Sun, 21 Aug 2022   Prob (F-statistic):           2.50e-11
Time:                        16:27:19   Log-Likelihood:                -742.49
No. Observations:                 186   AIC:                             1497.
Df Residuals:                     180   BIC:                             1516.
Df Model:                           5
Covariance Type:            nonrobust
==============================================================================
                 coef    std err          t      P>|t|      [0.025      0.975]
------------------------------------------------------------------------------
Intercept     714.7035     16.343     43.730      0.000     682.454     746.953
exptot         -0.0050      0.001     -3.353      0.001      -0.008      -0.002
scratio        -0.1079      0.367     -0.294      0.769      -0.833       0.617
special        -0.7163      0.280     -2.554      0.011      -1.270      -0.163
stratio        -2.6469      0.492     -5.384      0.000      -3.617      -1.677
salary          2.2107      0.374      5.914      0.000       1.473       2.948
==============================================================================
Omnibus:                        3.989   Durbin-Watson:                   2.049
Prob(Omnibus):                  0.136   Jarque-Bera (JB):                4.735
Skew:                          -0.095   Prob(JB):                       0.0937
Kurtosis:                       3.758   Cond. No.                     8.99e+04
==============================================================================

Notes:
[1] Standard Errors assume that the covariance matrix of the errors is cor-
rectly specified.
[2] The condition number is large, 8.99e+04. This might indicate that there are
strong multicollinearity or other numerical problems.
```

USE CASE: PROFIT FORECASTING USING LINEAR REGRESSION

Forecasting profits, revenues, debt levels, and a whole host of other metrics and analytics is crucial in business. Linear regression provides the most widely used tool kit for forecasting. As we have seen, linear regression is easy to understand, and we can use descriptive statistics to interpret how our model forecasts are, and whether we place a high or a low degree of trust in them as a result.

The financial performance of startup companies can be used to build a model to forecast profits. In this task, we assume that we are a provider of accounting and legal services to a wide range of startup companies, and part of our package is to extend credit to these companies. As a result, we must assess each startup's profitability; those with poor profitability we should remove from our platform, those with adequate profitability we retain, and to those with strong profitability we might extend further services on credit. In this task, we have three new startups to assess and need to forecast their profits given a range of other data. Would we add them to our platform and extend credit to them?

The dataset gives us a snapshot of annual data for a range of startup companies – research and development spending (R&D Spend), Administration expenses, Marketing Spend – and tells us the State the startup is based in, and the Profit generated:

Table 12.2 Startup companies

	R.D.Spend	Administration	Marketing.Spend	State	Profit
1	165349.2	136897.8	471784.1	New York	192261.8
2	162597.7	151377.6	443898.5	California	191792.1
3	153441.5	101145.6	407934.5	Florida	191050.4
4	144372.4	118671.9	383199.6	New York	182902
5	142107.3	91391.77	366168.4	Florida	166187.9
6	131876.9	99814.71	362861.4	New York	156991.1
7	134615.5	147198.9	127716.8	California	156122.5
8	130298.1	145530.1	323876.7	Florida	155752.6
9	120542.5	148719	311613.3	New York	152211.8
10	123334.9	108679.2	304981.6	California	149760
11	101913.1	110594.1	229161	Florida	146122

Our y-variable of interest is **Profit.**

New Startups

We will randomly select three new startups we want to assess from the dataframe. We will build the regression model based on 47 startups (we will term these the training data) and then test how well the model predicts for the three new startups (we will term these the test data):

R

```
startups = sample(1:nrow(final_df),3)
df_test = final_df[startups,]
df_train = final_df[-startups,]
```

Python

```
df_test = df.sample(n=3)
df_train = df[(df.index.isin(df_test) == False)]
```

Building the Model

We will use all numeric data to help us forecast this in a multiple linear regression model:

R

```
df = read.csv("50_Startups.csv")
reg1 = lm(Profit ~ .-State, data=df)
summary(reg1)
```

Python

```
lm = sm.OLS(df_train['Profit'], df_train[['R&D Spend',
    'Administration','Marketing Spend']])
 model = lm.fit()
 model.summary()
```

```
Call:
lm(formula = Profit ~ . - State, data = df_train)

Residuals:
   Min     1Q Median     3Q    Max
-33366  -4411    159   6703  17529

Coefficients:
                  Estimate Std. Error t value Pr(>|t|)
(Intercept)      4.945e+04  6.764e+03   7.311 4.57e-09 ***
R.D.Spend        7.977e-01  4.629e-02  17.232  < 2e-16 ***
Administration  -2.343e-02  5.259e-02  -0.445   0.6582
Marketing.Spend  2.959e-02  1.682e-02   1.759   0.0857 .
---
Signif. codes:  0 '***' 0.001 '**' 0.01 '*' 0.05 '.' 0.1 ' ' 1

Residual standard error: 9367 on 43 degrees of freedom
Multiple R-squared:  0.9508,     Adjusted R-squared:  0.9474
F-statistic:   277 on 3 and 43 DF,  p-value: < 2.2e-16
```

The results show that the R^2 of the model is 0.95, which is an excellent fit. The variable **R.D.Spend** is statistically significant. If we plot the model above, we get an impression of the strong relationship, shown by how similar predicted and fitted points are on the chart:

R

```R
plot(df_train$R.D.Spend,df_train$Profit,col="red",pch=16,xlab="R&D
Spend",ylab="profit")
points(df_train$R.D.Spend,reg1$fitted.values,col="blue",pch=16)
```

Python

```python
import statsmodels.api as sm

fig, ax = plt.subplots()
fig = sm.graphics.plot_fit(model, 0, ax=ax)
  plt.figure(figsize=(10, 10))

ax.set_ylabel("Profit")
ax.set_xlabel("R&D Spend")
ax.set_title("Linear Regression: Profit Forcasting")

plt.show()
```

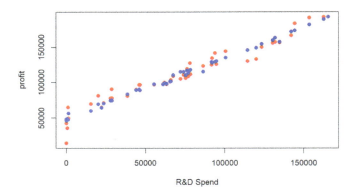

Figure 12.7 Similarity of predicted versus plotted points

Forecast Startup Profits

Finally, we can examine the three new startups to be assessed and evaluate how well the regression model predicts the profits of the three startups:

R

```R
df_test$prediction = predict.lm(reg1,df_test)
df_test
```

Python

```python
ypred = model.predict(df_test[['R&D Spend', 'Administration','Marketing
        Spend', 'New York', 'California', 'Florida']])
print(ypred)
```

```
df_new_startups = df_test.copy()
df_new_startups['Profit'] = ypred


df_new_startups
```

	RDSpend <dbl>	Administration <dbl>	Marketing.Spend <dbl>	State <chr>	Profit <dbl>	prediction <dbl>
11	101913.08	110594.1	229161.0	Florida	146122.0	134937.1
9	120542.52	148719.0	311613.3	New York	152211.8	151344.5
26	64664.71	139553.2	137962.6	California	107404.3	101847.2

Profit predictions are reasonable at first sight. If we now plot them versus our other startups, we will have a clearer idea if these profit expectations are reasonable, and we can decide what action to take. The Python code creates a bubble chart that allows us to scatter the data and add a linear interpolation line:

R

```
plot(df_train$R.D.Spend,df_train$Profit,col="red",pch=16,xlab="R&D
Spend",ylab="profit")
points(df_train$R.D.Spend,reg1$fitted.values,col="blue",pch=16)
points(df_test$R.D.Spend,df_test$prediction,col="yellow",pch=)
points(df_test$R.D.Spend,df_test$Profit,col="green",pch=16)
abline(v = df_test$R.D.Spend)
```

Python

```
# Function... plots bubble for the startup dataset
def bubble_startup_profits(df: pd.DataFrame, max_x: float = 0, max_y: float = 0):
    # Set the figure size
    plt.figure(figsize=(10, 10))


    #Scatter... size down some of the columns of data to get a good look
to the chart
    plt.scatter(df['R&D Spend']/1000, df['Profit']/1000, s=df['Marketing
Spend']/100, c=df['State'].cat.codes, cmap="Accent", alpha=0.4, edgecol-
ors="grey", linewidth=2)


    # Add titles (main and on axis)
    plt.xlabel("R&D Spend")
    plt.ylabel("Profit")
    #Axis Scaling...
    if(max_x==0): max_x = df['R&D Spend'].max()/1000
    if(max_y==0): max_y = df['Profit'].max()/1000
    plt.xlim(left=0, right=max_x)
    plt.ylim(bottom=0, top=max_y)
    plt.title("Profits: Driven by R&D Spend")
```

```
#Interpolation line....
lm = sm.OLS(df['Profit']/1000, sm.add_constant(df['R&D Spend']/1000)).
fit()
    #lm = sm.OLS(df['Profit'], df['R&D Spend']).fit()
    plt.plot(df['R&D Spend']/1000, df['R&D Spend']/1000 * lm.params[1] +
lm.params[0])

    # Show the graph
    plt.show()

#Run func
bubble_startup_profits(df_train)
```

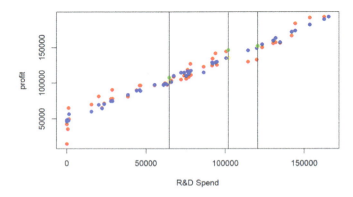

Figure 12.8　Profit predictions for the startups

Dealing with Categorical Data

Thus far, we have ignored the categorical (factor) variable **State** as it does lend itself directly for analysis. However, we can transform this to a numerical representation. One approach we will demonstrate is called 'one hot encoding' (otherwise called *dummy variables*). The following code takes the **State** column and constructs three new columns, called **'California'**, **'New York'**, **'Florida'**, the three categories in this column. Each column will now have a 1 or a 0 value, where for a New York startup, the **New York** column would have a value of 1, and the Florida and California startups would have a value of 0. It would be an interesting exercise to assess whether this categorical variable has an impact on profit prediction:

R

```
library(caret)
dummy = dummyVars(" ~ .", data=df)

final_df = data.frame(predict(dummy, newdata=df))
```

Python

```
one_hot_encodings_for_state = pd.get_dummies(df['State'])
```

b

	R.D.Spend <dbl>	Administration <dbl>	Marketing. Spend <dbl>	StateCalifornia <dbl>	StateFlorida <chr>	StateNew. York <chr>	Profit <dbl>
1	165349.2	136897.80	471784.1	0	0	1	192261.8
2	162597.7	151377.59	443898.5	1	0	0	191792.1
3	153441.5	101145.55	407934.5	0	1	0	191050.4
4	144372.4	118671.85	383199.6	0	0	1	182902.0
5	142107.3	91391.77	366168.4	0	1	0	166187.9
6	131876.9	99814.71	362861.4	0	0	1	156991.1

Summary

In this chapter, we developed regression models for numeric outcomes using the maximum likelihood principle. We discussed the interpretation of the results from regression and importantly analysed the key assumptions invoked and how these should provide caution in interpreting and actioning based on the regression results. In the next chapter, we will extend the regression analysis to consider binary and count outcomes.

Exercises

To complete the activity below, you will need to visit the companion website to the book and download the relevant dataset: https://study.sagepub.com/gopal

Read the file Diamonds.csv.

1   Using the maximum likelihood approach, develop a regression model for the outcome variable `price` based on the independent variables `carat`, `depth`, `table`, `x`, `y`, and `z`.
2   Compute the SST and SSE values. What is the R^2 value?
3   Plot the errors and visually examine if the errors are reasonably normal.
4   Based on a visual plot, assess if there is heteroscedasticity in the regression model.

Read the file UsedCars2017.csv.

1   Using the maximum likelihood approach, develop a regression model for the outcome variable **Price** based on the other variables in the dataframe.
2   Compute the SST and SSE values. What is the R^2 value?
3   Plot the errors and visually examine if the errors are reasonably normal.
4   Based on a visual plot, assess if there is heteroscedasticity in the regression model.

13

GENERAL LINEAR MODELS

Chapter Contents

In this chapter, we will extend the linear regression models we developed in the previous lesson to develop similar models for binary and count outcomes. When the outcome variable of interest in not numeric, it necessitates a different approach to estimate the parameters of interest. These are called general linear models.

BINARY OUTCOMES

Read the file called admit.csv:

R

```
admit = read.csv("admit.csv")
head(admit)
```

```
admit <int> gre <int> gpa <dbl> rank <int>
1      0      380      3.61      3
2      1      660      3.67      3
3      1      800      4.00      1
4      1      640      3.19      4
5      0      520      2.93      4
6      1      760      3.00      2
```

Python

```
admit = pd.read_csv("../data/admit.csv")
print(admit.dtypes)
admit.head(6)
```

```
admit        int64
gre          int64
gpa          float64
rank         int64
dtype: object
    admit      gre      gpa     rank
0     0        380      3.61      3
1     1        660      3.67      3
2     1        800      4.00      1
3     1        640      3.19      4
4     0        520      2.93      4
5     1        760      3.00      2
```

Our object of interest is the binary variable **admit**.

Baseline Model

The baseline model that we want to estimate is shown in the following figure:

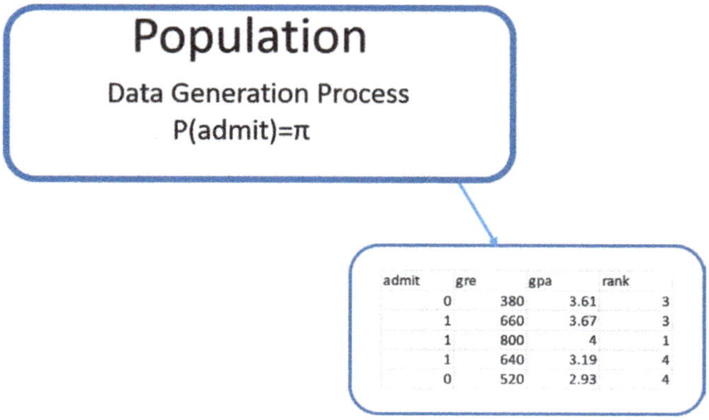

Figure 13.1   Data generation process in the base model

R

```
LLbinary = function(pi){
  p = ifelse(admit$admit == 1, pi, 1 - pi)
  LL = sum(log(p))
  return(-1*LL)
}


res1 = mle2(minuslogl = LLbinary, start = list(pi= .5))
summary(res1)



Maximum likelihood estimation

Call:
mle2(minuslogl = LLbinary, start = list(pi = 0.5))

Coefficients:
   Estimate  Std. Error   z value                      Pr(z)
pi 0.317500    0.023275    13.641 < 0.00000000000000022 ***
---
Signif. codes:  0 '***' 0.001 '**' 0.01 '*' 0.05 '.' 0.1 ' ' 1

-2 log L: 499.9765
```

Python

```
def LLbinary(pi):
    p = np.where(admit.admit == 1, pi, 1-pi)
    LL = np.sum(np.log(p))
```

```
    return(-1*LL)
res1 = scipy.optimize.minimize(LLbinary, x0 = .5, method = 'Nelder-Mead')
print(res1)

final_simplex: (array([[0.31748047],
       [0.31757812]]), array([249.98825913, 249.98826441]))
          fun: 249.98825912954734
      message: 'Optimization terminated successfully.'
         nfev: 26
          nit: 13
       status: 0
      success: True
            x: array([0.31748047])
```

As the result indicates, the point estimate for **admit** is 0.3175, which implies that the probability of admission for a randomly selected applicant is 0.3175. Now suppose we believe that the probability of admission is not the same for everyone and that it is determined by the variables **gre**, **gpa**, and **rank**. The data generation process is depicted in the following figure.

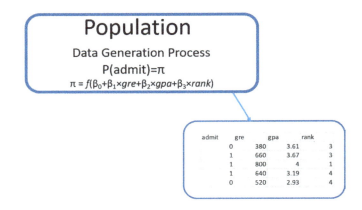

Figure 13.2 Data generation process in the improved model

Let us denote:

$$X = \beta_0 + \beta_1 \times gre + \beta_2 \times gpa + \beta_3 \times rank$$

What should the function be that links X with π? The issue here is that the two terms have different domains. The domain for π is [0,1]. The domain for X, however, is $(-\infty,\infty)$. For the function f that relates X to π, we need to be able to match the two domains. The function f is called the *link* function.

Logistic Regression

The following table illustrates the creation of one possible link function:

Table 13.1 Link function determination

Variable	Domain
X	$[-\infty,\infty]$
e^X	$[0,\infty]$
$\dfrac{e^X}{1+e^X}$	$[0,1]$

The specification linking π with X is the following:

$$\pi = \frac{e^X}{1+e^X}$$

Rearranging this gives us what is called the *logistic regression specification*:

$$\ln\left(\frac{\grave{A}}{1-\pi}\right) = X = \beta_0 + \beta_1 \times \text{gre} + \beta_2 \times \text{gpa} + \beta_3 \times \text{rank}$$

In terms of the terminology, π is the probability of *success*, $\frac{\pi}{1-\pi}$ is called the *odds*, and $\log\left(\frac{\pi}{1-\pi}\right)$ is the *log-odds*. The logistic regression specification essentially says that the log-odds are a linear function of the independent variables.

Now, let us write the code to estimate this:

R

```
LLbinary = function(b0,b1,b2,b3){
    X = b0 + b1*admit$gre + b2*admit$gpa + b3*admit$rank
    pi = exp(X)/(1+(exp(X)))
    p = ifelse(admit$admit == 1, pi, 1 - pi)
  LL = sum(log(p))
  return(-1*LL)
}

res2 = mle2(minuslogl = LLbinary, start = list(b0 = 0, b1 = 0, b2 = 0, b3 = 0))
summary(res2)


Maximum likelihood estimation

Call:
mle2(minuslogl = LLbinary, start = list(b0 = 0, b1 = 0, b2 = 0, b3 = 0))

Coefficients:
      Estimate  Std.Error z value       Pr(z)
b0 -3.3459553  1.1308047 -2.9589     0.003087 **
b1  0.0016874  0.0010866  1.5529     0.120443
```

```
b2   0.8804816   0.3290057   2.6762      0.007446 **
b3  -0.5967868   0.1279710  -4.6635 0.000003109 ***
---
Signif. codes:   0 '***' 0.001 '**' 0.01 '*' 0.05 '.' 0.1 ' ' 1

-2 log L: 459.8384
```

Python

```python
def LLbinary(params):
    b0, b1, b2, b3 = params
    X = b0 + b1*admit['gre'] + b2*admit['gpa'] + b3*admit['rank']
    pi = np.exp(X)/(1+np.exp(X))
    p = np.where(admit.admit == 1, pi, 1-pi)
    LL = np.sum(np.log(p))
    return(-1*LL)
res2 = scipy.optimize.minimize(LLbinary, x0 = [0, 0, 0, 0], method = 'Nelder-Mead')
print(res2)
```

```
          fun: 234.3219680023034
      message: 'Optimization terminated successfully.'
         nfev: 413
          nit: 232
       status: 0
      success: True
            x: array([-0.08354163,  0.00162173, -0.00901617, -0.66485216])
```

The estimated logistic regression is the following:

$$\ln\left(\frac{\pi}{1-\pi}\right) = -3.35 + 0.0017 \times \text{gre} + 0.88 \times \text{gpa} - 0.60 \times \text{rank}$$

The results indicate that **gre** is not statistically significant. A higher **gpa** increases the log-odds of admission, and higher rank lowers the log-odds of admission.

Let us try to understand the marginal effects. A unit increase in **gpa** increases the log-odds by 0.88. To understand this further, we can write:

$$\ln\left(\frac{\pi_1}{1-\pi_1}\right) - \ln\left(\frac{\pi}{1-\pi}\right) = 0.88$$

Rearranging this, we get:

$$\frac{\pi_1}{1-\pi_1} = \frac{\pi}{1-\pi}e^{0.88}$$

$$\frac{\pi_1}{1-\pi_1} = 2.41\frac{\pi}{1-\pi}$$

Thus, we can say that a unit increase in **gpa** increases the odds of admission by a factor of 2.41, which is the exponential of the estimated coefficient value.

Probit Regression

Another way to create the link function between X and π is to use the following:

$$\pi = \phi\,(X)$$

where $\phi(X)$ is a cumulative probability of a standard normal distribution. The specification works as the domain of any cumulative probability is [0,1]. This is called a *probit regression*. Let us code this:

R

```
LLbinary = function(b0,b1,b2,b3){
    X = b0 + b1*admit$gre + b2*admit$gpa + b3*admit$rank
   pi = pnorm(X)
    p = ifelse(admit$admit == 1, pi, 1 - pi)
   LL = sum(log(p))
  return(-1*LL)
}


res3 = mle2(minuslogl = LLbinary, start = list(b0 = 0, b1 = 0, b2 = 0, b3 = 0))
summary(res3)



Maximum likelihood estimation

Call:
mle2(minuslogl = LLbinary, start = list(b0 = 0, b1 = 0, b2 = 0,
    b3 = 0))

Coefficients:
      Estimate  Std. Error z value       Pr(z)
b0 -2.08427222  0.67170665 -3.1030     0.001916 **
b1  0.00093040  0.00064542  1.4415     0.149432
b2  0.55880127  0.19418973  2.8776     0.004007 **
b3 -0.35253287  0.07445794 -4.7347 0.000002194 ***
---
Signif. codes:  0 '***' 0.001 '**' 0.01 '*' 0.05 '.' 0.1 ' ' 1


-2 log L: 460.1186
```

Python

```
def LLbinary(params):
    b0, b1, b2, b3 = params
    X = b0 + b1*admit['gre'] + b2*admit['gpa'] + b3*admit['rank']
    pi = scipy.stats.norm.cdf(X)
    p = np.where(admit.admit == 1, pi, 1-pi)
    LL = np.sum(np.log(p))
    return(-1*LL)
```

```
res3 = scipy.optimize.minimize(LLbinary, x0 = [0, 0, 0, 0], method = 'Nelder-
Mead')
print(res3)
```

```
      fun: 235.06691094815426
  message: 'Optimization terminated successfully.'
     nfev: 365
      nit: 215
   status: 0
  success: True
        x: array([ 0.07532397,  0.00075881, -0.00146091, -0.40348545])
```

The results are quite similar to the logistic regression. The coefficients in a probit regression are a bit harder to interpret, and consequently the logistic regression is more commonly used.

COUNT OUTCOMES

Let us read the file student.csv. The variable of interest is the count variable **daysabs**, which captures the number of days a student has been absent from school:

R

```
student = read.csv("student.csv")
head(student)
```

```
id <int> gender <int> math <int> prog <int> daysabs <int>
1      1001     0      63     2       4
2      1002     0      27     2       4
3      1003     1      20     2       2
4      1004     1      16     2       3
5      1005     1       2     2       3
6      1006     1      71     2       136     1      760     3.00     2
```

Python

```
student = pd.read_csv("../data/student.csv")
print(student.dtypes)
student.head(6)
id         int64
gender     int64
math       int64
prog       int64
daysabs    int64
dtype: object
```

	id	gender	math	prog	daysabs				
0	1001	0	63	2	4				
1	1002	0	27	2	4				
2	1003	1	20	2	2				
3	1004	1	16	2	3				
4	1005	1	2	2	3				
5	1006	1	71	2	136	1	760	3.00	2

Baseline Model

Given that the outcome variable is of the type count, the baseline model is depicted below:

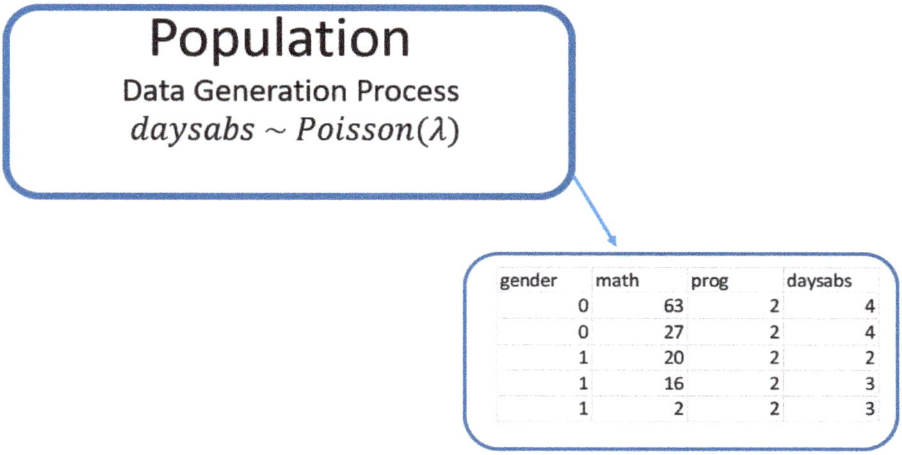

Figure 13.3 Data generation process (Poisson's) in the baseline model

The following estimates the population parameter λ:

R

```
LLpois = function(lam){
  p = dpois(x = student$daysabs, lambda = lam)
  LL = sum(log(p))
  return(-1*LL)
}

res4 = mle2(minuslogl = LLpois, start = list(lam=10))
summary(res4)
```

```
Maximum likelihood estimation

Call:
```

```
mle2(minuslogl = LLpois, start = list(lam = 10))


Coefficients:
    Estimate  Std.Error z value                 Pr(z)
lam 5.95542    0.13772   43.243 < 0.00000000000000022 ***
---
Signif. codes:  0 '***' 0.001 '**' 0.01 '*' 0.05 '.' 0.1 ' ' 1


-2 log L: 3101.018
```

Python

```
def LLpois(lam):
    p = scipy.stats.poisson.pmf(student['daysabs'], lam)
    LL = np.sum(np.log(p))
    return(-1*LL)
res4 = scipy.optimize.minimize(LLpois, x0 = 10, method = 'Nelder-Mead')
print(res4)

final_simplex: (array([[5.95544434],
        [5.9553833 ]]), array([1550.50922948, 1550.50922948]))
          fun: 1550.5092294752835
      message: 'Optimization terminated successfully.'
         nfev: 36
          nit: 18
       status: 0
      success: True
            x: array([5.95544434])
```

From the above results, we conclude that the average number of days absent in the student population is 5.96.

Poisson Regression

Now suppose we think that the number of days absent is influenced by the variables **gender**, **math**, and **prog**. The data generation process is depicted in the following figure:

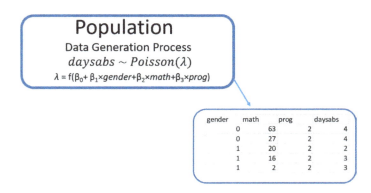

Figure 13.4 Data generation process (Poisson's) in the improved model

As the domain of λ is $(0,\infty)$ the link function is specified as $\lambda = e^x$. The following estimates the Poisson regression:

R

```
LLpois = function(b0, b1, b2, b3){
  X = b0 + b1*student$gender + b2*student$math + b3*student$prog
  lam = exp(X)
  p = dpois(x = student$daysabs, lambda = lam)
  LL = sum(log(p))
  return(-1*LL)
}

res5 = mle2(minuslogl = LLpois, start = list(b0 = log(5.96), b1 = 0, b2 = 0, b3 = 0))
summary(res5)


Maximum likelihood estimation

Call:
mle2(minuslogl = LLpois, start = list(b0 = log(5.96), b1 = 0,
    b2 = 0, b3 = 0))

Coefficients:
      Estimate  Std. Error  z value            Pr(z)
b0  3.25550431  0.08134145  40.0227 < 0.00000000000000022 ***
b1  0.23535492  0.04674158   5.0352        0.0000004773 ***
b2 -0.00766550  0.00092305  -8.3045 < 0.00000000000000022 ***
b3 -0.60676237  0.03619218 -16.7650 < 0.00000000000000022 ***
---
Signif. codes:  0 '***' 0.001 '**' 0.01 '*' 0.05 '.' 0.1 ' ' 1

-2 log L: 2648.787
```

Python

```
def LLpois(params):
    b0, b1, b2, b3 = params
    X = b0 + b1*student['gender'] + b2*student['math'] + b3*student['prog']
    lam = np.exp(X)
    p = scipy.stats.poisson.pmf(student['daysabs'], lam)
    LL = np.sum(np.log(p))
    return(-1*LL)
res5 = scipy.optimize.minimize(LLpois, x0 = [np.log(5.96), 0, 0, 0],
    method = 'Nelder-Mead')
print(res5)


        fun: 1324.3947078083743
    message: 'Optimization terminated successfully.'
```

```
     nfev: 254
      nit: 150
   status: 0
  success: True
        x: array([ 3.25203163,  0.23840155, -0.00763839, -0.60657528])
```

The Poisson regression equation is:

$$\ln(\lambda) = 3.26 + 0.24 \times \text{gender} - 0.0077 \times \text{math} - 0.607 \times \text{prog}$$

All variables are statistically significant. Let us understand the marginal effects. The coefficient for **gender** is 0.24. Gender is coded as 0 for females and 1 for males:

$$\ln(\lambda_1) - \ln(\lambda) = 0.24$$

With some algebra, we get:

$$\lambda_1 = e^{0.24}\,\lambda$$

and thus:

$$\lambda_1 = 1.27\lambda$$

This means that the average number of days a male student is absent is 1.27 times (which is the exponential of the estimated coefficient for **gender** 0.24) that of a female student.

MODEL FIT

With linear regression, R^2 is used as a measure of the model's performance. The same concept does not translate to binary and count models.

For a binary regression, a few metrics are useful to assess the model fit. The first is the likelihood, which is normally reported as −2LL (−2 loglikelihood). Note that we want this to be smaller. For the baseline model, the value of −2LL was 499.9765. For the logistic regression, it is 459.8384. Hence, the regression model is better than the baseline model. Two other metrics that are commonly used are *AIC* (Akaike Information Criterion) and *BIC* (Bayesian Information Criterion). They are defined as:

$$AIC = -2LL + 2k$$

$$BIC = -2LL + 2k\ln(n)$$

where *k* is the number of parameters to be estimated and *n* is the number of observations.

Let us compute these for the Poisson model:

Table 13.2 Metrics and model performance (baseline versus Poisson)

Metric	Baseline model	Poisson regression
-2LL	3101.018	2648.787
AIC	3103.018 ($k = 1$)	2656.787 ($k = 4$)
BIC	3112.517	2694.782

The metrics clearly indicate that the Poisson regression model is adding value over the baseline model.

FUNCTIONS IN R AND PYTHON

While we developed and estimated the binary and count models from first principles to derive deep intuition and understanding, R and Python provide functions that can be used to directly estimate the model.

R

The function to estimate a regression model with binary or count outcomes in R is **glm()**. The general syntax is:

```
glm(formula, family=familytype(link=linkfunction), data=)
```

Table 13.3 Distributions and link functions in R

Family	Default link function
binomial	(link = "logit")
gaussian	(link = "identity")
Gamma	(link = "inverse")
inverse.gaussian	(link = "1/mu^2")
poisson	(link = "log")
quasi	(link = "identity", variance = "constant")
quasibinomial	(link = "logit")
quasipoisson	(link = "log")

Python

The function to estimate a regression model with binary or count outcomes in Python is **sm.formula.glm()**. The general syntax is:

```
sm.formula.glm("formula", family= sm.families.<familyname>, data=)
```

Table 13.4 Distribution families in Python

Binomial()	Binomial exponential family
Gaussian()	Gaussian exponential family
NegativeBinomial()	Negative Binomial exponential family
Poisson()	Poisson exponential family
Gamma()	Gamma exponential family
Tweedie()	Tweedie family

The following code estimates the binary and the count models with our data.

R

```
res6 = glm(admit~gre+gpa+rank,family="binomial",data=admit)
summary(res6)


glm(formula = admit ~ gre + gpa + rank, family = "binomial", data = admit)

Deviance Residuals:
    Min       1Q   Median       3Q      Max
-1.5802  -0.8848  -0.6382   1.1575   2.1732

Coefficients:
             Estimate  Std. Error  z value  Pr(>|z|)
(Intercept) -3.449548    1.132846   -3.045   0.00233 **
gre          0.002294    0.001092    2.101   0.03564 *
gpa          0.777014    0.327484    2.373   0.01766 *
rank        -0.560031    0.127137   -4.405 0.0000106 ***
---
Signif. codes:  0 '***' 0.001 '**' 0.01 '*' 0.05 '.' 0.1 ' ' 1

(Dispersion parameter for binomial family taken to be 1)

    Null deviance: 499.98  on 399  degrees of freedom
Residual deviance: 459.44  on 396  degrees of freedom
AIC: 467.44
```

Python

```
res6 = sm.formula.glm("admit ~ gre + gpa + rank", family=sm.families.
       Binomial(), data=admit).fit()
res6.summary()


Generalized Linear Model Regression Results
Dep. Variable:    admit      No. Observations: 400
Model:            GLM        Df Residuals:     396
Model Family:     Binomial   Df Model:         3
Link Function:    Logit      Scale:            1.0000
```

```
Method:            IRLS            Log-Likelihood:     -229.72
Date:              Sat, 16 Jul 2022    Deviance:        459.44
Time:              21:21:57        Pearson chi2:       399.
No. Iterations: 4                  Pseudo R-squ. (CS):    0.09637
Covariance Type: nonrobust
coef         std err        z       P>|z|      [0.025 0.975]
Intercept    -3.4495       1.133    -3.045     0.002     -5.670    -1.229
gre           0.0023       0.001     2.101     0.036      0.000     0.004
gpa           0.7770       0.327     2.373     0.018      0.135     1.419
rank         -0.5600       0.127    -4.405     0.000     -0.809    -0.311
```

R

```
res7 = glm(daysabs~gender+math+prog,family="poisson",data=student)
summary(res7)


Call:
glm(formula = daysabs ~ gender + math + prog, family = "poisson",
    data = student)

Deviance Residuals:
    Min      1Q    Median      3Q      Max
-4.0728  -2.2685  -0.9698   0.7809   7.2922

Coefficients:
             Estimate Std. Error z value         Pr(>|z|)
(Intercept)  3.254816   0.081352  40.009 < 0.0000000000000002 ***
gender       0.235542   0.046747   5.039         0.000000469 ***
math        -0.007633   0.000923  -8.270 < 0.0000000000000002 ***
prog        -0.607277   0.036192 -16.779 < 0.0000000000000002 ***
---
Signif. codes:  0 '***' 0.001 '**' 0.01 '*' 0.05 '.' 0.1 ' ' 1


(Dispersion parameter for poisson family taken to be 1)

    Null deviance: 2217.7  on 313  degrees of freedom
Residual deviance: 1765.5  on 310  degrees of freedom
AIC: 2656.8
```

Python

```
res7 = sm.formula.glm("daysabs ~ gender + math + prog", family=sm.
        families.Poisson(), data=student).fit()
res7.summary()
```

```
Generalized      Linear Model        Regression Results
Dep. Variable:   daysabs             No. Observations:    314
Model:           GLM                 Df Residuals:        310
Model Family:    Poisson             Df Model:            3
Link Function:   Log                 Scale:               1.0000
Method:          IRLS                Log-Likelihood:      -1324.4
Date:            Sat, 16 Jul 2022    Deviance:            1765.5
Time:            21:21:57            Pearson chi2:        2.03e+03
No. Iterations:  5                   Pseudo R-squ. (CS): 0.7631
Covariance Type: nonrobust
coef          std err        z       P>|z|      [0.025 0.975]
Intercept     3.2548     0.081    40.008    0.000     3.095    3.414
gender        0.2355     0.047     5.039    0.000     0.144    0.327
math         -0.0076     0.001    -8.270    0.000    -0.009   -0.006
prog         -0.6073     0.036   -16.779    0.000    -0.678   -0.536
```

Summary

In this chapter, we developed regression models where the outcome of interest is either a binary or a count variable. The core principles remain the same as with linear regression, except that we need a link function to relate the independent variables with the outcome. Also, note that the issues of multicollinearity and omitted variables are also pertinent for binary and count outcomes. Therefore, be careful about interpreting the marginal effects as we discussed in this and the previous chapter. The next chapter will delve deeper into regression diagnostics to assess whether the underlying assumptions hold, followed by approaches to alter the structure of the regression model so that the assumptions are reasonably satisfied, and the overall performance of the model is improved.

Exercises

To complete the activity below, you will need to visit the companion website to the book and download the relevant dataset: https://study.sagepub.com/gopal

Read the file CA.COVID.csv.

1   Using the maximum likelihood approach, develop a Poisson regression model for the cumulative number of patient infections based on the cumulative number of staff infections and the number of available beds.

2   Are independent variables statistically significant? What is the marginal effect of the two independent variables? Are they practically significant? What do you conclude?

3   Compute the *AIC* and *BIC* values for both the Poisson regression model and the baseline model.
4   Does the Poisson regression model add value over the baseline model, based on *AIC* and *BIC* values?

Read the file Health.csv.

5   Using the maximum likelihood approach, develop a Poisson regression model for the outcome variable **ofp** based on variables **numchron**, **age**, **male**, **married**, and **employed**.
6   Which independent variables are statistically significant? What is the marginal effect of the statistically significant independent variables? Are they practically significant? What do you conclude?
7   Compute the *AIC* and *BIC* values for both the Poisson regression model and the baseline model.
8   Does the Poisson regression model add value over the baseline model, based on *AIC* and *BIC* values?

Read the file Credit.csv.

9   Using the maximum likelihood approach develop a logistic regression model for the outcome variable **Creditworthy** based on all the other variables in the dataframe.
10 Which independent variables are statistically significant? What is the marginal effect of the statistically significant independent variables? Are they practically significant? What do you conclude?
11 Compute the *AIC* and *BIC* values for both the logistic regression model and the baseline model.
12 Does the logistic regression model add value over the baseline model, based on *AIC* and *BIC* values?

14

REGRESSION DIAGNOSTICS AND STRUCTURE

Chapter Contents

Regression is one of the most popular approaches for building models and is often considered the 'workhorse' of analytics. In this chapter, we will conduct a variety of diagnostic tests to ensure that all the key assumptions invoked in developing the model are met and these use the diagnostic outcomes to aid in developing a 'good' structure for the regression model. In our context, 'good' refers to satisfying the assumptions and enhancing the fit of the model. This process also enables us to move the final regression structure we employ closer to the 'true' data generation process that creates the data we study.

DIAGNOSTICS

The basic regression model makes several assumptions, including the following.

1   Normality – errors are normally and independently distributed.
2   Homoscedastic – constant variance of errors or variance of the dependent variable does not vary with the levels of the independent variables.
3   Multicollinearity – the correlation between the independent variables is not strong enough to impact the parameter estimates.

When some of these assumptions are not met, the results obtained can be quite misleading and the prediction accuracy can be significantly reduced. In addition, we also need to concern ourselves with the following issues.

1   Extreme values – extremely large or small values, in comparison to other values in either independent or dependent variables, can have a disproportionate impact on the model outcomes and parameter values. We need approaches to detect and correct for such influential observations.
2   Linearity – the relationship between the independent and dependent variables is linear. While this is a simple depiction of the data generation process, we can explore more complicated structures that enhance the model performance.

To begin the diagnostics, let us examine a simple linear regression model where the key assumptions are met. Suppose the data generation process is as follows:

$$y = 250 + x + \epsilon, \epsilon \sim N(0, 10)$$

We will generate a sample of data from the above and examine the regression results and a plot of the residuals:

R

```
set.seed(987654321)
x = runif(500,1,100)
y = 250 + x + rnorm(500,0,10)
reg1 = lm(y~x)
coef(reg1)
```

```
plot(reg1$fitted.values,reg1$residuals)
abline(h = 0,col = "red")
```

```
(Intercept)              x
  249.606869       1.001227
```

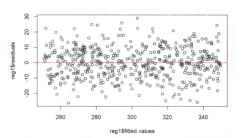

Python

```
np.random.seed(987654321)
x = np.random.uniform(1,100, size = 500)
y = 250 + x + np.random.normal(loc = 0, scale = 10, size = 500)
df = pd.DataFrame({'x':x, 'y':y})
reg1 = ols("y~x", data = df).fit()
reg1.params
```

```
Intercept     249.119728
x               1.042288
dtype: float64
```

```
plt.scatter(reg1.fittedvalues, reg1.resid)
plt.axhline(0, color = 'red')
plt.show()
```

In this 'proper' regression, the coefficient estimates based on a sample of 500 observations are quite close to the true population values. In addition, the plot of the residuals against predicted outcomes is generally uniformly spread around 0.

HETEROSCEDASTICITY

Now, let us consider a data generation process where the errors are heteroscedastic:

$$y = 100 + 2x + x\varepsilon, \ \varepsilon \sim N(0, 1)$$

In the above specification, the errors get larger as x and y values increase. Let us now generate a sample of data from the above and examine the regression outcomes:

R

```
set.seed(987654321)
x = runif(500,1,20)
y = 100+2*x + x*rnorm(500)
reg1 = lm(y~x)
```

```
coef(reg1)
plot(reg1$fitted.values,reg1$residuals)
abline(h = 0,col = "red")
```

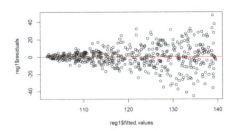

```
(Intercept)            x
  99.763920     1.991029
```

Python

```
np.random.seed(987654321)
x = np.random.uniform(1,20, size = 500)
y = 100 + 2*x + x*np.random.normal(size = 500)
df = pd.DataFrame({'x':x, 'y':y})
reg1 = ols("y~x", data = df).fit()
reg1.params

Intercept     98.784781
x              2.303887
dtype: float64

plt.scatter(reg1.fittedvalues, reg1.resid)
plt.axhline(0, color = 'red')
plt.show()
```

Despite heteroscedasticity, the coefficient estimates based on a sample of 500 observations are quite close to the true population values. The residual plot reveals that errors get larger as the outcome variable increases.

Let us look at a dataset where we do not know the true data generation process. Read the file cars.csv, which contains two variables: **speed** and **dist**. The variable **speed** refers to the speed of the car when brakes were applied to stop the car and **dist** refers to the distance the car then travelled before it came to a complete stop:

R

```
read.csv("cars.csv")
reg2 = lm(dist ~ speed, data = cars)
plot(reg2$fitted.values,reg2$residuals)
abline(h = 0,col = "red")
summary(reg2)$r.squared
coef(reg2)

[1] 0.6510794

(Intercept)        speed
 -17.579095     3.932409
```

Python

```
cars = pd.read_csv("../data/cars.csv")
reg2 = ols("dist ~ speed", data = cars).fit()
plt.scatter(reg2.fittedvalues, reg2.resid)
plt.axhline(0, color = 'red')
plt.show()
reg2.rsquared
```

```
0.6510793807582509
```

```
reg2.params
```

```
Intercept    -17.579095
speed          3.932409
dtype: float64
```

Visually, there appears to be heteroscedasticity. We can formally test for heteroscedasticity with a model that evaluates whether the variance of the errors is linearly related to independent variables. Such a model can be examined by regressing the squared residuals on the independent variables. If there is no statistical relationship in the model, it points to homoscedasticity. This called the *Breusch–Pagan test* and is implemented as follows:

R

```
library(car)
ncvTest(reg1)
ncvTest(reg2)
```

```
Non-constant Variance Score Test
Variance formula: ~ fitted.values
Chisquare = 161.1055, Df = 1, p = < 2.22e-16
```

```
Non-constant Variance Score Test
Variance formula: ~ fitted.values
Chisquare = 4.650233, Df = 1, p = 0.031049
```

Python

```
from statsmodels.compat import lzip
names = ['Lagrange multiplier statistic', 'p-value',
         'f-value', 'f p-value']

test1 = sm.stats.diagnostic.het_breuschpagan(reg1.resid, reg1.model.exog)
lzip(names, test1)

[('Lagrange multiplier statistic', 94.5833482166779),
 ('p-value', 2.3498677853334443e-22),
 ('f-value', 116.18296191020761),
```

```
('f p-value', 1.7179132159423896e-24)]
```

```
test2 = sm.stats.diagnostic.het_breuschpagan(reg2.resid, reg2.model.exog)
lzip(names, test2)
```

```
[('Lagrange multiplier statistic', 3.214879927174641),
 ('p-value', 0.07297154505407806),
 ('f-value', 3.2983614504820826),
 ('f p-value', 0.07559716486053959)]
```

In both models, the p-value is small enough (0.03 and 0.07) for us to reasonably reject the null hypothesis of homoscedasticity. The difference in the outcome is quite likely due to differences in the implementation of the test. What do we do when we detect heteroscedasticity? What we observe is that, in some regions, the errors are larger than in other regions. In the regions where the errors are large, our predictive power is poorer. The important thing is to recognize this fact and use the model appropriately. In the case of the *cars* dataframe, it is logical that the errors are larger when the speed is higher. When one hits the brakes at high speeds, several factors such as the road condition, state of the car tyres, weather, driver skills, etc. determine how far the car travels before it comes to a stop. At lower speeds, these factors likely do not have a large effect. Thus, the main takeaway is to recognize this and use the model appropriately.

In some cases, it might be possible to alleviate the problem of heteroscedasticity by transforming the dependent variable. The transformation that is often used is called the *Box Cox transformation*. The main purpose of the transformation is to make the resulting variable look as normally distributed as possible:

$$z_i = \begin{cases} \dfrac{y_i^{\lambda} - 1}{\lambda} & \text{if } \lambda \neq 0 \\ \log(y_i) & \text{if } \lambda = 0 \end{cases}$$

Box Cox transformation uses the maximum likelihood approach to find the value of λ that makes z_i as close to being normally distributed as possible:

R

```
library(caret)
BoxCoxTrans(y)

Box Cox Transformation

Estimated Lambda: -2


BoxCoxTrans(cars$dist)

Box Cox Transformation

Estimated Lambda: 0.5
```

Python

```
import scipy.stats
fitted_data1, fitted_lambda1 = scipy.stats.boxcox(y)
fitted_lambda1
```

```
-1.5741315427789888
```

```
fitted_data2, fitted_lambda2 = scipy.stats.boxcox(cars.dist)
print(fitted_lambda2)
```

```
0.4950761909055122
```

Let us employ the transformations as suggested and evaluate whether the two regressions models can be improved:

R

```
y1 = predict(BoxCoxTrans(y),y)
reg3 = lm(y1~x)
plot(reg3$fitted.values,reg3$residuals)
abline(h = 0,col = "red")
ncvTest(reg3)
summary(reg3)$r.squared
```

```
Non-constant Variance Score Test
Variance formula: ~ fitted.values
Chisquare = 85.66293, Df = 1, p = < 2.22e-16
[1] 0.4463459
```

Python

```
y1 = fitted_data1
df1 = pd.DataFrame({'x':x, 'y1':y1})
reg3 = ols("y1~x", data = df1).fit()
plt.scatter(reg3.fittedvalues, reg3.resid)
plt.axhline(0, color = 'red')
plt.show()
```

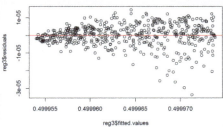

```
test3 = sm.stats.diagnostic.het_breuschpagan
        (reg3.resid, reg3.model.exog)
lzip(names, test3)
```

```
[('Lagrange multiplier statistic', 30.077635108296253),
 ('p-value', 4.1509084365023434e-08),
 ('f-value', 31.874759328348706),
 ('f p-value', 2.7656251542738505e-08)]
```

```
reg3.rsquared
```

```
0.5670580845119884
```

R

```
cars$dist1 = predict(BoxCoxTrans(cars$dist),cars$dist)
reg4 = lm(dist1~speed,data =cars)
plot(reg4$fitted.values,reg4$residuals)
abline(h = 0,col = "red")
ncvTest(reg4)
summary(reg4)$r.squared
coef(reg4)
```

```
Non-constant Variance Score Test
Variance formula: ~ fitted.values
Chisquare = 0.01205185, Df = 1, p = 0.91258
```

```
[1] 0.7094131
```

```
(Intercept)        speed
  0.5541004    0.6448250
```

Python

```
dist1 = fitted_data2
cars1 = pd.DataFrame({'speed':cars['speed'], 'dist1':dist1})
reg4 = ols("dist1 ~ speed", data = cars1).fit()
plt.scatter(reg4.fittedvalues, reg4.resid)
plt.axhline(0, color = 'red')
plt.show()


test4 = sm.stats.diagnostic.het_breuschpagan
        (reg4.resid, reg4.model.exog)
lzip(names, test4)
```

```
[('Lagrange multiplier statistic', 0.005927257689752885),
 ('p-value', 0.9386325459422038),
 ('f-value', 0.005690842003903435),
 ('f p-value', 0.9401800262578285)]
```

```
reg4.rsquared
```

```
0.7096882570316119
```

The results we obtained are quite interesting. There was no improvement in the first regression model where heteroscedasticity continues to be present even after the Box Cox transformation. However, for the **cars** dataframe, the transformation overcame the problem of heteroscedasticity and improved the R^2 value. Among the following two specifications for `dist`, the second one exhibits homoscedasticity and improves R^2, and thus is likely be closer to the true data generation process.

$$dist = -17.58 + 3.93 \text{ speed} + \epsilon$$

$$\frac{\sqrt{dist} - 1}{0.5} = 0.554 + 0.645 speed + \epsilon$$

Extreme Values

Let us assess the impact of an extreme value on the coefficient estimates with an example. Note that in the second case, we introduced an extreme value for a single x observation:

$$y = 250 + x + \epsilon, \epsilon \sim N(0, 10)$$

R

```
set.seed(987654321)
x = runif(500,1,100)
y = 250 + x + rnorm(500,0,10)
reg1 = lm(y~x)
reg1$coefficients
```

```
(Intercept)           x
 249.606869    1.001227
```

```
x[499] = 860
reg1 = lm(y~x)
reg1$coefficients
```

```
(Intercept)           x
278.4388931   0.4248577
```

Python

```
np.random.seed(987654321)
x = np.random.uniform(low = 1, high = 100, size = (500,))
y = 250 + x + np.random.normal(loc = 0,scale = 10,size = (500,))
df = pd.DataFrame({'x' :x, 'y' :y})
reg1 = ols("y~x", data = df).fit()
reg1.params
```

```
Intercept     249.119728
x               1.042288
dtype: float64
```

```
x[499] = 860
```

```
df = pd.DataFrame({'x':x, 'y':y})
reg1 = ols("y~x", data = df).fit()
reg1.params
```

```
Intercept    278.441160
x              0.439657
dtype: float64
```

The above clearly shows the potential effect of extreme values in the observations as they can significantly distort the coefficient estimates. *Cook's distance* is a commonly used metric to identify influential observations. Cook's distance measures the effect of deleting a given observation. The measure is constructed for each observation by computing the difference in the estimates of the outcome with and without that observation. Observations with a large Cook's distance merit closer examination due to their undue influence on the parameter estimates. Values greater than $4/n$, where n is the number of observations, are commonly treated as influential observations. The following table provides the requisite code to identify, plot, and remove highly influential observations:

R

```
cd = cooks.distance(reg1)
cutoff = 4/500
plot(reg1,which = 4,cook.levels = cutoff)
abline(h = cutoff,col="red")

reg2 = lm(y[-c(159,309,499)]~x[-c(159,309,499)])
reg2$coefficients
```

```
        (Intercept) x[-c(159, 309, 499)]
        249.7816250          0.9960175
```

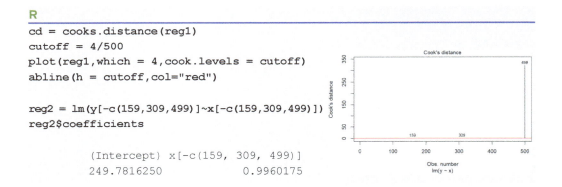

Python

```
cd = reg1.get_influence().cooks_distance
cutoff = 4/500
plt.plot(cd[0])
plt.axhline(cutoff, color = 'red')
plt.show()

reg2 = ols("y~x", data = df.drop
        (df.index[[159, 309, 499]])).fit()
reg2.params
```

```
Intercept    249.157346
x              1.041671
dtype: float64
```

Notice that removing the three most influential observations allowed us to obtain parameter estimates closer to the data generation process. The following provides an illustration for a binary regression:

R

```
breg1 = glm(admit~gre+gpa+rank,data = admit,family = "binomial")
round(breg1$coefficients,3)
z = cooks.distance(breg1)
cutoff = 4/nrow(admit)
plot(breg1,which = 4,cook.levels = cutoff)
abline(h = cutoff,col = "red")
```

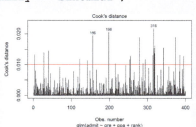

(Intercept)	gre	gpa	rank
-3.450	0.002	0.777	-0.560

```
breg1 = glm(admit~gre+gpa+rank,data =
        admit[-c(156,198,316),],family = "binomial")
breg1$coefficients
```

(Intercept)	gre	gpa	rank
-3.913	0.003	0.861	-0.607

Python

```
breg1 = sm.formula.glm("admit~gre+gpa+rank", data = admit, family =
        sm.families.Binomial()).fit()
np.round(breg1.params, 3)
```

```
Intercept    -3.450
gre           0.002
gpa           0.777
rank         -0.560
dtype: float64
```

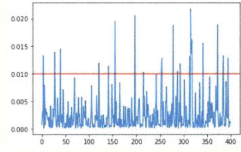

```
z = breg1.get_influence().cooks_distance
cutoff = 4/len(admit)
plt.plot(z[0])
plt.axhline(cutoff, color = 'red')
plt.show()
```

```
breg1 = sm.formula.glm("admit~gre+gpa+rank", data = admit.drop(admit.
index[[156, 198, 316]]), family = sm.families.Binomial()).fit()
breg1.params
```

```
Intercept   -3.598649
gre          0.002517
gpa          0.775080
rank        -0.552710
dtype: float64
```

It is often a good practice to detect outliers in the data before conducting formal statistical analysis. Boxplots, as we discussed earlier in the book, are a useful tool to detect outliers. An example is provided below:

R

```
library(ggplot2)
ggplot(admit, aes(x = gre)) +
  geom_boxplot(outlier.colour = "red", outlier.shape = 8,
               outlier.size = 4)
```

Python

```
import seaborn as sns
sns.boxplot(x = admit['gre'])
```

MULTICOLLINEARITY

We will assess the impact of multicollinearity through an example. Suppose the data generation process is as follows:

$$y = 2x_1 + x_2 + \epsilon, \epsilon \sim N(0, 10)$$

We will introduce correlation between the two variables through the variable `lambda` in the code below. You can experiment with the effects of multicollinearity by changing the values of `lambda`:

R

```
set.seed(987654321)
x1 = runif(500,1,10)
lambda = 0.7
x2 = (lambda*x1) + (1-lambda)*runif(500,1,10)
cor(x1,x2)
```

```
[1] 0.9193934
```

```
y = 2*x1 + x2 + rnorm(500,0,10)
reg1 = lm(y~x1+x2)
round(reg1$coefficients,3)
```

```
(Intercept)          x1          x2
      1.729       2.548       0.235
```

Python

```
np.random.seed(987654321)
x1 = np.random.uniform(low = 1, high = 10, size = (500,))
a = 0.7
x2 = a * x1 + (1-a)*np.random.uniform(low = 1, high = 10, size = (500,))
np.corrcoef(x1,x2)
```

```
array([[1.        , 0.92128094],
       [0.92128094, 1.        ]])
```

```
y = 2*x1 + x2 + np.random.normal(loc = 0,scale = 10,size = (500,))
df = pd.DataFrame({'x1':x1, 'x2':x2, 'y':y})
reg1 = ols("y~x1+x2", data = df).fit()
round(reg1.params,3)
```

```
Intercept    -2.480
x1            1.848
x2            1.671
dtype: float64
```

As discussed in Chapter 12, multicollinearity can distort the coefficient estimates of correlated variables, as illustrated in the above example.

The question, however, is how high should the correlation between two variables be before we get concerned with the effects of multicollinearity? A common approach for this is to calculate a *variance inflation factor* (VIF) for each independent variable. The variance inflation factor represents the proportion of variance in one variable explained by all the other predictors in the model. In our example, to compute the VIF for x_1, we estimate the following regression and compute the R^2 value:

$$x_1 = \alpha_0 + \alpha_1 x_2 + \epsilon$$

If R_1^2 is the R^2 value for the above regression, the VIF for x_1 is computed as:

$$VIF_1 = \frac{1}{1 - R_1^2}$$

When $R_1^2 = 0$, it indicates that x_2 has no effect on x_1 and thus there is no problem of multicollinearity. In this case, the VIF value is 1. As R_1^2 increases, the VIF value increases as well, with higher values of VIF suggesting increasing multicollinearity. A rule of thumb is that VIF values above 4 (some suggest cutoffs of 5 or 10 as well) are problematic. The following code illustrates the computation of VIF in our example:

R

```
reg2 = lm(x1~x2)
r2_1 = summary(reg2)$r.squared
r2_1
vif_x1 = 1/(1-r2_1)
vif_x1
```

```
[1] 0.8452842
[1] 6.463462
```

Python

```
reg2 = ols("x1~x2", data = df).fit()
r2_1 = reg2.rsquared
r2_1
```

```
0.8487585674194995
```

```
vif_x1 = 1/(1-r2_1)
vif_x1
```

```
6.611944775567602
```

A VIF value of 6.46 indicates multicollinearity in our example. Both R and Python have packages that provide functions to compute VIF and this is shown below for the case of a binary regression. Low values of VIF indicate that we do not have to worry about multicollinearity in such a case:

R

```
round(cor(admit[,-1]),3)
vif(breg1)
```

```
         gre     gpa    rank
gre    1.000   0.384  -0.123
gpa    0.384   1.000  -0.057
rank  -0.123  -0.057   1.000


     gre      gpa      rank
1.121310 1.123533 1.004103
```

Python

```
round(admit.corr(),3)
```

```
        admit     gre     gpa    rank
admit   1.000   0.184   0.178  -0.243
gre     0.184   1.000   0.384  -0.123
gpa     0.178   0.384   1.000  -0.057
rank   -0.243  -0.123  -0.057   1.000
```

If the objective of building a regression model is for predicting the outcome, then multicollinearity is not a significant problem. However, caution must be exercised, as we saw, in interpreting the coefficients as correctly capturing the marginal effect of the independent variable on the outcome. Doing so would be incorrect and inappropriate. In addition to attempting to obtain reasonable marginal effects, there are other reasons for trying to remove the problems arising from multicollinearity. One, when several independent variables are highly correlated, it is not necessary to include all of them in the regression as it would be redundant. Dropping some of the variables will not cause a large reduction in the performance of the model as other variables essentially capture the information content of the dropped variables. It will also enable construction of parsimonious regression models where only salient and important variables are used in the final model specification. Approaches for this include stepwise regression and subsets regression; we will discuss these later in the chapter. Another perspective is that highly correlated variables are likely capturing a higher-level concept or construct. For example, we often find **height** and **weight** of individuals to be highly correlated and might indicate a broader *body type* concept. Similarly, negative correlation between **exercise** and **body fat** is indicative of the *healthiness* of an individual. In such cases, it might be useful to combine the correlated variables and create new variables that do not exhibit multicollinearity. Approaches for this include summing up correlated variables into one new variable and conducting *principal components analysis*. Principal components analysis is a feature extraction technique that is particularly useful when the number of independent variables is large and there exists a significant degree of correlation among these variables. This technique creates *components*, where each component is a linear combination of the independent variables and the components themselves are uncorrelated to each other. We will not delve into principal components analysis here, but we will discuss stepwise regression and subsets regression to tackle multicollinearity.

REGRESSION STRUCTURE

In developing a linear regression model, we assume that (a) the independent variables we include impact the outcome variable, and that (b) the structure of the relationship is strictly linear. This structure, we assume, properly captures the data generation process which created the data we analyse. An example of that is the following:

$$Y = \beta_0 + \beta_1 x_1 + \beta_2 x_2 + \epsilon$$

Strictly speaking, to conduct the maximum likelihood analysis for regression, we need the structure of the regression to be 'linear in parameters' but not necessarily 'linear in variables'. Consider the following regression structures:

$$Y = \beta_0 + \beta_1 x_1 + \beta_2 x_2 + \beta_3 x_1 x_2 + \epsilon$$

$$y = \beta_0 + \beta_1 x_1^3 + \beta_2 log(x_2) + \beta_3 x_1 x_2 + \epsilon$$

$$y = \beta_0 + \beta_1 x_1 + \beta_2 \frac{1}{x_2} + \beta_3 x_1 x_2 + \epsilon$$

$$log(y) = \beta_0 + \beta_1 x_1^3 + \beta_2 log(x_2) + \beta_3 x_1 x_2 + \epsilon$$

While there is nonlinearity in the variables, all of the above exhibit 'linearity in parameters' that enable us to estimate the model using the maximum likelihood approach we developed for a linear regression. A simple way to see this is to replace nonlinear variables with a new variable, for example, in the first equation, we replace $x_1 x_2$ with z where $z = x_1 x_2$. With this new variable, the model then becomes a linear regression.

The 'true' data generation process that yields the data we examine is unknown and our objective in conducting robust analysis is to create a regression model that reasonably depicts the data generation process. Our first attempt at trying to depict the data generation process is through a simple regression that is linear in both parameters and in the variables. However, we have an opportunity to explore potential nonlinearities in variables to enhance the regression model. The reasons to do so are (1) to improve the fit of the model to enhance the predictive power, (2) to satisfy the key assumptions of a regression model so that the parameters are more reliably estimated, and (3) that an improved model is more likely to be 'closer' to the true data generation process than a simple linear structure.

To begin with, let us generate data that are inherently nonlinear and see what the results and the diagnostics look like when we conduct a simple linear regression:

$$y = 100 + 2x + \frac{x^2}{2} + \epsilon, \epsilon \sim N(0,1)$$

R

```
set.seed(987654321)
x = runif(500,1,20)
y = 100+2*x +0.5*x^2 + rnorm(500)
reg1 = lm(y~x)
summary(reg1)$r.squared
```

```
reg1$coefficients
plot(reg1$fitted.values,reg1$residuals)
abline(h = 0,col = "red")
```

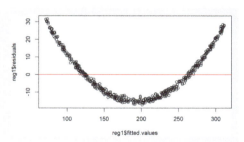

```
[1] 0.9657826


(Intercept)             x
   58.47326     12.66171
```

Python

```
np.random.seed(987654321)
x = np.random.uniform(low = 1, high = 20, size = (500,))
y = 100 + 2*x + 0.5*(x**2) + np.random.uniform(size = (500,))
df = pd.DataFrame({'x':x, 'y':y})
reg1 = ols("y~x", data = df).fit()
reg1.rsquared

0.9611678923423614

reg1.params

Intercept    60.724055
x            12.476621
dtype: float64
```

```
plt.scatter(reg1.fittedvalues, reg1.resid)
plt.axhline(0, color = 'red')
plt.show()
```

While the R^2 with a simple linear model is quite high, the coefficient values are meaningless in depicting the true (in this case, known) data generation process. A look at the residual plot offers us a first glimpse that our simple linear structure is not adequately capturing the data generation process. This is an excellent clue in practice where you do not know what is the true data generation process. Looking at the residual plot indicates potential nonlinearities that might exist.

Power Transformation

A useful technique to detect possible power transformations for the independent variables is to use the *Box–Tidwell transformation*. This is similar in spirit to the *Box–Cox transformation.* However, the difference is that the objective of the Box–Cox transformation is to achieve normality of the dependent variable, while the Box–Tidwell transformation estimates the λ values of the following specification to find the most appropriate power transformation for each of the independent variables.

$$y = \beta_0 + \beta_1 x_1^{\lambda 1} + \beta_2 x_2^{\lambda 2} + \beta_3 x_3^{\lambda 3} + \epsilon$$

R and Python provide packages for conducting the Box–Tidwell transformation:

R

```
Library(car)
boxTidwell(y~x)


MLE of lambda Score Statistic (z)  Pr(>|z|)
       1.8247                100.16 < 2.2e-16 ***
---
Signif. codes:  0 '***' 0.001 '**' 0.01 '*' 0.05 '.' 0.1 ' ' 1
```

Python

```
Currently there is no Python package that provides a function to directly
conduct the Box-Tidwell transformation as in R.
```

An estimated value of 1.824, as it is close to 2, suggests adding a square term to the regression specification. In this case, it is appropriate as the true data generation process includes a quadratic term. Let us do a more comprehensive analysis with the MASchools.csv file:

R

```
df = MASchools[,c(13,7,8,9,11,15)]
df1 = df[complete.cases(df),]
reg1 = lm(score4 ~ exptot + scratio + special + stratio + salary, data = df1)
summary(reg1)$r.squared
ncvTest(reg1)


[1] 0.2755063


Non-constant Variance Score Test
Variance formula: ~ fitted.values
Chisquare = 14.35983, Df = 1, p = 0.00015099


boxTidwell(score4 ~ exptot + scratio + special + stratio + salary, data = df1)


        MLE of lambda Score Statistic (z)  Pr(>|z|)
exptot        -1.6991                1.5080 0.1315588
scratio       -2.2424                0.3739 0.7084443
special       -1.7929                0.9977 0.3184028
stratio        4.5630               -2.9726 0.0029525 **
salary         6.4861                3.3145 0.0009182 ***
```

Python

```
MASchools = pd.read_csv("../data/MASchools.csv")
df = MASchools.iloc[:,[12,6,7,8,10,14]]
df1 = df.dropna()
reg1 = ols("score4~exptot + scratio + special + stratio + salary", data = df1).fit()
reg1.rsquared
```

```
0.2755062790920212
```

```
test1 = sm.stats.diagnostic.het_breuschpagan(reg1.resid, reg1.model.exog)
lzip(names, test1)
```

```
[('Lagrange multiplier statistic', 22.49849723455402),
 ('p-value', 0.0004208229288997204),
 ('f-value', 4.953752025177818),
 ('f p-value', 0.00028337744339731124)]
```

The Box--Tidwell transformation suggests adding a fourth power to the variable **stratio** and a sixth power to the variable **salary**. Does this improve the results?

R

```
reg2 = lm(score4 ~ exptot + scratio + special + stratio + salary +
        I(stratio^4) + I(salary^6),data = df1)
summary(reg2)$r.squared
ncvTest(reg2)
```

```
[1] 0.3352411
```

```
Non-constant Variance Score Test
Variance formula: ~ fitted.values
Chisquare = 5.040439, Df = 1, p = 0.024762
```

Python

```
df1['stratio_pow_4'] = np.power(df['stratio'], 4)
df1['salary_pow_6'] = np.power(df['salary'], 6)
reg2 = ols("score4 ~ exptot + scratio + special + stratio + salary +
        stratio_pow_4+salary_pow_6", data=df1).fit()
reg2.rsquared
```

```
0.33524106191662273
```

```
test2 = sm.stats.diagnostic.het_breuschpagan(reg2.resid, reg2.model.exog)
lzip(names, test2)
```

```
[('Lagrange multiplier statistic', 16.052973982783417),
```

```
('p-value', 0.02463676496571995),
('f-value', 2.4019496258843227),
('f p-value', 0.022600971587313713)]
```

There is a noticeable improvement in R^2. While heteroscedasticity is still present, the p-value has improved dramatically over the strictly linear specification.

Let us apply this for a logistic regression. Remember from the previous chapter that the linearity assumption is between the log-odds and the predictor variables:

R

```
breg1 = glm(admit ~ gre + gpa + rank,data = admit, family = "binomial")
logodds = breg1$linear.predictors
boxTidwell(logodds ~ gre + gpa + rank, data = admit)
```

	MLE of lambda	Score Statistic (z)	Pr(>|z|)
gre	1	0.4011	0.6883
gpa	1	-0.7051	0.4808
rank	1	-4.5164	6.29e-06 ***

Python

```
breg1 = sm.formula.glm("admit ~ gre + gpa + rank", data = admit,
        family = sm.families.Binomial()).fit()
logodds = breg1.predict(exog = admit)
```

No power transformation is recommended in this instance.

Interaction terms

In addition to a power transformation of independent variables, another common approach for incorporating nonlinearity is to add interaction terms between the independent variables.

Consider the following data generation process:

$$y = 1x_1 + 4x_2 + \frac{x_1 x_2}{2} + \epsilon, \epsilon \sim N(0,1)$$

What happens when we estimate a model without the interaction term from the data generated from the above data generation process?

R

```
set.seed(987654321)
x1 = runif(500,1,20)
x2 = runif(500,1,20)
y = x1+4*x2+0.5*x1*x2 + rnorm(500)
reg1 = lm(y~x1+x2)
reg1$coefficients
```

```
(Intercept)          x1          x2
 -53.290137    6.000533    9.242688
```

Python

```
np.random.seed(987654321)
x1 = np.random.uniform(low = 1, high = 20, size = (500,))
x2 = np.random.uniform(low = 1, high = 20, size = (500,))
y = x1 + 4 * x2 + 0.5 * x1 * x2 + np.random.uniform(size = (500,))
df = pd.DataFrame({'x1':x1, 'x2':x2, 'y':y})
reg1 = ols("y~x1+x2", data = df).fit()
reg1.params


Intercept    -58.605951
x1             6.334375
x2             9.435495
dtype: float64
```

Ignoring the interaction between the variables obviously resulted in a poor fit. R and Python provide very useful functions that evaluate possible interaction terms between the independent variables that can improve the fit:

R

```
res = step(reg1,~.^2)
res$anova


Start:  AIC = 2686.49
y ~ x1 + x2


Step:  AIC = 77.05
y ~ x1 + x2 + x1:x2
```

Python

```
Currently there is no Python package that provides a function to directly
conduct this analysis looking for interaction terms to add like in R.
```

The result indicates that adding an interaction term has benefits as *AIC* is significantly lowered. Remember that *AIC* is defined as:

$$AIC = -2LL + 2k$$

Higher values of loglikelihood (*LL*) and fewer parameters (*k*) indicate a superior model, and thus a lower value of *AIC* is indicative of a superior model. *AIC* is a useful measure to compare two competing models that have the same dependent variable.

Results from analysing the **MASchools** and **admit** data suggest inclusion of interaction terms as shown below:

R

```
reg2 = lm(score4 ~ exptot + scratio + special + stratio + salary +
       I(stratio^4) + I(salary^6),data = df1)
res = step(reg2,~.^2)
```

```
res$anova
```

```
Start:  AIC = 957.13
score4 ~ exptot + scratio + special + stratio + salary + I(stratio^4) +
        I(salary^6)

Step:  AIC = 930.57
score4 ~ exptot + scratio + special + stratio + I(stratio^4) + I(salary^6)
    + exptot:scratio + special:I(stratio^4) + scratio:special + exptot:
    I(stratio^4) + exptot:stratio + special:stratio + scratio:I(salary^6)
```

Python

```
reg2 = ols("score4 ~ exptot + scratio + special + stratio + salary +
        stratio_pow_4 + salary_pow_6", data = df1).fit()
```

Currently there is no Python package that provides a function to directly conduct this analysis looking for interaction terms to add like in R.

R

```
breg1 = glm(admit ~ gre + gpa + rank + gre:gpa,data = admit,family =
        "binomial")
step(breg1,direction = "both")$anova
```

```
Start:  AIC=467.44
admit ~ gre + gpa + rank
Step:  AIC=466.6
admit ~ gre + gpa + rank + gre:gpa
```

Python

```
breg1 = sm.formula.glm("admit ~ gre + gpa + rank + gre:gpa", data = admit,
        family = sm.families.Binomial()).fit()
```

Currently there is no Python package that provides a function to directly conduct this analysis looking for interaction terms to add like in R.

VARIABLE SELECTION

Going through the process of updating the regression structure often leads to adding several variables to the regression model. This can cause increased problems with multicollinearity. When there are several independent variables, it is useful to identify the most important variables to include in the final model to both reduce multicollinearity and to build a parsimonious model. *Stepwise regression* and *subsets regression* are two popular ways for variable reduction.

Stepwise Regression

Suppose we have a "true" data generation process as follows:

$$y = 2x_1 + x_2 + \epsilon, \epsilon \sim N(0, 10)$$

While the above data generation process is simple, suppose we estimate a more (unnecessarily) complicated model as follows:

$$y = \beta_0 + \beta_1 x_1 + \beta_2 x_2 + \beta_3 x_1 x_2 + \beta_4 x_1^2 + \beta_5 x_2^3 + \epsilon$$

Our objective is to go from our more complicated regression specification and remove variables that add little value to the model. *Stepwise regression* sequentially adds or drops variables until a certain stopping condition is met. In *forward* stepwise regression, the first step involves evaluating all the independent variables and selecting one variable that has the largest effect on the fit of the model (usually *AIC* is used as the measure of fit). Having included one variable, the next step involves adding the next best variable that improves the fit. This is repeated until adding the next variable does not improve the model. The *backward* stepwise regression uses a similar approach but starts with including all the variables and drops variables that contribute the least. A direction of *both* considers both adding and dropping in each step of the process. Let us evaluate this approach with the above example:

R
```
set.seed(987654321)
x1 = runif(500,1,10)
x2 = runif(500,1,10)
y = 2*x1 + x2 + rnorm(500,0,10)
reg1 = lm(y ~ x1 + x2 + x1:x2 + I(x1^2) + I(x^3))
step(reg1,direction = "backward")$anova
```

```
Start:  AIC=2383.39
y ~ x1 + x2 + x1:x2 + I(x1^2) + I(x^3)

          Df Sum of Sq   RSS    AIC
- x1:x2    1    13.763 57391 2381.5
- I(x^3)   1    22.701 57400 2381.6
- I(x1^2)  1    25.407 57402 2381.6
<none>                 57377 2383.4

Step:  AIC=2377.76
y ~ x1 + x2

         Df Sum of Sq   RSS    AIC
<none>                57419 2377.8
- x2      1    1931.6 59350 2392.3
- x1      1   13882.9 71301 2484.0
```

Python

```
np.random.seed(987654321)
x1 = np.random.uniform(low = 1, high = 10, size = (500,))
x2 = np.random.uniform(low = 1, high = 10, size = (500,))
y = 2*x1 + x2 + np.random.normal(loc = 0,scale = 10,size = (500,))
df = pd.DataFrame({'x1':x1, 'x2':x2, 'y':y})
df['x1_pow_2'] = np.power(df['x1'], 2)
df['x2_pow_3'] = np.power(df['x2'], 3)
reg1 = ols("y ~ x1 + x2 + x1:x2 + x1_pow_2 + x2_pow_3", data = df)
```

Currently there is no Python package that provides a function to directly conduct this analysis looking for interaction terms to add like in R.

As expected, the stepwise regression suggests dropping the nonlinear terms from the regression model. In the examples below, the stepwise regression approach does not recommend dropping any variables:

R

```
reg1 = lm(score4 ~ exptot + scratio + special + stratio + I(stratio^4) +
    I(salary^6) + exptot:scratio + special:I(stratio^4) + scratio:
    special + exptot:I(stratio^4) + exptot:stratio + special:stratio +
    scratio:I(salary^6),data=df1)
step(reg1,direction = "both")$anova
```

```
Start:  AIC = 930.57
score4 ~ exptot + scratio + special + stratio + I(stratio^4) + I(salary^6)
    + exptot:scratio + special:I(stratio^4) + scratio:special +
    exptot:I(stratio^4) + exptot:stratio + special:stratio +
    scratio:I(salary^6)
```

	Df	Sum of Sq	RSS	AIC
<none>			23820	930.57
- scratio:I(salary^6)	1	358.46	24178	931.35
- special:stratio	1	443.53	24263	932.00
- scratio:special	1	450.26	24270	932.05
- special:I(stratio^4)	1	1027.48	24847	936.42
- exptot:stratio	1	1195.85	25016	937.68
- exptot:scratio	1	1484.65	25304	939.81
- exptot:I(stratio^4)	1	1775.62	25595	941.94

```
breg1 = glm(admit ~ gre + gpa + rank + gre:gpa, data = admit, family = "binomial")
step(breg1,direction = "both")$anova
```

```
Start:  AIC = 466.6
admit ~ gre + gpa + rank + gre:gpa
```

	Df	Deviance	AIC

```
<none>            456.60 466.60
- gre:gpa   1     459.44 467.44
- rank      1     477.85 485.85
```

Python

```
reg1 = ols("score4 ~ exptot + scratio + special + stratio + salary +
       stratio_pow_4 + salary_pow_6 + \exptot:scratio+special:stratio_
       pow_4+scratio:special+exptot:stratio_pow_4+ \exptot:stratio+
       special:stratio+scratio:salary_pow_6", data = df1).fit()
```

Currently there is no Python package that provides a function to directly conduct this analysis looking for interaction terms to add like in R.

Subsets Regression

Stepwise regression is often criticized as it does not evaluate all possible regression models and thus may not find the best model. An alternative approach is to use *subsets regression*, where all possible combinations are considered. The caution here is that finding all subsets is very time consuming when there are several predictors.

The packages in R and Python provide functions to conduct subsets regression. Several metrics are available to make the selection of the best model. These include *BIC* (which is the same as *AIC* when alternate models all use the same number of observations), Adjusted R^2, and Mallows' Cp-statistic. Adjusted R^2 is a modification of R^2 with a penalty based on the number of parameters in the model (n is the number of observations and k is the number of independent variables). Here, $\bar{\sigma}^2$ is the estimated variance of the error term in the regression model. Higher values of Adjusted R^2 and low values of *BIC* and Mallows' Cp-statistic are preferred:

$$AdjR^2 = 1 - \frac{(1 - R^2)(n - 1)}{(n - 1 - k)}$$

$$Mallows'\,Cp = \frac{SSE}{\bar{\sigma}^2} - n + 2k$$

Let's consider the **MASchools** data:

R

```
library(leaps)
bestsub1 = regsubsets(score4 ~exptot + scratio + special+ I(stratio^4) +
           I(salary^6) + exptot:scratio + special:I(stratio^4) + scratio:
           special + exptot:I(stratio^4) + exptot:stratio + special:stratio +
           scratio:I(salary^6),data=df1,nvmax = 12)
summary(bestsub1)
names(summary(bestsub1))
cbind(
    Cp      = summary(bestsub1)$cp,
    r2      = summary(bestsub1)$rsq,
```

```
    Adj_r2 = summary(bestsub1)$adjr2,
    BIC    = summary(bestsub1)$bic
)
```

```
           Cp     r2 Adj_r2      BIC
 [1,] 87.539 0.158  0.154 -21.570
 [2,] 46.858 0.291  0.284 -48.408
 [3,] 41.016 0.316  0.305 -49.726
 [4,] 29.596 0.358  0.344 -56.261
 [5,] 23.554 0.383  0.366 -58.457
 [6,] 20.873 0.398  0.377 -57.691
 [7,] 18.349 0.412  0.389 -56.881
 [8,] 16.082 0.425  0.399 -55.917
 [9,] 15.811 0.432  0.403 -53.001
[10,] 12.400 0.449  0.418 -53.395
[11,] 11.290 0.459  0.425 -51.477
[12,] 13.000 0.460  0.422 -46.563
```

Python

```python
# perform a scikit-learn Recursive Feature Elimination (RFE)
from sklearn.feature_selection import RFECV
from sklearn.metrics import r2_score


X = df1[[,exptot', ,scratio', ,special','stratio','salary']]
y = df1[,score4']


pf1 = PolynomialFeatures(degree=2,interaction_only = False)
X = pf1.fit_transform(X1)
print(X.shape)


#OLS...
reg = LinearRegression().fit(X,y)
# Pass our ols model into RFECV
rfecv_mod = RFECV(estimator=reg)
# fit the model.
rfecv_mod = rfecv_mod.fit(X,y)


#Columns selected by RFE?
cols = pf1.get_feature_names_out()[rfecv_mod.support_]


print(f"Selected {len(cols)} columns:",str(list(cols)))
print("R2 = " + str(r2_score(y, y_hat)))


Selected 16 columns: ['exptot', 'scratio', 'special', 'stratio',
'salary', 'exptot scratio', 'scratio^2', 'scratio special', 'scratio stratio',
```

```
'scratio salary', 'special^2', 'special stratio', 'special salary', 'stratio^2',
'stratio salary', 'salary^2']
R2 = 0.4476800270450575
```

In R, based on **Cp** and **Adj_r2**, 11 variables are recommended to be used. The variable recommended for dropping is **salary**. The output created also indicates the best variables to use for a given number of variables to be included.

In Python, we have started with more features (all interaction and quadratic terms) and get a model with 16 variables. The R^2 coefficient is slightly lower because we did not include higher exponents as in the R example.

There are other approaches available for variable selection. An important class of these are called shrinkage or penalty-based methods. The idea here is to penalize regression coefficients (after standardizing them) if a variable does not contribute much, then impose a penalty to force the coefficient value towards 0. *Lasso regression* imposes linear penalties and *ridge regression* imposes quadratic penalties. These can be easily implemented with the available packages in R and Python (see Chapter 18).

USE CASE: PROFIT FORECASTING, STEPS FOR A SAFETY-FIRST LINEAR REGRESSION

Statistical tools implemented using R and Python are incredibly powerful for interpreting data and strengthening business decision making, but we have seen that there are pitfalls that must be avoided. A methodical approach to statistical testing is the best answer, taking steps to check all is well as we progress towards constructing a model.

We have examined profit forecasting using R&D and marketing spend in a parametric context, where we had a good idea what was the population distribution of profits, and a non-parametric approach when we were not sure. We now tackle the same challenge but using a 4-point safety first process:

1   Check the data
2   Check for collinearities
3   Check model fit
4   Check residuals

Check1: Check the data

Check1 is simply data exploration, examining distributions and relationships as we have seen in previous chapters. We also need to check for imbalances in the dataset, particularly in classification problems, where we might be forecasting credit card loan defaults from a dataset where only 5% of the rows represent defaults (we will address this later in the book). Can we take a view on what the population distribution is? If so, our model will always be more accurate if we use tests that assume distributions that most resemble the true population distribution of our data.

Check2: Check for Collinearities

In Check2, we need to make sure our driver variables are not correlated. If any two are, unstable and misleading results can occur. Collinearities, or correlations between independent variables, may cause unstable coefficients, as the job of one correlated input could potentially do the other's which could dramatically change these coefficients when the models are rerun. Simply calculating the pairwise correlations of your independent variables will be a good check:

R

```
cor(df_train[1:3])
corrgram(df_test[1:3],upper.panel = panel.pie)
```

Python

```
df_train[['R&D Spend', 'Administration','Marketing Spend']].corr()

# plot the heatmap
sns.heatmap(df_train[['R&D Spend', 'Administration','Marketing Spend']].corr())
```

	R&D Spend	Administration	Marketing Spend
R&D Spend	1.000000	0.241955	0.724248
Administration	0.241955	1.000000	−0.032154
Marketing Spend	0.724248	−0.032154	1.000000

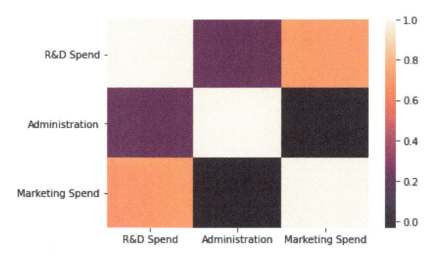

Figure 14.1 Checking for pairwise correlations of independent variables

We will use a rule of thumb that no two input variables should have a correlation coefficient of >0.5. You can see that R&D Spend and Marketing Spend have a correlation coefficient of 0.72 and so breach our rule of thumb. As the correlation is not perfect (i.e., it is not 1), there is probably still value in using both variables, and to do this, we can use an approach called *differencing*. This is where we simply deduct (or alternatively, divide) each R&D Spend data point by each corresponding Marketing Spend:

R

```
df_trn_dif = df_train
df_trn_dif$Marketing.Spend = df_trn_dif$Marketing.Spend - df_trn_
dif$R.D.Spend
cor(df_trn_dif[1:3])
```

Python

```
#Overweight Marketing Spending with a differenced series
df_trn_dif[,Marketing Spend'] = df_trn_dif[,Marketing Spend'] -
                        df_trn_dif[,R&D Spend']

# Run simple correlation matrix too
print("After Differencing Marketing Spend")
df_trn_dif[[,R&D Spend', ,Administration','Marketing Spend']].corr()
```

After Differencing Marketing Spend

	R&D Spend	Administration	Marketing Spend
R&D Spend	1.000000	0.241955	0.451477
Administration	0.241955	1.000000	−0.159130
Marketing Spend	0.451477	−0.159130	1.000000

After we have applied differencing to Marketing Spend, the correlation between R&D Spend and Marketing Spend has fallen to 0.45, which is more acceptable.

Check3: Check for Model Fit

We can now run the regression and assess the goodness of the model fit:

R

```
reg1 = lm(Profit ~ .-State, data = df_trn_dif)
summary(reg1)

plot(df_trn_dif$R.D.Spend,df_trn_dif$Profit,col = "red",pch = 16,xlab =
    "R&D Spend",ylab = "profit")
points(df_trn_dif$R.D.Spend,reg1$fitted.values,col = "blue",pch = 16)
```

Python

```
lm = sm.OLS(df_trn_dif['Profit'], df_trn_dif[['R&D Spend',
    'Administration','Marketing Spend']])
model = lm.fit()
model.summary()

# Regression plot
fig, ax = plt.subplots()
fig = sm.graphics.plot_fit(model, 0, ax = ax)
```

```
plt.figure(figsize = (10, 10))
ax.set_ylabel("Profit")
ax.set_xlabel("R&D Spend")
ax.set_title("Linear Regression: Profit Forecasting")
plt.show()
```

```
Call:
lm(formula = Profit ~ . - State, data = df_trn_dif)

Residuals:
Min     1Q Median     3Q     Max
-33366  -4411    159   6703   17529

Coefficients:
Estimate Std. Error t value Pr(>|t|)
(Intercept)      4.945e+04  6.764e+03   7.311 4.57e-09 ***
R.D.Spend        8.273e-01  3.540e-02  23.368  < 2e-16 ***
Administration  -2.343e-02  5.259e-02  -0.445   0.6582
Marketing.Spend  2.959e-02  1.682e-02   1.759   0.0857 .
---
Signif. codes:  0 '***' 0.001 '**' 0.01 '*' 0.05 '.' 0.1 ' ' 1

Residual standard error: 9367 on 43 degrees of freedom
Multiple R-squared:  0.9508, Adjusted R-squared:  0.9474
F-statistic:   277 on 3 and 43 DF,  p-value: < 2.2e-16
```

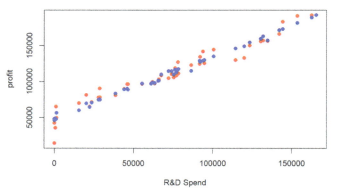

Figure 14.2 Goodness of model fit

Our first check should be the fit plot, which shows how well our forecasts fit the true data we are trying to forecast. We need to be satisfied that this is accurate enough for our needs, that is, forecasts across the range of outcomes are satisfactory. Looking carefully as if we are focused on high profitability outcomes and low profitability outcomes, as we are in this use case, we better be sure the fit is satisfactory at these high and low extremes. It does not matter that much that for middling profitability, the model fits well.

Next, we need to see a reasonable Adjusted R^2 (recall that Adjusted R^2 penalizes the R^2 the more input variables we have) and our rule of thumb here is that an Adjusted $R^2 > 0.7$ represents a good enough fit. We should also check the p-value for the F-Test, which is generally included in the outputs of most regression packages. Note that in some more noisy domains, this may be too low, and in other less noisy domains, too imprecise. A value of 0.7 makes sense in most business contexts. In this case, our model has both an Adjusted $R^2 > 0.7$ and a statistically significant F-statistics at the 5% level. Check.

Check4: Check Residuals

Finally, we need to sense check our model, to make sure there are no obvious biases or problems with it, and this is best done by examining the residuals of the model. These are the errors between our y variable and our forecasts (our y hat variable). We are looking for approximately normally distributed residuals, around a mean of zero. This should again be done using charts, plotting the y-variable against the residual, and also statistics. Our rule of thumb is that approximate normality, even weak normality, is fine so long as there are no strange patterns in the residuals:

R

```
plot(reg1$fitted.values, reg1$residuals, xlab = "Predicted Profit",
     ylab = "Residual")
abline(h = 0,col = "red")
```

Python

```
#Calculate the residuals:
y_pred = model.predict()
residuals = model.predict() - df_train[,Profit']
plt.scatter(y_pred,residuals)

plt.title("Model Residuals: y plotted against y_hat")
plt.axhline(0, color = 'red')

plt.xlabel("y_hat")
plt.ylabel("Residual")

plt.show()
```

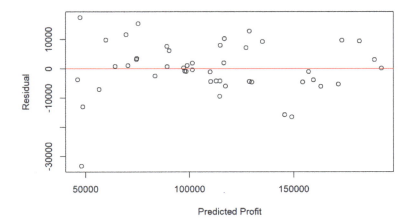

Figure 14.3 Plot of the residuals

We can see from the model residuals plot that residuals are approximately randomly distributed around a mean of zero, which is a good result.

R

```
plot(density(reg1$residuals))
shapiro.test(reg1$residuals)


Shapiro-Wilk normality test

data: reg1$residuals
W = 0.93664, p-value = 0.01332
```

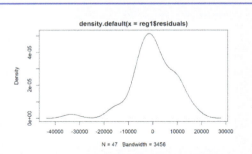

Python

```
# frequency distribution of residuals
plt.figure(figsize = (10,7))
plt.title('Residuals')
plt.hist(residuals, bins = 15)
from scipy import stats

# Normality test
results = stats.shapiro(residuals)

# Overall fit of the model: F-test
if results.pvalue < 0.9: print('Residuals are normally distributed): Check')
elif (1-results.pvalue) < 0.95: print('Residuals are normally distributed: Weak')
else: print('Residuals are normally distributed: Problem')

print("(Normality test: " + str(results.statistic) + ", p-val " +
      str(1-results.pvalue) +")")
```

The plot and the normality test indicate that the normality assumption is a bit weak.

Automating Model Construction: Stepwise/Subsets Regression

So far, we have manually chosen input variables, but packages exist to automate the selection of inputs. In the R code below, we will run the subsets regression to select the right input variables:

R

```
library(leaps)
bestsub1 = regsubsets(Profit ~ . - State, data = df_trn_dif,nvmax = 12)
summary(bestsub1)
```

```
names(summary(bestsub1))
round(cbind(
    Cp     = summary(bestsub1)$cp,
    r2     = summary(bestsub1)$rsq,
    Adj_r2 = summary(bestsub1)$adjr2,
    BIC    = summary(bestsub1)$bic),3)
```

```
Selection Algorithm: exhaustive
         R.D.Spend Administration Marketing.Spend
1 ( 1 ) "*"        " "            " "
2 ( 1 ) "*"        " "            "*"
3 ( 1 ) "*"        "*"            "*"
[1] "which" "rsq"   "rss"   "adjr2" "cp"    "bic"    "outmat" "obj"
        Cp    r2 Adj_r2      BIC
[1,] 4.195 0.946  0.945 -129.490
[2,] 2.198 0.951  0.948 -129.799
[3,] 4.000 0.951  0.947 -126.165
```

The results recommend using only 'R&D Spend' and 'Marketing Spend' as the input variables. Rerunning the regression model yields the following outcome which is an improvement over the initial regression model (for example, based on Adjusted R2 values):

R

```
reg2 = lm(Profit ~ R.D.Spend + Marketing.Spend, data = df_trn_dif)
summary(reg2)

Call:
lm(formula = Profit ~ R.D.Spend + Marketing.Spend, data = df_trn_dif)

Residuals:
   Min    1Q Median    3Q    Max
-33466  -4383   -323  6739  17371

Coefficients:
                 Estimate Std. Error t value Pr(>|t|)
(Intercept)     4.670e+04  2.753e+03  16.967  <2e-16 ***
R.D.Spend       8.217e-01  3.283e-02  25.028  <2e-16 ***
Marketing.Spend 3.194e-02  1.583e-02   2.018  0.0498 *
---
Signif. codes:  0 '***' 0.001 '**' 0.01 '*' 0.05 '.' 0.1 ' ' 1

Residual standard error: 9282 on 44 degrees of freedom
Multiple R-squared:  0.9506, Adjusted R-squared:  0.9483
F-statistic: 423.2 on 2 and 44 DF,  p-value: < 2.2e-16
```

We will now conduct the feature selection in Python. There are many different approaches available, and here we use Recursive Feature Elimination (RFE) to automatically choose our features. Additionally, we will use the *Scikit-Learn* implementation RFECV applied to profit forecasting in our use case. RFE refines a model by removing the least important independent variables. RFE runs by recursively considering smaller and smaller sets of features, and RFECV layers on an additional approach called *cross validation* to get a more robust result. We will again use the *sklearn* implementation, but many different learners are available to us with this approach. This approach will select the combinations of input variables that achieve the best fit:

Python

```python
from sklearn.feature_selection import RFE
from sklearn.feature_selection import RFECV

# set up our regressor. We will use the random forest
from sklearn.linear_model import LinearRegression

#OLS...
reg = LinearRegression().fit(df_trn_dif[['R&D Spend',
        'Administration','Marketing Spend']],df_trn_dif['Profit'])

# Pass our ols model, into RFECV, to get a model of best fit.
rfecv_mod = RFECV(estimator=reg)
# fit the model.
rfecv_mod = rfecv_mod.fit(df_trn_dif[['R&D Spend',
            'Administration','Marketing Spend']],df_trn_dif[,Profit'])
```

Having ran the model, we can now chart the results and show the Adjusted R^2:

Python

```python
#Columns selected by RFE?
cols = X.columns[rfecv_mod.support_]

#Predict
y = df_trn_dif[,Profit']
y_hat = rfecv_mod.predict(df_trn_dif[['R&D Spend',
        'Administration','Marketing Spend']])

#Chart
plt.figure(figsize=(8,6))
plt.title("RFECV Model Uses " + str(i+1) + " inputs : " + str([cols[i]
        for i in range(cols.__len__())]))
plt.scatter(y_hat, y,color = 'r')
plt.show()

#Get R2 for the regression model
print("R2 = " + str(r2_score(y, y_hat)))
```

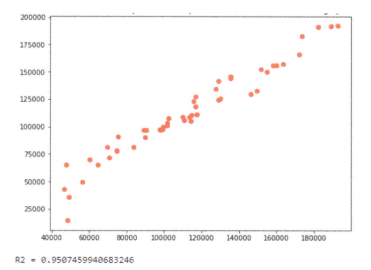

R2 = 0.9507459940683246

Figure 14.4 RFCEV model using three inputs

This particular feature selection approach we have used has actually selected all three possible input variables: R&D Spend, Administration, Marketing Spend. An important note is that while feature selection packages will mine for the best fit, no feature selection package will run our 4-point checks to ensure our model is on a good footing. It is essential we sense check what these 'clever' packages are telling us and never fully defer to them.

Summary

In this chapter, we started with a simple regression model that is linear in both parameters and in variables. Our goal was to transform the simplistic structure in an attempt to improve the fit, satisfy the key assumptions in regression modelling, and in the process, move closer to the true data generation process that produced the data we examined. The overall approach is to run appropriate diagnostics and then add terms to capture any inherent nonlinearities in the variables (while retaining linearity in parameters). This 'adding variables' step is followed by 'removing variables' that contribute little to the model. This process is as much art as science; there is no one prescribed set of steps. One can, for example, first add interaction terms and then power transformations, or reverse these steps. In going through the process, you should also be guided by your deeper understanding of the underlying problem domain and modifications you make to the model must be reasonable in the context of the underlying domain of study. Finally, it is very important to note that none of what we accomplished in this chapter eliminates the concerns with endogeneity. Despite improving the structure of the regression model, omitted variables continue to be a challenge and care must be exercised in interpreting and making decisions based on the model. The only sound approach to tackle endogeneity is through a robust randomized controlled experiment.

Exercises

To complete the activity below, you will need to visit the companion website to the book and download the relevant dataset: https://study.sagepub.com/gopal

1   Read the file Corn.csv. Develop an appropriate regression structure to predict **yield**.
2   Read the file women.csv. Develop an appropriate regression structure to predict **height**.
3   Read the file Boston.csv. Develop an appropriate regression structure to predict **medv**, which is the median value of incomes in neighbourhoods of the city of Boston.
4   Read the file student.csv. Develop an appropriate regression structure to predict **daysabs**. Note that the outcome is a count variable and therefore you must develop a Poisson regression for the problem.
5   Read the file Credit.csv. Develop an appropriate regression structure to predict the binary outcome **Creditworthy** based on all the other variables in the dataframe.

15

TIMESERIES AND FORECASTING

Chapter Contents

In this chapter, we will look at timeseries and how to forecast future events and data points. Timeseries, such as the changing level of profits quarter by quarter, or daily prices, are a central part of business analytics. Every timeseries can broadly be separated into three components: level; seasonality; and change. Each is crucial to consider when we forecast future profits, prices, or other timeseries. Consider the task of setting sales commissions and targets, where management needs to motivate an *increase* in sales (i.e., a change), rather than just rewarding a seasonal change (e.g., the run-up to Christmas), or the prevailing level or trend in sales (e.g., electric vehicle sales). Timeseries require us to think about trends and the dependence of present data points on past data points, as we see in the level of company debt – where a high value in the past indicates a higher likelihood of a high value today.

TIMESERIES MAKE-UP: TREND, SEASONALITY, AND NOISE

We can decompose timeseries into trend, seasonality, and noise using simple tools. Take US Vehicle Sales, sometimes used as a proxy for economic growth, which are inherently seasonal, as can be seen below in the jagged pattern than follows the overall movement in the timeseries. The Vehicle Sales timeseries exhibits seasonality for the simple reason that most vehicle sales are made in the spring and summer, and fewer sales generally occur in the winter, which you can see creates a repeating annual pattern, known as seasonality. It is important to understand these predictable, seasonal, fluctuations:

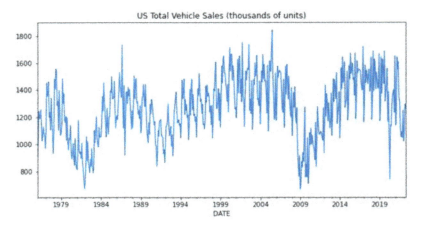

Figure 15.1   Seasonality in timeseries data

(Note that vehicle sales, like many economic series, can be downloaded as 'adjusted for seasonality' (or seasonality adjusted), and we will see how this is calculated below, whereas seasonality unadjusted can be seen in Figure 15.1.)

Packages such as *xts* in R and *statmodels* in Python libraries can automatically decompose a timeseries into seasonality, trend, and residual. This allows us to strip out seasonal variation. In this case, the trend is likely to be the most important component if we want to forecast the future level of sales in a year or more from now, as seasonality is predictable.

R

```
library(xts)
df = read_excel("TOTALNSA.xlsx")
df[['DATE']] = as.Date(df[['DATE']], format = '%Y-%m-%d')
df = ts(df$TOTALNSA, start = '1976', freq = 12)
plot(decompose(df))
```

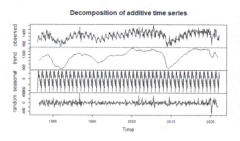

Python

```
import matplotlib as plt
from statsmodels.tsa.seasonal import seasonal_decompose

result = seasonal_decompose(df['TOTALNSA'], model='multiplicable')
result.plot()
plt.show()
```

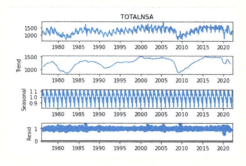

PREPARING THE DATA: STRIPPING AWAY SEASONALITY USING MOVING AVERAGES

The underlying pattern in a timeseries is usually the key to forecasting it. The simplest way of extracting this underlying pattern is by using a moving average (MA). To use an MA, you have to specify the number of data points (or the *window*) to average over, and below we simply use a 12-month (backward-looking) average, plotted for every point of the timeseries, which also has the effect of removing the seasonality:

R

```
library(forecast)
autoplot(df) + autolayer(ma(df, order = 12), colour = TRUE)
```

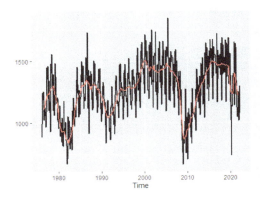

Python

```
import matplotlib as plt

plt.plot(df['TOTALNSA'].rolling(window = 12).mean())
plt.plot(df['TOTALNSA'])
plt.title('MA')
plt.show()
```

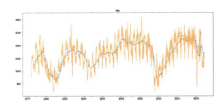

We can see that the 12-month MA captures the underlying level of the vehicles sales timeseries reasonably well, stripping out seasonality and noise. If we wanted to forecast the level of future vehicle sales, extrapolating this trend is a good starting point.

SIMPLE FORECASTING: EXTRAPOLATION

The simplest form of forecasting is to assume the same value continues to occur in the future. The next most simple is a straight line (or linear) forecast, extending a straight line fitted to the most recent data points into the future. More complex forecasts of curves can be carried out using polynomial extrapolation. In many cases, forecasts of this nature can be used as a 'base case' forecast or as a starting point before more complex forecasting approaches are used.

The code below illustrates the extrapolation functions. Note that forecasts from simple extrapolation may give an idea of the future direction, but it may not necessarily provide the most reliable forecasts. Simple extrapolation may be sufficient in some cases, but if the variable we are concerned with has important implications, it is worth expending additional effort to improving forecasting accuracy:

R

```
df_ma = ma(df, order = 12)
df_ma = ts(na.exclude(df_ma))
myforecast = forecast(df_ma, level = c(0), h = 36)
autoplot(myforecast)
```

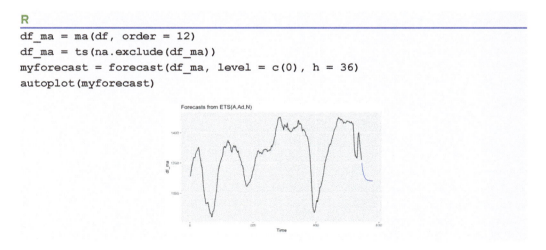

Python

```
from scipy import interpolate

x = range(0, df_ma.shape[0]) #[x for x in range(0, df.shape[0])]
x_extrap = range(0, df_ma.shape[0] + 36)
df_extr = interpolate.interp1d(x, df_ma['TOTALNSA'], fill_value = 'extrapolate'
```

TIME DEPENDENCE (AUTOCORRELATION), A FORECASTER'S BEST FRIEND

In many timeseries, the value tomorrow will be dependent on the value we see today (and perhaps values in the past too). This time dependency (or temporal dependency) can be represented by autocorrelation (or self-correlation), which is exploited by autoregressive (AR) models, that simply weight past data points to provide a forecast for future data points. We can see that autocorrelations exist in the Vehicle Sales dataset using the following Autocorrelation plot below. An autocorrelation plot shows the correlation on the vertical axis, between –1 and 1, while the horizontal axis shows the *lag* between the data points of the timeseries being compared. For example, the point on the horizontal axis at lag 100 shows the correlation of the latest part of the timeseries, and the earliest part of the timeseries, both separated by 100 data points, show a negative correlation of approximately –0.2:

R

```
acf_obs = acf(df_ma, lag.max = length(df_ma), plot = FALSE)
plot(acf_obs, type = "l")
```

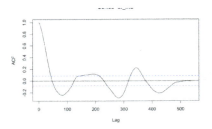

Python

```
from pandas.plotting import autocorrelation_plot
autocorrelation_plot(df_ma)
plt.title('autocorrelation_plot')
plt.show()
```

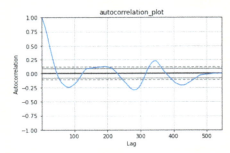

FORECASTING USING AUTOREGRESSION (AR)

Autoregressive (AR) models exploit autocorrelation, simply weighing past datapoints to provide a forecast for future datapoints. An AR(1) model solves for the weights and fits the model to our timeseries:

$$\hat{y} = b_0 + b_{1xt-1}$$

This is referred to as an AR(1) model, where 1 in this case indicates that the *order* of the AR model is 1. This is the simplest form of an AR model, just using the last data point to fit to the data, but we can have as many past values as are needed.

You can manually try different lag values as shown below:

R

```
ar(df_ma,order.max = 1)
```

```
Coefficients:
    1
```

```
0.9969
Order selected 1  sigma^2 estimated as  186.9
```

Python

```python
from statsmodels.tsa.ar_model import autoReg

# AR model
df_ma = df_ma.dropna()
res = autoReg(df_ma,lags = [1]).fit()
print(res.summary())
```

However, it is more sensible to use powerful functions to work out the best value of the lags for your AR model and forecast based on the best model:

R

```r
res = ar(df_ma,order.max = 12)
pred_ar = predict(res, n.ahead = 120)
autoplot(df_ma) +  autolayer(predict(res, n.ahead = 120)$pred)
```

Python

```python
from statsmodels.tsa.ar_model import ar_select_order
lags = ar_select_order(df, maxlag = 12, glob = True)
lags.ar_lags
df_ma = df_ma.dropna()
mod = AutoReg(df_ma,lags = lags.ar_lags).fit()
plt.plot(mod.forecast(120))
plt.plot(df_ma)
plt.title('AR ar_select_order and Fitted')
plt.show()
```

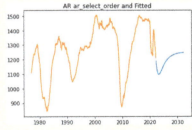

FORECASTING CHANGE: WHEN THE TREND IS NOT YOUR FRIEND

To forecast changes in a timeseries, a trend in our timeseries is usually not helpful, especially if the trend changes. For instance, for the US$ sales of a company, we may want to judge our sales team's performance over a long period, when there has been economic expansion and contraction. In this case, we do not want to consider the economic conditions that might naturally be driving all sales up (and down) across an economy (i.e., the trend), and more about the changes our sales team might affect. In other words, we would care about changes in the detrended timeseries.

In many cases, the trend is a distraction and, in some, downright misleading for timeseries forecasting models. To remove the distraction of the trend, we need to detrend our series. The simplest detrending approach is *differencing*, where we subtract each observation from the observation before (e.g., use this on vehicle sales), or divide each by the observation before (e.g., do this for prices, where the change is the price return). You need to decide which is most appropriate by estimating, whether the trend is better modelled as linear (subtract) or exponential (divide). The operation is very straightforward:

R

```
# Detrending
set1 = ts(df[1:length(df)-1], start = c('1976', '01'), frequency = 12)
set2 = ts(df[2:length(df)], start = c('1976', '02'), frequency = 12)


# Detrend by subtraction
df_detrended = set1 - set2


# Detrend by division
df_detrended2 = set1 / set2
```

Python

```
# Detrend by subtraction
df_detrended = df[:-1] - df[1:]
df_detrended = df_detrended.dropna()
# Detrend by division
df_detrended2 = df[:-1] / df[1:]
df_detrended2 = df_detrended2.dropna()
```

FORECAST KILLER: NONSTATIONARITIES

A strong trend in a timeseries can be more than misleading, it can distort forecasting models. Trending timeseries are known as nonstationary, meaning the mean and the variance change over time and this distorts most forecasting models. Put another way, most forecasting approaches cannot handle trends and so we need to detrend a timeseries before we conduct further analysis.

FORECASTING CHANGE: COMBINING AR AND MA (ARIMA)

If we combine the AR model and use a model of the MA to model how past deviations from the MA have an influence on future data points, we get an Autoregressive Integrated Moving Average (ARIMA) model. This is part of the AR family of models and one of the most popular for forecasting timeseries.

We need to define three parameters for an ARIMA: p is the order of the AR model, d controls the differencing to make the timeseries stationary, and q is the size of the moving average window, also known as the order of the moving average. As before, we can choose these parameters ourselves or employ a function that selects the best parameters, based on criteria such as *AIC*. This is illustrated with R below:

R

```
arima(df_ma, order = c(1,1,1))


Coefficients:
         ar1    ma1
      0.6240  1.000
s.e.  0.0336  0.005
sigma^2 estimated as 26.46: log likelihood = -1663.72,   aic = 3333.44
mod = auto.arima(df_ma,ic = "aic")
print(mod)
autoplot(forecast(mod, h = 120,level = 0))


Series: df_ma
ARIMA(1,1,0) with drift


Coefficients:
         ar1    drift
      0.8442  0.0001
s.e.  0.0231  1.7445


sigma^2 = 41.07:  log likelihood = -1778.79
AIC = 3563.57    AICc = 3563.62    BIC = 3576.46
```

Forecasts from ARIMA(1,1,0) with drift

Another approach to create a function is to carry out a grid search over p, d, and q, and find the set of parameters that offer the best fit. This is illustrated with Python below:

Python

```
# Auto ARIMA, solves p,d,q based on a minimization of AIC
# Auto ARIMA
def auto_ARIMA(srs: np.ndarray, p_max: int = 12, d_max: int = 12, q_max:
               int = 12) -> (ARIMA, []):
    max_aic = -999.999
    max_mod = None
    for p in range(1, p_max, int(p_max/10+1)):
        for d in range(0, d_max, int(d_max/10+1)):
            for q in range(0, q_max, int(q_max/10+1)):
                try:
                    mod = ARIMA(srs, order = (p,d,q)).fit()
                    if(mod.aic >= max_aic):
                        max_aic = mod.aic
                        max_mod = mod
                        max_order = [p,d,q]
                except:
                    pass
    return(max_mod, max_order)
# Auto ARIMA, solves p,d,q based on a maximization of AIC
mod,order = auto_ARIMA(df['TOTALNSA'].to_numpy())
print(mod.summary())


# one-step out-of sample forecast
forecast = mod.predict() #start = 0, end = 120)

#Plot 120 months of out of sample forecast
plt.plot(forecast)
plt.plot(df['TOTALNSA'].to_numpy())
plt.title('AR ar_select_order and Fitted')
plt.show()
```

ARIMA Model Results

```
==============================================================================
```

Dep. Variable:	D2.y	No. Observations:	554
Model:	ARIMA(1, 2, 0)	Log Likelihood	-4064.029
Method:	css-mle	S.D. of innovations	371.007
Date:	Tue, 09 Aug 2022	AIC	8134.058
Time:	18:02:05	BIC	8147.010
Sample:	2	HQIC	8139.118

```
==============================================================================
```

	coef	std err	z	P>|z|	[0.025	0.975]
const	0.5760	9.222	0.062	0.950	-17.499	18.651
ar.L1.D2.y	-0.7105	0.030	-23.718	0.000	-0.769	-0.652

Roots

```
========================================================================
               Real        Imaginary         Modulus        Frequency
------------------------------------------------------------------------
AR.1          -1.4074         +0.0000j          1.4074          0.5000
------------------------------------------------------------------------
```

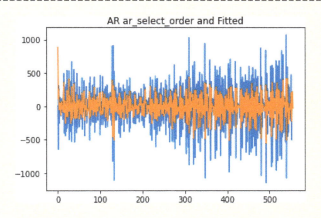

```
# Fit AR model
#mod = ARIMA(df, order = (1,1,1)).fit()


mod = ARIMA(df['TOTALNSA'], order = (order[0],order[1],order[2])).fit()
print(mod.summary())



#Plot 120 months of out of sample forecast
plt.plot(mod.predict(start = df.shape[0], end = df.shape[0]+36))
plt.plot(df)
plt.title('AR ar_select_order and Fitted')
plt.show()
```

```
                          ARIMA Model Results
========================================================================
Dep. Variable:          D2.TOTALNSA   No. Observations:            554
Model:                  ARIMA(1, 2, 0) Log Likelihood         -4064.029
Method:                     css-mle   S.D. of innovations      371.007
Date:           Tue, 09 Aug 2022      AIC                     8134.058
Time:                    18:02:05     BIC                     8147.010
Sample:                 03-01-1976    HQIC                    8139.118
                       - 04-01-2022
========================================================================
                   coef    std err        z     P>|z|   [0.025   0.975]
------------------------------------------------------------------------
const            0.5760      9.222    0.062     0.950  -17.499   18.651
ar.L1.D2.TOTALNSA -0.7105     0.030  -23.718     0.000   -0.769   -0.652
                              Roots
========================================================================
               Real        Imaginary         Modulus        Frequency
------------------------------------------------------------------------
AR.1          -1.4074         +0.0000j          1.4074          0.5000
------------------------------------------------------------------------
```

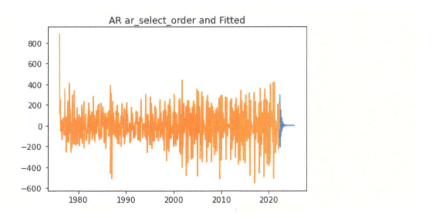

A note of caution is warranted. While functions such as our `auto_ARIMA` are very powerful, it is essential that we still check the goodness of fit and check the distribution of residuals. One particularly acute risk for timeseries models to check for is heteroscedasticity in our residuals, where the variance of a variable changes over time.

Summary

In this chapter, we introduced timeseries and how to forecast future events and data points. We explain how to remove the distortions of seasonality, or predictable changes by season, first decomposing a timeseries into trend, seasonality, and noise and then removing seasonality using moving averages (MA). We then learned how to produce a simple timeseries forecast by extending a timeseries into the future using a straight-line plot, known as linear extrapolation. While linear extrapolation is quick and simple to run, for complex timeseries that tend not to follow a straight line themselves, the results can be inaccurate. We then saw how dependencies between timepoints, autocorrelation, can help us and we introduced autoregressive (AR) forecasting models that exploit these dependencies. We saw how, for a variable timeseries that does not follow an approximate straight-line, AR forecasts can produce more realistic forecasts than simple linear extrapolation. We note that a forecaster needs to decide whether to forecast the trend of a timeseries or the changes in a timeseries. For forecasts of changes, the trend is not always a forecaster's friend. Trends in timeseries, known as non-stationarities, can make forecasts of changes inaccurate. To fix non-stationarities, we can use differencing – where the next data point is divided by or deducted from the previous one – as a way of eliminating a trend from a timeseries to more accurately create a forecasting model for changes. Finally, we introduced one of the most popular forecasting models in business, the ARIMA model, which combines both MA and AR approaches to forecast timeseries. Powerful approaches available in R and Python allow us to build forecasting models quickly and easily, but we stress that you also need to check the goodness of fit, and check the residuals of the model for a lack of normality.

Exercises

To complete the activity below, you will need to visit the companion website to the book and download the relevant dataset: https://study.sagepub.com/gopal

Read the file TOTALNSA.csv.

1   Decompose the series into trend, seasonality, and noise.

2   We want to know the trend growth in vehicle sales over the past 5 years, with seasonality removed. Use an MA to do this and calculate the average trend growth as a number. The timeseries is seasonal. Remove the seasonality from the timeseries using *statsmodels* **seasonal_decompose** function to create a seasonality adjusted (SA) vehicle sales timeseries. Use linear extrapolation, using the **statsmodel.interpolate** function or similar, applied to SA vehicle sales, to forecast vehicle sales in 12 months' time.

3   Remove the trend from SA vehicles sales you calculated using differencing.

4   Use our **auto_ARIMA** function on the SA vehicles sales, forecast seasonally adjusted, changes in detrended sales in 24 months' time. Also plot residuals of your model and present statistics showing the goodness of fit.

16

INTRODUCTION TO MACHINE LEARNING

Chapter Contents

Machine learning is a relatively new field compared to probability theory and statistics. The underlying idea is to have a system, or a software program, that learns based on data, i.e., it produces a more effective behaviour or software output. With this goal in mind, we can use probabilities and distributions, but we do not have to do that. We can also relax assumptions, e.g., like those about linearity that we used in Chapter 13. We can use any method that optimizes the output that we care about, as long as we have a way of measuring the quality of the output and a way of optimizing.

Learning in animals or humans is an important inspiration for machine learning, but most machine learning does not actually aim to model natural learning. Human learning, in particular, is far from understood by science, but a full understanding of human learning is not needed to build effective machine learning systems.

Supervised machine learning is the most common form of machine learning, and it is similar to estimation (see Chapters 11–13). It is based on an *input* value (the independent variable) and one or more *label* or *target* values (the dependent variable) that we try to estimate or predict, as it is more commonly called in machine learning. We use a set of data with labels to establish a mapping from the input values to the label, which is typically called the *model* and adapting the model to the data is called *training*. Estimation techniques such as linear or logistic regression are generally considered as machine learning techniques. However, there are alternative techniques that take a simpler approach, such as our first example here: decision trees.

In the following, we will go through a machine learning lifecycle, which includes preparing a dataset, training a model, and evaluating its *generalization*, i.e., how well it performs on new data that was not used for training.

EXAMPLE 1: FITTING A DECISION TREE FOR CLASSIFICATION

We start by loading a dataset called *iris*, which provides measurements of flower petal and sepal sizes as inputs and the species, which are three variants of iris, as the class labels. Each input item contains multiple attribute values, usually called *features*. Each input/target pair is called a sample, data item, or a data point.

We start below by loading the dataset with a ready-made function **data(iris)** provided by the library **datasets** in **R** and by **load_iris** provided by *Scikit-Learn* in Python. It returns the dataset object and we print the **iris$Species** values, the column names, and the number of items in datasets (in R).

R

```
library(datasets)
data(iris)
print(unique(iris$Species))
print(names(iris[,1:4]))
print(nrow(iris))
```

```
[1] setosa     versicolor virginica
```

```
"Sepal.Length" "Sepal.Width" "Petal.Length" "Petal.Width"

150
```

```
print(iris[1,])
```

```
Sepal.Length Sepal.Width Petal.Length Petal.Width Species
1    5.1    3.5    1.4    0.2   setosa
```

The last output is the first sample, printed as an input/target pair. In **R**, the dataframe has no predefined feature or target values.

In Python, we have a slightly different structure, more specifically designed for machine learning, with the attributes **target_names** (the list of class labels) and **feature_names** (the list of attributes).

Python

```python
from sklearn.datasets import load_iris
iris = load_iris()
print(iris.target_names)
print(iris.feature_names)
print(,no of samples: ,,len(iris.data))'m'
```

```
['setosa' 'versicolor' 'virginica']
['sepal length (cm)', 'sepal width (cm)', 'petal length (cm)', 'petal width (cm)']
no of samples:  150
```

```python
print('sample 0 - input: ',iris.data[0], ', target: ',iris.target[0])
```

```
sample 0 - input:  [5.1 3.5 1.4 0.2] , target:  0
```

The **target** value relates to the **target_names**, e.g., 0 in the example above indicates class 'setosa'. The task of predicting one of the 3 target values is called classification.

The **input** values relate to the **feature_names**, e.g., the first element ('5.1') is the 'sepal length' in cm.

We are now going to divide the dataset into two parts, the *training set* for fitting the model (i.e., learn) and the *test set* that we use later to evaluate our model. We use here a ready-made function **train_test_split** from *Scikit-Learn* in Python and the corresponding **createData Partition** in R, that generates those sets for us, but is it easy to do it yourself (see the exercises below):

R

```r
library(caret)
set.seed(121)
index = createDataPartition(iris$Species,p=0.5,list=FALSE)
```

```
train = iris[index,]
test = iris[-index,]
```

```
from sklearn.model_selection import train_test_split
X = iris.data
y = iris.target
X_trn, X_tst, y_trn, y_test = train_test_split(X, y, test_size =.5,
    random_state=538)
```

We can now fit a decision tree to the samples in our dataset. In **R**, there is a function **rpart** that creates a fitted classifier, while in Python a we use a class `DecisionTreeClassifier` with its constructor and its `fit` function. This classifier follows the simple principle that it selects a feature and searches for a threshold so that it is most effective at discriminating the samples belonging to different classes. Read the text box **Decision Tree Learning** to understand in more detail how this is done. In the example below, there are several parameters, that basically ensure that the decision tree is trained to fully fit to the training data.

```
library(rattle)
library(rpart)
clf_full = rpart(Species~., data = train,
    control = rpart.control(minsplit=2, minbucket = 1, cp=0))
fancyRpartPlot(clf_full)
```

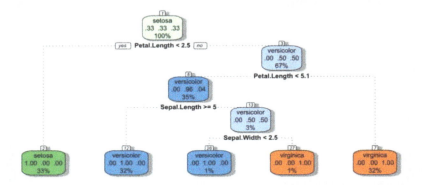

```
from sklearn import tree
import matplotlib.pyplot as plt
clf_full = tree.DecisionTreeClassifier(random_state = 0)
clf_full.fit(X_trn,y_trn)
plt.figure(figsize = (18,10))
tree.plot_tree(clf_full,fontsize=12,feature_names = iris.feature_names,
    class_names = iris.target_names,filled = True)
pass # this prevents printing of a textual tree representation
```

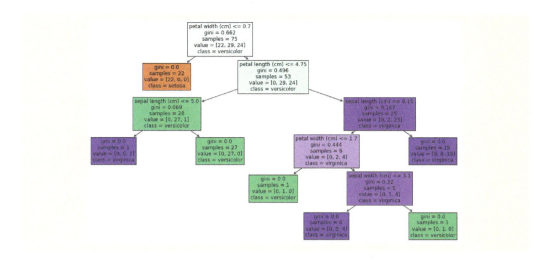

The diagrams above show the structure of the tree. We can see that the visualisation and the structure of the trees are somewhat different between R and Python although they were trained on the same data. This happens often in machine learning and for different reasons, such as differences in algorithms, or implementation details, different data splits, or random elements.

Each internal node has a split rule that determines whether samples go into the left or right node below. When a node has no nodes connected below, it is called a *leaf* and has no split rule. The *Gini* coefficient is an indicator how diverse the data in that node are, where a Gini value of 0 indicates that there is only one class present. We focus here on the tree diagrams generated in Python.

PREDICTION AND ACCURACY

The trained model can then be used to predict the class for new input values. The `DecisionTreeClassifier` class in *Scikit-Learn* has a method `predict()` for that. We use the test set samples and compare the true class (from `y_test`) with the predicted class. In the case below, they are the same, so the prediction is correct.

In R, we print the first element of the test dataset. Then we use the `predict()` function, which provides the class names and the value 1 indicates the predicted class. The label value and the prediction result in the case below they are the same, so the prediction is correct.

R

```
print(test[1,])
predict(clf_full, newdata = test[1,])


Sepal.Length Sepal.Width Petal.Length Petal.Width Species
4.7          3.2          1.3          0.2
setosa versicolor virginica
  1        0          0
```

In Python, use the class **DecisionTreeClassifier** from Scikit-Learn, which has a method **predict()**. We print the test samples and compare the true class (from **y_test**) with the predicted class.

Python

```
print(X_tst[0],y_test[0],clf_full.predict(X_tst[0:1]))
[6.3 2.3 4.4 1.3] 1 [1]
```

As a measure of prediction quality, we calculate the *classification accuracy*, which is the proportion of correctly predicted class labels for a dataset. This can be programmed with a loop as shown below for the training set:

R

```
total = nrow(train)
correct = 0
for(i in 1:total){
  if(train$Species[i] == predict(clf_full, newdata = train[i,],
     type = "class")){
    correct = correct + 1
  }
}
accuracy = correct / total
accuracy
1
```

Python

```
total = len(X_trn)
correct = 0
for i in range(total):
    if y_trn[i] ==
      clf_full.predict(
        X_trn[i:i+1]):
        correct = correct + 1
accuracy = correct / total
accuracy

1.0
```

As we can see, the training set predictions are all correct, as was already clear from the diagram.

GENERALIZATION, OVERFITTING, AND REGULARIZATION

As long as the class labels are the same for items with equal input values, it is possible to break down each node so that any leaf contains only one class, as can be seen in the example above. The actual goal of machine learning is, however, to make good predictions on new data, assuming it is of the same nature as the training data or, probabilistically speaking, that it was drawn from the same distribution as the training set. To measure this capability in practice, we use an empirical approach with a separate dataset for testing.

We created a separate test set earlier, which contains data from the same source as our training set, but that was not used in training. We can now calculate the accuracy of our trained model on that test set. We use below the vectorized form, which is simpler but is equivalent to the code above:

R

```
sum(predict(clf_full, newdata = test, type = "class") == test$Species)/nrow(test)
```

```
0.88
```

Python

```
import numpy as np
np.sum(np.equal(clf_full.predict(X_tst),y_test))/len(X_tst)
```

```
0.88
```

As we can see, the model gets only 88% of the test set right in Python and in R. This performance on unseen data (i.e., data not used in training the model) is called *generalization*. The generalization performance is typically lower than the training set performance. This can be attributed to missing information in the input, i.e., missing features that would help the prediction, and to truly random components in the target data that we cannot predict.

A model that fits perfectly to data in a training set is often not ideal as it learns the specifics of the training set which do not necessarily apply to other data, as in our test set. For example, in the tree shown above, we have one example of a 'versicolor' iris with a long and wide petal but a short and wide sepal in the lower right corner of the Python version. This is not typical, however, as most 'versicolor' samples have short wide petals and long sepals. The special rule for one example is unlikely to help for new samples. This effect is called *overfitting* a model.

Regularization is a general term for techniques that prevent models from overfitting by limiting their ability to adapt. With a decision tree, a simple form of regularization is to make the tree smaller.

EXAMPLE 2: IMPROVING GENERALIZATION BY REGULARIZING THE MODEL

Below we allow only two levels in the tree when we fit it to the training set. We see that two of the three leaves contain samples of multiple classes, so the model fits slightly worse to the training data and training accuracy will be lower:

R

```
clf_small = rpart(Species~., data =train, control = rpart.control(maxdepth = 2))
fancyRpartPlot(clf_small)
```

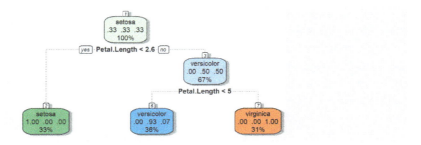

Python

```
clf_small = tree.DecisionTreeClassifier(max_depth = 2,random_state = 0)
clf_small.fit(X_trn,y_trn)
plt.figure(figsize = (15,5))
tree.plot_tree(clf_small,fontsize = 12,feature_names = iris.feature_names,
            class_names = iris.target_names,filled = True)
pass
```

When we calculate the test and training set accuracy for this simpler model on our test set, we see that the values are much closer and the test result on the training set is particularly better. This indicates that we have reduced overfitting and created a model that generalizes better.

R

```
train_acc = sum(predict(clf_small, newdata = train, type = "class") ==
            test$Species)/nrow(train)
test_acc = sum(predict(clf_small, newdata = test, type = "class") ==
            test$Species)/nrow(test)
print(cat("Training accuracy: ", train_acc, "Test accuracy: ", test_acc))
Training accuracy:  0.9733333 Test accuracy:  0.9466666
```

Python

```
# Training set accuracy
train_acc = 1-np.sum(np.abs(clf_small.predict(X_trn)-y_trn))/len(X_trn)
```

```
# Test set accuracy
test_acc = 1-np.sum(np.abs(clf_small.predict(X_tst)-y_test))/len(X_tst)
print("Training accuracy: ", train_acc, ", Test accuracy: ",test_acc)

Training accuracy:  0.96,
Test accuracy:  0.9466666666666667
```

═══════════════ **Box 16.1** ═══════════════

Decision Tree Learning

In this example, we build the decision tree with an algorithm implemented in R in the `rpart` function and in Python in the class `DecisionTreeClassifier` when using the method fit. There are many variants of algorithms for decision tree building. The simplest one, which we use here, has a few simple steps and uses only a few concepts.

Dataset partitioning - splitting the set of data items into two sets, based on an attribute value. Impurity metric - a metric for the lack of classification quality for a given set. Splitting criterion - a rule when to stop growing the tree

The simplest version of the process is this (in pseudocode):

- select an impurity metric and a splitting criterion;
- start with the whole dataset assigned to the root node of the tree and call the method `split` on it:

> split(node) Select an attribute of the samples at random.
> Split the samples in the current node into two subsets,
> > left and right, depending on whether the sample's
> > attribute value is below some threshold or not.
> Determine the threshold value for that attribute
> > that maximises your metric
> If you can improve over previous metrics:
> > Create two new child nodes, left and right,
> > and assign the left and right subsets to them.
> > Call split(left) and split(right)

- `Split` calls itself recursively as it generates more child nodes.
- Once all calls are executed, we have a tree, where each node is associated with: (a) an attribute and threshold; (b) a subset of the data; (c) its impurity value; and (d) its most frequent class.
- For a new data item, we apply the attribute and threshold to traverse through the tree from the root (depicted on top) to a leaf of the tree and assign the most frequent class of that leaf to the item.

In our examples, every node has also the distribution of classes in its subset shown as `value`. We can use that as an estimate of class probabilities, but for a small tree like in our examples, that would be unreliable.

(Continued)

The metric used in our examples is the *Gini Impurity*, I_G. It measures the probability of a random element labelled with a random class to have the wrong label. It is calculated for i in a set: $I_G(p) = \sum_i p_i(1-p_i) = 1 - \sum_i p_i^2$, where p_i which is the proportion of samples of a class in the set. To aggregate over two nodes after splitting, we take the average weighted by the number of items in each set.

The corresponding splitting criterion for the Gini Impurity is the *Gini Gain*, G_G. It is defined as the difference between *Gini Impurity* of the original set *all* and the weighted average of the impurities of the *left* and *right* sets. It is calculated as:

$$G_G = \frac{I_G(left) \times |left| + I_G(left) \times |right|}{|all|} - I_G(all)$$

where $|\cdot|$ is the cardinality (number of items) of a set. A higher gain indicates a better split.

Dangers of Overfitting

Overfit is a key risk for model development and using regularization helps, but most important for avoiding it is our model development hygiene. A model can only be judged by its out-of-sample performance, i.e., data it has not seen before. It is vital to ensure that we keep our training data distinct from our testing data, using separate test sets or cross-validation, as will be shown in the following chapters.

It easily happens during data pre-processing that information from the test data is include in the model, e.g., through data sampling or through dependencies within the dataset. We will see a practical example of this in Chapter 19 on resampling as a method to address class imbalance. If the test data are not actually unseen, we will be overestimating model performance without knowing it and that would set our model up for underperformance in practice.

Summary

Machine learning approaches the problems of learning form data in a direct way, often avoiding the treatment of probabilities and distributions and relaxing underlying assumptions.

The most common form of machine learning is supervised learning, where we have labelled data that we use to fit (train) the model. The general setting is to train a model on a training dataset that can be used to predict an unknown label. A common task is classification, i.e., discrete labels, where we can measure the prediction quality as the proportion of correct predictions, the accuracy.

The accuracy of the model on the training set gives us an indication how well the model fits the data. To evaluate the quality of our model, we need to measure the prediction quality of a test set. This is called the generalization performance of the model.

A common problem is that the model fits the training data very well, but not the test data. This is called overfitting. One possible approach to tackle overfitting is regularization. Regularization means that we limit the complexity of the model, which can prevent the model from overfitting, especially if there is not much training data available. A regularized model often performs better on unseen data.

INTRODUCTION TO MACHINE LEARNING

Exercises

Complete the activity below, using the iris dataset: https://study.sagepub.com/gopal

1   Implement your own version of **`train_test_split`**, so that it generates three sets (train, validation, test). You should accept two arguments, **`train_size`** and **`validation_size`**. You then need to internally determine the **`test_size`**.
2   What is a necessary condition for the arguments to the function created in Exercise 1 to be valid? Implement a test and print an error message if the arguments are not valid.
3   Implement **`train_test_split`** version with *stratified sampling*, i.e., sample such that you have an approximately equal distribution of class labels in each output set.

17

MODEL SELECTION AND CROSS-VALIDATION

Chapter Contents

In machine learning, having fewer assumptions and restrictions means that we have many options for choosing and adapting models. One important part of machine learning is therefore to select the models and to tune them so that we get good generalization.

Model selection is about finding a model that will give good predictions for new data from the same underlying distribution. It can also be about reflecting the process that we are modelling, but that is usually less of a focus in machine learning. The underlying distribution is usually unknown, and without making assumptions, we can only use the empirical approach introduced in the previous chapter.

There are several ways to select among the vast number of choices for models and for evaluating their performance. Machine learning is often formulated as some form of optimization, i.e., minimizing an error metric or maximizing likelihood. The optimization process can be a closed form calculation (linear regression), an iterative algorithm (logistic regression), or a search process (decision tree splits).

It is important, however, that the quantity we are ultimately interested in – the prediction quality on unseen data – is, by definition, not directly available to an optimization procedure. We therefore need to set up specific approaches to the model optimization and selection processes to make sure we optimize for the right target.

MODEL SELECTION

In machine learning, we fit models to training data, but since the goal is to have good predictions for new input data, the performance on the training data is not a good indicator of model quality. Therefore, we hold out part of the available data as a test dataset.

There are sometimes cases where we have an effectively infinite supply of labelled data (e.g., text on the internet). However, in most cases, labelled data are not easy to obtain and we need to make the most of the data we have. To illustrate this approach, we will now look at two different models and how to determine which one is more suitable for a problem.

Wine Dataset

This time, we will look at a different, but also well-known, dataset containing information about wine. It contains 13 different chemical measurements as features and three types of wine as classes. See https://archive.ics.uci.edu/ml/datasets/wine for more information.

R

```
print(names(wine))
print(nrow(wine))
```

```
[1] "Type" "Alcohol" "Malic" "Ash" "Alcalinity" "Magnesium" "Phenols"
"Flavanoids" "Nonflavanoids" "Proanthocyanins" "Color" "Hue" "Dilution"
"Proline"
[1] 178
```

```
set.seed(123456)
```

```
index = caret::createDataPartition(wine$Type,p = 0.8,list = FALSE)
train_wi = wine[index,]
test_wi = wine[-index,]
test_category = test_wi[["Type"]]
train_category = train_wi[["Type"]]
```

Python
```
from sklearn.datasets import load_digits, load_wine
dataset = load_wine()
#dataset = load_digits()
print(dataset.feature_names)
sprint(len(dataset.target)) # samples

X = dataset.data
y = dataset.target

['alcohol', 'malic_acid', 'ash', 'alcalinity_of_ash', 'magnesium', 'total_
phenols', 'flavanoids', 'nonflavanoid_phenols', 'proanthocyanins', 'color_
intensity', 'hue', 'od280/od315_of_diluted_wines', 'proline']

178

from sklearn.model_selection import train_test_split
seed = 0
X_trn, X_tst, y_trn, y_test = train_test_split(X, y, test_size = .2,
    random_state = seed)
```

ANOTHER CLASSIFIER - NEAREST NEIGHBOUR

We now use another classifier: the K-Nearest-Neighbour (KNN) classifier. This classifier is very simple: it views the feature values of an item as a vector. For a new feature vector, we calculate the k closest feature vectors in our training set. We then look up the classes belonging to these k feature vectors and choose the most frequent one as our KNN prediction. The number k determines the behaviour. In the simplest case, we can choose 1, which makes it easy to select the predicted class (no ties). This is a very simple classifier, but it can be quite effective.

Our question now is whether we should use a KNN or a Decision Tree (DT) classifier. We start by training both models on our training set and calculate the performance on the test set.

R
```
set.seed(0)
model_tree = rpart(Type ~ ., data = train_wi, control = rpart.control
            (maxdepth = 5))
predicted_dt = predict(model_tree, type = "class")
```

```
pred_tst_dt = predict(model_tree, test_wi, type = "class")

paste("dt test:",
    confusionMatrix(reference = test_wi$Type, data = pred_tst_dt)$overall[1],
    "dt train:",
    confusionMatrix(reference = train_wi$Type, data = predicted_dt)$overall[1])

model_knn = knn3(train_wi,train_wi$Type)
predicted_knn = predict(model_knn, train_wi, type ='class')
pred_tst_knn = predict(model_knn, test_wi, type ='class')

paste("knn test:",
    confusionMatrix(reference = test_wi$Type, data = pred_tst_knn)$overall[1],
    "knn train:",
    confusionMatrix(reference = train_wi$Type, data = predicted_knn)$overall[1])

[1] "dt test: 0.985714285714286 dt train: 0.972222222222222"
[1] "knn test: 0.714285714285714 knn train: 0.768518518518518"
```

Python

```
from sklearn.neighbors import KNeighborsClassifier

dtc = DecisionTreeClassifier(max_depth = 5, random_state = 0)
dtc.fit(X_trn, y_trn)

knn = KNeighborsClassifier()
knn.fit(X_trn, y_trn)

# helper functions
def accuracy(X, y, predictor):
    return np.sum(np.equal(predictor.predict(X), y))/len(X)

def trainValTestAcc(predictor):
    return ['train: ', accuracy(X_trn,y_trn,predictor), 'test: ',
        accuracy(X_tst,y_test,predictor)]

print(" DT: ", trainValTestAcc(dtc))
print("KNN: ", trainValTestAcc(knn))

DT: {'train': 1.0, 'test': 0.9722222222222222}
KNN: {'train': 0.7887323943661971, 'test': 0.8055555555555556}
```

We see that a DT seems to work better than KNN on the test set. However, this is just on 20% of the data in our test set. To test whether data selection is the cause of the difference, we can look at different ways to split the data by changing the value of the **seed** variable above. That has the effect of changing the results of `train_test_split`. We can try it out with the notebooks provided with this book, but here are some results to study (created with Python):

Table 17.1 Performance of the classifiers

Seed	Classifier	Accuracy-train	Accuracy-test
1	DT	0.9295	0.8611
	KNN	1	0.75
2	DT	0.9295	0.9166
	KNN	1	0.7222
3	DT	0.9436	0.7777
	KNN	1	0.6666
4	DT	0.9295	0.8888
	KNN	1	0.8333
5	DT	0.9366	0.7222
	KNN	1	0.75

In most cases, the DT produces higher accuracy, but in the last one, the KNN is better. We can also see that there is significant variation between the different splits that we created by using different seeds. The question we need to answer now is whether the better performance of the DT is due to the underlying process, i.e., the true distribution of model performances on data from underlying distribution, or whether it is likely be the result of random variation. To gain some evidence, we need two things: more measurements and a statistical test.

Cross-validation

The measurements we are taking are based on randomly selected training and test splits. As we increase the number of splits to test, we will increasingly have overlap between them, because the same data points will be reused. To obtain multiple independent test datasets, we would ideally use newly collected data. However, getting more data is often not feasible. A method to make most use of small datasets is called *cross-validation*. The idea of cross-validation is to divide the data systematically such that each data item is used only in one test set.

The most common type is *k-fold cross-validation*, where we divide the whole dataset into k subsets, called folds, of approximately equal size. Each fold is used once as the test set, while the remaining $k-1$ folds are combined and used as the training set. In this way, we get k different samples of the performance. Commonly used values for k are between 3 and 10, and sometimes 20. In the extreme case of $k = n$, where n is the size of the dataset, it is called *leave-one-out cross-validation*.

There are ready-made implementati ons of k-fold cross-validation available. However, In R we use a self-made function in the notebook, that implements simple cross-validation.[1] In Python, the function **cross_validate** is available in *Scikit-Learn*. It is left as an exercise to implement your own version of **cross_validate** (see below).

R

```
acc = cross_val(wine,10)
paste('10-fold-CV mean:',mean(acc),'sd:', sd(acc))
```

---

[1]The **caret** package offers only stratified cross-validation, but here we are interested in plain cross-validation.

```
acc = cross_val(wine,20)
paste('20-fold-CV mean:',mean(acc),'sd:', sd(acc))

acc = cross_val(wine,nrow(wine))
paste('Leave-one-out-CV mean:',mean(acc),'sd:', sd(acc))

[1] "10-fold-CV mean: 0.624509803921569 sd: 0.225653009748211"

[1] "20-fold-CV mean: 0.653472222222222 sd: 0.226273155937941"

"Leave-one-out-CV mean: 0.713483146067416 sd: 0.453409185554118"
```

Python

```
from sklearn.model_selection import cross_validate, KFold, LeaveOneOut

cv = KFold(10)
scores = cross_validate(knn, X, y, cv = cv, scoring ='accuracy',
    return_trn_score = True)
# code for printing
print('10-fold CV, test accuracy, mean:', scores['test_score'].mean(),
    'std dev:', scores['test_score'].std())

cv = KFold(20)
# adapt the code above for printing

cv = LeaveOneOut()
# adapt the code above for printing

10-fold CV, test accuracy, mean: 0.6310457516339869 std dev: 0.21593098615373252

20-fold CV, test accuracy, mean: 0.6590277777777779 std dev: 0.23288129990550768

Leave-one-out, test accuracy, mean: 0.6966292134831461 std dev:
0.45971398978604006
```

We also see that the leave-one-out CV produces higher accuracy results. There are two contributing factors here, the larger size of the training set (n–1 versus $0.8n$) and the avoidance of class imbalances in the training sets. When taking a random sample, we will get variation in the distribution of classes between the folds. This can skew the accuracy measurements, because some classes may be harder to predict than others and because the class distribution between the training and test sets can be different.

We can ensure that the class distribution in all folds is approximately the same, which is called stratified sampling and leads to *Stratified Cross-Validation*. This is implemented in *Scikit-Learn* as **StratifiedKFold** and can be used exactly as KFold and in caret package in R it is always used when selected for `trainControl` (with `method = 'cv'`).

R

```
model_knn_strt = train(Type ~ ., data = wine, method ='knn', metric = "Accuracy",
                trControl = trainControl(method = 'cv',number = 10))
```

```
paste("Stratified CV accuracy = ", mean(model_knn_strat$resample$Accuracy))
paste("Stratified CV std dev = ", sd(model_knn_strat$resample$Accuracy))


[1] "Mean for stratified sample =  0.705825593395253"
[1] "std for stratified sample =  0.0818242752478426"
```

Python

```python
from sklearn.model_selection import StratifiedKFold, LeaveOneOut

cv = StratifiedKFold(10, shuffle = True, random_state = 0)
scores = cross_validate(knn, X, y, cv = cv, scoring ='accuracy')
print('10-fold Stratified CV, test accuracy, mean: ', scores['test_score'].mean(), ',',
    std dev:', scores['test_score'].std())


10-fold Stratified CV, test accuracy, mean: 0.6748366013071896 , std dev:
0.06665785537054658
```

We observe that standard deviation of the test accuracy is lower with stratified sampling, as expected because of the more stable class distribution. We also see an increased accuracy, almost as high as with the leave-one-out CV, which indicates that the effect of the class imbalance was stronger than that of the smaller training sets when comparing *k*-fold to leave-one-out CV.

Significance of Model Differences

When trying to assess whether an ML model is better, we can use CV (or multiple datasets) to create multiple independent measurements and test for significance of their difference. Given that we have no good reasons to assume normality of the distribution of the accuracy values, it is safest to use a non-parametric test. In Chapter 9, we discussed the Wilcoxon signed rank test for medians. Alternatively, a pairwise t-test could be used, but the normality of the distribution should be tested beforehand. Normality can typically not be shown, at least for smaller datasets.

We will now apply both KNN and DT and apply the Wilcoxon test to the test accuracy results per fold. The p-value gives the probability that a difference between the models of this size or more could have been observed when the underlying distribution had the same median. We normally accept the models as being different when the p-value is below 5%. For significance tests, it is better to have more independent measurements. We can therefore increase the number of folds, as the resulting smaller test sets do not increase the variation between measurements too much, as happened in the leave-one-out CV above. A value of 20 seems like a good guess, as it still leaves approximately 35 samples in every fold.

R

```r
model_dt_cv20 = train(Type ~ ., data = wine, method ='rpart',metric =
              "Accuracy", trControl = trainControl(method = 'cv',
              number = 20))
paste("Mean accuracy of KNN = ",mean(model_knn_cv_20$results$Accuracy))
```

```
paste("Mean accuracy of DT = ",mean(model_dt_cv_20$results$Accuracy))
wilcox.test(model_dt_cv_20$resample$Accuracy,model_knn_
cv_20$resample$Accuracy)
```

```
[1] "KNN Mean Accuracy:  0.775138888888889"
[1] "Decision Tree Mean Accuracy:  0.855694444444444"

Wilcoxon signed rank test with continuity correction

data:  fit_dt_20fold$resample$Accuracy and fit_knn_20fold$resample$Accuracy
V = 129.5, p-value = 0.05796
alternative hypothesis: true location shift is not equal to 0
```

Python
```
cv = KFold(20)

scores_knn = cross_validate(knn, X, y, cv = cv, scoring = 'accuracy')
scores_dtc = cross_validate(dtc, X, y, cv = cv, scoring = 'accuracy')
print('avg accuracy KNN:', scores_knn['test_score'].mean(), ', DT: ',
scores_dtc['test_score'].mean())

wilcoxon(scores_dtc['test_score'], scores_knn['test_score'], mode ='approx')

avg accuracy KNN: 0.6590277777777779, DT: 0.8777777777777779
WilcoxonResult(statistic=6.0, pvalue=0.003074168162550741)
```

The results show that the show that the p-value is clearly below 0.05, difference is significant, i.e., the DT is significantly better than the KNN model at predicting the Wine type from the chemical measurements. The implementations and settings for R and Python are different, therefore we get different model performance.

We can also test whether Stratified CV leads to less variation (standard deviation) and better accuracy:

R
```
mdl_knn_strt = train(Type ~ ., data = wine, method = 'knn',metric = "Accuracy",
            trControl = trainControl(method = 'cv',number = 20))
mdl_dt_strt = train(Type ~ ., data = wine, method = 'rpart',metric = "Accuracy",
            trControl = trainControl(method = 'cv',number = 20))
paste("Mean accuracy KNN = ",mean(mdl_knn_strt$results$Accuracy))
paste("Mean accuracy DT = ",mean(mdl_dt_strt$results$Accuracy))
paste("std accuracy KNN = ", mdl_knn_strt$results$AccuracySD))
paste("std accuracy DT = ",sd(mdl_dt_strt$results$AccuracySD))
wilcox.test( mdl_knn_strt$results$Accuracy, mdl_dt_strt$results$Accuracy )
[1] "Mean accuracy KNN =  0.720436507936508"
[1] "Mean accuracy DT =  0.845416666666667"
```

```
[1] "std accuracy KNN =  0.144239152073144"
[1] "std accuracy DT =  0.109156756546209"

Wilcoxon rank sum test with continuity correction

data:  model_knn_strat$resample$Accuracy and model_dt_strat$resample$Accuracy
W = 2417, p-value = 2.082e-10
alternative hypothesis: true location shift is not equal to 0
```

Python

```python
cv = StratifiedKFold(20)

scores_knn = cross_validate(knn, X, y, cv = cv, scoring ='accuracy')
scores_dtc = cross_validate(dtc, X, y, cv = cv, scoring ='accuracy')
print('avg accuracy KNN mean:', scores_knn['test_score'].mean(), ', DT: ',
      scores_dtc['test_score'].mean())
print('avg accuracy KNN std:', scores_knn['test_score'].std(),', DT: ',
      scores_dtc[,test_score'].std())

wilcoxon(scores_dtc['test_score'], scores_knn['test_score'], mode ='approx')
avg accuracy KNN mean: 0.7041666666666667 , DT: 0.9111111111111111
avg accuracy KNN std: 0.13088758016700938 , DT: 0.11439589045541111
WilcoxonResult(statistic=12.0, pvalue = 0.0004792877798731423)
```

As we can see, all expected effects of Stratified CV occur: lower standard deviation, higher accuracy, and lower p-value, i.e., a more significant result.

HYPER-PARAMETER TUNING

In addition to selecting a model-type, we also need to set values that control the training process, e.g., regularization parameters, or the size and structure of the model (e.g., the maximal depth of a decision tree). The settings are usually called hyper-parameters to distinguish them from the parameters within a model that are optimized during training (e.g., the feature thresholds in a decision tree).

The approach is very similar to model selection, we can indeed view models with different hyper-parameters as different models and apply the same technique. In practice, however, the tuning of hyper-parameters and the selection of a models type are treated separately because the separate implementation is easier, and then they are compared after optimization.

An important and common hyper-parameter is the regularization strength, as we saw in the last chapter. We can tune regularization by testing several parameter values and selecting the one that creates the best value in CV. It is often informative to view the performance for different hyper-parameter values. This whole process is available in a single function in *Scikit-Learn* called `validation_curve`. It takes a model, varies multiple parameters, and records the training and test performance ready to plot. In R, we can use factor variables to achieve this.

R

```
folds = createMultiFolds(train_wi$Type, k = 20)
model_dt_strat_fold = train(Type ~ ., data = train_wi, method ='rpart2',
    metric = "Accuracy", trControl = trainControl(index = folds),
    tuneGrid = expand.grid(maxdepth = 1:10))
folds = createMultiFolds(train_wi$Type, k = 2)
model_dt_strat_nofold = train(Type ~ ., data = train_wi, method ='rpart2',
    metric ="Accuracy", trControl = trainControl(index = folds),
    tuneGrid = expand.grid(maxdepth = 1:10))

df1 = model_dt_strat_nofold$results[,c(1,2)]
df1$foldtype = as.factor("Training")
df2 = model_dt_strat_fold$results[,c(1,2)]
df2$foldtype = as.factor("Cross-validation")
df = rbind(df1,df2)
ggplot(data = df,aes(x = maxdepth,y = Accuracy,color = foldtype)) + geom_line()
```

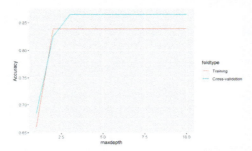

Python

```
import matplotlib.pyplot as plt
from sklearn.model_selection import validation_curve

cv = StratifiedKFold(10, shuffle = True, random_state = 1)
param_range = list(range(1, 10))
train_scores, test_scores = validation_curve( dtc, X, y, cv = cv,
    param_name = "max_depth", param_range = param_range, scoring = "accuracy")

train_scores_mean = np.mean(train_scores, axis = 1)
test_scores_mean = np.mean(test_scores, axis = 1)

plt.title("Validation Curve with DT")
plt.xlabel("max_depth")
plt.ylabel("Accuracy")

plt.plot(param_range, train_scores_mean, label = "Training accuracy")
plt.plot(param_range, test_scores_mean, label = "Cross-validation accuracy")
plt.show()
```

```
Mean test score per fold: [0.64607843 0.82058824 0.90457516 0.89346405
    0.89901961 0.89346405  0.89346405 0.89346405 0.89346405]
Best value: 3
```

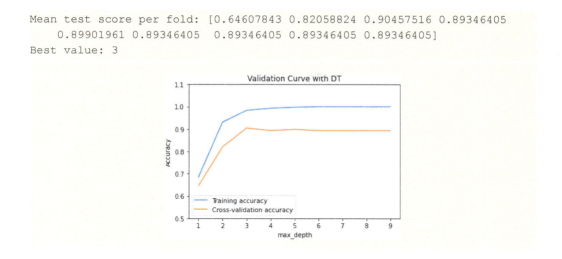

The curve shows us that the training accuracy keeps increasing as we allow deeper decision trees. However, the cross-validation accuracy reaches a peak at a depth of 3 and then decreases in Python. The best value for **max_depth** for a decision tree on this dataset is therefore 3. In R, we have slightly different implementations that behave slightly differently: the best test accuracy is reached at depth 2 and then stays constant. Given the choice of many models with the same performance we choose the one simplest model, i.e. the lowest tree depth value. This means, we select the most efficient model (smaller trees need less computation) and the model that is least likely to overfit when tested on new data. This approach of choosing the simplest model is called *Occam's Razor*.

We could go even further in estimating the **max_depth** by applying the CV to the *k* training sets in a *k*-fold cross-validation (this is called *nested cross-validation*), so that we get more measurements and have an independent test set for each cross-validated estimate. This would indeed maximize the use of the data. However, it would multiply the effort needed to optimize the parameter by the factor *k*, and for small *k*, we might overestimate the need for regularization, as our training sets become even smaller. Whether this is worth doing in practice depends on how critical the model performance is in the application scenario. In general, there is a trade-off between making the most of a limited dataset and the computational cost of doing so. If performance is very important, it is, in practice, often the better option to collect more training data, as that is typically more effective in increasing performance without excessive additional computation.

ESTIMATING THE MODEL PERFORMANCE

The evaluation of an ML model should include an estimate of the performance on new data. To get an unbiased estimate, the data we use to estimate model performance on new data must actually be new to the model. That means that any information used in the evaluation cannot be used to optimize or select our model. This applies to training, model selection, and hyperparameter tuning, extending the principle of division into training and test data.

The best way to do this is to use nested cross-validation as explained in the previous section. However, that is often not practical and instead, we take a single separate test set (often called a hold-out set) of data that is not used in training, tuning, or selection of models. The hyper-parameter tuning and the selection of the best model is then done using a separate data set (taken out of the training set if no new data are available), which is called the validation set.

R

```
df = data.frame()
folds = createMultiFolds(train_wi$Type, k = 2)
for (md in 1:10){
    model_dt_strat_nofold = train(Type ~ ., data = train_wi,
                        method = 'rpart2',
            metric = "Accuracy",trControl = trainControl(index = folds),
                        tuneGrid = expand.grid(maxdepth = md))
    df = rbind(df,c(md,"Training",model_dt_strat_nofold$results$Accuracy))
    pred = predict(model_dt_strat_nofold,newdata = test_wi)
    t1 = table(test_wi$Type,pred)
    accu = sum(t1[1,1]+t1[2,2]+t1[3,3])/nrow(test_wi)
    df = rbind(df,c(md,"Validation",accu))
}
colnames(df) = c("maxdepth","foldtype","Accuracy")
df$maxdepth = as.numeric(df$maxdepth)
df$Accuracy = as.numeric(df$Accuracy)
ggplot(data = df,aes(x = maxdepth,y = Accuracy,color = foldtype)) + geom_line()
```

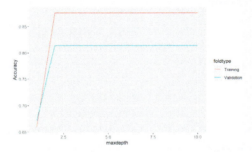

Python

```
X_trn2, X_val, y_trn2, y_val = train_test_split(X, y, test_size=0.2,
                        random_state = seed, stratify = y)

train_scores = []; val_scores = []
for md in param_range:
    dtc.max_depth = md
    dtc.fit(X_trn2, y_trn2)
    train_scores.append(np.sum(np.equal(dtc.predict(X_trn2),
        y_trn2))/len(y_trn2))
    val_scores.append(np.sum(np.equal(dtc.predict(X_val),
        y_val))/len(y_val))
```

```
plt.title("Validation Curve with DT")
plt.xlabel("max_depth")
plt.ylabel("Accuracy")

plt.plot(param_range, train_scores, label = "Training accuracy")
plt.plot(param_range, val_scores, label = "Validation accuracy")
plt.show()
```

We see in Python that the curve is less stable because it is based only on one validation set. The best HP value is also different (4 instead of 3). Instead of using a single validation set, we can use CV on the training set, as we did before on the whole set:

R

```
df = data.frame()
folds = createMultiFolds(train_wi$Type, k = 20)
for (md in 1:10){
    model_dt_strat_fold = train(Type ~ ., data = train_wi,  method ='rpart2',
                         metric = "Accuracy",trControl = trainControl(index
                         = folds), tuneGrid = expand.grid(maxdepth = md))
    df = rbind(df,c(md,"Training",model_dt_strat_fold$results$Accuracy))
    pred = predict(model_dt_strat_fold,newdata = test_wi)
    t1 = table(test_wi$Type,pred)
    accu = sum(t1[1,1]+t1[2,2]+t1[3,3])/nrow(test_wi)
    df = rbind(df,c(md,"Validation",accu))
}
colnames(df) = c("maxdepth","foldtype","Accuracy")

df$maxdepth = as.numeric(df$maxdepth)
df$Accuracy = as.numeric(df$Accuracy)

ggplot(data = df,aes(x = maxdepth,y = Accuracy,color = foldtype))+
  geom_line()
```

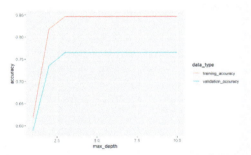

Python

```
cv = StratifiedKFold(10, shuffle = True, random_state = 1)
train_scores, test_scores = validation_curve( dtc, X_trn, y_trn, cv = cv,
                    param_name = "max_depth", param_range = param_
                    range, scoring = "accuracy")


train_scores_mean = np.mean(train_scores, axis =1)
test_scores_mean = np.mean(test_scores, axis =1)


plt.title("Validation Curve with DT")


plt.plot(param_range, train_scores_mean, label = "Training accuracy")
plt.plot(param_range, test_scores_mean, label = "Cross-validation accuracy")
plt.show()
```

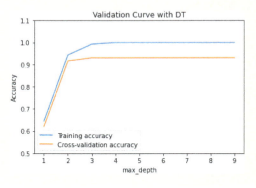

With CV on the training set, the curve of the validation accuracy is visually more similar to that on the whole set and the best HP value is now the same as we had with CV on the whole set. This illustrates that we can achieve more reliable results when using CV instead of a single split. With that HP value, we can now fit the whole training set and estimate the accuracy on the test set:

R

```
folds = createMultiFolds(train_wi$Type, k = 2)
model_dt_strat_nofold = train(Type ~ ., data = train_wi, method ='rpart2',
                metric = "Accuracy", trControl = trainControl(index
                = folds), tuneGrid = expand.grid(maxdepth = 3))
```

```
pred = predict(model_dt_strat_nofold,newdata = test_wi)
t1 = table(test_wi$Type,pred)
accu = sum(t1[1,1] + t1[2,2] + t1[3,3])/nrow(test_wi)
paste("Accuracy = ", accu)
[1] "Accuracy =  0.814285714285714"
```

Python

```
dtc.max_depth = 3
dtc.fit(X_trn, y_trn)
np.sum(np.equal(dtc.predict(X_tst), y_test))/len(y_test)
```

```
0.9722222222222222
```

This estimate seems potentially overoptimistic, as it is better than the cross-validation accuracy. It is helpful to cross-check this against a cross-validated performance with our selected *max_depth* values over the whole dataset (remember, this may also be over-optimistic, as the testing now included data that were used to optimize this value).

R

```
folds = createMultiFolds(wine$Type, k = 20)
model_dt_strat_fold = train(Type ~ ., data = wine, method ='rpart2',
                    metric = "Accuracy",trControl = trainControl(index =
                    folds), tuneGrid = expand.grid(maxdepth = 3))
paste("CV Accuracy - Mean = ", mean(model_dt_strat_fold$resample$Accuracy))
paste("CV Accuracy - sd = ", sd(model_dt_strat_fold$resample$Accuracy))
[1] "CV Accuracy - Mean =  0.867472222222222"
[1] "CV Accuracy - sd =  0.116981760776662"
```

Python

```
dtc.max_depth = 3
from sklearn.model_selection import cross_val_score
test_score = cross_val_score(dtc, X, y, cv = cv)
print("CV test accuracy mean: ", np.mean(test_score), ", std: ", np.std
      (test_score))
```

```
CV test accuracy mean: 0.9045751633986928 , std: 0.04339888967590594
```

The value that we see here is clearly lower than our single test set estimate of 0.97, and the distance to is almost 2 standard deviations. Therefore, we cannot be sure about this performance estimate. In practice, we can and should now do a full nested cross-validation.

By tuning the hyper-parameter *max_depth* on data that is independent of the final test, we can be confident that we have not introduced selection bias in the process. However, using a single estimate for the performance prediction is prone to noise, especially for small datasets and needs to be treated with care. It is important not to take raw measurements as predictions and cross-check results after model selection.

USE CASE: DECISION TREES TO MODEL APP RATINGS

As we have seen before, decision trees (DT) can overfit easily, and they are notorious for overfitting to the quirks of a dataset. However, they can be a very useful tool to understand dynamics in complex systems quickly if used carefully.

Let us assume that we are private equity analysts, providing support and advice to a tech company in our portfolio. One portfolio company provides tax and investment services targeting family wealth and the company seeks to launch an Android app to promote its brand name. The app will be a scheduling app for families. If the app only garners poor ratings, the project will be a waste of time, so we need to understand which types of apps tend to get the best ratings from users. We can then attempt to reverse engineer into our app these important, ratings-boosting features from the most successful apps. The GooglePlay App store data gives us a basis with which to work. The problem is that the data are messy and much data wrangling will be needed.

Data Wrangling

First, we load our data and start to clean it:

R

```
df = read.csv("googleplaystore.csv")
```

Python

```
df =  pd.read_csv("googleplaystore.csv")
```

To build a DT, we need a categorical variable to predict (rating), and numeric variables to drive the prediction. We notice that these data contain categorical columns, such as 'Content Rating', in some of the numeric fields there are characters, for example in 'Installs' there is a '+' suffix we will have to remove. This is a time-consuming process.

First remove characters from numeric columns and convert the datatypes of these columns to numeric. We are removing any non-digit characters and missing values are replaced with zeros:

R

```
#remove text characters from numeric columns
df$Price = str_replace(df$Price,",","")
df$Price = str_replace(df$Price,"\\$","")
df$Price = as.numeric(df$Price)
df$Price = as.numeric(str_replace_na(df$Price,0))
```

Python

```
#remove text characters from numeric columns
df['Price'] = df['Price'].str.replace(', ',,'')
df['Price'] = df['Price'].str.replace('$', '')
#Force conversion of the column to a numeric
df['Price'] = pd.to_numeric(df['Price'], errors ='coerce').fillna(0).
        astype('float')
```

	App	Category	Rating	Reviews	Size	Installs	Type	Price	Content rating	Genres	Last updated	Current ver	Android ver
0	Photo Editor & Candy Camera & Grid & Scrap Book	ART_AND_DESIGN	4.1	159	19M	10,000+	Free	0	Everyone	Art & Design	January 7, 2018	1.0.0	4.0.3 and up
1	Colouring book moana	ART_AND_DESIGN	3.9	967	14M	500,000+	Free	0	Everyone	Art & Design;Pretend Play	January 15, 2018	2.0.0	4.0.3 and up
2	U Launcher Lite - FREE Live Cool Themes, Hide ...	ART_AND_DESIGN	4.7	87510	8.7M	5,000,000+	Free	0	Everyone	Art & Design	August 1, 2018	1.2.4	4.0.3 and up
3	Sketch - Draw & Paint	ART_AND_DESIGN	4.5	215644	25M	50,000,000+	Free	0	Teen	Art & Design	June 8, 2018	Varies with device	4.2 and up

Now do one hot encoding for categorical variables, remembering that we need to convert the column's datatype to **category** in *Pandas* before we use the `get_dummies` function.

We now need to convert the 'Rating', which is a numeric value into a categorical column which will be our *y* variable. All the other columns we can use as our *x* variables. We can wrap this up as a function, which bins the Ratings into high/mid/low categories (labelled as '0', '1', '2' in the code):

R

```
x = ifelse(is.nan(df$Rating),0,df$Rating)
brakepoints = quantile(x,probs= c(0,0.33,0.67,1))
x = cut(x,breaks = brakepoints,labels = c("lowest","middle","highest"))
x = ifelse(is.na(x),"1",x)
df$Rating = x
df$Reviews = as.numeric(df$Reviews)
df$Installs = as.numeric(df$Installs)
df$Size = as.numeric(df$Size)
df = df[-c(1,11,12,13)]
#Final check to ensure no missing values
table(complete.cases(df))
```

Python

```
# Prepare our X and y variables and wrap as a function
def get_X_and_y(df: pd.DataFrame, bins_to_use: int = 3):
    # Define X variables
    cols = list(df.columns)
    cols.remove("Rating")
    X_trn = df[cols]
    # Define y variables (rating): lowest 33% as 0, middle as 1, highest 2
    bins_to_use = 3
    y_trn = pd.qcut(df['Rating'], q = bins_to_use+1, labels = [str(i)
            for i in range(bins_to_use)], duplicates = 'drop')
    return (X_trn, y_trn)

#Run the func
X_trn, y_trn = get_X_and_y(df)
```

Tree of Truth? Inferring from Decision Tree

Our data are prepared and we can run the DT across all genres of apps to take a high pass on the problem to see what generally drives higher and lower ratings for apps. We apply now a different regularization technique by forcing the DT to have a minimum of 1% of samples at each leaf node with the `min_samples` parameter. We can wrap the DT creation function in our own wrapper-function, so we can reuse our implementation easily:

R

```
dtmodel = train(Rating ~ ., method = "rpart", data = df)
fancyRpartPlot( dtmodel$finalModel,main = "Decision Tree",sub = "" )
```

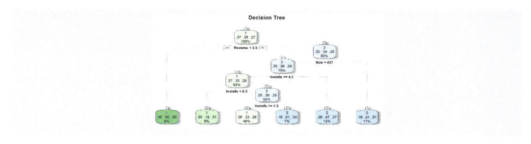

Python

```
from sklearn.tree import DecisionTreeClassifier
from sklearn import tree

# function to create, fit, and plot a decision tree
def make_dt(X_trn: pd.DataFrame, y_trn: pd.DataFrame):
    dtc = DecisionTreeClassifier(max_depth = 3, random_state = 0, \
          min_samples_leaf = int(X_trn.shape[0]*0.01))
    dtc.fit(X_trn, y_trn)
    fig = plt.figure(figsize =(25, 20))
    tree.plot_tree(dtc, feature_names = X_trn.columns, \ class_names =
                   list(y_trn.unique()), filled = True)
    return dtc

#Run the func
make_dt(X_trn, y_trn)
```

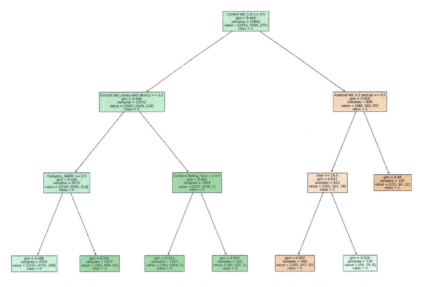

Figure 17.1 Drivers of ratings on apps (decision tree generated with *scikit-learn*)

As explained in Chapter 16, each node in the DT represents a decision. The top node 'Curr_
Ver_1.0 < 0.5' relates to a one hot encoding column, where a '1' value indicates the app runs on
Version 1.0, and '0' says it does not. The rule 'Curr_Ver_1.0 < 0.5' says to follow the left-hand
branch if the value of this column is '0', and to follow the right if the value is '1'.

From the tree, we can see that the DT algorithm has found some helpful and some unhelpful splits. More useful, and generic, is that Android version and also app size appear to be related to the rating, which could be a proxy for complexity and functionality – perhaps the more complex an app is, the more likely it is to have a better rating.

Now we can drill into the Family apps specifically. We can run the functions to quickly reproduce the DT but for Family apps only:

R

```
dtmodel_family = train(Rating ~ ., method = "rpart", data = df[df$Category
            == "FAMILY",])
fancyRpartPlot(dtmodel_family$finalModel,main = "Decision Tree",sub = "")
```

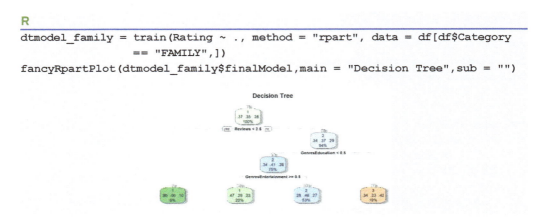

Python

```
# Family App specific
df_family = df[(df[,Category_FAMILY'] == 1)]

X_trn, y_trn = get_X_and_y(df_family)
dtc = make_dt(X_trn, y_trn)
```

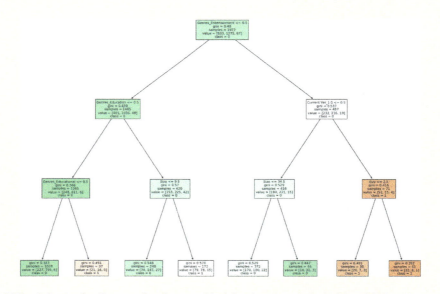

Figure 17.2 Drivers of ratings on Family apps (decision tree generated with *scikit-learn*)

Our DT was trained only on Family apps shows that Family apps of the Educational genre tend to be higher rated, and of those, the larger, more substantial apps tend to be better rated. More analysis is needed but based on this high pass, we have been able to establish that our app probably needs to be Educational to have the best chance of gaining higher ratings.

Finally, we can examine the accuracy of our DT approach, to double check that our model was not overfitting.

R

```
result = dtc.predict(X_trn)
scores = accuracy_score(y_trn, result)
print('Mean ', scores)
```

```
Mean:  0.6678
```

Python

```
from sklearn.metrics import accuracy_score

result = dtc.predict(X_trn)
scores = accuracy_score(y_trn, result)
print('DT, mean: ', scores)
```

```
DT, mean:  0.6668356997971603
```

The training set accuracy is 0.67 (rounded). Let us compare that to the test accuracy we achieve with cross-validation:

R

```
dtmodel = train(Rating ~ ., method = "rpart", data = df,
        trControl = trainControl(method = 'cv',number = 10))
paste("Mean accuracy in 10 fold cv = ",mean(dtmodel$results$Accuracy))
paste("sd of accuracy in 10 fold cv = ",sd(dtmodel$results$Accuracy))
dtmodel = train(Rating ~ ., method = "rpart", data = df,
        trControl=trainControl(method = 'cv',number = 20))
paste("Mean accuracy in 20 fold cv = ",mean(dtmodel$results$Accuracy))
paste("sd of accuracy in 20 fold cv = ",sd(dtmodel$results$Accuracy))
```

```
[1] "Mean accuracy in 10 fold cv =  0.431048647415384"
[1] "sd of accuracy in 10 fold cv =  0.0391426057872761"
[1] "Mean of accuracy in 20 fold cv =  0.437196564003099"
[1] "sd of accuracy in 20 fold cv =  0.0391836484321515"
```

Python

```
from sklearn.model_selection import cross_validate, KFold, LeaveOneOut

cv = KFold(10)
```

```
scores = cross_validate(dtc,X_trn,y_trn,cv = cv,scoring ='accuracy')
print('10-fold CV, test accuracy, mean: ',scores['test_score'].mean(),',
      std dev:',scores['test_score'].std())

cv = KFold(20)
scores = cross_validate(dtc,X_trn,y_trn,cv = cv,scoring = 'accuracy')
print('20-fold CV, test accuracy, mean: ',scores['test_score'].mean(),',
      std dev:',scores['test_score'].std())

10-fold CV, test accuracy, mean:  0.6494026560016408 , std dev:
0.10617636783598784
20-fold CV, test accuracy, mean:  0.6457792207792207 , std dev:
0.12631281958925833
```

We can see that accuracy using cross-fold validation is close to that on the training data before, so we can be confident that the models have not overfitted.

Summary

Overall, we found that a decision tree is better suited for the wine dataset. We can use a significance test on the differences between models in cross-validation results to select the best model type. We can apply the same approach to optimize hyper-parameters. By keeping a hold-out set, we can get an unbiased estimate of the model performance on new data.

Exercises

To complete the activity below, you will need to visit the companion website to the book and download the Diabetes dataset: https://study.sagepub.com/gopal

1   Implement the model selection and HP tuning as above for the iris dataset.
     a   Vary the **n_neighbors** parameter for KNN.
     b   Plot the validation curve.
2   Implement nested cross-validation for tuning the *max_depth* of the decision tree on the wine dataset.
3   Implement a validation curve plot that shows the accuracies plus and minus the standard deviation.
4   Tune a KNN model on the *Abalone dataset* with the hyper-parameters *k* (number of neighbours), and *p* (metric exponent). Evaluate the results in a two-dimensional grid search with cross-validation. Make sure to avoid overfitting and estimate model performance.
5   Tune a DT to classify web pages in the *Website Phishing* dataset with the hyper-parameters minimum numbers to split a leave, maximum tree depth, minimum number of samples in a leaf. Evaluate the results in a three-dimensional grid search with cross-validation. Make sure to avoid overfitting and estimate model performance.

18

REGRESSION MODELS IN MACHINE LEARNING

Chapter Contents

So far, we have addressed machine learning with classification tasks, i.e., where there is a finite discrete set of target labels, the classes. The other main task in supervised machine learning is regression, where the task is to predict a continuous value. Regression leads to different metrics and algorithms, as well as some new concepts such as loss functions and regularization terms, as it is closer to optimization.

LOSS MINIMIZATION VERSUS MODEL ESTIMATION

Estimation, as introduced in Chapter 11, has the goal of finding the best parameter values for a model that represents the data generation process. In machine learning, the focus is typically more on the quality of the predictions generated by the model. The quality of the predictions is measured by a loss function, which describes the deviation of the predictions from the actual values we have observed. A lower loss value means a better quality of prediction, so the machine learning process should therefore minimize the loss. This can be equivalent to maximizing a likelihood of the data under some assumptions and in a regression setting, this is often the case.

In a regression setting, where we work with continuous values, we can also use calculus to find the optimal parameter values, which can be very effective.

LINEAR REGRESSION

The most common regression model is a linear regression, where we calculate our predicted labels $\hat{y}$ for a given D-dimensional input vector $X = (x_1, ..., x_D)$ as a sum weighted with $W = (w_1, ..., w_D)$:

$$\hat{y} = \sum_{d=1}^{D} w_d x_d$$

or in vector notation:

$$\hat{y} = w^T x$$

Often, an intercept or bias b is included $\hat{y} = \sum w_d x_d + b$, but that can be integrated into the vectorized solution by adding an element with constant value 1 to the data vectors $X = (x_1, ..., x_D, 1)$ and making b part of $W = (w_1, ..., w_D, b)$. We will from now on assume that the bias is included in the data vectors and it can be treated like other data dimensions, unless otherwise indicated.

With a dataset of N input/label pairs, we can write the dataset as an input matrix X of row

$$\S = \begin{bmatrix} x_1 \\ \cdots \\ x_n \end{bmatrix} = \begin{bmatrix} x_1 1 & \cdots & x_1 d \\ \vdots & \ddots & \vdots \\ x_1 1 & \cdots & x_n d \end{bmatrix}$$

and the labels as a vector $y = (y_1, ..., y_n)$. The prediction vector $\hat{y}$ can then be calculated as:

$$\hat{y} = Xw$$

LEAST SQUARES OPTIMIZATION

The most common loss function for regression functions is the *sum of squared errors* (SSE). It is calculated as:

$$\text{SSE} = \sum_{k=1}^{d}(y_k - \hat{y}_k)^2 = (y - \hat{y})^{\mathsf{T}}(y - \hat{y}) = (\mathbf{y} - X\mathbf{w})^{\mathsf{T}}(\mathbf{y} - X\mathbf{w})$$

In the case of SSE with a linear model, there is a closed-form solution. As a sketch, it can be found as follows. We need the gradient of SSE with respect to W:

$$\nabla_{\omega}\text{SSE} = 2(\S^{\mathsf{T}}\S\,\mathbf{w} - \S^{\mathsf{T}}\mathbf{y})$$

Setting the gradient to 0, we can work out the optimal $\hat{y}$:

$$X^{\mathsf{T}}X\hat{w} = X^{\mathsf{T}}y$$

From there, we can find the solution:

$$\hat{w} = (X^{\mathsf{T}}X\hat{w})^{-1} X^{\mathsf{T}}y$$

A more rigorous mathematical treatment can be found, e.g., in James, Gareth, Daniela Witten, Trevor Hastie, and Robert Tibshirani. *An Introduction to Statistical Learning*. Vol. 112. New York: Springer, 2013.

In practice, we often take the average SE per sample, *the mean squared error* (MSE):

$$\text{MSE} = \frac{SSE}{N} = \frac{1}{N}\sum_{k=1}^{N}\left(y_n - \hat{y}_n\right)^2$$

The MSE has the advantage over the SSE that it is comparable between datasets of different sizes. You may have noticed that the MSE is the population variance if the mean of the residuals is 0. In other words, the variance of the data is the MSE of a predictor that predicts the mean of the labels.

Another frequently used error metric is the *root mean squared error* (RMSE):

$$\text{RMSE} = \sqrt{\frac{SSE}{N}} = \sqrt{\frac{1}{N}\sum_{k=1}^{N}\left(y_k - \hat{y}_k\right)^2}$$

The RMSE metric is on the same scale as the label data, so that we can interpret the RMSE in units of the measured quantity, e.g., physical or financial units. Since the standard deviation is the square root of the variance, the RMSE is the population-based standard deviation of the residuals if they have a mean of 0.

━━━━━ **Box 18.1** ━━━━━

Least Squares as Maximum Likelihood

Minimizing SSE fits with the following model formulation for normally distributed target values:

$$p(y|x) = N (y - w^T x, \sigma^2)$$

with x and W as above.

The total log-likelihood is:

$$LL\left(w, \sigma^2\right) = \sum_{n=1}^{N} \log N(y_n - w^T x_n, \sigma^2) = \sum_{n=1}^{N} \log N(y_n - \hat{y}_n, \sigma^2)$$

Written into the definition, this can be worked out as:

$$LL\left(x\right) = \sum_{n=1}^{N} \log \frac{1}{\sqrt{\sigma^2 2\pi}} \, exp\left(-\frac{\left(y_n - \hat{y}_n\right)^2}{2\sigma^2}\right)$$

$$= \frac{1}{2\sigma^2} \sum_{n=1}^{N} \left(y_n - \hat{y}_n\right)^2 + \frac{N}{2} \log(2\pi\sigma^2)$$

In a full model estimation, we would optimize for W and σ^2. However, for producing predictions, it is sufficient to just optimize for W. For this purpose, the terms relating to σ^2 can be seen as constants that do not influence the optimization, so that the term to maximize looks like this:

$$-C_1 \sum_{n=1}^{N} \left(y_n - \hat{y}_n\right)^2 + C_2$$

where the only relevant term is the negative SSE. Therefore, minimizing the SSE maximizes the LL if we assume that the errors are normally distributed.

This assumption may often not be true in practice, so that the estimates of W (or σ^2) may not be valid as probabilistic model parameters. However, if the main goal is to optimize prediction quality, minimizing SSE is still useful. For a more detailed probabilistic treatment of machine learning, see Murphy, K., *Probabilistic Machine Learning: An Introduction*. MIT Press, 2022.

REGRESSION EXAMPLE

In this chapter, we will use the diabetes dataset. This dataset has 10 attributes about a patient as features, and disease progression after a year as the target. The dataset contains data for 442 patients. This means that in R we have 11 dimensions in the dataset, including the target variable:

R

```
dataset = read.csv(,../../diabetes.csv', header = TRUE)
dim(dataset)
```

[1] 442 11

Python

```python
from sklearn.datasets import load_diabetes
dataset = load_diabetes()

X = dataset.data
y = dataset.target

print(X.shape,y.shape)

(442, 10) (442,)
```

Generally, cross-validation is the appropriate method for this dataset, but for simplicity, we will operate with single training, validation, and test sets for now:

R

```r
set.seed(123456)
N = nrow(dataset)
cut1 = floor(0.6*N)
cut2 = floor(0.8*N)
index = sample(1:N)
train_index = index[1:cut1]
val_index = index[(cut1+1):cut2]
test_index = index[(cut2+1):N]
df_trn1 = dataset[train_index,]
df_val1 = dataset[val_index,]
df_tst1 = dataset[test_index,]
sapply(list(df_trn1,df_val1,df_tst1),nrow)

[1] 265  88  89
```

Python

```python
from sklearn.model_selection import train_test_split
seed = 0 # avoid randomness in demo

X_trn, X_rest, y_trn, y_rest = train_test_split(X, y,
    test_size=.4,random_state=seed)

X_tst, X_val, y_test, y_val = train_test_split(X_rest, y_rest,
    test_size=.5,random_state=seed)
print(len(y_trn),len(y_val),len(y_test))
265 89 88
```

In this chapter, we will use mostly numeric optimization and most numeric optimization works better on scaled data. We used standardization, where we ensure that the training data has a mean of 0 and a standard deviation of 1. We transform the validation and test data too, but we do not fit the scaling to them, as that would not be possible with new data that would not be available at training time:

R

```
means = apply(df_trn1[-11],2,mean)
sds = apply(df_trn1[-11],2,sd)
scalefun = function(x){return((x-means)/sds)}
df_trn[-11] = data.frame(sapply(df_trn1[-11],scalefun))
df_val[-11] = data.frame(sapply(df_val1[-11],scalefun))
df_tst[-11] = data.frame(sapply(df_tst1[-11],scalefun))

printfun = function(s, x){
  means = apply(x[-11],2,mean)
  sds = apply(x[-11],2,sd)
  print(paste(s," mean: ",mean(means)," std: ",mean(sds)))
}
printfun("train unscaled", df_trn1)
printfun("train scaled", df_trn)
printfun("val unscaled", df_val1)
printfun("val scaled",df_val)

[1] "train unscaled  mean:  -0.000339411866430797  std:  0.0479598862553068"
[1] "train scaled  mean:  0.000554679590602047  std:  1.00044596359934"
[1] "val unscaled  mean:  -0.00126893653928781  std:  0.0470232437451337"
[1] "val scaled  mean:  -0.0182516281305545  std:  0.980027926607645"
```

Python

```
from sklearn.preprocessing import StandardScaler
sclr = StandardScaler()

X_trn_scl = sclr.fit_transform(X_trn) # scale all 3 sets:
X_val_scl = sclr.transform(X_val)
X_tst_scl = sclr.transform(X_tst)
X_scl = sclr.transform(X)
print("train unscaled mean: ", np.mean(X_trn), " std ", np.std(X_trn))
print("train scaled mean: ", np.mean(X_trn_scl), " std ", np.std(X_trn_scl))
print("val unscaled mean: ", np.mean(X_val), " std ", np.std(X_val))
print("val unscaled mean: ", np.mean(X_val_scl), " std ", np.std(X_val_scl))

train unscaled mean:  0.0003187069681085489  std  0.04878424857498195
train scaled mean:  5.362586684981888e-17  std  1.0000000000000002
val unscaled mean:  -0.0009806367715719235  std  0.04656471364346283
val unscaled mean:  -0.026560745236608264  std  0.9586114379045836
```

With the available programming libraries in R and Python, linear regression is very easy to use, just like the models we used previously for classification, which have fit and predict methods, so that the code is very similar to the previous chapter:

R

```
# Helper function for preparing
# dataframes (merging target and
# features)
```

```r
df_prep = function(features_df,
    target_df) {
    output_df = merge(target_df,
        features_df,
        by = 'row.names',
        all = TRUE)
    rownames(output_df) =
        output_df$Row.names
    output_df$Row.names = NULL
    return(output_df)
}


# Prepare dataframe
train_df = df_prep(X_trn_scl, y_trn)

# Train a linear model
lr = lm(target ~ ., data = train_df)

# helper functions to calculate the prediction metrics
mse = function(X, y, predictor) {
    output = mean( as.matrix(
        predict(predictor, X)-y)^2)
    return(output)
}
rmse = function(X, y, predictor){
    return(
        mse(X,y,predictor)^0.5)
}
print( paste("Train RMSE:",
    rmse(X_trn_scl, y_trn,lr))
paste("Validation RMSE:",
    rmse(X_val_scl, y_val, lr))
print( paste("Test RMSE:", rmse(X_tst_scl, y_test, lr)) )

[1] "Train RMSE: 52.3696480202681"
[1] "Validation RMSE: 53.1913833973054"
[1] "Test RMSE: 60.249180462483"
```

Python

```python
from sklearn.linear_model import LinearRegression
import numpy as np

# train a linear model
lr = LinearRegression()
lr.fit(X_trn_scl,y_trn)

# helper functions to calculate the rmse
def rmse(X,y,predictor):
    return ( mse( X, y,
```

```
        predictor))**.5

# helper functions mes
def mse(X,y,predictor):
    return (
        (predictor.predict(X) - y)**2).mean()
# helper functions to calculate the R^2 coefficient
def R_2(X,y,predictor):
    mean_v = np.repeat(np.mean(y), len(y))
    SST = np.var(y)
    SSE = np.var(y - predictor.predict(X))
    return (1-(SSE/SST))


def trainValTestMse(predictor):
    vals = {}
    vals['train'] = rmse(X_trn_scl, y_trn, predictor)
    vals['val'] = rmse(X_val_scl, y_val, predictor)
    vals['test'] = rmse(X_tst_scl, y_test, predictor)
    return vals


print("Linear regression RMSE ", "results: ", trainValTestMse(lr))


Linear regression RMSE results:  {,train': 51.78004290628544, ,val':
55.43725846881888, 'test': 58.26522006034281}
```

The numbers can be put into context by looking at the distribution of the target data, the predictions, and the residuals and calculating the R^2 (coefficient of determination):

R

```
y_trn_hat = lr$fitted.values
res = lr$residuals

print("Training set:")
paste("label mean: ", mean(df_trn$target), "std: ", sd(df_trn$target),
    "var: ", var(df_trn$target))
paste("residuals mean: ", mean(res), "RMSE: ", mean(res^2)^.5,
    "MSE: ", mean(res^2))
paste("R^2: ", 1 - ( mean(res^2) / var(df_trn$target)))
y_val_hat = predict(lr, df_val[-11])
res_val = y_val_hat - df_val$target
mse_val = mean(res_val^2)
print("Validation set:")
paste("label mean:", mean(df_val$target), "std: ", sd(df_val$target),
    "var: ", var(df_val$target))
paste("residuals mean: ", mean(res_val), "RMSE: ", mse_val^.5,
    "MSE: ", mse_val)
paste("R^2: ", 1-(mse_val/var(df_val$target)))
```

```
[1] "Training set:"
[1] "label mean:  155.098113207547 std:  79.1712626031953
var:  6268.08882218411"
[1] "residuals mean: -0.0000000000000202131288646082 RMSE: 51.5635296643493
MSE:  2658.79759144623"
[1] "R^2:  0.575820051873519"
[1] "Validation set:"
[1] "label mean: 148.170454545455 std:  72.3179794485103
var:  5229.89015151515"
[1] "residuals mean:  6.04162475381114
RMSE:  58.8839655941469
MSE:  3467.32140409268"
[1] "R^2:  0.337018311352456"
```

Python

```python
y_trn_hat = lr.predict(X_trn_scl)
resid = y_trn_hat-y_trn

print("Training Set")
print('label mean: ', y_trn.mean(),', std: ', y_trn.std(),', var: ',
      y_trn.var())
print('residuals  mean: ', resid.mean(),', RMSE: ', ((resid**2).mean())**.5, ',
      MSE:', (resid**2).mean() )
print(,R^2: ', 1 -((resid**2).mean() np.var(y_trn)))

y_val_hat = lr.predict(X_val_scl)
resid_val = y_val_hat-y_val
mse_val = (resid_val**2).mean()
print("Validation Set")
print('label mean: ', np.mean(y_val),', std: ', np.std(y_val),', var:',
      np.var(y_val))
print('residuals  mean:', resid_val.mean(),', RMSE: ', mse_val**.5,',
      MSE: ', mse_val)
print('R^2: ', 1-(mse_val/np.var(y_val)))

Training Set
label mean: 152.3811320754717 , std: 79.81375740069201 ,
var:  6370.235870416519
residuals  mean:  1.7160277391942042e-15 ,
RMSE:  51.78004290628544 ,
MSE:  2681.172843376761
R^2:  0.5791093300283947
Validation Set
label mean:  147.22471910112358 , std:  66.47255965222679 ,
var:  4418.601186718849
residuals   mean:  10.53236014358034 ,
RMSE:  55.43725846881888 ,
MSE:  3073.289626538631
R^2:  0.30446548654897165
```

We can see that the average of the residuals is very close to 0 on the training data, so our model has (almost) no bias for over- or under-predicting. The R^2 on the training set is over 50%, and on the validation set, it is over 30%, i.e., the error is reduced compared to a model always predicting the mean. Similarly, the RMSE is lower than the standard deviation of the label data, but there is clearly room for improvement.

FEATURE EXPANSION TO ADDRESS UNDERFITTING

A lack of precision of the predictions on the training set is called *underfitting*, i.e., the model does not adapt well to the data. This is typically caused by the model not being flexible enough. One way to increase the flexibility of the model is by processing the data, so that we have more features that relate to the input in different ways. The most common way to achieve this is to create polynomial features that include products of input features. For example, for two inputs x_1, x_2, the polynomial features up to a maximal degree of 2 would be $1, x_1, x_2, x_1^2, x_1 x_2, x_2^2$. In other words, we are adding interaction terms (products of two different variables) and quadratic terms to the regression equation, so that the number of coefficients (i.e., the weights $w_1, ..., w_m$) increases. For higher degrees, max_d, the features will contain all possible polynomials of degrees up to max_d. This leads to exponential growth of the number of features with max_d and is therefore only possible for small values of max_d.

This is implemented in *sklearn* in the class `PolynomialFeatures`, which also offers a method `get_feature_names_out`, that describes the generated features. Using degree = 1 just generates one additional feature of degree 0, i.e., a constant feature1:

R

```
X_trn_sc_pf1 = model.matrix(target ~ ., data = train_df)
print(colnames(X_trn_sc_pf1))
```

```
[1] "(Intercept)" "age"      "sex"      "bmi"      "bp"       "s1"
[7] "s2"          "s3"       "s4"       "s5"       "s6"
```

Python

```
from sklearn.preprocessing import PolynomialFeatures
pf1 = PolynomialFeatures(degree=1)
X_trn_sc_pf1 = pf1.fit_transform(X_trn_scl)
print(pf1.get_feature_names_out())
```

```
['1' 'x0' 'x1' 'x2' 'x3' 'x4' 'x5' 'x6' 'x7' 'x8' 'x9']
```

By increasing to degree = 2, we add all possible polynomials of degree 2 so that we get 66 features in total:

R

```
# Degree 2 polynomial feature generation function
pf2_transform = function(df, target_name='target') {
    # formula for intercept, raw, squared, and interaction features
```

```
        formula_pf2 = as.formula(paste(target_name, ,~ .^2 +',
            paste('poly(', colnames(df)[-c(1)], ',2,
                raw=TRUE)[, 2]', collapse = ' + ')))
        output = model.matrix(formula_pf2, data = df)
        # Rewrite column names for readability
        colnames_pf2 = c("1", colnames(df)[-1], # exclude target
            paste0(colnames(df)[-1],"^2"), # include squares
            colnames(output)[-(1:(length(df)*2-1))]) # include interactions
        colnames(output) = colnames_pf2 # Convert to dataframe
        output_df = data.frame(output) # Exclude intercept column
        output_df[,1] = NULL
        return(output_df)
}
# Degree 2 polynomial feature generation
X_trn_sc_pf2 = pf2_transform(train_df)
print(colnames(X_trn_sc_pf2))
print(dim(X_trn))
print(dim(X_trn_sc_pf2))
```

```
[1] "age"     "sex"      "bmi"     "bp"      "s1"      "s2"      "s3"
"s4"      "s5"
[10] "s6"      "age.2"    "sex.2"   "bmi.2"   "bp.2"    "s1.2"    "s2.2"
"s3.2"    "s4.2"
[19] "s5.2"    "s6.2"     "age.sex" "age.bmi" "age.bp"  "age.s1"  "age.s2"
"age.s3"  "age.s4"
[28] "age.s5"  "age.s6"   "sex.bmi" "sex.bp"  "sex.s1"  "sex.s2"  "sex.s3"
"sex.s4"  "sex.s5"
[37] "sex.s6"  "bmi.bp"   "bmi.s1"  "bmi.s2"  "bmi.s3"  "bmi.s4"  "bmi.s5"
"bmi.s6"  "bp.s1"
[46] "bp.s2"   "bp.s3"    "bp.s4"   "bp.s5"   "bp.s6"   "s1.s2"   "s1.s3"
"s1.s4"   "s1.s5"
[55] "s1.s6"   "s2.s3"    "s2.s4"   "s2.s5"   "s2.s6"   "s3.s4"   "s3.s5"
"s3.s6"   "s4.s5"
[64] "s4.s6"   "s5.s6"
```

```
[1] 265  10
[1] 265  65
```

Python

```
pf2 = PolynomialFeatures(degree=2)
X_trn_sc_pf2 = pf2.fit_transform(X_trn_scl)
print(pf2.get_feature_names_out())
print(X_trn.shape)
X_trn_sc_pf2.shape
```

```
['1' 'x0' 'x1' 'x2' 'x3' 'x4' 'x5' 'x6' 'x7' 'x8' 'x9' 'x0^2' 'x0 x1'
 'x0 x2' 'x0 x3' 'x0 x4' 'x0 x5' 'x0 x6' 'x0 x7' 'x0 x8' 'x0 x9' 'x1^2'
```

```
'x1 x2' 'x1 x3' 'x1 x4' 'x1 x5' 'x1 x6' 'x1 x7' 'x1 x8' 'x1 x9' 'x2^2'
'x2 x3' 'x2 x4' 'x2 x5' 'x2 x6' 'x2 x7' 'x2 x8' 'x2 x9' 'x3^2' 'x3 x4'
'x3 x5' 'x3 x6' 'x3 x7' 'x3 x8' 'x3 x9' 'x4^2' 'x4 x5' 'x4 x6' 'x4 x7'
'x4 x8' 'x4 x9' 'x5^2' 'x5 x6' 'x5 x7' 'x5 x8' 'x5 x9' 'x6^2' 'x6 x7'
'x6 x8' 'x6 x9' 'x7^2' 'x7 x8' 'x7 x9' 'x8^2' 'x8 x9' 'x9^2']
(265, 10)
(265, 66)
```

We can now train a model with the transformed dataset:

R

```
lr2 = lm(target ~ ., data = trn_sc_pf2)
paste("Poly2 train RMSE: ", rmse(trn_sc_pf2[-10],df_trn$target,lr2))
paste("Poly 2 val   RMSE: ", rmse(val_sc_pf2[-10],df_val$target,lr2))
paste("Poly 2 test  RMSE: ", rmse(tst_sc_pf2[-10],df_tst$target,lr2))


[1] "Poly2 train RMSE:  44.9480294133388"
[1] "Poly2 val   RMSE:  71.0445319217037"
[1] "Poly2 test  RMSE:  77.2455828915384"
```

Python

```
X_val_sc_pf2 = pf2.transform(X_val_scl)
X_tst_sc_pf2 = pf2.transform(X_tst_scl)

# train a linear model
lr2 = LinearRegression()
lr2.fit(X_trn_sc_pf2,y_trn)

print('Poly2 Features,  train  RMSE:  ', rmse(X_trn_sc_pf2,y_trn,lr2),',',
    val RMSE:', rmse(X_val_sc_pf2,y_val,lr2),',', test RMSE: ', rmse(X_tst_
    sc_pf2,y_test,lr2))
Poly2 Features, train RMSE:  44.509225398475564 , val RMSE:  67.55361367535333 ,
    test RMSE:  63.2999076381296
```

The results show a much-reduced error on the training set, but a large error on the validation set. If you inspect the coefficients, you will see what is happening (see exercise below). This is an extreme case of *overfitting*.

Too much flexibility of the model can apparently lead to problems too, specifically to overfitting. This can be understood by thinking of a very flexible model that can perfectly reproduce the training data. Apart from the fact that memorizing the data is not too useful, polynomials of higher degrees also have the property that they produce steeper slopes and thus a large variation of values between data points.

Another problem is that with a higher number of variables, there is a higher chance for numerical problems in the optimization. Especially, if there are more features than data points, the system is underdetermined and there is no unique solution. The implementations in `lm` (R) and `LinearRegression` (Python) are numerically very robust and can deal with underdetermined systems, but that is not guaranteed in general.

L_2 and L_1 Regularization

Both the overfitting and potential numerical problems can be addressed by regularization. The general concept of regularization as a way to reduce model flexibility, as introduced in the previous chapters, has very popular implementations for linear regression and related models, including general linear models (Chapter 13) and neural networks. Because these models use numeric optimization methods, we can introduce additive terms in the loss function that relate to the model, and will be minimized together with the prediction loss. The most common such loss terms are L_1 and L_2 norms of the weights.

The term *norm* describes ways of calculating the length of the vector. The standard norm is the Euclidian norm or L_2 norm, which can also be written as W_2, which is defined for a D-dimensional vector W as $\sqrt{\sum_{d=1}^{D} w_d^2}$ and describes the length in physical space for $d = 3$. The L_1 norm is defined as $\sum_{d=1}^{D} \text{abs}(w_d)$, where abs sets the sign of the argument to positive. The L_1 norm can be interpreted as the distance on a rectangular grid and is also called the *Manhattan norm*.

The L_2 norm regularizing loss l_r, also called Tikhonov regularization, is defined as follows:

$$loss_2 = \sum_d \left(\hat{y}_d - y \right)^2 + \rho \sum_d w_d^2 = \left| Xw - y \right|_2^2 + \rho \left| w \right|_2^2$$

and the L_1 loss as

$$loss_1 = \sum_d \left(\hat{y}_d - y \right)^2 + \rho \sum_d \text{abs}\left(w_d \right) = \left| Xw - y \right|_2^2 + \rho \left| w \right|_1 \ ,$$

where $|\cdot|_2$ is the norm and $|\cdot|_1$ is the norm. The parameter p controls the strength of the regularization.

In both cases, the idea is that the optimizer reduces the size of the model coefficients, so that weights that contribute little to reducing the prediction error will be kept small.

For simple linear regression, there are specific names: L_2- and L_1-regularized regressions are called *ridge* and *lasso* regression, respectively, and in both cases, the term *shrinkage* is also used (as the regularization shrinks the coefficients). L_2-regularization is often very effective as it penalizes larger weight values more. L_1-regularization has the positive property of leading to sparse coefficients.

Parameter Shrinkage with Ridge Regression

Let us start by applying L_2 (i.e., ridge) regression. In R, we use the `glmnet` package to train a linear model, which has α and λ variables that control the lasso and ridge regularization. α defines whether L_2 is used ($\alpha = 0$) or L_1 ($\alpha = 1$) or a weighted average ($0 < \alpha < 1$), which is often called *Elastic Net*. The λ value determines the strength of the regularisation, it corresponds to p in the equation above. In Python we can use the predictor class **Ridge** in *Scikit-Learn*, which has a parameter alpha that corresponds to *p* above. One practical aspect is important here, which is to not have an intercept (or bias) term in the data, but to have it calculated by the ridge model (default in glmnet and ridge), because we do not want the intercept to be regularized:

R

```
ridge = glmnet(trn_sc_pf2[-10], trn_sc_pf2$target, alpha=0, lambda = 1)
paste("Ridge train RMSE: ", rmse(as.matrix(trn_sc_pf2[-10]),df_trn$target,
      ridge))
paste("Ridge val   RMSE: ", rmse(as.matrix(val_sc_pf2[-10]),df_val$
      target,ridge))
```

```
Data           RMSE
Training       46.67
Validation     59.98
```

Python

```
from sklearn.linear_model import Ridge

pf2n = PolynomialFeatures(include_bias=False)
X_trn_sc_pf2 = pf2n.fit_transform(X_trn_scl)
X_val_sc_pf2 = pf2n.fit_transform(X_val_scl)
X_tst_sc_pf2 = pf2n.fit_transform(X_tst_scl)

# train a linear model
lr_rd1 = Ridge(fit_intercept=True)
lr_rd1.fit(X_trn_sc_pf2,y_trn)

print('Ridge train RMSE: ',rmse(X_trn_sc_pf2,y_trn,lr_rd1))
print('Ridge val   RMSE: ',rmse(X_val_sc_pf2,y_val,lr_rd1))

Ridge train RMSE:  45.0006645588884
Ridge val   RMSE:  61.94445869321387
```

We can see that the errors on the training data have gone up slightly and on the validation data, they have gone down greatly. We still have room to improve, so let us try stronger regularization with a higher λ (α in Python) value. This is a hyper-parameter to tune, like in the previous chapter. We could use the cross-validation plot, but for brevity, we will just use a value that was found by a grid search (see below). Implementing a grid search on the train/validation split and a CV grid search are left as exercises for the reader.

R

```
ridge_best = caret::train(y = train_sc_pf2$target, x = train_sc_pf2[-10],
            method = 'glmnet',
```

```
        tuneGrid = expand.grid(alpha = 0, lambda = 25))
paste("Ridge train RMSE:", rmse(train_sc_pf2$target, train_pred))
paste("Ridge val RMSE:", rmse(val_sc_pf2$target, val_pred))


[1] "Ridge train RMSE: 51.2267915661586"
[1] "Ridge val RMSE: 57.0049295299758"
```

Python

```
lr_rd2 = Ridge(alpha=300,fit_intercept=True)
lr_rd2.fit(X_trn_sc_pf2, y_trn)


print("Ridge train RMSE:", rmse(X_trn_sc_pf2, y_trn,lr_rd2))
print(("Ridge val RMSE:", rmse(X_val_sc_pf2, y_val,lr_rd2))


Ridge train RMSE: 53.23942319481683
Ridge val RMSE: 51.64815860679413
```

We see that with a suitable α/λ value, we can indeed reduce overfitting and obtain a better model, also in terms of the R^2 coefficient:

R

```
paste("Ridge2 train R^2: ", R_2(as.matrix(trn_sc_pf2[-65]),
      trn_sc_pf2$target,ridge2))
paste("Ridge2 train R^2: ", R_2(as.matrix(val_sc_pf2[-65]),
       val_sc_pf2$target,ridge2))
paste("Ridge2 train R^2: ", R_2(as.matrix(tst_sc_pf2[-65]),
      tst_sc_pf2$target,ridge2))


[1] "Ridge2 train R^2:  0.582148502794092"
[1] "Ridge2 train R^2:  0.364354550693784"
[1] "Ridge2 train R^2:  0.458062729927458"
```

Python

```
print('Ridge2 trn R^2: ', R_2(X_train_sc_pf2, y_train,lr_rd2))
print('Ridge2 val R^2: ', R_2(X_val_sc_pf2, y_val,lr_rd2))
print(,Ridge2 tst R^2: ', R_2(X_test_sc_pf2, y_test,lr_rd2))


Ridge2 trn R^2: 0.6234935649566713 Ridge2 val R^2: 0.3792545799603789 Ridge2
tst R^2: 0.4124346702270759
```

Feature Selection with Lasso Regression

As mentioned, L_1-regression can lead to sparse coefficients. That means, it drives weights equally towards 0 even if they are very small (as opposed to L_2, where the regularization term gets quadratically smaller for smaller coefficient values). This leads to many coefficients actually reaching 0 after fitting them to the model, so that they have no influence on the predictions.

This allows us to understand easily which features are most important for predicting the target. Also, it means that we do not need to gather values for these 0-weighted features in future applications of the model. This can save time, money, and computation cost in actual applications.

Let us try this on the diabetes dataset. Again, there is a convenient method in R, **glmnet**, and a class in *Scikit-Learn*, **Lasso,** that allow us to create and fit a model with minimal code changes:

R

```
# Train a lasso model
lasso <- glmnet( as.matrix(trn_sc_pf2[-65]), trn_sc_pf2$target, alpha = 1)

paste("Lasso train RMSE:", rmse(as.matrix(trn_sc_pf2[-65]), trn_sc_
      pf2$target,lasso))

paste("Lasso val RMSE:", rmse(as.matrix(val_sc_pf2[-65]), val_sc_pf2
      $target,lasso))

[1] "Lasso train RMSE: 50.8524264650375"
[1] "Lasso val   RMSE: 60.776589560245"
```

Python

```
from sklearn.linear_model import Lasso

# train a linear model
lr_lso = Lasso()
lr_lso.fit(X_trn_sc_pf2,y_trn)
print('Lasso train RMSE): ', rmse(X_trn_sc_pf2, y_trn,lr_lso))
print('Lasso val RMSE):   ', rmse(X_val_sc_pf2, y_val,lr_lso))

Lasso train RMSE):   47.37809431050939
Lasso val RMSE):     55.61032458728394
```

Although there is a worse fit than with ridge regression, we can still try to choose better hyperparameters. With a little testing, we can find that 5 or 10 are good values for the parameter. Determining this value systematically is again left as an exercise:

R

```
# Train a linear model
lasso2 <- glmnet( as.matrix(trn_sc_pf2[-65]), trn_sc_pf2$target,
                  alpha = 1, lambda = 4)
paste("Lasso2 train RMSE:", rmse(as.matrix(trn_sc_pf2[-65]), trn_sc_
      pf2$target,lasso2))
paste("Lasso2 val   RMSE:", rmse(as.matrix(val_sc_pf2[-65]), val_sc_
      pf2$target,lasso2))

[1] "Lasso2 train RMSE: 51.7950222076933"
[1] "Lasso2 val   RMSE: 57.5298424353424
```

Python

```
# train a linear model
lr_lso2 = Lasso(alpha=10)
lr_lso2.fit(X_trn_sc_pf2,y_trn)

print('Lasso alpha=300 train RMSE): ',rmse(X_trn_sc_pf2,y_trn,lr_lso2))
print('Lasso alpha=300 val RMSE):   ',rmse(X_val_sc_pf2,y_val,lr_lso2))

Lasso alpha=10 train RMSE):   54.393944437527104
Lasso alpha=10 val RMSE):     52.807267316335164
```

This error value is slightly higher than with the ridge regression, as can also be seen in the R^2 value. However, on the test set, the lasso model comes out slightly better, which is some evidence that the true difference of model performance is very small:

R

```
y_trn_hat = predict(lr_lso2, newx=as.matrix(X_trn_sc_pf2), s=best_lambda_lso)
res_lso2 = y_trn_hat - y_trn$target
print("Training set")
paste('R^2: ', 1-(var(res_lso2)/ var(y_trn$target)))

y_val_hat = predict(lr_lso2, newx = as.matrix(X_val_sc_pf2), s = best_
          lambda_lso)
res_val_lso2 = y_val_hat - y_val
paste("Validation set R^2: ", 1-(var(res_val_lso2)/var(y_val)))

y_tst_hat = predict(lr_lso2, newx = as.matrix(X_tst_sc_pf2), s = best_
          lambda_lso)
res_tst_lso2 = y_tst_hat - y_test
print("Test set")
print( paste('R^2: ', 1-(var(res_tst_lso2)/var(y_test))))
print(mean((res_tst_lso2$target)^2)^.5)

[1] "Training set"
[1] "R^2:  0.0951301235847977"
[1] "Validation set"
[1] "R^2:  0.0225884290452385"
[1] "Test set"
[1] "R^2:  -0.0529938490901436"
[1] 83.47607
```

Python

```
y_trn_hat = lr_lso2.predict(X_trn_sc_pf2)
resid = y_trn_hat-y_trn
print("Training Set")
print('R^2: ',1-(np.var(resid)/np.var(y_trn)))
```

```
y_val_hat = lr_lso2.predict(X_val_sc_pf2)
print("Validation Set")
print('R^2: ',1-(np.var(y_val_hat-y_val)/np.var(y_val)))

y_tst_hat = lr_lso2.predict(X_tst_sc_pf2)
print("Test Set")
print('R^2: ', 1-(np.var(y_tst_hat-y_test)/np.var(y_test)))
((y_tst_hat-y_test)**2).mean()**.5


Training Set
R^2:   0.5355429136913058
Validation Set
R^2:   0.37642565670267825
Test Set
R^2:   0.4209717108265886
59.49520079118262
```

For more reliable results, cross-validation should be applied and a significance test conducted. Even if the Lasso model is slightly worse, depending on the application, it may be more valuable to be able to get predictions with fewer measures. For example, it may allow you to take measurements more often.

We can extract the coefficients and see which features have non-zero coefficients. In the case of the diabetes data, we can see that only six of the original features (X0,X1,X2,X5,X7,X9) are actually used:

R

```
coef_vect = coef(lr_lso2)[,1]
print("Lasso coefficients:")
print(coef_vect)
print("Positions of non-zero coefficients:")
print(seq(1:length(coef_vect))[coef_vect!=0])
print("Names and values of non-zero coefficients:")
print(coef_vect[coef_vect!=0])


[1] "Lasso coefficients:"
(Intercept)      age       sex       bmi         bp        s1       s2        s3
152.2057866   2.9276331   0.0000000   0.0000000   0.0000000   -7.6713441
0.0000000     0.0000000
s4        s5        s6      age.2     sex.2      bmi.2      bp.2       s1.2
0.0000000   0.0000000   0.0000000   0.0000000   0.0000000   -1.6375100
0.0000000   0.0000000
s2.2      s3.2      s4.2      s5.2      s6.2      age.sex      age.bmi
age.bp
0.0000000   0.0000000   0.0000000   0.0000000   0.0000000   0.0000000
0.0000000   5.5668135
age.s1    age.s2    age.s3    age.s4    age.s5    age.s6      sex.
bmi       sex.bp
```

```
0.0000000    0.0000000    0.0000000    0.0000000    0.0000000    0.0000000
0.0000000    0.0000000
sex.s1       sex.s2       sex.s3       sex.s4       sex.s5       sex.s6       bmi.bp
bmi.s1
-7.1348581   0.0000000   -4.7624488    0.0000000    0.0000000    0.0000000
-3.1661206   0.0000000
bmi.s2       bmi.s3       bmi.s4       bmi.s5       bmi.s6       bp.s1        bp.s2
bp.s3
0.0000000    0.0000000    0.0000000    0.0000000    0.0000000    0.0000000
0.0000000    0.0000000
bp.s4        bp.s5        bp.s6        s1.s2        s1.s3        s1.s4        s1.s5
s1.s6
-1.2971684   0.0000000   -2.3558529    0.0000000    0.0000000    0.0000000
0.0000000    0.0000000
s2.s3        s2.s4        s2.s5        s2.s6        s3.s4        s3.s5        s3.s6
s4.s5
0.0000000    0.0000000    0.0000000   -0.9212003    0.0000000    0.0000000
0.0000000    0.0000000
s4.s6        s5.s6
0.0000000    0.0000000
[1] "Positions of non-zero coefficients:"
[1]   1   2   6 14 24 33 35 39 49 51 60
[1] "Names and values of non-zero coefficients:"
(Intercept)         age           s1         bmi.2        age.bp        sex.s1
sex.s3       bmi.bp
152.2057866    2.9276331   -7.6713441   -1.6375100    5.5668135   -7.1348581
-4.7624488   -3.1661206
     bp.s4        bp.s6         s2.s6
-1.2971684   -2.3558529   -0.9212003
```

Python

```python
print('Lasso coefficients',lr_lso2.coef_)
print('Positions of non-zero coefficients',np.nonzero(lr_lso2.coef_))
nz_feature_names = pf2.get_feature_names_out()[np.nonzero(lr_lso2.coef_)]
nz_feature_values = lr_lso2.coef_[np.nonzero(lr_lso2.coef_)]
print('Names and values of non-zero coefficients',list(zip(nz_feature_
names,nz_feature_values)))
```

```
Lasso coefficients [ 0.         -0.          21.09885135  7.25809404 -0.         -0.
 -4.66809785  0.          23.92567557  0.           0.          2.284511
  0.          0.          -0.         -0.          -0.          0.
  0.          0.          -0.          0.           0.          0.
 -0.          0.          -0.          0.           0.          2.11981431
  0.         -0.          -0.         -0.          0.          0.
  0.          2.1011182   0.         -0.          0.          -0.
  0.          0.          -0.         -0.          0.          -0.
```

```
  -0.          0.         -0.          0.         -0.         -0.
   0.         -0.          0.          0.         -0.         -0.
  -0.          0.          0.          0.          0.          ]
Positions of non-zero coefficients (array([ 2,  3,  6,  8, 11, 29, 37]),)
Names and values of non-zero coefficients [('x1', 21.098851350283923), ('x2',
7.258094039818483), ('x5', -4.668097852769056), ('x7', 23.925675570857106),
('x0^2', 2.2845109952089255), ('x1 x9', 2.1198143136713385), ('x2 x9',
2.1011182026125352)]
```

OPTIMIZING NONLINEAR MODELS

Above, we have used a polynomial extension of the model on the input side by extracting inter-action and quadratic combinations. When the parameters in these feature extractors are fixed, the model is still linear with respect to the feature values. However, using nonlinear functions on the input side with learnable parameters can make models much more flexible while retaining control over the number of parameters in the model. This approach is used, e.g., in neural networks.

Gradient Descent

For nonlinear models, there is, in general, no closed-form solution available to fit the model parameters to the data. In the general case (so called non-convex optimization problems), there is no algorithm for finding the optimal solution or even for knowing if we found it. The most common idea for optimizing nonlinear models is to use a technique called gradient descent. For this, we calculate the gradient of our loss function with respect to the parameters. The gradient tells us whether the error will increase if we change the parameters in a particular direction by an arbitrarily small amount. By moving in the opposite direction, we hope to obtain a reduction in the loss. As the gradient changes size and direction as we change the parameters, we make only small changes and repeat the process until we find that the gradient approaches zero and we cannot improve the error. In so-called convex problems, which include linear regression, this will lead us to an optimal solution. However, most linear models are not convex, so we cannot be sure that change will lead us to the best solution. The main problem is that we may find a local minimum, which may be far from optimal. Despite these problems, for complex problems and large datasets, nonlinear models tend to perform better.

Neural Networks

The most commonly used continuous nonlinear model is probably a neural network. We will start with a simple neural network for regression. It is like a linear regression with k features, where each is a linear combination of the input data followed by a nonlinear activation function f:

$$\hat{y} = \sum_k w2_k f\left(\sum_d w1_{kd} x_d\right)$$

where w1 is the weight vector of the output, $\hat{y}$, and w2 is the matrix of weights for the k features. Popular choices for f are the logistic function that we used in Chapter 13 for logistic regression and the rectified linear function (ReLu): $f(x) = \max(0, x)$.

In neural networks, the output and feature values are seen as the activation levels of connected neurons. These neurons were originally meant as models of biological neurons, but today they are generally used as building blocks for computational learning systems. The neurons are organized in layers. In our case, there is an input layer, the input data, one hidden layer, the k features, and the output layer, containing only our output value.

This structure is called a multi-layer perceptron (MLP). It has been proven mathematically that with enough hidden neurons, there exists a weight configuration such that the model approximates any function on a compact interval with arbitrary precision. That does not, however, mean that our learning algorithms find that weight configuration for a given set of data points.

In practical terms, we can use an MLP similarly to a linear regression, with two main differences: the MLP can learn nonlinear functions but to achieve good results, we need to find a good setting for the many hyper-parameters of an MLP.

Let us try to use an MLP on the diabetes dataset with polynomial features, as above. Again, there is a convenient class for using MLPs in *Scikit-Learn*. We will use the default settings (of 100 hidden neurons, $\alpha = 0.001$) except for the solver where we use 'sgd', which stands for *Stochastic Gradient Descent*. The stochastic element of sgd is that it selects a subset of the data at every iteration. This is computationally efficient and can also help to move out of a local minimum of the error function:

R

```
library(RSNNS)

mlp = mlp(as.matrix(trn_sc_pf2[-65]), trn_sc_pf2$target,size=50, linOut =
        TRUE, learnFunc="Rprop")
paste("MLP trn RMSE:", rmse(as.matrix(trn_sc_pf2[-65]), trn_sc_pf2$
    target,mlp))
paste("MLP val RMSE:", rmse(as.matrix(val_sc_pf2[-65]),val_sc_pf2$
    target,mlp))

[1] "MLP trn RMSE: 20.2772326821243"
[1] "MLP val RMSE: 72.2670999395802"
```

Python

```
from sklearn.neural_network import MLPRegressor

mlp = MLPRegressor(random_state = 0,solver = 'sgd')
mlp.fit(X_trn_sc_pf2, y_trn)
print('MLP train RMSE: ',rmse(X_trn_sc_pf2,y_trn,mlp))
print('MLP val RMSE: ',rmse(X_val_sc_pf2,y_val,mlp))

MLP train RMSE:   12.834870456539784
MLP val RMSE:     79.61163998684314
```

The results show that the MLP can adapt very well to the training data, but the high validation error indicates strong overfitting.

There are several things we can do now to reduce the overfitting. One is to not use the expanded features. Since the MLP can calculate any function, we are not limiting the space of possible solutions. In addition, we can reduce the number of hidden neurons and increase the α parameter (which works like for linear regression). Here is an example of a more suitable setting:

R

```
mlp2 = mlp(as.matrix(trn_sc_pf2[-65]), trn_sc_pf2$target,size=5,
        linOut = TRUE, learnFunc="Rprop")
paste("MLP trn RMSE:", rmse(as.matrix(trn_sc_pf2[-65]), trn_sc_pf2$
      target,mlp2))
paste("MLP val RMSE:", rmse(as.matrix(val_sc_pf2[-65]), val_sc_pf2$
      target,mlp2))
paste("MLP tst RMSE:", rmse(as.matrix(tst_sc_pf2[-65]), tst_sc_pf2$
      target,mlp2))


[1] "MLP trn RMSE: 61.3454431642162"
[1] "MLP val RMSE: 66.6098161585488"
[1] "MLP tst RMSE: 62.0920659730219"
```

Python

```
mlp = MLPRegressor(random_state = 0,solver = 'sgd',alpha = .1,hidden_
      layer_sizes = 5)
search = mlp.fit(X_trn_scl, y_trn)
print('MLP train, val, test RMSE:', trainValTestMse(mlp))


MLP train, val, test RMSE: {'train': 45.73266797551563, 'val':
56.84115094558477, 'test': 59.36947997304398}
```

We see that the validation error is a bit higher than for the previous models. However, the test error is in the same range as the lasso and ridge regression.

Regression Trees

Another approach to regression is to not use weighted sums at all, but to divide the data up according to feature thresholds. This approach is used in regression trees, which operate very much like decision trees, with the exception that they use the variance of the labels in a node. For example, they split the nodes such that the average variance in the split nodes is as low as possible. For inference, a new input sample is processed until it reaches a leaf and then the average label value of that leaf is returned:

R

```
library(rpart)

dtr = rpart(target ~ ., data = train_df)
```

```
print("DT Regression:")
paste("DT train RMSE:", rmse(X_trn_scl, y_trn, dtr))
paste("DT val    RMSE:", rmse(X_val_scl, y_val, dtr))
paste("DT test   RMSE:", rmse(X_tst_scl, y_test, dtr)) )

[1] "DT Regression:"
[1] "DT train RMSE: 49.5964464839434"
[1] "DT val    RMSE: 66.6188884636543"
[1] "DT test   RMSE: 63.9043336325445"
```

Python

```
from sklearn.tree import DecisionTreeRegressor

dtr = DecisionTreeRegressor()
dtr.fit(X_trn_scl,y_trn)

print("DT regression: ",
  trainValTestMse(dtr))

DT regression:  {'train': 0.0, 'val': 82.63878350584454, 'test':
81.69093640612213}
```

The training error is 0 because every training example occurs in a leaf with only its label. However, this leads to strong overfitting. Like in the previous chapter, we can reduce overfitting by reducing the tree depth:

R

```
dtr2 = rpart(target ~ ., data = train_df, control = list(maxdepth = 2))

print("DT Regression:")
paste("DT train RMSE:", rmse(X_trn_scl, y_trn, dtr2)))
paste("DT val    RMSE:", rmse(X_val_scl, y_val, dtr2)))
paste("DT test   RMSE:", rmse(X_tst_scl, y_test, dtr2)))

[1] "DT Regression:"
[1] "DT train RMSE: 57.9426972395778"
[1] "DT val    RMSE: 67.5150929022346"
[1] "DT test   RMSE: 68.6018092546154"
```

Python

```
dtr = DecisionTreeRegressor(max_depth = 2)
dtr.fit(X_trn_scl,y_trn)

print("DT regression:", trainValTestMse(dtr))

DT regression: {'train': 57.111047461837266, 'val': 58.7492928396893,
'test': 61.059915268263936}
```

The tree regressor performs slightly worse than the other models we tested, but still fairly similar.

Summarizing over the experiments so far, the most important aspect of modelling is to avoid overfitting. Even with feature expansion and nonlinear modelling, no model is significantly better than the linear models. This result seems to indicate that linear regression is a good model for the underlying process, and that a large part of the variance in the data is randomly generated. At least, the nonlinear models tried here apparently do not learn how to predict it.

A HARDER LEARNING PROBLEM

The diabetes dataset shows that the choice of model makes little difference. This is a typical situation for a small dataset, where there may not be enough information for nonlinear patterns to be learnt.

However, datasets with nonlinear generating processes can benefit strongly, as the following example shows. Here, we use a dataset on the energy used by buildings for heating, which is roughly twice the size of the diabetes dataset. We try the same model types as before, but this time there are clear differences in performance:

R

```r
dataset = read.csv('data/ENB2012_data.csv')

X = dataset[,1:7]
y = dataset[,9, drop = FALSE]
print(dim(X))
print(dim(y))

SEED = 0
smp_size = floor((1-0.3) * nrow(X))
set.seed(SEED)
train_ind = sample(seq_len(nrow(X)), size = smp_size)
cX_trn = X[train_ind, ]
cX_tst = X[-train_ind, ]
cy_trn = y[train_ind, , drop=FALSE]
cy_test = y[-train_ind, , drop=FALSE]
cX_trn = sclr_fit_transform(cX_trn)
cX_tst = sclr_fit_transform(cX_tst, cX_trn)

c_trn_df = df_prep(cX_trn, cy_trn)
c_tst_df = df_prep(cX_tst, cy_test)

c_lr = lm(Y1 ~ ., data = c_trn_df)

paste("LR train RMSE",
  rmse(cX_trn, cy_trn, c_lr))
paste("LR val RMSE",
  rmse(cX_tst, cy_test, c_lr)))
```

```
cX_trn_p2 = sclr_fit_transform(pf2_transform(c_trn_df, 'Y1'))
cX_tst_p2 = sclr_fit_transform(pf2_transform(c_tst_df, 'Y1'), cX_trn_p2)

print("shape original:")
print(dim(c_trn_df))
print("poly 2:")
print(dim(cX_trn_p2))

c_rdg = glmnet(as.matrix(cX_trn_p2), cy_trn$Y1, alpha = 0)
paste("Ridge train RMSE:", rmse(as.matrix(cX_trn_p2), cy_trn,c_rdg))
paste("Ridge test RMSE:", rmse(as.matrix(cX_tst_p2), cy_test,c_rdg))

c_lso = glmnet(as.matrix(cX_trn_p2), cy_trn$Y1, alpha = 1)

paste("Lasso train RMSE:", rmse(as.matrix(cX_trn_p2), cy_trn,c_lso))
paste("Lasso test  RMSE:", rmse(as.matrix(cX_tst_p2), cy_test,c_lso))

c_mlp = mlp(as.matrix(cX_trn_p2), cy_trn$Y1, size = 200, maxit = 5000)

paste("MLP train RMSE:", rmse(cX_trn_p2, cy_trn, c_mlp))
paste("MLP test  RMSE:", rmse(cX_tst_p2, cy_test, c_mlp))

c_dtr = rpart(Y1 ~ ., data = c_trn_df, control = list(maxdepth=7))

paste("DT regression train RMSE:", rmse(X_trn_scl, y_trn, dtr2))
paste("DT regression test  RMSE:", rmse(X_tst_scl, y_test, dtr2))

[1] 768    7
[1] 768    1
[1] "LR train RMSE 2.90923888455245"
Warning message:
In predict.lm(predictor, X) :
  prediction from a rank-deficient fit may be misleading
> print( paste("LR val RMSE", rmse(cX_tst, cy_test, c_lr)))
[1] "LR val RMSE 4333.34381593216"
Warning message:
In predict.lm(predictor, X) :
prediction from a rank-deficient fit may be misleading
[1] "shape original:"
[1] 537    8
[1] "poly 2:"
[1] 537   35
[1] "Ridge train RMSE: 10.1359195546934"
[1] "Ridge test   RMSE: 9.96227889721586"
[1] "Lasso train RMSE: 10.1359195546934"
[1] "Lasso test  RMSE: 9.96227889721586"
[1] "MLP train RMSE: 23.6744609506434"
```

```
[1] "MLP test  RMSE: 23.33471539197"
[1] "DT regression train RMSE: 57.9426972395778"
[1] "DT regression test  RMSE: 68.6018092546154"
```

Python

```python
dataset = pd.read_csv('/data/ENB2012_data.csv')


X = np.array(dataset.iloc[:,0:7])
y = np.array(dataset.iloc[:,8])
print(X.shape,y.shape)


cX_trn, cX_tst, cy_trn, cy_test = train_test_split(X,y,test_size=0.3,
                                 random_state=0)
scl = StandardScaler()
cX_trn = scl.fit_transform(cX_trn)
cX_tst = scl.transform(cX_tst)


c_lr = LinearRegression()
c_lr.fit(cX_trn, cy_trn)

print(,LR train RMSE: ', rmse(cX_trn,cy_trn,c_lr))
print(,LR val RMSE: ', rmse(cX_tst,cy_test,c_lr))


eb_pf = PolynomialFeatures(degree=2)
eb_sc = StandardScaler()
cX_trn_p2 = eb_sc.fit_transform(eb_pf.fit_transform(cX_trn))
cX_tst_p2 = eb_sc.transform(eb_pf.transform(cX_tst))
print("shape original: ", cX_trn.shape, ", poly 2: ", cX_trn_p2.shape)


c_rdg = Ridge(alpha=0.001)
c_rdg.fit(cX_trn_p2, cy_trn)

print(,Ridge train RMSE: ', rmse(cX_trn_p2,cy_trn,c_rdg))
print(,Ridge test RMSE: ', rmse(cX_tst_p2,cy_test,c_rdg))


c_lso = Lasso(alpha=0.0001, max_iter=20000,tol=0.005)
c_lso.fit(cX_trn_p2, cy_trn)

print(,Lasso train RMSE: ', rmse(cX_trn_p2,cy_trn,c_lso))
print(,Lasso test RMSE: ', rmse(cX_tst_p2,cy_test,c_lso))

mlp = MLPRegressor(random_state = 0, hidden_layer_sizes = [200],
      solver = 'sgd',alpha = 0.1, max_iter = 5000)
mlp.fit(cX_trn,cy_trn)

print(,MLP train RMSE: ', rmse(cX_trn,cy_trn,mlp))
```

```
print(,MLP test RMSE: ', rmse(cX_tst,cy_test,mlp))

dtr = DecisionTreeRegressor(max_depth=7)
dtr.fit(cX_trn,cy_trn)

print('DT regression train RMSE: ', rmse(cX_trn,cy_trn,dtr))
print("DT regression test RMSE: ", rmse(cX_tst,cy_test,dtr))

(768, 7) (768,)
LR train RMSE:   2.8845432092602943
LR val RMSE:     3.0691740564862515
shape original:  (537, 7) , poly 2:  (537, 36)
Ridge train RMSE:  1.078126013175186
Ridge test RMSE:   1.1961322051387506
Lasso train RMSE:  1.0946864267308754
Lasso test RMSE:   1.2207293031861808
MLP train RMSE:  0.4657702247907204
MLP test RMSE:   0.529752250510767
DT regression train RMSE:  0.4081012046829919
DT regression test RMSE:  0.5915688077343915
```

Summary

Regression is a very common task in ML. The main approach is to optimize parameters to minimize a loss function calculated empirically on training data. In many cases, the optimization can be interpreted as a maximum likelihood estimation of a probability distribution. Since the ML approach makes very few assumptions, the main method of finding models that generalize is to apply them to test data.

Avoiding overfitting and choosing an appropriate model for the data are important and require careful selection of candidate models and hyper-parameter values as they can make a substantial difference, but the cost of evaluating many models can be high.

Exercises

To complete the activity below, you will need to visit the companion website to the book and download the Diabetes dataset: https://study.sagepub.com/gopal

1   Inspect the coefficients of the linear model trained on the polynomial features. Find the coefficient responsible for the large error and explain why it has an especially strong effect on the polynomial features.
2   Implement a grid search for the alpha parameter of a linear regression on the train/validation split with the poly 2 features of the diabetes data.
3   Implement a grid search for the alpha parameter of a linear regression using cross validation with the poly 2 features of the diabetes data. Use the *Scikit-Learn* class **GridSearchCV**.

(Continued)

4   Load the California Housing dataset (either with `sklearn.datasets.fetch_california_housing` or from *here*) and predict the house price (as a regression). Use different models, expand the features, tune the hyper-parameters, select the best model, and estimate its performance on new data. Justify the choices or methods and models.

5   Load the Temperature Prediction Bias dataset from https://archive.ics.uci.edu/ml/datasets/Bias+correction+of+numerical+prediction+model+temperature+forecast and predict the difference between predicted and actual next day temperatures. Model this regression problem with different models and determine their optimal hyper-parameters, select the best model, and estimate its performance on new data. Justify the choices or methods and models.

19

CLASSIFICATION MODELS AND EVALUATION

Chapter Contents

In the last chapter, we introduced the approach to directly minimize a loss function in a continuous model. In this chapter, we will apply this method to classification with some adaptations and also alternative approaches.

CLASSIFICATION AND PROBABILITIES

The main difference between classification and regression is that in regression, the target values are continuous, while in classification, the values are categorical. The metric we have used in Chapters 16 and 17 for classification was accuracy, i.e., the proportion of correctly classified items in a dataset. However, accuracy is a discrete function (based on binary input of classification success). Optimization methods using gradients (like linear regression or gradient descent) need continuous functions and cannot directly be applied.

A way to avoid this problem and also gain a richer representation of the classifiers output is to predict probabilities. We have actually done this already in the logistic regression example.

We will leave the details of the optimization aside mostly, as there are many excellent textbooks that address the mathematical and computational details, e.g., Murphy, Kevin P., *Probabilistic Machine Learning: An Introduction*. MIT Press, 2022; James, Gareth, Daniela Witten, Trevor Hastie, and Robert Tibshirani. *An Introduction to Statistical Learning*. Vol. 112. New York: Springer, 2013; Bishop, Christopher M. and Nasser M. Nasrabadi. *Pattern Recognition and Machine Learning*. Vol. 4, no. 4. New York: Springer, 2006. Instead, we will focus on how to use these models.

Logistic Regression and Cross-entropy

Binary logistic regression was defined in Chapter 13 through this link function:

$$\pi(x) = \sigma(a) = \frac{e^a}{1 + e^{-x}} = \frac{1}{1 + e^{-x}}$$

where π is the *probability of success* (i.e., class 1) and σ is called the *logistic function*, and a = wTx. The logistic function is useful for probabilities, as it has a range of (0,1). As discussed in Chapter 13, a represents the *log-odds*. They are often called *logits* in machine learning.

For a maximum likelihood estimate of the model, we view the class labels y_k as 1 and 0 probabilities of success, as we assume them to be correct. The likelihood of our data $\pi(X)$ is then

$$\mathcal{L} = \prod_k \pi(x_k) y_k + (1 - \pi(x_k))(1 - y_k)$$

In this expression, one summation element is always zero; which one depends on whether the true class y_k is 1 or 0. The negative loglikelihood is then

$$NLL = -\sum \log(\pi(x_k)) y_k + \log(1 - \pi(x_k))(1 - y_k)$$

The elements of the summation are called the *cross-entropy* of the prediction $\pi(x)$ with respect to true value y_k, also written as

$$H\left(y,\pi\left(\mathbf{x}_k\right)\right) = -\log\left(\pi\left(\mathbf{x}_k\right)\right)y_k + \log(1 - \pi\left(\mathbf{x}_k\right)(1 - y_k)$$

Therefore, minimizing the cross-entropy maximizes the probability of our predictions. Since all the functions involved are differentiable, we can directly optimize the parameters. In general, there are no closed form solutions for this problem, but many different algorithms that use different gradient-based methods, including stochastic gradient descent that we used in the previous chapter. For a more detailed discussion, see Murphy, Kevin P. *Probabilistic Machine Learning: An Introduction.* MIT Press, 2022 or James, Gareth, Daniela Witten, Trevor Hastie, and Robert Tibshirani. *An Introduction to Statistical Learning.* Vol. 112. New York: Springer, 2013.

From Logistic Regression to Neural Networks

We can extend the logistic regression model by replacing $a = \mathbf{w}^T\mathbf{x} = \sum_d w_d x_d$ with $a = \sigma(\sum_k w2_k b_k)$, where $b_k = f\left(\sum_d w1_{kd} x_d\right)$, similar to the regression MLP in the last chapter.

This is again a neural network with one input layer (the x_d), one hidden layer (the b_k), and one output neuron. The activation function f can be a sigmoid function, which would make all neurons use the same activation function, but that is not required. Other nonlinear continuous functions are also possible and are used in practice. The only general difference of a classification MLP, compared to the regression MLP used in the last chapter, is that the final output is processed by a sigmoid function and that we are using cross-entropy as our loss function.

Multi-class Classification

The formulation above assumes that there are only two classes (success or not). For multiple classes, we cannot predict the probability of one class π and calculate the other class probability as $1-\pi$, because there are multiple other classes. There are different approaches that can be taken, such as training one classifier per class, but the most common one for neural networks is to use a softmax function, which is similar to the logistic function, but extended to multiple classes. For logistic regression, this setup is called multinomial logistic regression. The central element is to have a *logit (log-odds)* value a_m for every class m. For each logit, we take the exponential and then normalize so that all exponentials add up to 1, to form a probability distribution:

$$P\left(y_m = 1\right) = \frac{e^{w2_m^T \mathbf{x}}}{\sum_k e^{w2_k^T \mathbf{x}}}$$

where the label y is a one-hot encoded vector, i.e., all elements are 0 except for element m to indicate class m.

This function is called the *softmax* and it is calculated for each class m to yield the class probability vector $\pi(\mathbf{x})$. The related loss function is the cross-entropy, but formulated for arbitrary class numbers: $H(y,\pi(\mathbf{x})) = -\sum_m \log(P(\mathbf{x}))y_m$. Since all elements y_m are 0 except for the true class, the cross-entropy is the negative predicted probability of the true class.

Alternative Approach

Although numeric optimization of parameters in a continuous model is the most popular approach in machine learning, there are alternatives.

Generative Models – Naive Bayes

Naive Bayes classification is a popular classifier, because the idea behind it is straightforward and it is computationally efficient. The general idea is to take the distribution of the features given the classes in the training data to infer the probability of the classes given the features. This is achieved using Bayes' theorem, which is in general stated as

$$P(A \mid B) = \frac{P(B \mid A)P(A)}{P(B)}$$

In our case, A is the class value and B the feature vector.

$P(A)$ can be obtained by counting the class labels and estimating the distribution. The values of $P(B)$ are typically more difficult to estimate, as there are usually many more possible feature value combinations than data points. Fortunately, the value of $P(B)$ is not required since it is independent of class A. Therefore, we can just calculate the numerators and then normalize so that they add up to 1, as is required for a probability distribution. The value of $P(B|A)$ is the most difficult part, as even in the simplest case of discrete features, there are typically many more possible values of A and B than we have data points. We can work around that problem by making the assumption that gave the method its name: we assume that the elements B_d of B are independently distributed, so that $P(B \mid A) = \prod P(B_d \mid A)$. This makes the estimation practical as there are typically enough data points to estimate $P(B_d|A)$, i.e., the distribution of each feature dimension individually per class. This independence assumption is called naive because it is typically not true or uncertain. In practice, it has, however, been observed that naive Bayes classification produces good results even if there are dependencies in the distribution of $P(B_d|A)$.

The estimation of $P(B_d|A)$ can be just relative frequencies for categorical features. In that case, Lagrangian smoothing is often used, which means that we add one to the observation count of every category, to avoid probability values of 0. For continuous valued features, we need to estimate a continuous distribution, e.g., Gaussian or Bernoulli.

COMPARING DIFFERENT CLASSIFIERS

Let us try out a few of the classifiers that we have discussed on a somewhat larger dataset. This dataset contains greyscale images of the faces of 40 people. Each image has 64 × 64 pixels, with values in the range [0, 1]. There are multiple images per person and the goal is to recognize the person, so that we have 40 classes. There are 10 pictures of each person, so 400 training samples. This is a small dataset by modern standards, but still useful for trying out some models.

Most numeric optimization methods work better with standardized data; therefore, we standardize the feature data for all models here. For neural networks and sometimes for logistic regression, training can often take many iterations to converge, i.e., reach a stable state. The default maximum of 200 iterations is often not sufficient, so that we set it here to 2000.

R

```
index <- createDataPartition(oli_sc$Label,p = 0.8,list = FALSE)
train <- oli_sc[index,]
test <- oli_sc[-index,]

log_reg = multinom(class ~ ., train)

lr_prd_train = predict(log_reg, train)
lr_prd_test = predict(log_reg, test)
trn_accuracy = caret::confusionMatrix(lr_prd_train,train$Label)$overall[1]
tst_accuracy = caret::confusionMatrix(lr_prd_test,test$Label)$overall[1]
print(paste("Multinomial Regression Accuracy: Training = ", trn_accuracy,",
            Test = ", tst_accuracy))
 [1] "Multinomial Regression Accuracy: Training = 0.925, Test = 0.9"


# run multiple models in a loop
for (mdl in c("rpart","naive_bayes","mlp"))
{
    mdl <- caret::train(Label ~ ., method = mdl,
       trControl = trControl, data = train,  metric = "Accuracy")
    mdl_prd_tst = predict(mdl, test)
    mdl_prd_trn = predict(mdl, train)
    trn_acc = caret::confusionMatrix(mdl_prd_trn,
       train$Label)$overall[1]
    tst_acc = caret::confusionMatrix(mdl_prd_tst,
       test$Label)$overall[1]
  paste("Model ", mdl, " Accuracy: ", "Training = ",
      trn_acc, " Test = ",tst_acc)
}


[1] "Model  rpart  Accuracy:  Training =  0.6  Test =  0.6"
[1] "Model  naive_bayes  Accuracy:  Training =  1  Test =  1"
[1] "Model  mlp  Accuracy:  Training =  0.925  Test =  0.9"
```

Python

```python
import numpy as np
import time

from sklearn.datasets import fetch_olivetti_faces
from sklearn.model_selection import train_test_split
from sklearn.preprocessing import StandardScaler

from sklearn.linear_model import LogisticRegression
from sklearn.naive_bayes import GaussianNB
from sklearn.neural_network import MLPClassifier
```

```
from sklearn.tree import DecisionTreeClassifier

dset = fetch_olivetti_faces()
X = dset.data
y = dset.target
print(X.shape,y.shape)
X_trn,X_tst,y_trn,y_test = train_test_split(X,y,)
sclr = StandardScaler()
sclr.fit(X_trn) # scale to 0 mean and std dev 1 on training data

X_trn = sclr.fit_transform(X_trn) # scale both sets:
X_tst = sclr.fit_transform(X_tst)

dtc = DecisionTreeClassifier()
gnb = GaussianNB()
lr = LogisticRegression(max_iter = 2000,random_state = 0)
mlp = MLPClassifier(max_iter = 2000,random_state = 0)

print("Start fitting models")
for mdl in [dtc, gnb, lr,  mlp]:
    mdl.fit(X_trn,y_trn)
    print(mdl, mdl.score(X_trn,y_trn), mdl.score(X_tst,y_test))

(400, 4096) (400,)
Start fitting models
DecisionTreeClassifier() 1.0 0.46
GaussianNB() 1.0 0.79
LogisticRegression(max_iter = 2000, random_state = 0) 1.0 0.95
MLPClassifier(max_iter = 2000, random_state = 0) 1.0 0.93
```

We can observe that different models not only show different levels of adaptation and generalization, but need also different times for training the model. As usual, we can tune the hyperparameters, but that does not change the overall picture by much:

R

```
# Code up to here as in the previous example
dtc = DecisionTreeClassifier(max_depth = 32)
gnb = GaussianNB(var_smoothing = 1e-4)
lr = LogisticRegression(C = 1, max_iter = 2000,random_state = 0)
mlp = MLPClassifier(alpha = 1, max_iter = 2000,random_state = 0)

print("Start fitting models")
for mdl in [dtc, gnb, lr,  mlp]:
    t = time.perf_counter()
    mdl.fit(X_trn,y_trn)
    t = time.perf_counter()-t
    print(mdl)
```

```
print(f"accuracy train: {mdl.score(X_trn,y_trn):.4f}, test: ", f"{mdl.
    score(X_tst,y_test):.4f}, train time, {t:.4f}")

DecisionTreeClassifier(max_depth = 32)
accuracy train: 0.9767, test: 0.5400, train time, 1.8726
GaussianNB(var_smoothing = 0.0001)
accuracy train: 1.0000, test: 0.8100, train time, 0.0087
LogisticRegression(C = 1, max_iter = 2000, random_state = 0)
accuracy train: 1.0000, test: 0.9700, train time, 8.1514
MLPClassifier(alpha = 1, max_iter = 2000, random_state = 0)
accuracy train: 1.0000, test: 0.9600, train time, 3.2387
```

Python

```
# code up to here as in previous example
dtc = DecisionTreeClassifier(max_depth = 32)
gnb = GaussianNB(var_smoothing=1e-4)
lr = LogisticRegression(C = 1, max_iter = 2000,random_state = 0)
mlp = MLPClassifier(alpha = 1, max_iter = 2000,random_state = 0)

print("Start fitting models")
for mdl in [dtc, gnb, lr,  mlp]:
    t = time.perf_counter()
    mdl.fit(X_trn,y_trn)
    t = time.perf_counter()-t
    print(mdl)
    print(f"accuracy train: {mdl.score(X_trn,y_trn):.4f}, test: ",
        f"{mdl.score(X_tst,y_test):.4f}, train time, {t:.4f}")

(400, 4096) (400,)
Start fitting models
DecisionTreeClassifier(max_depth = 32)
accuracy train: 0.9767, test: 0.5400, train time, 1.8726
GaussianNB(var_smoothing = 0.0001)
accuracy train: 1.0000, test: 0.8100, train time, 0.0087
LogisticRegression(C = 1, max_iter = 2000, random_state = 0)
accuracy train: 1.0000, test: 0.9700, train time, 8.1514
MLPClassifier(alpha = 1, max_iter = 2000, random_state = 0)
accuracy train: 1.0000, test: 0.9600, train time, 3.2387
```

However, when we try the same models on the iris dataset from Chapter 17, we get a very different picture:

R

```
index <- caret::createDataPartition(iris$Species,p = 0.5,list = FALSE)
train_iris <- iris[index,]
```

```r
test_iris <- iris[-index,]
trControl <- trainControl(method = "cv", number = 2)
for (mdl in c("multinom","rpart","naive_bayes","mlp"))
{
    mdl_model <- caret::train(Species ~ .,
            method = mdl,
            trControl  = trControl,
            data = train_iris,
            metric     = "Accuracy")
    mdl_pred_test = predict(mdl_model,test_iris)
    mdl_pred_train = predict(mdl_model,train_iris)
    train_accuracy =
      caret::confusionMatrix(mdl_pred_train,train_iris$Species)$overall[1]
    test_accuracy =
      caret::confusionMatrix(mdl_pred_test,test_iris$Species)$overall[1]
    print(paste("Model ", mdl, " Accuracy: ",
                "Training = ", train_accuracy,
                " Test = ",test_accuracy))
}
```

```
[1] "Model    multinom   Accuracy:   Training = 0.973333333333333   Test =
0.973333333333333"
[1] "Model    rpart    Accuracy:    Training = 0.973333333333333    Test =
0.946666666666667"
[1] "Model    naive_bayes Accuracy:  Training =  0.96  Test =  0.96"
[1] "Model    mlp Accuracy:   Training =  0.96  Test =  0.96"
```

Python

```python
from sklearn.datasets import load_iris

dset = load_iris()
X = dset.data
y = dset.target
X_train,X_test,y_train,y_test = train_test_split(X,y,)
sclr.fit(X_train) # scale to 0 mean and std dev 1 on training data

X_train = sclr.fit_transform(X_train) # scale both sets:
X_test = sclr.fit_transform(X_test)

dtc = DecisionTreeClassifier(max_depth = 32)
gnb = GaussianNB(var_smoothing = 1e-4)
lr = LogisticRegression( max_iter = 2000,random_state = 0)
mlp = MLPClassifier( max_iter = 2000,random_state = 0)

for mdl in [dtc, gnb, lr,  mlp]:
    print(mdl)
```

```
    print(f"accuracy train: {mdl.score(X_train,y_train):.4f}, test: ",
        f"{mdl.score(X_test,y_test):.4f}")
```

```
DecisionTreeClassifier(max_depth = 32)
accuracy train: 1.0000, test:  0.8421
GaussianNB(var_smoothing = 0.0001)
accuracy train: 0.9732, test:  0.8684
LogisticRegression(max_iter = 2000, random_state = 0)
accuracy train: 0.9643, test:  0.8947
MLPClassifier(max_iter = 2000, random_state = 0)
accuracy train: 0.9821, test:  0.8947
```

Ultimately, different models show different performances and have different computational costs. Since we aim to choose the best models or the ones with the best cost-performance ratio, we would like to determine why some models are performing better than others, if we can know beforehand which models will perform well, and if there are some models that are generally better than others. These are fundamental questions in machine learning and especially the question of why models perform differently is the subject of research. Although general answers are not available, there are some general concepts that will be illustrated with two small synthetic data examples.

SYNTHETIC DATA EXAMPLE 1

We will use small artificial dataset examples to illustrate how differences in the data affect different models. *Scikit-learn* provides functions to generate datasets according to specific distributions. The first example has two-dimensional input vectors and two classes. The class distribution is according to a Gaussian distribution around zero. This type of data exposes a limit of linear models (including logistic regression). We can understand this by considering the decision boundary, i.e., where the probability $\sigma(a)$ is 0.5, i.e., $a = 0$. For a linear model, this is a straight line at $0 = w^Tx = w_1x_1 + w_2x_2 + w_3$, where w_3 is the intercept (bias). The Gaussian distribution means that the class boundary of the generating process is on a circle. Since there is no straight line that separates the inside from the outside of a circle, there is no linear model that adequately represents the generating process.

The following code generates the dataset and plots the data points with the class labels indicated by colours. Then a logistic regression model is trained and used to make predictions on the training set, which are again plotted:

R

```
x <- as.data.frame(rmvnorm(n = 400, sigma = matrix(c(1,0,0,1), ncol = 2)))
x$class = factor(ifelse((x$V1>-1 & x$V1<1 )&(x$V2>-1 & x$V2<1 ), 0, 1))
index <- caret::createDataPartition(x$class,p = 0.5,list = FALSE)
train_x <- x[index,]
test_x <- x[-index,]
ggplot(train_x) + geom_point(aes(V1, V2, color = class))
```

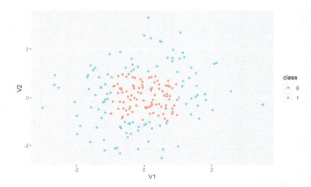

```
log_reg = multinom(class ~ ., data = train_x)
log_reg_pred_train = predict(log_reg, train_x)
log_reg_pred_test = predict(log_reg, test_x)
train_accuracy = sum(log_reg_pred_train == train_x$class)/nrow(train_x)
test_accuracy = sum(log_reg_pred_test == test_x$class)/nrow(test_x)
paste("Multinomial Regression Accuracy: ",
      "Training = ", train_accuracy, " Test = ",test_accuracy)
ggplot(test_x) + geom_point(aes(V1, V2, color = log_reg_pred_test))
```

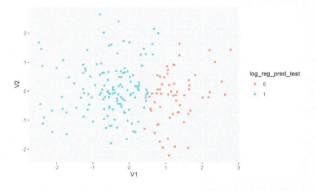

```
[1] "Multinomial Regression Accuracy:  Training = 0.477611940298507  Test
    = 0.361809045226131"
```

Python

```
from sklearn.datasets import make_gaussian_quantiles
from sklearn.linear_model import LogisticRegression
from sklearn.model_selection import train_test_split
from matplotlib import pyplot as plt

X1, y1 = make_gaussian_quantiles(n_features = 2, n_classes = 2, n_samples = 400)
    X1_train, X1_test, y1_train, y1_test =
        train_test_split(X1,y1,train_size = 0.5,random_state = 0)

plt.scatter(X1_train[:, 0], X1_train[:, 1], marker = "o", c = y1_train, s  = 30)
plt.show()
```

```
lgr = LogisticRegression()
lgr.fit(X1_train,y1_train)
y1_train_hat = lgr.predict(X1_train)
plt.scatter(X1_train[:,0], X1_train[:, 1], marker = "o", c = y1_train_hat,
s = 30)
plt.show()
print("LGR accuracy - train: ",lgr.score(X1_train,y1_train),", test",
    lgr.score(X1_test,y1_test))
```

```
LGR accuracy - train:  0.55 , test 0.54
```

We can see clearly that the decision boundary of the logistic regression model is very different from the true classes. This leads to low accuracy on the training data and on unseen test data, commonly described as *underfitting*.

Next, we use an MLP classifier, which has a nonlinear hidden layer so that it can approximate any function within the output range, as mentioned in the last chapter:

R

```
mlp = nnet(class ~ ., data = train_x, size = 100, maxit = 2000)
mlp_pred_train = predict(mlp, train_x)
mlp_pred_test = predict(mlp, test_x)
train_accuracy = sum(mlp_pred_train == train_x$class)/nrow(train_x)
test_accuracy = sum(mlp_pred_test == test_x$class)/nrow(test_x)
paste("MLP: Training = ", train_accuracy, " Test = ",test_accuracy)
ggplot(test_x) + geom_point(aes(V1, V2, color = mlp_pred_test))
```

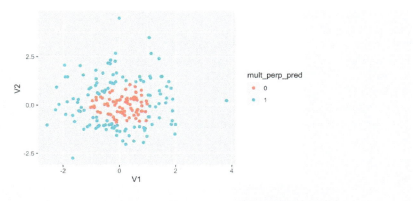

```
[1] "MLP: Training = 0.975124378109453  Test = 0.939698492462312"
```

Python

```python
mlpc = MLPClassifier(activation = 'relu', max_iter = 2000, random_state = 1)
mlpc.fit(X1_train,y1_train)
y1_train_hat = mlpc.predict(X1_train)
plt.scatter(X1_train[:, 0], X1_train[:, 1], marker = "o",
    c = y1_train_hat, s = 30)
plt.show()
print("MLPC train: ",mlpc.score(X1_train,y1_train),", test",
    mlpc.score(X1_test,y1_test))
```

```
MLPC train:  0.99, test 0.985
```

The results are visually very similar to the true labels and the accuracy on both training and test data is high. We can conclude that MLP is a good choice. When running the code, you may notice that fitting the model takes a bit longer. This can be reduced somewhat by reducing the size of the model, but it may be necessary to invest more computation for using a more complex model.

SYNTHETIC DATA EXAMPLE 2

As a contrast, we will now create a dataset that is generated by a process that fits a linear model. We make this dataset relatively small and add some so-called label noise by changing the class label on 30% of the data using the **flip_y** parameter. The dataset is generated as two clusters of points, one for each class. A line between the cluster centres is the ideal classification boundary, so that a linear model seems like a good choice:

R

```
x <- as.data.frame(rmvnorm(n = 400, sigma = matrix(c(1,0,0,1), ncol = 2)))
x$class1 = ifelse(x$V1<0,0,1)
x$class2 = ifelse(x$class1 == 0,1,0)
x$flip = ifelse(runif(nrow(x))<0.3,1,0)
x$class = factor(ifelse(x$flip == 1,x$class2,x$class1))
x = x[,c(1,2,6)]

index <- caret::createDataPartition(x$class,p = 0.5,list = FALSE)
train_x <- x[index,]
test_x <- x[-index,]
ggplot(train_x) + geom_point(aes(V1, V2, color = class))
```

```
log_reg = multinom(class ~ ., data = train_x, maxit = 100)
log_reg_pred_train = predict(log_reg, train_x)
log_reg_pred_test = predict(log_reg, test_x)
train_accuracy = sum(log_reg_pred_train == train_x$class)/nrow(train_x)
test_accuracy = sum(log_reg_pred_test == test_x$class)/nrow(test_x)
paste("Logistic Regression Accuracy: Train = ", train_accuracy, " Test =
",test_accuracy)
ggplot(test_x) + geom_point(aes(V1, V2, color = log_reg_pred_test))
```

```
[1] "Logistic Regression Accuracy: Train = 0.691542288557214
    Test =   0.668341708542714"
```

Python

```
from sklearn.datasets import make_classification

X2, y2 = make_classification(
  n_features = 2,  n_redundant = 0,
  n_informative = 2,  class_sep = .5,
  flip_y = 0.3, random_state = 0,
  n_clusters_per_class = 1,
  n_samples = 100)
X2_train, X2_test, y2_train, y2_test = train_test_split(X2,y2,
    train_size = 0.5,random_state = 0)

plt.scatter(X2_train[:, 0], X2_train[:, 1], marker = "o", c = y2_train)
plt.show()

#lgr = LogisticRegression(penalty = 'none')
lgr = LogisticRegression()
lgr.fit(X2_train,y2_train)
y2_trn_hat = lgr.predict(X2_train)
plt.scatter(X2_train[:, 0], X2_train[:, 1], marker = "o", c = y2_trn_hat)
plt.show()
print("LGR train: ",lgr.score(X2_train,y2_train),", test", lgr.score(X2_
test,y2_test))
```

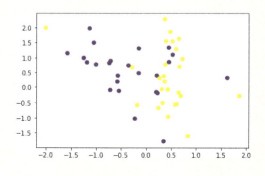

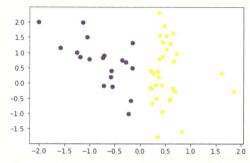

```
LGR train: 0.78, test 0.7
```

The results show that the trained logistic regression model indeed separates the classes along a line that (according to visual inspection) lies between the clusters. The accuracy values are lower than in the last example. However, considering that 30% of the labels have been flipped, an accuracy of 0.7 is as good as we can expect the result to be.

For comparison, we will now try an MLP classifier without regularization. This much more flexible model should be able to adapt well to the training data. The question is what will happen with previously unseen data:

R

```
mlp = nnet(class ~ ., data = train_x, size = 50)
mlp_pred_train = predict(mlp, train_x)
mlp_pred_test = predict(mlp, test_x)
train_accuracy = sum(mlp_pred_train == train_x$class)/nrow(train_x)
test_accuracy = sum(mlp_pred_test == test_x$class)/nrow(test_x)
print(paste("MLP: Train = ", train_accuracy, " Test = ",test_accuracy))
ggplot(test_x) + geom_point(aes(V1, V2, color = mlp_pred_test))
```

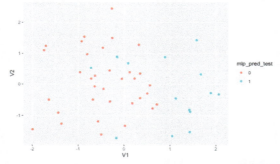

```
[1] "MLP: Train = 0.95049504950495  Test = 0.505050505050505"
```

Python

```
mlpc = MLPClassifier(alpha = 0,max_iter = 2000)
mlpc.fit(X2_train,y2_train)
y2_trn_hat = mlpc.predict(X2_train)
plt.scatter(X2_train[:, 0], X2_train[:, 1], marker = "o", c = y2_trn_hat)
plt.show()
print("MLPC train: ", mlpc.score(X2_train,y2_train),",   test",
      mlpc.score(X2_test,y2_test))
```

```
MLPC train: 0.88, test 0.66
```

The results show that the model adapts very well to the training data, given that the class areas are overlapping. A good example is the single point on the far right with the purple label in the Python version above. Given that the underlying process is based on one cluster per class, this point has its label flipped with high probability. Therefore, the model is adapting to the label noise, which is unpredictable and should be ignored by the model. This is reflected in the lower accuracy on the test set.

One way to address this is by using regularization. The alpha parameter sets the weight of the L_2 regularization, which is by default set to 0.001. With a value of 0.1, we can expect a noticeable effect:

R

```
mlp_reg = nnet(class ~ ., data = train_x, size = 50, decay = c(.1))
mlp_reg_pred_train = predict(mlp_reg, train_x, type = "class")
mlp_reg_pred_test = predict(mlp_reg, test_x, type = "class")
train_accuracy = sum(mlp_reg_pred_train == train_x$class)/nrow(train_x)
test_accuracy = sum(mlp_reg_pred_test == test_x$class)/nrow(test_x)
print(paste("MLP reg: Train = ", train_accuracy, " Test = ",test_accuracy))
ggplot(test_x) + geom_point(aes(V1, V2, color = mlp_reg_pred_test))
```

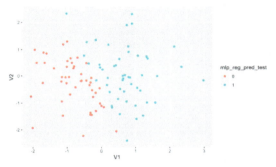

```
[1] "MLP reg: Train = 0.643564356435644  Test = 0.656565656565657"
```

Python

```
mlpc = MLPClassifier(alpha = .1,max_iter = 2000,random_state = 4)
mlpc.fit(X2_train,y2_train)
y2_trn_hat = mlpc.predict(X2_train)
plt.scatter(X2_train[:, 0], X2_train[:, 1], marker = "o", c = y2_trn_hat)
plt.show()
print("MLP reg train: ",mlpc.score(X2_train,y2_train),", test",
      mlpc.score(X2_test,y2_test))
```

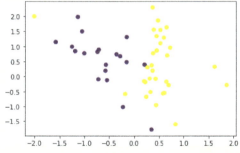

```
MLP reg train:  0.86, test 0.68
```

The test accuracy is improved as expected, but still much lower than the training accuracy. Using a more complex model and performing some hyper-parameter tuning, we still have a slightly lower generalization.

A GLIMPSE INTO MACHINE LEARNING THEORY

This little experiment illustrated that the effectiveness of machine learning models depends on the nature of the data. How to design and evaluate machine learning models to be effective, efficient, and robust is a topic of extensive research. While there has been a recent focus on deep neural networks trained on big data, there are theoretical reasons to keep developing new modelling methods and to use human knowledge and insight in the design and application of machine learning models.

Inductive Bias and the No Free Lunch Theorem

If we have no prior knowledge about the data, it can indeed be shown that there is no learning algorithm that is generally better than others, which is stated in the so-called *No Free Lunch Theorem* (Wolpert, D. The lack of a priori distinctions between learning algorithms. *Neural Computation*, 1996, 8(7): 1341–1390).

Different algorithms have different propensities and limitations in how they adapt to the data, this is called their *inductive bias*. If we do not know the structure of the data, we have to use experimentation to find the most suitable models. However, an exhaustive search of learning models and/or feature extractions is intractable even for datasets of moderate size. The two main things that can help here are experience, from published literature or practitioners, and a good understanding of the task and the data. Prior knowledge or hypotheses about the structure of the data and an understanding of the nature of the models can be very useful in choosing good models and hyper-parameters, which saves effort and computation time and leads to more robust models.

Machine Learning with Big Data and Deep Learning

Notwithstanding the value of prior knowledge, the most influential trend in machine learning over the last decade has been the use of deep neural networks on vast amounts of data. This trend has been driven by the availability of vast amounts of data and by increased availability of computational power, particularly Graphics Processing Units, which have been re-purposed for machine learning and more recently specialized processors for neural networks.

The main change in approach was away from engineered features, e.g., edge detectors in computer vision, to models that learn feature extraction from raw data. This approach led to great progress on many hard problems, including speech recognition, image analysis, and natural language processing.

However, the fundamental problems of machine learning are still to find or design the correct model for a given task, understanding the structure of the task, and using inductive biases of the models to make them efficient and robust.

Practical Classification Modelling and Evaluation

In practice, our development of machine learning models for classification is driven by evaluation. We have so far focused on classification accuracy, but there are additional considerations, when the classes are not equally distributed or the task is not symmetric regarding the importance or treatment of different classes.

Confusion matrix

A confusion matrix is a fantastic way of understanding the performance of a classification model, and are widely used in machine learning. We have already seen that imbalances in datasets can distort accuracy statistics and confusion matrices address this by showing how many samples are in each of four categories: true positives, false positives, true negatives, and false negatives. We will use our fraud detection example to illustrate:

Table 19.1   Binary classification outcomes

Classification outcomes	Meaning
True positive (tp)	Fraud is accurately predicted
False positive (fp)	Fraud is predicted incorrectly
True negative (tn)	A 'no fraud' is predicted accurately
False negative (fn)	A 'no fraud' is predicted incorrectly

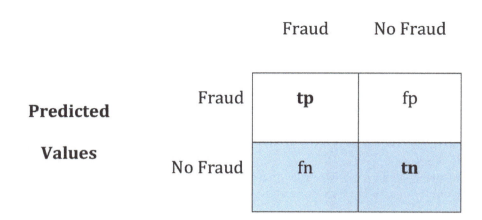

Figure 19.1   A confusion matrix

A confusion matrix allows us to see the specific distribution of predictions, which gives us more insight than a metric-like accuracy. For example, if our model is simply predicting everything as a non-fraud, we would see high numbers in the blue cells, fn and tn, indicating the model is biased towards predicting 'no fraud'. Ideally, we would see a high number in the diagonal cells, tp, tn, with no predictions in the off-diagonal fn, fp. We will see more about confusion matrix in our use case.

Class Imbalances

Class imbalances are a specific problem for classification tasks that we may need to address in the data before applying classification approaches. This is crucial. If, for instance, we have a dataset to forecast loan defaults, cancer diagnoses, frauds, cyber-attacks, and so on, only a minority of the observations will represent the effect we are trying to detect, e.g., fraud. These imbalances can significantly distort the training and performance of our models. For instance, if frauds represent only 5% of observations in a dataset where 95% of observations do not have fraud, a classification model for {'fraud', 'no fraud'} that simply forecasts 'no fraud' every time will be 95% accurate. We can address this by up-sampling or down-sampling the training data to bring the classes into near 50%/50% balance before we train and test our model.

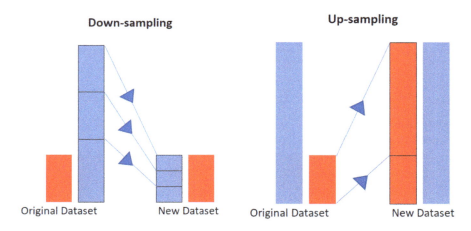

Figure 19.2 Class re-balancing with up- and down-sampling

Down-sampling is the process of removing samples from the majority class, for example occurrences of 'no fraud'. We should make sure the samples we are removing are chosen so as they span the characteristics of the dataset and leave us with a heterogeneous, reduced dataset for model training and testing. This is known as stratified sampling and has been introduced for the class attribute in Chapter 17, but it can also be applied to other attributes, e.g., the representation of countries in the sampled dataset. As a rule, though, removing data from the training of our models is a bad idea.

Up-sampling adds samples in the minority class to bring the data into 50%/50% balance, for example, adding more 'fraud' samples. We can achieve this by simply duplicating the 'fraud' samples we already have, a process called resampling. We again need to stratify our choices to avoid overrepresenting one type of fraud data, which could bias our model to only identifying this type of fraud. More complex methods exist to up-sample, where a data-generating process is used to create new samples that obey the same distributions as the minority class observations. We will elaborate in our use case.

There is a risk if you do not up-sample correctly. If you do the up-sampling before separating the training and testing set, you may have copies of your training samples in your test set and *vice versa*, an effect known as *data-snooping*, which would lead to us overfitting the model and overestimating test performance without noticing at test time. This would lead to undereperformance in applications. As a best practice, up-sample only the training data and *after* this has been separated from the test set.

Precision, Recall, and F1 Score

We have already seen that accuracy can be distorted by imbalanced datasets. The F1 score, also known as F-score or F-measure, is designed to better deal with this problem. We will discuss accuracy, precision, and recall to build up to the F1 score as a way of measuring the power of a classification model in a more detailed way.

Accuracy measures the number of predictions that are correct as a percentage of the total we are trying to predict, *ignoring the number of cases that we are not trying to predict*. In our fraud example, say we are trying to predict 'no fraud' rather than 'fraud', a model that always predicts 'no fraud' would have an accuracy of 90%, where 90% of the time 'no fraud' is a true positive:

$$Accuracy = \frac{\# \, of \, true \, positives}{\# \, of \, observations}$$

Precision tells us *in all those cases that are predicted as positive, how successful is the model?* In the case of customer credit screening, precision would help find good customers (true positive), as we care more about misidentifying a bad customer as a good customer (false positive) and losing money, than we do about missing out on a good customer (false negative):

$$Precision = \frac{\# \, of \, true \, positives}{\# \, of \, true \, positives + \# \, of \, false \, positives}$$

Recall tells us *in all those cases that are actually positive, how successful is the model?* In the case of product recalls, recall is helpful, as we want to identify as many faulty items as possible (minimizing false negatives), and we care less if we incorrectly identify items (false positives):

$$Recall = \frac{\# \, of \, true \, positives}{\# \, of \, true \, positives + \# \, of \, false \, negatives}$$

The F1 score takes both these measures (a harmonic mean) and provides a good single measure we can use for our classification models:

$$F1 = 2 \cdot \frac{Precision \cdot Recall}{Precision + Recall}$$

$$F1 = 2 \times \frac{Precision \times Recall}{Precision + Recall}$$

A high F1 score will result if both precision and recall are high. A low F1 score will result if either precision *or* recall is low. We will see more in our use case. As a rule of thumb, an F1 score of <0.5 is considered poor.

USE CASE: CREDIT RISK - IDENTIFYING BAD CREDITS

Credit is vital in business to avoid capital impairments in banks, but also to avoid losses for small medium-sized enterprises (SMEs) in the course of their business. Credit risk is present when you pre-deliver to your customers, vendor financing, paying suppliers before delivery, and so on.

In this example, we aim to predict bad consumer credits, and we develop a classification model for this purpose, driven by loan and debtor attributes. We would use this model to accept or reject a customer's business. If our business had a ready stream of customers, we would be far more concerned about correctly identifying bad credits (true positive), than we are about incorrectly identifying bad credits (false positive), making *recall* the best performance metric for our model. If, however, customers were very hard to come by, we would be more concerned about rejecting customers incorrectly (false positive), making *precision* a more appropriate performance measure. Clearly, in practice, we want to avoid rejecting customers and we want to minimize credit losses, and in this case, F1 is a good performance measure.

Data Preparation

First, we load our dataset and carry out data wrangling, convert columns data types of numeric values to floats and int where appropriate, make one hot encodings for categorical columns, and so on. We then construct our X and y variables for the training and test data-sets, where w\e will train our model on the **X_trn** and **y_trn** and will test its performance out-of-sample on the **X_tst** and **y_test** data the model training process will not have seen. Our y variable is a value of {0,1}, where '1' indicates a bad credit and '0' indicates an, as yet, good credit.

R

```
cols  = list(df.columns)
cols.remove('class')

# Contains only numerics
X = df[cols]
y = df['class']

#Test and train set
X_trn, X_tst, y_trn, y_test = train_test_split(X, y, test_size = 0.3,
                        random_state = None)
```

Python

```python
# Define X and y variables
cols  = list(df.columns)
cols.remove('class')

# Contains only numerics
X = df[cols]
y = df['class']

#Test and train set
X_trn, X_tst, y_trn, y_test = train_test_split(X, y, test_size = 0.3,
                               random_state = None)
```

We will now create five classifiers and a function to plot training and test accuracy:

R

```
dtc = DecisionTreeClassifier(max_depth = 5,random_state = 0)
gnb = GaussianNB()
lr = LogisticRegression(C = .1,max_iter = 2000,random_state = 0)
rf = RandomForestClassifier(max_depth = 5,random_state = 0)
mlp = MLPClassifier(max_iter = 2000,random_state = 0)
all_models = [dtc, gnb, lr, rf, mlp]

def model_compare(all_models,X_trn,y_trn,X_tst,y_test):
    mdl_trn_scr = []
    mdl_tst_scr = []

    for mdl in all_models:
        mdl.fit(X_trn,y_trn)
        mdl_trn_scr.append(mdl.score(X_trn,y_trn))
        mdl_tst_scr.append(mdl.score(X_tst,y_test))

    x = np.arange(len(all_models))  # the label locations
    width = 0.35  # the width of the bars

    fig, ax = plt.subplots()
    rects1 = ax.barh(x + width/2, mdl_trn_scr, width, label = 'Train')
    rects2 = ax.barh(x - width/2, mdl_tst_scr, width, label = 'Test')

    ax.bar_label(rects1, padding = 3)
    ax.bar_label(rects2, padding = 3)

    ax.set_xlabel('Accuracy')
    ax.set_yticks(x, all_models)
    ax.legend()
    plt.show()
```

Python

```python
from sklearn.metrics import f1_score
from sklearn.metrics import precision_score
from sklearn.metrics import recall_score
```

```
dtc = DecisionTreeClassifier(max_depth = 5,random_state = 0)
gnb = GaussianNB()
lr = LogisticRegression(C = .1,max_iter = 2000,random_state = 0)
rf = RandomForestClassifier(max_depth = 5,random_state = 0)
mlp = MLPClassifier(max_iter = 2000,random_state = 0)
all_models = [dtc, gnb, lr, rf, mlp]

def model_compare(all_models,X_trn,y_trn,X_tst,y_test):
    mdl_trn_scr = []
    mdl_tst_scr = []

    for mdl in all_models:
        mdl.fit(X_trn,y_trn)
        mdl_trn_scr.append(mdl.score(X_trn,y_trn))
        mdl_tst_scr.append(mdl.score(X_tst,y_test))

    x = np.arange(len(all_models))  # the label locations
    width = 0.35  # the width of the bars

    fig, ax = plt.subplots()
    rects1 = ax.barh(x + width/2, mdl_trn_scr, width, label='Train')
    rects2 = ax.barh(x - width/2, mdl_tst_scr, width, label='Test')

    ax.bar_label(rects1, padding=3)
    ax.bar_label(rects2, padding=3)

    ax.set_xlabel('Accuracy')
    ax.set_yticks(x, all_models)
    ax.legend()
    plt.show()

model_compare(all_models,X_trn,y_trn,X_tst,y_test)
```

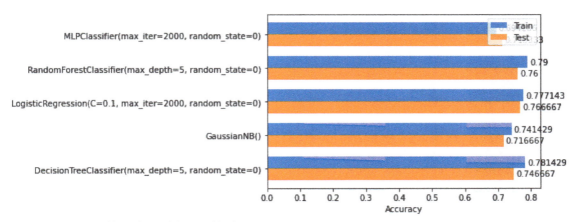

Figure 19.3 Classifiers for training and test accuracy

Comparing the classifiers, we can see that the models are in a similar ballpark, but the logistic regression has the best test accuracy, albeit by a small margin.

We now create a function to calculate accuracy, recall, precision, and F1 scores, and one function to plot a confusion matrix. Then we apply them to our trained logistic regression:

R

```
X_trn, y_trn, X_tst, y_test):

    y_trn_hat = mdl.predict(X_trn)
    y_tst_hat = mdl.predict(X_tst)


    # Print score
    print(mdl)
    print(f"Accuracy   train:   {mdl.score(X_trn,y_trn):.4f},   test:   ",
        f"{rf.score(X_tst,y_test):.4f}")
    print(f"Precision train: {precision_score(y_trn, y_trn_hat):.4f}, test: ",
        f"{precision_score(y_test,y_tst_hat):.4f}")
    print(f"Recall train: {recall_score(y_trn, y_trn_hat):.4f}, test: ",
        f"{recall_score(y_test,y_tst_hat):.4f}")
    print(f"F1 train: {f1_score(y_trn, y_trn_hat):.4f}, test: ",
        f"{f1_score(y_test,y_tst_hat):.4f}")

def cnfsn_mtrx(mdl, X_tst, y_test):

#   y_trn_hat = mdl.predict(X_trn)
    y_tst_hat = mdl.predict(X_tst)



    #Print confusion matrix...
    cf_matrix = confusion_matrix(y_test, y_tst_hat, labels = [0, 1])
    cf_matrix_norm = cf_matrix.astype('float') # / cf_matrix.sum(axis = 1)
[:, np.newaxis]
```

Python

```
def classification_metrics(mdl, X_trn, y_trn, X_tst, y_test):

    y_trn_hat = mdl.predict(X_trn)
    y_tst_hat = mdl.predict(X_tst)

    # Print score
    print(mdl)
    print(f"Accuracy train: {mdl.score(X_trn,y_trn):.4f}, test: ",
      f"{rf.score(X_tst,y_test):.4f}")
    print(f"Precision train: {precision_score(y_trn, y_trn_hat):.4f}, test: ",
        f"{precision_score(y_test,y_tst_hat):.4f}")
    print(f"Recall train: {recall_score(y_trn, y_trn_hat):.4f}, test: ",
        f"{recall_score(y_test,y_tst_hat):.4f}")
    print(f"F1 train: {f1_score(y_trn, y_trn_hat):.4f}, test: ",
        f"{f1_score(y_test,y_tst_hat):.4f}")
```

```
def cnfsn_mtrx(mdl, X_tst, y_test):

    y_tst_hat = mdl.predict(X_tst)


    #Print confusion matrix...
    cf_matrix = confusion_matrix(y_test, y_tst_hat, labels=[0, 1])
     cf_matrix_norm = cf_matrix.astype('float') # / cf_matrix.sum(axis = 1)
                    [:, np.newaxis]

    ax = sns.heatmap(cf_matrix_norm, annot = True, cmap = 'Blues', fmt = 'g')
    ax.set_title('Confusion Matrix\n\n');
    ax.set_xlabel('\nPredicted Values')
    ax.set_ylabel('Actual Values ,);
    plt.show()

mdl = all_models[2]
classification_metrics(mdl, X_trn, y_trn, X_tst, y_test)
cnfsn_mtrx(mdl, X_tst, y_test)
```

Here is the output for our classifier:

```
LogisticRegression(C = 0.5, max_iter = 2000, random_state = 0)
Accuracy train: 0.7929, test:  0.7300
Precision train: 0.6949, test:  0.5833
Recall train: 0.5748, test:  0.4070
F1 train: 0.6292, test:  0.4795
```

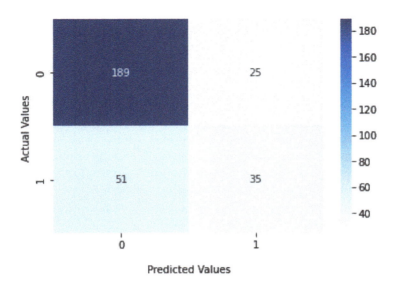

Figure 19.4 Confusion matrix

On the test set, the model generates precision (0.40) and F1 score (0.48), indicating that there could be a bias in the prediction. This is not reflected in the accuracy of 0.73. From the confusion matrix, it can be seen that the model predicts '0', or 'no defaults', with good precision (189/(189+51)=79%), but it can also be seen that there is a bias in the model in that '0' was predicted for 240 (189+51) observations in the test data, whereas '1' was predicted for only 60 observations (25+35). That means that 1 is only predicted for 20% or the samples while 29% of the samples actually have class 1. We should reject this model, examine the class balance of the dataset, and start again.

DEALING WITH CLASS IMBALANCES

If we chart the number of '1' and '0' classes in the data, we see a problem:

R

```
def pie_of_imbalance(df: pd.DataFrame, class_col: str = 'class'):
    print('Imbalanced dataset....')
    print(df[class_col].value_counts())
    df.groupby(class_col).size().plot(kind='pie', y = 'class', label =
        "Type",  autopct = '%1.1f%%')


#run func
pie_of_imbalance(df)
```

Python

```
#Pie chart of imbalances wrapped as a func as we will use it a few times..
def pie_of_imbalance(df: pd.DataFrame, class_col: str = 'class'):
    print('Imbalanced dataset....')
    print(df[class_col].value_counts())
    df.groupby(class_col).size().plot(kind='pie', y = 'class', label =
        "Type",  autopct = '%1.1f%%')


#run func
pie_of_imbalance(df)
```

30% of observations are labelled '1', a credit problem, and 70% are labelled '0'. There is clearly an imbalance and we need to address this.

There are two straightforward strategies to bring the training data into 50/50% balance: up-sample items labelled '1' or down-sample items labelled '0'. We will try two types of up-sampling: simply resampling the existing data labelled '1'; and using a more sophisticated approach that uses the distribution of the training data to generate new training samples.

Note that we need to do this sampling on our training data only. If we use the full data set, then split test data out of it, the training data will most likely contain some test data. This is known as data snooping, and is a cardinal sin of modelling because it leads to overestimation of the test set performance.

```
Imbalanced dataset....
0    700
1    300
Name: class, dtype: int64
```

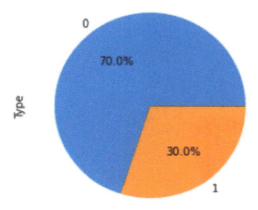

Figure 19.5 Pie chart of imbalances

Up-sampling: Simple Resampling

We need to generate enough samples for the '1' labelled data to bring the training data into balance. We can see that this is now the case:

R

```
# minority class
# note that n_samples = the number of samples the imbalance represents.
X_upsampled, y_upsampled = resample(X_trn[y_trn == 1],y_trn[y_trn == 1],
replace = True, n_samples = (X_trn[y_trn == 0].shape[0]-X_trn[y_trn == 1].
shape[0]), random_state = None)


#Combine train with upsampled
X_upsampled = X_trn.append(X_upsampled)
y_upsampled = y_trn.append(y_upsampled)
```

Python

```
from sklearn.utils import import resample


# Create up-sampled data set for minority class
# note that n_samples = the number of samples the imbalance represents.
X_upsampled, y_upsampled = resample(X_trn[y_trn == 1],y_trn[y_trn == 1],
replace=True, n_samples=(X_trn[y_trn == 0].shape[0]-X_trn[y_trn == 1].
shape[0]), random_state=None)
```

```
#Combine train with upsampled
X_upsampled = X_trn.append(X_upsampled)
y_upsampled = y_trn.append(y_upsampled)
```

```
Imbalanced dataset....
1    487
0    487
Name: class, dtype: int64
```

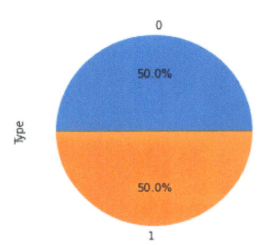

Figure 19.6 Up-sampling for balanced training data

With the up-sampled data, we can re-fit our model and inspect the metrics and confusion matrix. We now have a better F1 score for our test data, 0.54, and we can additionally see that the number of '0' and '1' predictions look more balanced. However, we have now a worryingly high number of false positives (true class 0 predicted as 1, in the upper right quadrant), which is reflected in a low precision (0.45).

R

```
classification_metrics(mdl, X_upsampled, y_upsampled, X_tst, y_test)

Accuracy train: 0.7582, test:  0.8000
Precision train: 0.7515, test:  0.4504
Recall train: 0.7716, test:  0.6860
F1 train: 0.7614, test:  0.5438
```

Python

```
mdl.fit(X_upsampled, y_upsampled)
classification_metrics(mdl, X_upsampled, y_upsampled, X_tst, y_test)
```

```
LogisticRegression(C=0.5, max_iter=2000, random_state=0)
Accuracy train: 0.7582, test:  0.8000
Precision train: 0.7515, test:  0.4504
Recall train: 0.7716, test:  0.6860
F1 train: 0.7614, test:  0.5438
```

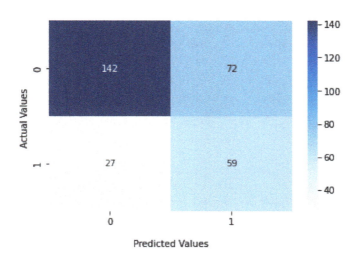

Figure 19.7   Confusion matrix for up-sampled data

Up-sampling: Synthetic Minority Over-sampling Technique (SMOTE)

Now we use a more sophisticated approach which generates new synthetic samples that follow the distribution of our data. SMOTE uses a nearest neighbour approach to generate samples that are very similar in their distribution to the real dataset:

R

```
extra_samples = (y_trn.value_counts().values[0]-y_trn.value_counts().
               values[1])
X_upsampled, y_upsampled = resample(X_trn[y_trn == 1],y_trn[y_trn == 1],
   n_samples = extra_samples, random_state = None)

# Generate SMOTE samples
upsampler_smote = SMOTE()
X_upsampled_smote, y_upsampled_smote = upsampler_smote.fit_resample
  (X_trn, y_trn)
```

Python

```
from imblearn.over_sampling import SMOTE

#How many samples do we need to balance?
```

```
extra_samples = (y_trn.value_counts().values[0]-y_trn.value_counts().
                values[1])
X_upsampled, y_upsampled = resample(X_trn[y_trn == 1],y_trn[y_trn == 1],
                          n_samples = extra_samples, random_state = None)
```

```
# Generate SMOTE samples
upsampler_smote = SMOTE()
X_upsampled_smote, y_upsampled_smote = upsampler_smote.fit_resample(X_trn, y_trn)
```

First, let us look at the distribution of SMOTE's synthetic data to get an idea of how accurately it represents the true training data. We take three data columns, which contain continuous data, and we plot the real data and the synthetic data on a 3D scatter. You can see that the distribution of SMOTE's synthetic data is a good representation of our real data:

R

```
fig = plt.figure(figsize = (10, 7))
ax = fig.add_subplot(111, projection = '3d')

ax.scatter(X_trn['credit_amount'],X_trn['age'], X_trn['duration'],
    marker = "o", s = 10, c = 'blue', label = 'Real datapoints')
ax.scatter(X_upsampled_smote['credit_amount'],X_upsampled_smote['age'],
    X_upsampled_smote['duration'], marker = "+", s = 50, c = 'red',
    label = 'SMOTE datapoints')

# set axes range
plt.xlim(0, 11000)
plt.ylim(20, 60)

ax.set_xlabel('credit_amount')
ax.set_ylabel('age')
ax.set_zlabel('duration')

plt.title('How SMOTE Samples are Distributed vs Real Data Points')
plt.legend(loc = 1,framealpha = 1, fontsize = 8)
plt.show()
```

Python

```
from matplotlib import pyplot as plt
from mpl_toolkits.mplot3d import Axes3D


fig = plt.figure(figsize = (10, 7))
ax = fig.add_subplot(111, projection='3d')

ax.scatter(X_trn['credit_amount'],X_trn['age'], X_trn['duration'],
    marker = "o", s = 10, c = 'blue', label = 'Real datapoints')
ax.scatter(X_upsampled_smote['credit_amount'],X_upsampled_smote['age'],
    X_upsampled_smote['duration'], marker = "+", s = 50, c = 'red',
    label = 'SMOTE datapoints')
```

```
# set axes range
plt.xlim(0, 11000)
plt.ylim(20, 60)

ax.set_xlabel('credit_amount')
ax.set_ylabel('age')
ax.set_zlabel('duration')

plt.title('How SMOTE Samples are Distributed vs Real Data Points')
plt.legend(loc = 1,framealpha = 1, fontsize = 8)
plt.show()
```

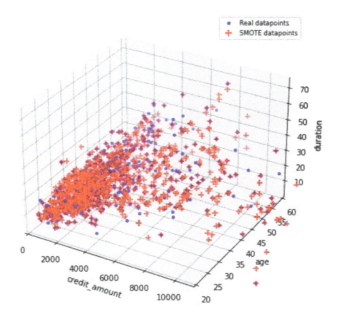

Figure 19.8   Distribution of SMOTE samples versus real data

Retraining and evaluating our model with the SMOTE data, we can see the F1 score on our test data has improved again, to 0.599. This tells us that the prediction of both '1', credit issues, and '0' is performing better. The prediction is not perfect, but looking at the confusion matrix, we can see that now the true positives and negatives have clearly the highest numbers in the matrix.

```
LogisticRegression(C = 0.5, max_iter = 2000, random_state = 0)
Accuracy train: 0.8539, test:  0.8000
Precision train: 0.8805, test:  0.5824
Recall train: 0.8189, test:  0.6163
F1 train: 0.8486, test:  0.5989
```

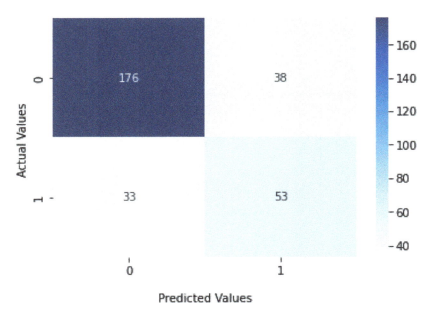

Figure 19.9 Confusion matrix for the retrained model on SMOTE data

Down-sampling

We now use down-sampling to reduce the majority category, '0', to bring the training data into balance. This is not an ideal approach as it removes valuable data from the training process. However, if we did not trust resampling, or SMOTE, to up-sample, this could remain an option for us. One reason we might prefer down-sampling is a specific feature distribution that SMOTE could not reproduce or if we had large amounts data.

R

```
# Randomly downsample rows in the majority class
rus = RandomUnderSampler(random_state = 42)
X_downsampled, y_downsampled = rus.fit_resample(X_trn, y_trn)
```

Python

```
from imblearn.under_sampling import RandomUnderSampler

# Randomly downsample rows in the majority class
rus = RandomUnderSampler(random_state = 42)
X_downsampled, y_downsampled = rus.fit_resample(X_trn, y_trn)
```

We retrain and evaluate again with these results:

```
LogisticRegression(C = 0.5, max_iter = 2000, random_state = 0)
Accuracy train: 0.7593, test:  0.8000
Precision train: 0.7534, test:  0.4532
```

```
Recall train: 0.7710, test:  0.7326
F1 train: 0.7621, test:  0.5600
```

Confusion Matrix

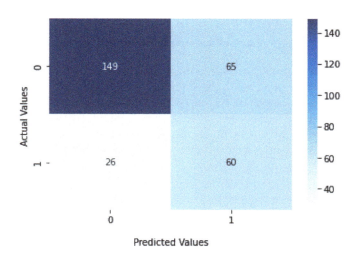

Figure 19.10   Confusion matrix for down-sampling

We can see that down-sampling on the training data shows a slightly better F1 score on the test data, 0.56, than we saw in standard up-sampling, but lower than SMOTE. However, it is still superior to the classifier trained on the imbalanced data.

We can conclude that for imbalanced data, a careful strategy of balancing data using an appropriate method is very beneficial. In this specific use case, the profitability benefit we would gain from better identifying bad credits could be significant. Balancing the training data (and avoiding data snooping) was part of the solution.

Selecting Classifiers

After resampling the data, we can train and test our classifiers again.

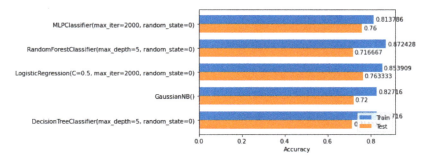

Figure 19.11   Classifiers trained on balanced data

We find that we now have, on average, better accuracy, although the test data are now differently distributed than the training data regarding the classes. It is, however, a common observation that classifiers trained on class balanced data perform better overall, especially if the data are highly imbalanced.

Summary

Classification is another common machine learning problem. In addition to the non-parametric approaches seen earlier (decision trees, k-nearest neighbour), we discussed here the most common approach of modelling class probabilities. This can be treated as a numeric optimization problem, similar to regression, with some re-formulation leading to logistic regression, based on linear regression, and neural network classification with MLPs, based on a neural network regressor. Alternatively, we can directly estimate class conditional feature distribution and apply naive Bayes classification.

We find that the different models behave differently, and we need to select and tune suitable models. That leads to the question whether there is a generally best or most efficient machine learning algorithm, and the answer is there is unfortunately no general best model, and we have to use experimentation to find and validate models. However, using prior knowledge about the task and the data, and experience with models, help in shortening the search. This becomes increasingly relevant with larger datasets and larger models that can be very powerful, but also require more time and resources to design, train, and validate.

Exercises

To complete the activity below, you will need to visit the companion website to the book and download the relevant dataset: https://study.sagepub.com/gopal

1   Implement your own version of the classification metrics precision, recall, and F1 score.
2   Load the *digits* dataset and test the classifiers introduced in this chapter on it.
3   Implement parameter tuning on the digits datasets for the logistic regression and the MLP classifier.
4   Formulate a small MLP classifier yourself and use a general optimizer to train it like the general linear models in Chapter 13.
5   Load the *Wisconsin breast cancer* dataset (either with `sklearn.datasets. load_breast_cancer` or from *here*) and predict the tumour type. Use different models, tune their hyper-parameters, select the best model, and estimate its performance on new data. Justify the choices or methods and models.
6   Load the *Covertype* dataset (either with `sklearn.datasets.fetch_covtype` or from *here*) and predict the classes. Model this multi-class problem with different models and determine their optimal hyper-parameters, select the best model, and estimate its performance on new data. Justify the choices or methods and models.

20

AUTOMATED MACHINE LEARNING

Chapter Contents

In the last few chapters, we have used machine learning approaches for regression and classification, and much of the work has been wrapped up into powerful functions and libraries. However, there are still many more machine learners we have available to use, such as Random Forest, Support Vector Machine (SVM), and Gradient Boosted Tree (GBT). Which one is the more appropriate for our problem? We also have many pre-processing steps we can take with our data, normalizing it, standardizing it, and balancing class data. We can also take multiple learners and combine their output, known as *ensembling*, which can create more stable results in many applications. Which is most appropriate for our data? What we end up with is a *pipeline* or different steps in our modelling process and we can conduct a huge grid-search to work out the most effective steps to take. This is the essential idea of automated machine learning (AutoML). AutoML aims to find the most effective way to process our data, model, and even combine learners to achieve the best fit to our data. The principle is to automate the model development process and automatically generate the full modelling pipeline. Used carefully and with caution, AutoML can help provide effective machine learning.

In this chapter, we will step through model selection and feature selection concepts, and then we will dive into AutoML proper, briefly showing simple AutoML approaches. This is an advanced chapter for specific uses of machine learning and, here, all code will be in Python owing to the prevalence of Python in this field.

AUTOMATING THE MODELLING PIPELINE

AutoML attempts to automate the steps a data scientist takes to complete a project, ideally reducing the time, risk, and biases in model development. Similarly, it allows business analysts to apply ML with little engagement with the underlying ML algorithms. The motivation for AutoML is to increase the productivity of analysts and to reduce the probability of model selection biases and errors during model development. However, great care must be taken to apply data processing methods and learning algorithms appropriately. AutoML is not a way to outsource our need for due diligence and care, and does not replace an understanding of the concepts and principles of statistics, data science, and machine learning.

AutoML uses exhaustive search over given options, also called 'brute force', or heuristics, i.e., established guesses that are not necessarily optimal but are known to work often. Some AutoML systems now learn to associate different types and shapes of input data – metadata – with pre-processing and model selection choices that have been effective in the past. This is described as learning to learn, or meta-learning. We will explore an opensource AutoML called Auto-Sklearn.

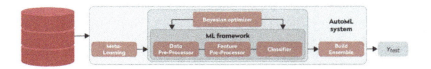

Figure 20.1 An AutoML system for classification based on Auto-Sklearn

Automating Pre-processing Steps

AutoML examines the data we pass to it and attempts to decide on what pre-processing to use. Auto-Sklearn has most of the options we would want to consider.

```
from autosklearn.pipeline.components.feature_preprocessing import
FeaturePreprocessorChoice
for name in FeaturePreprocessorChoice.get_components():
    print(name)
densifier
extra_trees_preproc_for_classification
extra_trees_preproc_for_regression
fast_ica
feature_agglomeration
kernel_pca
kitchen_sinks
liblinear_svc_preprocessor
no_preprocessing
nystroem_sampler
pcs
polynomial
random_trees_embedding
select_percentile_classification
select_percentile_regression
select_rates_classification
select_rates_regression
truncatedSVD
```

Clearly, there are many options here. The AutoML will search the most appropriate ones using an efficient search based on meta-learning. However, it may still not always be optimal.

Automating Model Selection

The selection of the correct learner can be a time-consuming process. The advantages and disadvantages of the many different learners available, applied to a given dataset, can ultimately only be appreciated through trial and error. It is possible to program a model selection function to do this in an automated way. Again, we need to be very careful that we do not conceal biases and issues in a black-box, so for a function of this sort, we need to use diagnostic information that could reveal any issues, and write clear, readable, code with documentation to implement it, so that its operation and the justification for selections made can be understood by others.

Avoiding Model Design Biases in Consumer Credit Modelling

In Chapter 19, we looked at the use case of consumer credit prediction. We had a choice of classifiers: random forest, decision tree, naïve Bayes, MLP, logistic regression. However, we picked a classifier that seemed best suited at the time based on a few experiments that were clearly not exhaustive. This choice of learner is open to biases, most commonly where the model most familiar to the data scientist is selected. We revisit this problem but this time developing a model selection approach.

We can write a function that tests each of these classifiers in turn using the F1 score on the validation dataset as a way of picking the best (note that we call this the validation set in practice, because these data are generally used to perfect the model). The learner with the highest F1 score will be selected as the classifier of choice. This will make the model selection process systematic and reusable, although we could question the use of F1 as the singular metric for choosing a model:

```python
from sklearn.metrics import f1_score
from sklearn.metrics import precision_score
from sklearn.metrics import recall_score
from imblearn.over_sampling import SMOTE


# Func to wrap up running these selected classification learners
def auto_classifier_selection(X_trn: pd.DataFrame, X_val:
  pd.DataFrame, y_trn: pd.DataFrame, y_val: pd.DataFrame):
    upsampler_smote = SMOTE() # balance classes
    X_upsampled_smote, y_upsampled_smote = \
      upsampler_smote.fit_resample(X_trn, y_trn)

    sclr = StandardScaler()
    sclr.fit(X_trn) # scale to 0 mean and std dev 1 on training data

    X_trn = sclr.fit_transform(X_upsampled_smote) # scale both sets:
    X_val = sclr.fit_transform(X_val)

    dtc = DecisionTreeClassifier(max_depth = 5)
    gnb = GaussianNB()
    lr = LogisticRegression(max_iter = 2000,random_state = 0)
    mlp = MLPClassifier(max_iter = 2000,random_state = 1, early_stopping = True)
    rf = RandomForestClassifier(max_depth = 3,random_state = 0)
    all_mdls = [dtc,gnb,lr,mlp,rf]

    max_f1 = 0
    for mdl in all_mdls:
        mdl.fit(X_upsampled_smote,y_upsampled_smote)
        y_trn_hat = mdl.predict(X_upsampled_smote)
        y_val_hat = mdl.predict(X_val)

        print(mdl)   # Output model selection information
        print(f"F1 train: {f1_score(y_val, y_val_hat)[1]:.4f},   test: ",
            f"{f1_score(y_val,y_val_hat, \
            average=None)[1]:.4f}")

        this_f1 = f1_score(y_upsampled_smote,y_trn_hat)[1]
```

```
            if this_f1 > max_f1: # store model and f1 if best so far
                max_f1 = this_f1
                max_mdl = mdl

    # evaluate the best model
    y_trn_hat = max_mdl.predict(X_upsampled_smote)
    y_val_hat = max_mdl.predict(X_val)
    print('\nWinner\n', type(max_mdl))
    print(f"Accuracy train: {max_mdl.score(X_trn,y_upsampled_smote):.4f},\
            validation: ", f"{max_mdl.score(X_val,y_val):.4f}")
        print(f"Precision train: {precision_score(y_upsampled_smote, \
            y_trn_hat).4f}, validation: ", \
            f"{precision_score(y_val,y_val_hat).4f}")
        print(f"Recall train: {recall_score(y_upsampled_smote, y_trn_
            hat).4f}, validation: ",
            f"{recall_score(y_val,y_val_hat).4f}")
    print(f"F1 train: {f1_score(y_upsampled_smote, y_trn_hat).4f}, validation: ",
        f"{f1_score(y_val,y_val_hat).4f}")

    #Print confusion matrix...
    cf_matrix = confusion_matrix(y_val, y_val_hat, labels=[0, 1])
    cf_matrix_norm = cf_matrix.astype('float')

    ax = sns.heatmap(cf_matrix_norm, annot = True, cmap = 'Blues', fmt = 'g')
        ax.set_title('Confusion Matrix\n\n');    ax.set_xlabel('\n
        Predicted Values')    ax.set_ylabel('Actual Values'); plt.show()
    return max_mdl, all_mdls
#Run our function....autoselect the best classifier wrt F1
max_mdl, all_models = auto_classifier_selection(X_trn, X_tst, y_trn, y_test)


DecisionTreeClassifier(max_depth=5)
F1 train: 0.8321, test:  0.5526
GaussianNB()
F1 train: 0.7558, test:  0.0000
LogisticRegression(max_iter=2000, random_state=0)
F1 train: 0.8401, test:  0.5407
MLPClassifier(max_iter=2000, random_state=1)
F1 train: 1.0000, test:  0.5896
RandomForestClassifier(max_depth=3, random_state=0)
F1 train: 0.8287, test:  0.5810


Winner
 <class ,sklearn.neural_network._multilayer_perceptron.MLPClassifier'>
Accuracy train: 1.0000, validation:  0.6333
Precision train: 1.0000, validation:  0.4438
Recall train: 1.0000, validation:  0.8778
F1 train: 1.0000, validation:  0.5896
```

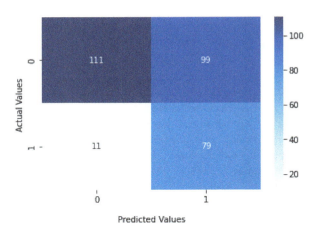

Not only have we been able to select a model, based on performance on our dataset, we have also been able to include the ***SMOTE*** to balance the training dataset to contain a 50%/50% balance between '1' and '0' classifications.

Diagnostic information generated by our function as it looped through each classifier tells us that the most effective leaner on the training data was ''MLPClassifier'' with an F1 = 1 on the training and an F1 = 0.59 on the test data.

Automated Feature Selection

We can select the most effective model based on our specified criteria, but what about the specification of the learner itself, such as which input variables it should use? We saw in earlier chapters how to refine the input variables, and we have already seen RFE, which eliminates those variables that do not make a good contribution to the fit of the model. Feature selection is therefore something that can also be automated to some extent. The first step in automated feature selection is to determine how influential each of our input variables is on our model predictions, and then remove the least helpful. These approaches for '''parameter importance''' can act upon almost any learner and we can plot the results.

First, let us get our data in good shape by up-sampling using SMOTE, and scaling the data. (Note that this was all wrapped into our ***auto_classifier_selection*** meaning that ***X_trn*** and so on are generated only within the scope of the function, so we need to run this code again but outside of the function to gain access to ***X_trn***.)

```
#import SMOTE object
from imblearn.over_sampling import SMOTE

#Balance training data....
# Generate SMOTE samples and use this to train
upsampler_smote = SMOTE()
X_upsampled_smote, y_upsampled_smote = upsampler_smote.fit_resample
    (X_trn, y_trn)
```

```
sclr = StandardScaler()
sclr.fit(X_trn) # scale to 0 mean and std dev 1 on training data


X_trn = sclr.fit_transform(X_upsampled_smote) # scale both sets:
y_trn = y_upsampled_smote
X_tst = sclr.fit_transform(X_tst)
```

Now we can use *sklearn*'s **permutation_importance** to find the most important input variables for our model by altering the training set to establish how sensitive the model is to each input variable:

```
from sklearn.inspection import permutation_importance

# Get the importance of each input variable
result = permutation_importance(max_mdl, X_tst, y_test, n_repeats=10, \
                                random_state=42)
sorted_idx_full = result.importances_mean.argsort()

# Top 10 parameters...
sorted_idx = sorted_idx_full[-5:]

#Chart...
fig = plt.figure(figsize=(10, 5))
ax = fig.subplots()
ax.boxplot(result.importances[sorted_idx].T, vert=False, labels =
           X.columns[sorted_idx])
ax.set_title("Permutation Importances (test set)")
fig.tight_layout()

plt.show()
```

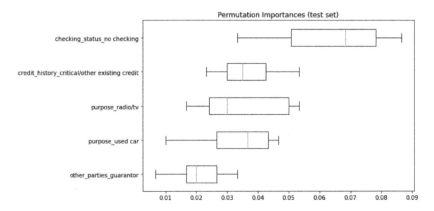

Figure 20.2 Permutation importances

Looking at the five most important input variables, we see that **checking_static_no_checking** is the most important input variable. It would now be possible to refine the input variables going into our classifier using this information. As we will see, AutoML also includes this process.

AutoML

We will use Auto-Sklearn to explore the potential of AutoML. Auto-Sklearn attempts to provide the optimal pipeline for a given dataset, from data pre-processing, model selection, and by combining different learners in an ensemble. Auto-Sklearn is mainly using *scikit-learn* models, and at the time of writing provides 15 classifiers, 14 pre-processing methods, 4 data pre-processing methods, and an optimization tool.

First, the setup details. Auto-Sklearn runs on Linux and will not run in the Windows or MacOS environment. We can install it on Google Colab (or other services that run on Linux), for instance, as follows:

```
# Install
!sudo apt-get install build-essential swig
!curl https://raw.githubusercontent.com/automl/auto-sklearn/master/
requirements.txt | xargs -n 1 -L 1 pip install
!pip install auto-sklearn

import autosklearn.classification
```

Next, we import the package and run the system with our data (consumer credit data). It takes only three lines of code for AutoML to perform pre-processing, model selection, before optimizing and generating a full pipeline for our problem. We use the latest version 2 and set parameters to use all processors (**n_jobs=−1**), optimize for F1 (**metric=autosklearn.metrics.f1**), and limit the processing time to 20 minutes (**time_left_for_this_task=1200**):

```
from autosklearn.experimental.askl2 import AutoSklearn2Classifier
automl_mod = AutoSklearn2Classifier(n_jobs=-1, \
   time_left_for_this_task=1200, metric=autosklearn.metrics.f1)
automl_mod.fit(X_trn, y_trn)
predictions = automl_mod.predict(X_tst)
```

After 20 minutes, we can examine the leaderboard of pipelines, viewing the pre-processing selected model selection, balancing schemes chosen by the AutoML. *PipelineProfiler* generates an interactive screen where we can view different elements of the leaderboard:

```
import PipelineProfiler
# Get an interactive screen, which we can view the pre-processing, model
selection, balancing schemes chosen by the AutoML
profiler_data= PipelineProfiler.import_autosklearn(automl_mod)
PipelineProfiler.plot_pipeline_matrix(profiler_data)
```

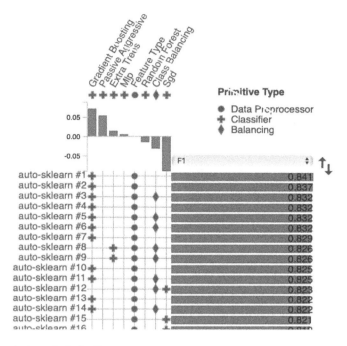

Figure 20.3 Leaderboard of pipelines

Our AutoML has found that the most effective learner is the Gradient Boosting classifier. If anything is unfamiliar, we should first research it and decide if the AutoML's choices are sensible.

Now we can run our pipeline on our test data for the consumer credit use case:

```
y_trn_hat = automl_mod.predict(X_trn)
y_tst_hat = automl_mod.predict(X_tst)
```

Output the results to a confusion matrix as before:

```
#Confusion matrix for the AutoML model
cf_matrix = confusion_matrix(y_test, y_tst_hat, labels=[0, 1])
cf_matrix_norm = cf_matrix.astype('float') # / cf_matrix.sum(axis=1)[:,
np.newaxis]

# Output model selection information....
print(automl_mod)
print(f"F1 train: {f1_score(y_trn, y_trn_hat).4f}, test: ",
f"{f1_score(y_test,y_tst_hat).4f}")

ax = sns.heatmap(cf_matrix_norm, annot=True, cmap='Blues', fmt='g')
ax.set_title('Confusion Matrix\n\n');
ax.set_xlabel('\nPredicted Values')
ax.set_ylabel('Actual Values ');
plt.show()
```

```
AutoSklearn2Classifier(metric=f1, n_jobs=-1, per_run_time_limit=240,
                       time_left_for_this_task=1200)
F1 train: 1.0000, test:  0.6042
```

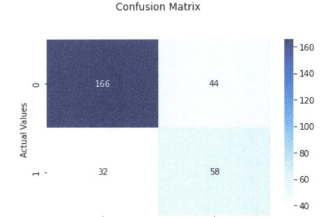

The LDA model with the pipeline features introduced by the AutoML has produced F1 = 0.60 on the test data, slightly better than our simple model selection earlier. In particular, we can see that the frequency of false positives (upper right quadrant) has been reduced.

Dangers of AutoML

An important health warning is required that AutoML uses data to construct a modelling pipeline, and while this is supposed to be an objective process, there are clear risks that the system does not do what it is intended to do. It might not deal with the data sensibly, it might select the wrong learners, and it may result in a predictive model that simply does not work. In other words, applying the principles you have learned in this book cannot be safely replaced by AutoML.

Summary

AutoML is a cutting-edge area of machine learning that can reduce the time spent on a modelling task hugely, reduce the probability of data and model specification errors, and remove the subjectivities of analysts. We have seen how to install, apply, and analyse the results of an AutoML approach. We have seen how, in principle, models can be selected using a performance metric, where we selected the best performing classifier based on the F1 score. We have also seen how input variables for the selected learner can be selected, feature selection, using a systematic process. Finally, we saw how an AutoML was able to generate the entire modelling pipeline from data pre-processing, model selection, through to optimization and ensembling.

We stress the dangers of deferring the design of models to a blackbox. AutoML is an effective tool if used responsibly, but an analyst deferring to a system that they do not understand is dangerous. An effective use of AutoML is to run it in parallel with your own work on model development. The results may inform changes you can introduce in your own pipeline, or even what to avoid.

Exercises

To complete the activity below, you will need to visit the companion website to the book and download the relevant dataset: https://study.sagepub.com/gopal

Read the file credit-g.csv.

1   Run our model selection function **auto_classifier_selection**. Which model is the best performing?
2   However, we care more about getting a 'bad credit flag' wrong as the cost of a bad credit is high. Alter the function **auto_classifier_selection** to select models based on recall rather than F1 score. Which model is best performing?
3   We use our model to reject customers, where a bad credit would be rejected. However, customers are hard to come by and bad credit costs have fallen. Alter the function **auto_classifier_selection** to select models based on recall rather than F1 score. Which model is best performing?
4   Install and run Auto-Sklearn on our problem.
5   Produce the AutoML leaderboard of pre-processing options and learners the AutoML has found.
6   Calculate the F1 score for the AutoML pipeline.

INDEX